THE
WHITE MAN'S
BURDEN

Also by William Easterly

*The Elusive Quest for Growth: Economists' Adventures
and Misadventures in the Tropics*

THE
WHITE MAN'S
BURDEN

*Why the west's efforts to aid the
rest have done so much ill
and so little good*

William Easterly

OXFORD
UNIVERSITY PRESS

OXFORD

UNIVERSITY PRESS

Great Clarendon Street, Oxford OX2 6DP

Oxford University Press is a department of the University of Oxford.
It furthers the University's objective of excellence in research, scholarship,
and education by publishing worldwide in

Oxford New York

Auckland Cape Town Dar es Salaam Hong Kong Karachi
Kuala Lumpur Madrid Melbourne Mexico City Nairobi
New Delhi Shanghai Taipei Toronto

With offices in

Argentina Austria Brazil Chile Czech Republic France Greece
Guatemala Hungary Italy Japan Poland Portugal Singapore
South Korea Switzerland Thailand Turkey Ukraine Vietnam

Oxford is a registered trade mark of Oxford University Press
in the UK and in certain other countries

Published in the United States
by The Penguin Press, 2006

© William Easterly, 2006

British Library Cataloguing in Publication Data

Data available

Library of Congress Cataloging-in-Publication Data
Easterly, William Russell.
The white man's burden : why the West's efforts to aid the rest have done
so much ill and so little good / William Easterly.
p. cm.
Includes bibliographical references and index.
1. Economic assistance—Developing countries. 2. Poverty—Prevention. I. Title.
HC59.7.E22 2006
338.91'1713—dc22
2005055516
Printed in the United States of America

Typeset by SPI Publisher Services, Pondicherry, India
Printed in Great Britain
on acid-free paper by
Clays Ltd., St Ives plc., Suffolk

ISBN 0-19-921082-9   978-0-19-921082-4
1 3 5 7 9 10 8 6 4 2

For Rachel, Caleb, and Grace, as always
To Lizzie, with love and respect

Contents

Amaretch

I am driving out of Addis Ababa, Ethiopia, to the countryside. An endless line of women and girls is marching in the opposite direction, into the city. They range in age from nine to fifty-nine. Each one is bent nearly double under a load of firewood. The heavy loads propel them forward almost at a trot. I think of slaves driven along by an invisible slave driver. They are carrying the firewood from miles outside of Addis Ababa, where there are eucalyptus forests, and across the denuded lands encircling the city. The women bring the wood to the main city market, where they will sell it for a couple of dollars. That will be it for their day's income, as it takes all day for them to heft firewood into Addis and to walk back.

I later found that BBC News had posted a story about one of the firewood collectors. Amaretch, age ten, woke up at 3:00 a.m. to collect eucalyptus branches and leaves, then began the long and painful march into the city. Amaretch, whose name means "beautiful one," is the youngest of four children in her family. She says: "I don't want to have to carry wood all my life. But at the moment I have no choice because we are so poor. All of us children carry wood to help our mother and father buy food for us. I would prefer to be able to just go to school and not have to worry about getting money."[1]

When another group of Western television cameramen encountered the depths of poverty in Ethiopia for the first time, they went back to their hotel rooms and cried their eyes out.[2] That is the right response. What can be more important? I dedicate this book to Amaretch, and to the millions of children like her around the world.

CHAPTER ONE

Planners Versus Searchers

United Kingdom Chancellor of the Exchequer Gordon Brown is eloquent about one of the two tragedies of the world's poor. In January 2005, he gave a compassionate speech about the tragedy of extreme poverty afflicting billions of people, with millions of children dying from easily preventable diseases. He called for a doubling of foreign aid, a Marshall Plan for the world's poor, and an International Financing Facility (IFF) against which tens of billions more dollars toward future aid could be borrowed to rescue the poor today. He offered hope by pointing out how easy it is to do good. Medicine that would prevent half of all malaria deaths costs only twelve cents a dose. A bed net to prevent a child from getting malaria costs only four dollars. Preventing five million child deaths over the next ten years would cost just three dollars for each new mother. An aid program to give cash to families who put their children in school, getting children like Amaretch into elementary school, would cost little.[3]

Gordon Brown was silent about the other tragedy of the world's poor. This is the tragedy in which the West spent $2.3 trillion on foreign aid over the last five decades and still had not managed to get twelve-cent medicines to children to prevent half of all malaria deaths. The West spent $2.3 trillion and still had not managed to get four-dollar bed nets to poor families. The West spent $2.3 trillion and still had not managed to get three dollars to each new mother to prevent five million child deaths. The West spent $2.3 trillion, and Amaretch is still carrying firewood and not going to school. It's a tragedy that so much well-meaning compassion did not bring these results for needy people.

In a single day, on July 16, 2005, the American and British economies delivered nine million copies of the sixth volume of the Harry Potter children's book series to eager fans. Book retailers continually restocked the shelves as customers snatched up the book. Amazon and Barnes & Noble shipped preordered copies directly to customers' homes. There was no Marshall Plan for Harry Potter, no International Financing Facility for books about underage wizards.[4] It is heartbreaking that global society has evolved a highly efficient way to get entertainment to rich adults and children, while it can't get twelve-cent medicine to dying poor children.

This book is about that second tragedy. Visionaries, celebrities, presidents, chancellors of the exchequer, bureaucracies, and even armies address the first tragedy, and their compassion and hard work deserve admiration. Many fewer address the second tragedy. I feel like kind of a Scrooge pointing out the second tragedy when there is so much goodwill and compassion among so many people to help the poor. I speak to many audiences of good-hearted believers in the power of Big Western Plans to help the poor, and I would so much like to believe them myself. I often feel like a sinful atheist who has somehow wound up in the meeting of the conclave of cardinals to choose the successor to the saintly John Paul II. Where there is a lot of consensus for Big Plans to help the poor, the audience receives my doubts about these plans about as well as the cardinals would receive my nomination of the pop singer Madonna to be the next Pope.

But I and many other like-minded people keep trying, not to abandon aid to the poor, but to make sure it reaches them. Rich countries have to address the second tragedy if they are going to make any progress on the first tragedy. Otherwise, the current wave of enthusiasm for addressing world poverty will repeat the cycle of its predecessors: idealism, high expectations, disappointing results, cynical backlash.

The second tragedy is due to the mistaken approach that traditional Western assistance takes toward world poverty. So has this book finally found, after all these years, the right Big Plan to reform foreign aid, to enrich the poor, to feed the hungry, and to save the dying? What a breakthrough if I have found such a plan when so many other, much smarter, people than I have tried many different plans over fifty years, and have failed.

You can relax; your author has no such delusions of grandeur. All the hoopla about having the right plan is itself a symptom of the misdirected approach to foreign aid taken by so many in the past and so many still today. The right plan is to have no plan.

Planners' Failure, Searchers' Success

Let's call the advocates of the traditional approach the Planners, while we call the agents for change in the alternative approach the Searchers. The short answer on why dying poor children don't get twelve-cent medicines, while healthy rich children do get Harry Potter, is that twelve-cent medicines are supplied by Planners while Harry Potter is supplied by Searchers.

This is not to say that everything should be turned over to the free market that produced and distributed Harry Potter. The poorest people in the world have no money to motivate market Searchers to meet their desperate needs. However, the mentality of Searchers in markets is a guide to a constructive approach to foreign aid.

In foreign aid, Planners announce good intentions but don't motivate anyone to carry them out; Searchers find things that work and get some reward. Planners raise expectations but take no responsibility for meeting them; Searchers accept responsibility for their actions. Planners determine what to supply; Searchers find out what is in demand. Planners apply global blueprints; Searchers adapt to local conditions. Planners at the top lack knowledge of the bottom; Searchers find out what the reality is at the bottom. Planners never hear whether the planned got what it needed; Searchers find out if the customer is satisfied. Will Gordon Brown be held accountable if the new wave of aid still does not get twelve-cent medicines to children with malaria?

A Planner thinks he already knows the answers; he thinks of poverty as a technical engineering problem that his answers will solve. A Searcher admits he doesn't know the answers in advance; he believes that poverty is a complicated tangle of political, social, historical, institutional, and technological factors. A Searcher hopes to find answers to individual problems only by trial and error experimentation. A Planner believes outsiders know enough to impose solutions. A Searcher believes only insiders have enough knowledge to find solutions, and that most solutions must be homegrown.

Columbia University professor and director of the United Nations Millennium Project Jeffrey Sachs is an eloquent and compassionate man. I am always moved when I listen to him speak. Unfortunately, his intellectual solutions are less convincing. Professor Sachs offers a Big Plan to end world poverty, with solutions ranging from nitrogen-fixing leguminous trees to replenish soil fertility, to antiretroviral therapy for AIDS, to specially programmed cell phones to provide real-time data to health planners, to rainwater harvesting, to battery-charging stations, to twelve-cent medicines for children with malaria—for a total of 449 interventions. Professor Sachs has played an important role in calling upon the West to do more for the Rest, but the implementation strategy is less constructive. According to Professor Sachs and the Millennium Project, the UN secretary-general should run the plan, coordinating the actions of officials in six UN agencies, the UN country teams, the World Bank, the International Monetary Fund, and a couple of dozen rich-country aid agencies. This Plan is the latest in a long string of Western plans to end poverty.

So for the twelve-cent medicines, the Planners are distracted by simultaneously doing the other 448 interventions; they don't have enough local information to know how many children in each locale have malaria and how many doses of medicine are needed at each of the myriad health clinics; they don't have agents motivated to get those doses there; the local health workers are poorly paid and poorly motivated; many different aid agencies are doing many different interventions on the health system and on malaria; nobody knows who or what to blame if the twelve-cent medicines are out of stock in the local health clinic and do not reach the dying children; and the local parents don't even have a way of communicating to the Planners whether the medicines have reached them.

Searchers have better incentives and better results. When a high willingness to pay for a thing coincides with low costs for that thing, Searchers will find a way to get it to the customer.

The market rewarded book retailers, wholesalers, and publishers who got Harry Potter to those fanatically awaiting the latest installment on July 16, 2005. Those retailers, wholesalers, and publishers have a strong incentive to have Harry Potter always in stock. Myriad children's book authors search for compelling characters and narratives that will attract readers and earn them income. When J. K. Rowling, a Scottish single mother on welfare, hit upon the story of a teenage wizard who triumphs over evil, she became one of the richest women in the world.

Searchers could find ways to make a specific task—such as getting medicines to dying children—work if they could concentrate on that task instead of on Big Plans. They could test whether a specific task had a high payoff for the poor, get rewarded for achieving high payoffs, and be accountable for failure if the task didn't work. We will see some areas where Searchers have already achieved tangible benefits, but they have had little chance to deliver in the area of global poverty because foreign aid has been dominated by the Planners.

The Planners have the rhetorical advantage of promising great things: the end of poverty. The only thing the Planners have against them is that they gave us the second tragedy of the world's poor. Poor people die not only because of the world's indifference to their poverty, but also because of ineffective efforts by those who do care. To escape the cycle of tragedy, we have to be tough on the ideas of the Planners, even while we salute their goodwill.

Big Problems and Big Plans

Almost three billion people live on less than two dollars a day, adjusted for purchasing power.[5] Eight hundred and forty million people in the world don't have enough to eat.[6] Ten million children die every year from easily preventable diseases.[7] AIDS is killing three million people a year and is still spreading.[8] One billion people in the world lack access to clean water; two billion lack access to sanitation.[9] One billion adults are illiterate.[10] About a quarter of the children in the poor countries do not finish primary school.[11] So Amaretch is enslaved to a load of firewood instead of playing and learning in a school yard.

This poverty in the Rest justifiably moves many people in the West. The Western effort deploys a variety of interventions besides foreign aid, including technical advice and lending from the International Monetary Fund and the World Bank, the spread of the knowledge of capitalism and democracy, scientific interventions to cure disease, nation-building, neo-imperialism, and military intervention. Both the Right and the Left participate in this effort.

Who is "the West"? It is the rich governments in North America and Western Europe who largely control international agencies and the effort to transform poor nations. Although, over time, some non-Western nations (Japan) and professionals from all over the world have also become involved.

The tragedy of the poor inspires dreams of change. President James Wolfensohn of the World Bank put on the wall of the lobby of the World Bank headquarters the words **our dream is a world free of poverty**. He has written about this dream with inspiration and eloquence:

> *If we act now with realism and foresight,*
> *if we show courage,*
> *if we think globally and*
> *allocate our resources accordingly,*
> *we can give our children a*
> *more peaceful and equitable world.*
> *One where suffering will be reduced.*
> *Where children everywhere*
> *will have a sense of hope.*
> *This is not just a dream.*
> *It is our responsibility.*[12]

In the world's capital, New York, the United Nations had an inspirational dream of its own at the start of the new millennium. It got "the largest-ever gathering of heads of state" to promise "to eradicate poverty, promote human dignity and equality and achieve peace, democracy and environmental sustainability."[13]

Political leaders from around the world specifically agreed then on the Millennium Development Goals (MDGs). The eight MDGs for 2015 are (1) eradicate extreme poverty and hunger, (2) achieve universal primary-school enrollment, (3) promote gender equality and empower women, (4) reduce child mortality, (5) improve maternal health, (6) combat HIV/AIDS, malaria, and other diseases, (7) ensure environmental sustainability, and (8) develop a global partnership for development. These are beautiful goals.

At Davos in January 2005, British prime minister Tony Blair called for "a big, big push forward" in Africa to reach the Millennium Development Goals, financed by an increase in foreign aid.[14] Blair commissioned a "Report for Africa," which released its findings in March 2005, likewise calling for a "big push."

Gordon Brown and Tony Blair put the cause of ending poverty in Africa at the top of the agenda of the G8 Summit in Scotland in July 2005. Bob Geldof assembled well-known bands for "Live 8" concerts on July 2, 2005, to lobby the G8 leaders to "Make Poverty History" in Africa. Veterans of the 1985 Live Aid concert, such as Elton John and Madonna, performed, as did a younger generation's bands, such as Coldplay. Hundreds of thousands marched on the G8 Summit for the cause. Live 8's appeals for helping the poor and its dramatizations of their sufferings were moving, and it is great that rock stars donate their time for the needy and desperate.

Yet helping the poor today requires learning from past efforts. Unfortunately, the West already has a bad track record of previous beautiful goals. A UN summit in 1990, for example, set as a goal for the year 2000 universal primary-school enrollment. (That is now planned for 2015.) A previous summit, in 1977, set 1990 as the deadline for realizing the goal of universal access to water and sanitation. (Under the Millennium Development Goals, that target is now 2015.)[15] Nobody was held accountable for these missed goals.

In July 2005, the G8 agreed to double foreign aid to Africa, from twenty-five billion dollars a year to fifty billion for the big push, and to forgive the African aid loans contracted during previous attempts at a "big push."

The current enthusiasm for big plans got new life with the the "war on terror." After defeating Saddam Hussein's army, President George W. Bush enthused in a graduation ceremony at the Coast Guard Academy in May 2003: "These goals—advancing against disease, hunger and poverty... are... the moral purpose of American influence.... President Woodrow Wilson said, 'America has a spiritual energy in her which no other nation can contribute to the liberation of mankind.' In this new century, we must apply that energy to the good of people everywhere."[16] The new military interventions are similar to the military interventions of the cold war, while the neo-imperialist fantasies are similar to old-time colonial fantasies. Military intervention and occupation show a classic Planner's mentality: applying a simplistic external answer from the West to a complex internal problem in the Rest.

Similarly, the aid-financed Big Push is similar to the early idea that inspired foreign aid in the 1950s and 1960s, when central planning and a "Big Push" were all the rage. This legacy has influenced the planning approach to economic development by the World Bank, regional development banks, national aid agencies such as the United States Agency for International Development (USAID), and the United Nations agencies. At first, these agencies called for the planning of poor countries' economies. Later they shifted toward advocacy of the free market for these countries, yet in many ways the agencies themselves continued to operate as Planners (and still today, the UN, World Bank, and IMF advocate a kind of national plan they call a Poverty Reduction Strategy Paper).

Jeffrey Sachs wrote a fascinating book in 2005 called *The End of Poverty*. He sees the world's poor as caught in a "poverty trap," in which poor health, poor education, and poor infrastructure reinforce one another. But there is hope from a Big Plan. "Success in ending the poverty trap," Sachs writes in the book, "will be much easier than it appears."

But if rich people want to help the poor, they must face an unpleasant reality: If it's so easy to end the poverty trap, why haven't the Planners already made it history?

The Backward Question That Cripples Foreign Aid

How can the West end poverty in the Rest? Setting a beautiful goal such as making poverty history, the Planners' approach then tries to design the ideal aid agencies, administrative plans, and financial resources that will do the job.

Sixty years of countless reform schemes to aid agencies and dozens of different plans, and $2.3 trillion later, the aid industry is still failing to reach the beautiful goal. The evidence points to an unpopular conclusion: Big Plans will always fail to reach the beautiful goal.

I am among the many who have tried hard to find the answer to the question of what the end of poverty requires of foreign aid. I realized only belatedly that I was asking the question backward; I was captive to a planning mentality. Searchers ask the question the right way around: What can foreign aid do for poor people?

Setting a prefixed (and grandiose) goal is irrational because there is no reason to assume that the goal is attainable at a reasonable cost with the available means. It doesn't make sense to have the goal that your cow will win the Kentucky Derby. No amount of expert training will create a Derby-winning race cow. It makes much more sense to ask, "What useful things can a cow do?" A cow can nicely feed a family with a steady supply of milk, butter, cheese, and (unfortunately for the cow) beef. Of course, you could win the Kentucky Derby if you had a championship-caliber horse, but this book will review the decades of experience that show aid agencies to be cows, not racehorses.

Likewise, we will see in this book that aid agencies cannot end world poverty, but they can do many useful things to meet the desperate needs of the poor and give them new opportunities. For example, instead of trying to "develop" Ethiopia, aid agencies could devise a program to give cash subsidies to parents to keep their children in school. Such a program has worked in other places, so it could take children like Amaretch out of the brutal firewood brigade and give her hope for the future. But right now much aid goes astray because we keep trying to train the aid agency cow to win the Kentucky Derby.

Searchers look for any opportunity to relieve suffering—e.g., the cash-for-school program—and don't get stuck on infeasible objectives. One of the key predictions about Planners that we will see confirmed over and over in this book is that they keep pouring resources into a fixed objective, despite many previous failures at reaching that objective, despite a track record that suggests the objective is infeasible or the plan unworkable. We will see that Planners even escalate the scope of intervention when the previous intervention fails. They fail to search for what *does* work to help the poor. The second tragedy continues. Yet Searchers in aid are already finding things that help the poor, and we will see that they could find many more if the balance of power in aid is shifted from Planners to Searchers.

Setting goals may be good for motivation, but it is counterproductive for implementation. The free market operates without fixed specific goals, only general goals (e.g., businessmen making profits, consumers achieving satisfaction). *The Art of What Works* is a marvelous book by Columbia Business School professor William Duggan. He quotes Leonardo da Vinci: "As you cannot do what you want, / Want what you can do."[17] Duggan points out with numerous examples that business success does *not* come from setting a prefixed goal and then furiously laboring to reach it. Rather, successful businessmen are Searchers, looking for any opportunity to make a profit by satisfying the customers. They evaluate the chance of reaching many different goals and choose the one that promises the highest expected benefit at the lowest cost (in other words, the highest profits). Book publishers did not fixate on the goal of selling books about teenage wizards until after J. K. Rowling found a way to please customers with such a book.

Bill Duggan gives the example of Ray Kroc. Kroc was a salesman peddling the Multimixer, a machine that mixes six milkshakes at a time. His original idea was to sell as many Multimixers as possible. In 1954, he visited a restaurant called McDonald's in San Bernardino, California. He noticed that the McDonald brothers kept eight Multimixers operating at full capacity around the clock. At first, he wanted to recommend their methods to his other clients, increasing the demand for his Multimixers. But then he changed his mind. He saw that preparing hamburgers, fries, and milkshakes on an assembly-line basis was a way to run a successful chain of fast-food restaurants. He forgot all about the Multimixer, and the rest is a history of Golden Arches stretching as far as the eye can see. How many Ray Krocs has foreign aid lost by its emphasis on plans?

Getting Bed Nets to the Poor

At the World Economic Forum in Davos in 2005, celebrities from Gordon Brown to Bill Clinton to Bono liked the idea of bed nets as a major cure for poverty. Sharon Stone jumped up and raised a million dollars on the spot (from an audience made up largely of middle-aged males) for more bed nets in Tanzania. Insecticide-treated bed nets can protect people from being bitten by malarial mosquitoes while they sleep, which significantly lowers malaria infections and deaths. But if bed nets are such an effective cure, why hadn't Planners already gotten them to the poor? Unfortunately, neither celebrities nor aid administrators have many ideas for how to get bed nets to the poor. Such nets are often diverted to the black market, become out of stock in health clinics, or wind up being used as fishing nets or wedding veils.

The nonprofit organization Population Services International (PSI), headquartered in Washington, D.C., gets rewarded for doing things that work, which enables it to attract more funding. This makes it act more like a Searcher than a Planner. PSI stumbled across a way to get insecticide-treated bed nets to the poor in Malawi, with initial funding and logistical support from official aid agencies. PSI sells bed nets for fifty cents to mothers through antenatal clinics in the countryside, which means it gets the nets to those who both value them and need them. (Pregnant women and children under five are the principal risk group for malaria.) The nurse who distributes the nets gets nine cents per net to keep for herself, so the nets are always in stock. PSI also sells nets to richer urban Malawians through private-sector channels for five dollars a net. The profits from this are used to pay for the subsidized nets sold at the clinics, so the program pays for itself. PSI's bed net program increased the nationwide average of children under five sleeping under nets from 8 percent in 2000 to 55 percent in 2004, with a similar increase for pregnant women.[18] A follow-up survey found nearly universal use of the nets by those who paid for them. By contrast, a study of a program to hand out free nets in Zambia to people, whether they wanted them or not (the favored approach of Planners), found that 40 percent of the recipients didn't use the nets. The "Malawi model" is now spreading to other African countries.

The Washington headquarters of PSI, much less the Davos World Economic Forum, did not dictate this particular solution. The local PSI office in Malawi (which is staffed mostly by Malawians who have been with the program for years) was looking for a way to make progress on malaria. They decided that bed nets would do the job, then hit upon the antenatal clinic and the two-channel sales idea. This scheme is not a magical panacea to make aid work under all circumstances; it is just one creative response to a particular problem.

Philosophy of Social Change

The debate between Planners and Searchers in Western assistance is the latest installment in a long-standing philosophical divide in Western intellectual history about social change. The great philosopher of science Karl Popper described it eloquently as "utopian social engineering" versus piecemeal democratic reform.[19] This is pretty much the same divide as the one Edmund Burke described in the late eighteenth century as "revolution" versus "reform" (the French Revolution was a bloody experiment in utopian engineering). Social engineering experiments have been applied since then in such diverse contexts as compulsory resettlement of Tanzanians into state villages and Communist five-year plans to industrialize in the Soviet Union and Eastern Europe. Ironically, social engineering surfaced again as "shock therapy" in the transition from communism (after the five-year plans had failed) to capitalism, which eschewed the alternative of "gradualism." Social engineering showed up in Africa and Latin America in the eighties and nineties as IMF/World Bank–sponsored comprehensive reforms called "structural adjustment." Military intervention to overthrow evil dictators and remake other societies into some reflection of Western democratic capitalism is the extreme of contemporary utopian social engineering. The plan to end world poverty shows all the pretensions of utopian social engineering.

Democratic politics is about searching for piecemeal solutions: a local group engages in political action to campaign for a missing public service, such as trash collection; and a politician recognizes an opportunity for political gain from meeting these needs and winning over this particular group.

Even when our politicians are not exactly the sharpest tools in the shed, rich democracies somehow work. Political scientist Charles Lindblom in a classic article described rich-country politics as the "science of muddling through." He noted that in rich democracies "actual policy practice is a piecemeal process of limited comparisons, a sequence of trials and errors followed by revised trials, [and] reliance on past experience."[20] In other words, politicians in rich countries are Searchers at home.

Burke and Popper recognized the economic and political complexity of society. That complexity dooms any attempt to achieve the end of poverty through a plan, and no rich society has ended poverty in this way. It is only when rich-country politicians gaze at the non-voters in the rest of the world that they become Planners. This is another clue to the likelihood of planning: outsiders are more likely to be Planners, while insiders are forced by their fellow insiders to be Searchers.

Feedback and Accountability

Two key elements that make searches work, and whose absence is fatal to plans, are feedback and accountability. Searchers know if something works only if the people at the bottom can give feedback. This is why successful Searchers have to be close to the customers at the bottom, rather than surveying the world from the top. Consumers tell the firm that "this product is worth the price" by buying it, or they decide the product is worthless and return it to the store. Voters tell their local politician that "public services suck," and the politician tries to fix the problem.

Lack of feedback is one of the most critical flaws in existing aid. It comes about because of the near-invisibility of efforts and results by aid agencies in distant parts of the world. The rest of the book explores how to begin addressing this flaw, from employing local "watchers" of aid projects to doing independent evaluation of those projects.

Of course, feedback works only if somebody listens. Feedback without accountability is like the bumper sticker I once saw on an eighteen-wheeler: DON'T LIKE MY DRIVING? CALL 1-800-SCREW-YOU. Once Searchers implement the results of a search, they take responsibility for the outcome. Profit-seeking firms make a product they find to be in high demand, but they also take responsibility for the product—if the product poisons the customer, they are liable, or at least they go out of business. A political reformer takes responsibility for the results of the reform. If something goes wrong, he pays politically, perhaps by losing office. If the reform succeeds, he gets the political rewards.

Although all governments include bureaucracy, in well-developed democratic governments, the bureaucrats are somewhat more specialized and accountable for specific results to the citizens (although God knows they try hard not to be). The bureaucrats gradually make improvements through what Lindblom called "disjointed incrementalism." Active civic organizations and political lobbies operate from the bottom up to hold leaders and bureaucrats accountable, correcting missteps and rewarding positive ones. Rich voters complain if municipal trash collectors don't pick up their discarded shipping boxes after Amazon delivers Harry Potter; politicians and bureaucrats have political incentives to correct any breakdown in trash collection. Feedback guides democratic governments toward supplying services that the market cannot supply, and toward providing institutions for the markets to work.

At a higher level, accountability is necessary to motivate a whole organization or government to use Searchers. In contrast, Planners flourish where there is little accountability. Again, outsiders don't have much accountability, and so they are Planners; insiders have more accountability and are more likely to be Searchers.

We will see some of the helpful changes that can happen in aid when accountability is increased, shifting power from Planners to Searchers. Aid agencies can be held accountable for specific tasks, rather than be given the weak incentives that follow from collective responsibility for broad goals. Aid workers now tend to be ineffective generalists; accountability would make them into more effective specialists.

To oversimplify by a couple of gigawatts, the needs of the rich get met because the rich give feedback to political and economic Searchers, and they can hold the Searchers accountable for following through with specific actions. The needs of the poor don't get met because the poor have little money or political power with which to make their needs known and they cannot hold anyone accountable to meet those needs. They are stuck with Planners. The second tragedy continues.

Why Are Planners So Popular?

In any human endeavor, the people paying the bills are the ones to keep happy. The big problem with foreign aid and other Western efforts to transform the Rest is that the people paying the bills are rich people who have very little knowledge of poor people. The rich people demand big actions to solve big problems, which is understandable and compassionate. The Big Plans at the top keep the rich people happy that "something is being done" about such a tragic problem as world poverty. In June 2005, the *New York Times* ran an editorial advocating a Big Plan for Africa titled "Just Do Something." Live 8 concert organizer Bob Geldof said, "Something must be done; anything must be done, whether it works or not."[21] Something, anything, any Big Plan would take the pressure off the rich to address the critical needs of the poor. Alas, if ineffective big plans take the pressure off the rich to help the poor, there's the second tragedy, because then the effective piecemeal actions will not happen.

The prevalence of ineffective plans is the result of Western assistance happening out of view of the Western public. Fewer ineffective approaches would survive if results were more visible. The Big Plans are attractive to politicians, celebrities, and activists who want to make a big splash, without the Western public realizing that those plans at the top are not connected to reality at the bottom.

Popular books, movies, and television shows are full of plotlines that feature a hero, the chosen one, who saves the world. The Harry Potter series is a particularly successful variation on this plotline: an ordinary teenager who triumphs over evil with courage and compassion.

We all love the fantasy of being the chosen one. Is part of the explanation for the Big Plan's Western popularity that it stars the rich West in the leading role, that of the chosen people to save the Rest?

The Planners-versus-Searchers divide is not equal to Left versus Right. The Big Plans show remarkable bipartisan support from both the rich-world

Left and the rich-world Right. The Left likes the idea of a big state-led effort to fight global poverty. The Right likes the idea of benevolent imperialism to spread Western capitalism and subdue opposition to the West. So, as this book will explore, we get a bizarre conjuncture of foreign aid on the left and military interventions on the right (although each might disavow the other). Few military crusaders or aid advocates can resist the temptation to play Harry Potter.

Likewise, the critique of the Big Plan mainstream comes from dissidents on both the Left and the Right. The right-wing dissident says that hope for the poor will come mainly from homegrown markets and democracy. The left-wing dissident doesn't like the Western imperialists trying to remake the poor in the West's image. Both right-wing and left-wing dissidents are on the right track. The Searchers in the middle agree that neither the Big Plans of the Left nor those of the Right (neither foreign aid nor foreign military intervention) can end poverty in the Rest—let's just find some specific things that help poor people.

To be sure, many people who work on world poverty are distant from the fantasies and really just want to help the poor and try hard to do their jobs well. Planners come in many varieties, which are sometimes in sharp disagreement, and many of them do not embrace the extremes cited here. Yet the fondness for the Big Goal and the Big Plan is strikingly widespread. It's part of the second tragedy that so much goodwill and hard work by rich people who care about the poor goes through channels that are ineffective.

The working-level people in aid agencies or nongovernmental organizations (NGOs) are more likely to be Searchers than Planners. Unfortunately, the political realities of rich countries—the bipartisan support for Big Plans—foist on these workers these plans, taking money, time, and energy away from the doable actions that workers discover in their searching.

Utopianism

Nineteenth-century utopian socialist Robert Owen was excited about the industrial revolution. Anticipating the world leaders' Millennium Declaration a century and a half later, he said in a book in 1857, "Let not the leading powers of the world longer hesitate what course to take." If only they embrace the right plan, "the human race shall be perpetually well born, fed, clothed, lodged, trained, educated, employed, and recreated, locally and generally governed, and placed to enjoy life in the most rational matter on earth, and to best fit them for whatever change may occur after death."[22] Owen has been discredited ever since as a utopian. Yet with the exception of the reference to preparing for life after death, there are strong parallels between his nineteenth-century rhetoric and that of a modern Planner such as Jeffrey Sachs (see below). Utopia is making a comeback today.

ROBERT OWEN, 1857	JEFFREY SACHS, 2005
"if you will now agree among yourselves to call a Congress of the leading governments of the world, inviting those of China, Japan, Burmah, &c., . . . a new state of rational existence for men shall arise, when truth, peace, harmony, perpetual prosperity, and happiness shall reign triumphant"	"in September 2000 [was] the largest gathering of world leaders in history. . . The document . . . adopted by the assembled leaders . . . surveys the issues of war and peace, health and disease, and wealth and poverty, and commits the world to a set of undertakings to improve the human condition" (pp. 210–11).*
"through the progress of physical and mental science . . . all the . . . means in superabundance to well-feed, clothe, lodge, train, educate, amuse and govern the human race in perpetual progressive-prosperity—without war . . . these results may now, for the first time in the history of the world, be accomplished"	"technological progress enables us to meet basic human needs . . . and to achieve a margin above basic needs unprecedented in history" (p. 347). . . . "our breathtaking opportunity . . . [is to] spread the benefits of science and technology . . . to all parts of the world . . . to secure a perpetual peace . . ." (pp. 351–52).
"when . . . they shall have imbibed the spirit of universal love and charity . . . then will be the direct path to the permanent superior happiness of our race . . . be attainable"	"The world community has at its disposal the . . . human courage and compassion to make it happen" (introduction to *Millennium Project Report,* January 2005)
"these results may now . . . be accomplished . . . with far less difficulty and in less time than will be imagined"	"success in ending the poverty trap will be much easier than it appears" (p. 289)
"all the petty isolated schemes hitherto proposed by well-intentioned but inexperienced and short-sighted reformers will be abandoned as useless for the ultimate objects to be attained"	"to do things piecemeal is vacuous" (*Washington Post,* March 27, 2005). "Even more to the point, success in any single area, whether in health, or education, or farm productivity, depends on investments across the board" (p. 256)

*Page numbers are in Sachs's book *The End of Poverty: Economic Possibilities for Our Time* (New York: Penguin Press, 2005)

Unfortunately, the new fondness for utopia is not just harmless inspirational rhetoric. The setting of utopian goals means aid workers will focus efforts on infeasible tasks, instead of the feasible tasks that will do some good.

Desperate Needs

The effort wasted on the plans is all the more tragic when we consider some of the simple, desperate needs of the poor, which Searchers could address piecemeal. In a typical country in Africa, one third of the children under five have stunted growth due to malnutrition. A group of women in Nigeria report that they were too weakened by hunger to breast-feed their babies. Throughout Africa, there is a long "hungry season," when the stores from the last harvest run out and the new crop becomes available. Even in a more prosperous region such as Latin America, one fifth of the children suffer from malnutrition. Malnutrition lowers the life potential of children and makes them more vulnerable to killer diseases. As a woman in Voluntad de Dios, Ecuador, put it, children get sick "because of lack of food. We are poor. We have no money to buy or to feed ourselves."[23]

In Kwalala, Malawi, wells break down during the rainy season because of lack of maintenance. Villagers are forced to take their drinking water from the lake, even though they know it is contaminated with human waste from the highlands. This practice causes diseases such as diarrhea and schistosomiasis.[24] Schistosomiasis is caused by parasitic worms passed along through contaminated water; it causes damage to the lungs, liver, bladder, and intestines.[25]

An old man in Ethiopia says: "Poverty snatched away my wife from me. When she got sick, I tried my best to cure her with tebel [holy water] and woukabi [spirits], for these were the only things a poor person could afford. However, God took her away. My son, too, was killed by malaria. Now I am alone."[26]

Surveys of Brazilian *favelas* find terrible sewage problems. In Nova California, "The sewage running in front of the houses causes disease, and no one can stand the smell. When it rains, it comes in the front door, and one has to take everything up off the floor." In Vila União, "In the winter, the sewers overflow and the streets flood, to say nothing of the mosquito invasion. And here in the *favela* some houses do not have toilets, so people use the street." In Morro da Conceição, sewage causes the children to get sick and creates "a terrible smell."[27]

Chinwe Okoro, twenty-six, lives in the farming village of Okpuje, in southeastern Nigeria. Chinwe's widowed mother cut his schooling short so he could contribute to the family income from farm jobs and harvesting oil palm. Besides oil palm, Okpuje also produces cassava, yam, and handicrafts. Bad roads out of the village make the cost of transport of local goods to the market about five times higher than it would be with good roads, lowering Chinwe's income and opportunities. The isolation caused by bad roads makes health workers and teachers reluctant to accept postings in Okpuje. I have been on corrugated, potholed, and muddy roads in Africa, and they are indeed agony. The villagers also must travel on the bad roads to get water, since the thirteen-year-old local well broke down four years ago and hasn't been repaired. Women and children walk up to eight kilometers to get spring water; some travel twenty-two kilometers on the bad roads to the nearest town to buy water.[28]

Some success stories show that aid agencies can make progress on problems like these. There have been successful programs feeding the hungry, which means children have been able to get food in Voluntad de Dios, Ecuador. Success on expanding access to clean water helped the villagers of Kwalala, Malawi. In Mbwadzulu, Malawi, in fact, the drilling of two new boreholes has allowed villagers to discontinue using polluted lake water, and has led to a decline in cholera.[29] The Ethiopian man's tragedy could have been avoided with cheap medicines. Brazilian *favelas* could get proper sanitation; in fact, there has already been progress there on sanitation compared with a decade ago. The isolation of Okpuje, Nigeria, could be alleviated by building and maintaining a good road. Broken-down wells can be repaired in Kwalala and Okpuje. Aid agencies could do much more on these problems if they were not diverting their energies to utopian Plans and were accountable for tasks such as getting food, roads, water, sanitation, and medicines to the poor.

White Man's Burden: Historical Cliffs Notes

As the example of Robert Owen shows, the fondness for utopian solutions to the Rest's problems is not new—it is a theme throughout the history of the West and the Rest. The Big Plans that would one day become foreign aid and military intervention appeared as early as the eighteenth century. Most accounts stress an abrupt transition from colonialism to foreign aid and benevolent military intervention, and of course there were major changes in the attitudes and policies of the West. Yet it is instructive also to see the themes that persist. From the beginning, the interests of the poor got little weight compared with the vanity of the rich. The White Man's Burden emerged from the West's self-pleasing fantasy that "we" were the chosen ones to save the Rest. The White Man offered himself the starring role in an ancien régime version of Harry Potter.

The Enlightenment saw the Rest as a blank slate—without any meaningful history or institutions of its own—upon which the West could inscribe its superior ideals. As the Comte de Buffon put it, "It is through the European that civilization arrives... precisely because of their superiority, the civilized peoples are responsible for an evolving world." The Marquis de Condorcet said, "These vast lands... need only assistance from us to become civilized."[30]

Even when making beneficial piecemeal reforms, such as the British anti-slave trade campaign in the late eighteenth and early nineteenth centuries, white arrogance was not going to disappear anytime soon. British Tory Sir Robert Peel said in a speech in June 1840 that unless whites stopped the slave trade, they never would convince Africans "of the superiority of their European fellow men."[31]

As one of the leaders of the antislavery movement, William Wilberforce, subsequently said about India, "Must we not then... endeavour to raise these wretched beings out of their present miserable condition?"[32] James Mill in 1810 said, "For the sake of the natives" in India, the British could not "leave them to their own direction."[33]

Even the Berlin Conference of 1885, which divided Africa among European colonizers—who resembled children scrambling for candy as the piñata breaks open—included some altruistic language. The signatories were to "aim at instructing the natives and bringing home to them the blessings of civilization."[34]

A rare dissenter, Mark Twain, satirized the civilizing effort as of 1901: "The Blessings of Civilization... could not be better, in a dim light.... With the goods a little out of focus, they furnish this desirable exhibit: Law and Order... Liberty... Honorable Dealing... Protection to the Weak... Education... is it good? Sir, it is pie. It will bring into camp any idiot that sits in darkness anywhere."[35]

The covenant of the League of Nations adopted after World War I promised the "peoples not yet able to stand by themselves" that "the well-being and development of such peoples form a sacred trust of civilization." Therefore, "the tutelage of such peoples should be entrusted to advanced nations."[36] Only a few doubters wondered whether such tutelage might be "a greater trial to subject races than a more primitive... form of exploitation."[37]

A shift in language (and also in thought) occurred after World War II. Verbiage about racial superiority, the tutelage of backward peoples, and people not ready to rule themselves went into the wastebasket. Self-rule and decolonization became universal principles. The West exchanged the old racist coinage for a new currency. "Uncivilized" became "underdeveloped." "Savage peoples" became the "third world." There was a genuine change of heart away from racism and toward respect for equality, but a paternalistic and coercive strain survived. Later chapters of this book will examine the lessons of colonial history for today's "nation-building."

Meanwhile, the enterprise of the West transforming the Rest got a new name: foreign aid. Foreign aid began with the Point Four Program of Harry S Truman. His inaugural address on January 20, 1949, said (anticipating Jeffrey Sachs and the UN Millennium Project by half a century), "We must embark on a bold new program for...the improvement and growth of underdeveloped areas. More than half the people of the world are living in conditions approaching misery.... For the first time in history, humanity possesses the knowledge and the skill to relieve the suffering of these people." Truman ignored past Westernization attempts as if they were hick relatives at a Park Avenue wedding: "for the first time in history" we know how to help the Rest ("these people").

Truman broke the ground. Soon was born the development expert, the heir to the missionary and the colonial officer. A United Nations group of experts two years after Truman concluded that "a 2 percent increase in the per capita national incomes" required foreign aid of "about $3 billion a year." In 1960, Walt Rostow's bestselling book *The Stages of Economic Growth* proclaimed that "an increase of $4 billion in external aid would be required to lift all of Asia, the Middle East, Africa, and Latin America into regular growth, at an increase of per capita income of say, 1.5% per annum." There was some self-interest at work here. Rostow subtitled his book *A Non-Communist Manifesto*. The West (the first world) competed with the Communists (the second world) to offer the third world the One Path. The West strove to convince the Rest that material prosperity was more feasible under freedom (private property, free markets, and democracy) than under communism. Sometimes the West's military had to make sure the Rest stayed on the path to prosperity. The cold war would influence the Western effort for decades to come (just as the war on terrorism influences foreign assistance today).

Rostow was an adviser to John F. Kennedy, who declared in 1961 that "existing foreign aid programs and concepts are largely unsatisfactory...we intend during this coming decade of development to achieve a decisive turnaround in the fate of the less-developed world, looking toward the ultimate day...when foreign aid will no longer be needed."

Implementing this crusade brought an alphabet soup of agencies created after World War II: the International Monetary Fund, the World Bank, the United States Agency for International Development (USAID), the United Kingdom's Department for International Development (DFID), the Inter-American Development Bank (IDB), the African Development Bank (AFDB), the Asian Development Bank (ADB), the United Nations Development Program (UNDP), the World Health Organization (WHO), the Food and Agriculture Organization (FAO), the International Labour Organization (ILO), the United Nations Children's Fund (UNICEF), and many more.

Not just foreign aid was involved; the West promoted advice, diplomatic relations, and military intervention as part of the crusade to transform the Rest. Cold warriors sent spies, soldiers, and guns to poor countries to try to save them from communism and implement capitalism.

A whole new field of economics was invented called "development economics." A Polish-born economist named Paul Rosenstein-Rodan in the 1940s called for a "Big Push" to move the third world into the first. Scholars in politics and sociology and many other fields studied "development" of the poor countries.

Economist, sociologist, and later Nobel laureate Gunnar Myrdal said in 1956 that the answer to poverty was a plan: "It is now commonly agreed that an underdeveloped country should have ... an overall integrated national plan ... under the encouraging and congratulating applause of the advanced countries." Myrdal used dramatic language in favor of such plans, language that echoes today's (italics in original): *"The alternative to making the heroic attempt is continued acquiescence in economic and cultural stagnation or regression which is politically impossible in the world of today."*[38] Amen to that, except that the heroic plan failed to end economic stagnation or even to realize its potential to address simpler needs.

With some fluctuations in intellectual favor since, these are the same ideas that inspire today's version of the White Man's Burden. A rare early dissenter was the Hungarian-British economist Peter Bauer, who four decades ago presciently predicted the failure of planning "development" through foreign aid.[39]

The fallacy is to assume that because I have studied and lived in a society that somehow wound up with prosperity and peace, I know enough to plan for other societies to have prosperity and peace. As my friend April once said, this is like thinking the racehorses can be put in charge of building the racetracks.

The Poor Help Themselves

In his introduction to Sachs's *The End of Poverty,* Bono said, "It's up to us." Sachs writes of "our generation's challenge." Gordon Brown, in announcing his Big Push aid plan, saw himself telling Africans: "We have to say," 'We will help you build the capacity you need to trade. Not just opening the door but helping you gain the strength to cross the threshold.' "[40]

The most infuriating thing about the Planners is how patronizing they are (usually unconsciously). Here's a secret: anytime you hear a Western politician or activist say "we," they mean "we whites"—today's version of the White Man's Burden. (This is not automatic for any Western effort to help the poor; there are other rich people who genuinely care about the poor and are not patronizing.)

Cameroonian lawyer and journalist Jean-Claude Shanda Tonme protested in a July 2005 *New York Times* Op-Ed column about the Live 8 concert organizers that "they still believe us to be like children that they must save," with "their willingness to propose solutions on our behalf."

We will see in the rest of the book the refreshing changes that can happen once the patronizing mind-set is abandoned—from ending conditions placed on aid and IMF loans, to ending military interventions, to giving matching grants that increase the opportunities of individuals rather than coddle bad governments.

The world's poor do not have to wait passively for the West to save them (and they are not so waiting). The poor are their own best Searchers. While Western Planners were discussing whether to increase foreign aid by $50 billion for all poor countries, the citizens of just two large poor countries— India and China—were generating an increase in income for themselves of $715 billion every year.[41] The Gang of Four—Hong Kong, Korea, Singapore, and Taiwan—went from third world to first over the last four decades. China, India, and the Gang of Four did this through the efforts of many decentralized agents participating in *markets* (the ideal vehicle for feedback and accountability) without significant Western assistance as a share of their income, with some efforts by their own governments (at their own top), and without the West telling them what to do. The developing countries that are in the bottom fourth in terms of aid receipts as a percent of their income have had no trouble achieving healthy growth rates, seeing a 2.5-fold increase in income over the last four decades.

Homegrown development does not always work, as the poverty and political chaos in various parts of the world shows. Yet even when national development fails, the poor are more resourceful than Planners give them credit for. In Ethiopia, Etenesh Ayele, thirty-eight, spent twelve years carrying firewood into Addis Ababa. Now she is trying to help women and girls like Amaretch. She runs the Association of Former Women Fuelwood Carriers, whose members teach girls so those girls can stay out of the firewood brigade. Etenesh Ayele and her colleagues also teach women alternative skills, such as weaving, and give them small loans for start-up capital. "Most women know how to weave but do not have enough money to buy materials," says Ayele, "so we provide that and we also help them with new and different designs so that they can sell the shawls and dresses that they make more easily."[42] This association is no panacea—it still has not reached Amaretch—but it shows the kind of homegrown effort that foreign donors could support much more.

Poor people have already accomplished far more for themselves than the Planners have accomplished for them, as we will see in a chapter on "homegrown development." Although the West could help alleviate more of the poor's sufferings if it relied more on Searchers in aid agencies and those on the ground such as Etenesh Ayele, the West cannot transform the Rest. It is a fantasy to think that the West can change complex societies with very different histories and cultures into some image of itself. The main hope for the poor is for them to be their own Searchers, borrowing ideas and technology from the West when it suits them to do so.

We have to separate two questions that are usually lumped together: What can Western aid do? How can long-run prosperity be achieved in the Rest? This book is only about question one, except to argue that Western aid is *not* the answer to question two.

Question two is certainly worth asking! It will continue to be a fertile area of exploration for researchers and policymakers. For readers understandably impatient to answer the Big Question of "What can we do *now* to achieve prosperity?" let's just note that the previous fifty years of research have not yielded any simple answers. If there were such simple answers, there would be many more development success stories than there are now. There have been many little answers to particular parts of the Big Question, and further progress is likely to continue in the same way—not through a frontal assault on the Big Question. As Sir Francis Bacon said in the seventeenth century, "So it cometh often to pass, that mean and small things discover great better than great can discover small."[43] This book is about those little answers that can be implemented through Western aid.

One of those uncommon success stories was the country that registered the world's highest per capita growth rate from 1960 to the present. This

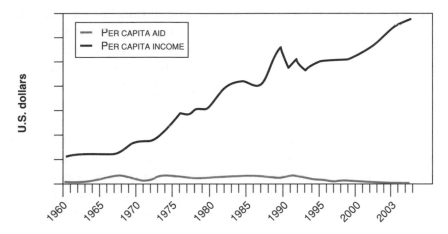

Fig. 1. Income and Aid in Botswana

country is not in East Asia; it is in Africa. Botswana registered 6 percent per capita growth over this period, a historically unprecedented number for so long a period. How much of Botswana's success was due to foreign aid? In the early years, per capita aid was a significant fraction of per capita income. But then aid declined while income soared (see figure 1). While aid may have played some formative role early in independent Botswana's history, the era of rapid growth soon made it an afterthought. Botswana was lucky to have rich diamond mines, but many other poor countries had natural resources but squandered rather than developed them. What was more uncommon for a poor country was that Botswana embraced democracy.

Moving Forward

As for the actions of the West, asking the aid agencies and development workers to attain utopian ideals makes them much worse at achieving the doable things called for by the Searchers. It also makes them much less accountable for making specific things work, as the focus on the Big Goals of the Big Plan distracts everyone's attention from whether more children are getting twelve-cent medicines. Acknowledging that development happens mainly through homegrown efforts would liberate the agencies of the West from utopian goals, freeing up development workers to concentrate on more modest, doable steps to make poor people's lives better.

Idealists, activists, development workers of the world, you have nothing to lose but your utopian chains. Let's give more power and funds to the many Searchers who are already working in development. You don't have to immediately eliminate world poverty, bring world peace, or save the environment. You just have to do whatever you discover works with your modest resources to make a difference in the lives of poor people.

If you want to work on issues at a higher level, there should also be Searchers for how to make piecemeal changes to the foreign aid system to give more power and money to the working-level Searchers. One piecemeal change is honest and independent evaluation of aid agencies, which would make possible rewards for finding things that work and redirection of money to do more of those things. Searchers could think of mechanisms to let the poor themselves show what they want most and what they don't. We will see that there is much scope for improvement just by having the West follow the rule "First do no harm." This book will offer plenty more suggestions for experimental improvements to Western assistance, but don't expect a Big Plan to reform foreign aid. The only Big Plan is to discontinue the Big Plans. The only Big Answer is that there is no Big Answer.

Only an elite few in the West can be Planners. People everywhere, not just in the West, can all be Searchers. Searchers can all look for piecemeal, gradual improvements in the lives of the poor, in the working of foreign aid, in the working of private markets, and in the actions of Western governments that affect the Rest. Many Searchers can watch foreign aid at work in many locales around the world and let their voices be heard when it doesn't deliver the goods. It is time for an end to the second tragedy of the world's poor, which will help make progress on the first tragedy. Searchers can gradually figure out how the poor can give *more* feedback to *more* accountable agents on what *they* know and what *they* most want and need. The big plans and utopian dreams just get in the way, wasting scarce energies. Can't the Searchers just look for how the agents of charity *can* get twelve-cent medicines to children to keep them from dying of malaria, *can* get four-dollar bed nets to the poor to prevent malaria, *can* get three dollars to each new mother to prevent child deaths, *can* get Amaretch into school?

Ghana across a Lifetime

A Volkswagen Beetle creeps through a small town in Ghana along the road from Accra to Cape Coast. It is night. It is hot. The Beetle is small for its five passengers. The air smells of wood smoke. There are no streetlights. The driver—my father—picks his way through the Ghanaian walkers on the road. The car hits frequent potholes. Unlighted vehicles pass us going in the opposite direction. We come out of the town and are in the bush. The smells are now of tropical flowers. We come to the guesthouse where we will spend the night. The bungalow has no light. Somebody lights a kerosene lantern. The odor of kerosene drives out every other smell. For the rest of my life, whenever I smell kerosene, I think of Ghana. My brother, sister, and I stumble sleepily into the wooden guesthouse with verandas, a leftover from British colonizers. My nervous mother, to whom every blind curve in the road was an existential crisis, copes with tropical disorder. The bungalow has only one bedroom; the rest of us make do with sofas or chairs pushed together. We are skittish after sighting a few insects and even bats in the bungalow. We go to sleep anyway, to the rhythms of drums in nearby villages and surf on the nearby coast. My father is a biology professor at the University College of Cape Coast, Ghana, part of the American program to lend knowledge to the development of Africa. We are a family of five from Bowling Green, Ohio. We are white people and we have come to save you. I am twelve years old.

Thirty-five years later, I am again on the road from Accra to Cape Coast. I am a development economics professor, having spent many of the intervening years working on the quest to transform the poor countries of the world, sixteen of them working for the World Bank. Our car is bumping along on one of the worst roads I have ever seen; the donors are building a new road next to the wretched road. Our car swings into the small town of Mprumem, a village of mud huts with thatched roofs. My traveling companion knows the chief of Mprumem, who curiously enough is a Ghanaian immigrant to the United States, working as a university professor in Akron, Ohio. He spends part of every year in Mprumem.

The village elders come to greet us, marching in a dignified file with ceremonial robes and carved walking sticks, scattering goats and chickens, followed by a crowd of curious children. As part of the welcoming ceremony, the elders pass around a glass of schnapps. Each of us in turn (excluding the children) drinks half the contents of the glass and throws the rest on the ground; the attendant then refills the glass for the next person.

The older village elders tell us about how life has changed over time. Many villagers used to suffer from Guinea worm disease when they had to get their water from a contaminated water hole. Guinea worm disease is caused by a tiny water flea that contains the worm larvae. When people drink water containing such fleas, they get infected with the larvae. The larvae hatch inside their bodies, eventually growing to worms as long as three feet. The worms eventually emerge from open sores on the skin. They take weeks to emerge, during which the victim is in agony and cannot work or attend school.[44]

Now the villagers get piped water from the nearby city of Winneba, and there is no Guinea worm. The expansion of water services was financed partly by foreign aid. Even though the water supply is periodically interrupted, the chief has built a water reservoir (financed by Western donations) to store water to tide the people over during water cutoffs. Children are healthier. What's more, the returning chief has also built a junior high school, also financed by Western donations.

Night falls. With only a few homes with electricity, the village is deep in a darkness that few Western urbanites could imagine. The Milky Way is visible in the sky overhead. Walking along the main street of the village, I try not to bump into other walkers in the darkness. A little light comes from vendors selling omelets by candlelight on the street. Fifty people are gathered around to watch television outdoors on one of the few electric hookups. They are watching a funeral. Another part of the funeral occasion that I don't fully comprehend: across the street, speakers are booming out heavy metal, quite a change from the drums of thirty-five years ago. Even the few electric hookups are an improvement from thirty-five years ago (although I personally prefer drums to heavy metal), when so many villages had no electricity at all. Accommodation for the night is basic, but free of insects or bats.

This snapshot, like the other ones interspersed throughout the book, shows anecdotal evidence of how Searchers, like the chief from

Akron, Ohio, or some in the aid agencies, find piecemeal improvements that work, such as electric power, piped water, a water reservoir, the wiped-out Guinea worm, a junior high school. I mean these anecdotes to be suggestive, not "proof" that aid Searchers do better than Planners. (The main text of the book addresses that big issue.) Few of the small interventions that I will describe have been rigorously evaluated, which the book will argue is necessary to make progress. But few things have been rigorously evaluated in foreign aid, period. We have to start somewhere to get ideas on things that could work.

There is still so much more that could be done in Ghana to prevent needless tragedy. Only 46 percent of infants with diarrhea receive the cheap treatment of oral rehydration therapy that dramatically lowers the risk of death. Twenty-nine percent of children are still stunted from malnutrition, which could be alleviated with timely treatment of anti-diarrhea programs, feeding programs, and nutritional supplements. Thirty-one percent of children do not receive the cheap immunizations against childhood killer diseases.[45]

These interventions always seem puny compared with the grand visions of the Planners. Yet if you multiply the Searchers exponentially and contrast their numerous interventions to plans that don't actually work, if you consider the doable things that don't get done because aid does not have enough Searchers, you have a way of thinking about aid that will help the poor more than Gordon Brown's eloquence.

PART I

WHY PLANNERS
CANNOT BRING
PROSPERITY

CHAPTER TWO

The Legend of the Big Push

It is undesirable to believe a proposition when there is no ground whatsoever for supposing it is true.

Bertrand Russell

Why do ineffectual utopian plans dominate the debate on economic development? We have already seen that it is partly explained by the political appeal of utopian plans to rich-country politicians. In addition, the Planners' intellectual inspiration was an old legend about how Western efforts could achieve long-run development, which has come back with a vengeance.

The legend dates back to the 1950s. Many things have changed since the 1950s—we now have air-conditioning, the Internet, new life-saving drugs, and sex in movies. Yet one thing is unchanged: the legend that inspired foreign aid in the 1950s is the same legend that inspires foreign aid today.

The first chapter in this book presents parts of the legend. The full version goes like this: The poorest countries are in a *poverty trap* (they are poor *only* because they started poor) from which they cannot emerge without an aid-financed *Big Push*, involving investments and actions to address all constraints to development, after which they will have a *takeoff* into self-sustained growth, and aid will no longer be needed. This was exactly the legend that gave birth to foreign aid in the 1950s; it is exactly the legend that the advocates of a massive aid increase are telling today. This chapter will test this legend against the evidence that has accumulated over the past fifty years in between the original legend and its remake a half century later. I will tell you up front what you have already guessed: the evidence does not support the legend. This is a classic example of trying again something that didn't work before, one of the traits of Planners.

Let's examine each of the component parts of the legend of development.

LEGEND PART ONE:
THE POOREST COUNTRIES ARE STUCK IN A POVERTY TRAP FROM WHICH THEY CANNOT EMERGE WITHOUT AN AID-FINANCED BIG PUSH

The Big Push of massive aid flow was supposed to get poor countries out of what the UN Millennium Project calls a "poverty trap," which automatically prevents very poor countries from growing. As Jeffrey Sachs explains it in his 2005 book, *The End of Poverty,* "When people are . . . utterly destitute, they need their entire income, or more, just to survive. There is no margin of income above survival that can be invested for the future. This is the main reason why the poorest of the poor are most prone to becoming trapped with low or negative economic growth rates. They are too poor to save for the future and thereby accumulate the capital that could pull them out of their current misery" (pp. 56–57).

We can check this story out. As shown in table 1, we have data on per capita income from 1950 to 2001 for 137 countries, from a statistical compilation done by the economist Angus Maddison. (I exclude Communist economies and Persian Gulf oil producers as special cases.) We rank countries according to their per capita income in 1950. Did the poorest countries in 1950 remain stuck in poverty over the next half century? Well, no. The poorest fifth of countries in 1950 increased their income over the next five decades by a factor of 2.25. The other four fifths increased their incomes by a factor of 2.47. The difference in growth rates between the two groups is not statistically distinguishable from random fluctuation. We can statistically reject that the growth rate of the poorest countries as a group was zero. The only period that fits the legend is 1985–2001, to which I will return.

Table 1. Testing the Poverty Trap for Long Periods

Average per capita growth per year for:	1950–2001	1950–1975	1975–2001	1980–2001	1985–2001
Poorest fifth at beginning of period indicated	1.6	1.9	0.8	0.5*	0.2*
All others	1.7	2.5†	1.1	0.9	1.3†
Reject stable income for poorest fifth	Yes	Yes	Yes	Yes	Yes
Fail to reject unstable income for poorest fifth	Yes	Yes	Yes	Yes	Yes

* Poorest fifth not statistically distinguishable from zero.

† All others' growth statistically distinguishable from poorest fifth.

Sample: 137 countries. Statistical tests exclude 12 transition economies and Persian Gulf oil states.

There are further statistical tests we can do to assess the poverty trap legend. If the legend holds, then the poorest countries should have stagnant income at a very low level. Income will fluctuate randomly around this level, but will always tend to return to it. There are two ways we can test whether there is a cursed stability of low income (known as "stationarity" in statistics jargon). We can assume stagnation and see whether the data reject that assumption, or we can assume instability of income—positive per capita growth is a nice form of instability—and see whether the data are consistent with that assumption (the data fail to reject instability). When we do a test for the stagnation of income over the subsequent half century for the poorest fifth of countries in 1950, we decisively reject the hypothesis of stagnation. When we assume instability—such as positive growth—the data provide no evidence against that assumption.

Perhaps it was aid that enabled poor countries to break out of stagnant income? When I break the sample in half into those poor countries that had above-average foreign aid and those that had below-average foreign aid, I find identical results for 1950–2001 in both halves as with the above tests of stable income. Over 1950–2001, countries with below-average aid had the same growth rate as countries with above-average foreign aid. Poor countries without aid had no trouble having positive growth.

This is a critical finding—the poorest countries *can* grow and develop on their own. Since foreign aid received does not explain these successes, perhaps they happened for entirely homegrown reasons. The Searchers among the poor can find a way toward higher living standards; they do not have to wait for the West to save them.

To be sure, among the poorest countries, there were individual poor countries that failed to grow. Chad had zero growth from 1950 to 2001. Zaire/Democratic Republic of the Congo (DRC) actually had negative per capita growth over this period. Aid still has a role to play to help those unlucky enough to be born into a stagnant economy—even if it doesn't help the overall economy escape stagnation.

The stagnant economies were offset by such success stories as Botswana, which was the fourth poorest in 1950, but which increased its income by a factor of thirteen by 2001. Lesotho was the fifth poorest in 1950, but increased its income by a factor of five over the half century. Two other subsequent success stories who were among the poorest in 1950 are China and India.

Let us keep looking for confirmation of the two main predictions of the poverty trap legend: (1) that growth of the poorest countries is lower than other countries, and (2) that per capita growth of the poorest countries is zero or negative. The poorest did have lower growth than the others in an earlier period, 1950–1975. However, this was not a poverty trap, as average growth of the poorest during 1950–1975 was still a very healthy 1.9 percent per year (roughly the same as the long-run growth rate of the American economy, for example).

There is no evidence of lower growth for the poorest countries for recent periods, such as 1975–2001 or 1980–2001. Their growth was disappointing—much worse than in the previous period—but so was growth in middle-income countries. The poorest fifth of countries at the beginning of those periods had growth performance over the subsequent period that was statistically indistinguishable from the other four fifths of countries. Only when the starting point is put at 1985 does there finally appear evidence that the poorest did worse.

The evidence that Jeffrey Sachs adduces for the poverty trap in his book *The End of Poverty* is from this later period. So, from 1985 to the present, it is true that the poorest fifth of countries have had significantly lower per capita growth than other countries, about 1.1 percentage points lower. The next section will consider further whether this period fits the classic legend of the poverty trap.

The numbers in table 1 don't seem to add up. The poorest countries did not have lower growth in the whole period 1950–2001, but they had slightly lower growth in 1950–1975, and much lower growth in more recent periods. The solution to the conundrum is that the identities of the poorest countries at the start of each period shown keeps changing. It doesn't help the poverty trap legend that eleven out of the twenty-eight poorest countries in 1985 were *not* in the poorest fifth back in 1950. They got into poverty by declining from above, rather than from being stuck in it from below, while others escaped. If the identity of who is in the poverty trap keeps changing, then it must not be much of a trap.

Other scholars have also failed to find any evidence for a "poverty trap."[1] One of the requirements for a poverty trap is the idea that saving is very low for poor people, increasing only at some intermediate level of income. Aart Kraay and Claudio Raddatz, in a January 2005 paper, studied the savings rate in all countries with data and found that that saving does *not* behave the way the poverty trap requires at low income. The reasons countries stay poor must lie elsewhere.

It is still possible that some countries are in a poverty trap; it is just that the average poor country is not. The theory of poverty traps is quite appealing: there are many ways in which we could think that countries are caught in traps. In a previous book, I give an example of how low average skills in the population could discourage new entrants to the labor force from getting skills, perpetuating a low-skill trap. Traps can also form at higher levels of income if there is some factor missing, such as high-quality formal institutions (which may itself be a consequence of insufficient income), keeping an economy stuck at a middle-income level.

With so many possible kinds of traps, it is not possible to definitively prove or refute the existence of traps in general. I can only test the specific form of the poverty trap discussed in the aid debates on the poorest countries, which predicts that being poor means a country will not grow without external assistance. This the data *can* reject.

LEGEND PART TWO:
WHENEVER POOR COUNTRIES HAVE LOUSY GROWTH, IT IS BECAUSE OF A POVERTY TRAP RATHER THAN BAD GOVERNMENT

What about the period of lower growth and stagnation in poor countries in 1985–2001 shown in table 1? The UN Millennium Project argues that it is the poverty trap rather than bad government that explains the poor growth of those countries and their failure to make progress toward the Millennium Development Goals (MDGs). Jeffrey Sachs says, "The claim that Africa's corruption is the basic source of the problem [the poverty trap] does not withstand practical experience or serious scrutiny."[2] Likewise the Millennium Project says, "Many reasonably well governed countries are too poor to make the investments to climb the first steps of the ladder."[3]

Why does it matter whether it is bad government or a technological poverty trap? The case for Planners is even weaker if they must deal with the complexities of bad government. (We will see in chapter 4 just how difficult it has been.) So aid advocates desperately want to disbelieve the bad government explanation for poverty, which is something akin to the church youth group minister who wants to believe that his charges are all virgins. Bad government is also bad for fund-raising for aid. Jeffrey Sachs worries in *The End of Poverty:* "If the poor are poor because... their governments are corrupt, how could global cooperation help?"[4]

Let us test bad government against the poverty trap as an explanation for poor economic growth. The earliest rating we have on corruption is from 1984, from the International Country Risk Guide. We have a rating on democracy for the same year from a research project at the University of Maryland called Polity IV. Let's take countries that have the worst ratings on both corruption and democracy, and call these countries "bad governments." While poor countries did worse, it's also true that the twenty-four countries with bad governments in 1984 had significantly lower growth from 1985 to the present: 1.3 percentage points slower than the rest. There is some overlap between these two stories, as poor countries are much more likely to have bad government. So which is it, bad government or the poverty trap? When we control both for initial poverty and for bad government, it is bad government that explains the slower growth. We cannot statistically discern any effect of initial poverty on subsequent growth once we control for bad government. This is still true if we limit the definition of bad government to corruption alone. The recent stagnation of the poorest countries appears to have more to do with awful government than with a poverty trap, contrary to the UN/Sachs hypothesis. Actually if those preparing the UN Millennium Project report about escaping the well-governed poverty trap had looked at the Millennium Project's own country studies, they would have found interesting clues to this result, such as the following vignette on Cambodian schoolteachers: "Many supplement their income by soliciting bribes from students, including the sale of examination questions and answers. . . . [T]he end result is a high dropout rate."[5]

There is another piece of evidence that we have to consider that looks like it *does* support the poverty trap story. Over the last two centuries, there *has* been a widening gap between rich and poor nations. This is what World Bank economist Lant Pritchett calls in a famous article "Divergence, Big Time." There is historical data on about fifty countries from the economist Angus Maddison. The gap between the richest and poorest countries has widened drastically over the last two centuries, with the ratio of the max to the min going from about six to one two hundred years ago to about seventy to one today. There *is* a positive correlation between per capita growth from, say, 1820 to 2001 and the initial level of income in 1820.

Was this because the poor countries were stuck in a poverty trap? Well, first of all, the data do not fit our definition of a poverty trap—per capita growth of the poorest countries was not zero. The predicted level of annual per capita growth for the poorest countries in the sample in 1820 was 1.05 percent, with a margin of error of .25 percent. One limitation may be that African countries are not in the sample. However, Maddison gives an estimate for per capita income in the continent as a whole in 1820—per capita growth in Africa from 1820 to 2001 is 0.7 percent per annum, a 3.5-fold increase, not a poverty trap.

Still, let us consider the slower growth of the poorest countries as suggestive of a poverty trap. The alternative explanation to the "poverty trap" is that Europe and its offshoots had better government than the Rest. Good government could be correlated with per capita income in 1820, and that could explain why countries that were richer in 1820 subsequently grew faster. The poor countries were stuck with authoritarian governments (or another form of authoritarian rule: colonial occupation). This could imply a bad-government poverty trap, but not the savings-and-technology poverty trap favored by the UN/Sachs story.

I test this story by using again the data from the Polity IV research project, which covers democracy since 1820. I average whatever Polity data are available on each country over the period 1820–2001.[6] It turns out that average democracy is significantly correlated with long-term growth in most specifications, and the positive relationship of growth with initial per capita income declines or even turns negative once you control for quality of government. The latter results would suggest that poor countries grow faster than rich countries if they have a good government (using democracy as a proxy for good government)—contrary to the Millennium Project idea that "many reasonably well governed countries are too poor to make the investments to climb the first steps of the ladder." These results hold up when you control for possible reverse causality going from economic growth to bad government. There is no evidence that initially poor countries are at a disadvantage once you control for good government. The Big Push is not going to work if the problem is bad government rather than a poverty trap. We will see in chapter 4 what tortured conundrums foreign aid encounters when dealing with bad governments.

LEGEND PART THREE:
FOREIGN AID GIVES A BIG PUSH TO COUNTRIES TO ACHIEVE A TAKEOFF INTO SELF-SUSTAINED GROWTH

There is now a regular cycle in the literature on foreign aid and growth. Someone will survey the evidence and find that foreign aid does not produce growth. There will be some to-and-fro in the literature, in the course of which a few studies will find a positive effect of aid on growth. Foreign aid agencies will then seize upon the positive effect, usually focusing on only one study, and will publicize it widely. Researchers will examine the one positive result more carefully and find that it is spurious. Then there will be more to-and-fro in the literature, and a new twist will be discovered under which aid has a positive effect on growth. Aid agencies will seize on this result again, and the cycle will begin all over again.

We have already had a test of old and new theories of the Big Push in Africa. For a region as poor as Africa, aid receipts have *already* been large enough to constitute a Big Push. The typical African country received more than 15 percent of its income from foreign donors in the 1990s. Figure 2 shows the overall outcome for aid and growth in Africa. Aid accelerated as

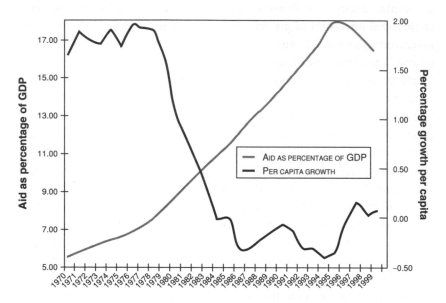

Fig. 2. Aid and Growth in Africa (ten-year moving averages)

growth fell. Note that African growth over the previous ten years had been a respectable 2 percent up to about 1975 (with modest aid), contradicting the idea that Africa is always and everywhere condemned to low growth without aid. There is a negative association, but I don't think the increase in aid *caused* the fall in growth. Rather, the fall in growth probably caused the increase in aid. But the surge of aid was not successful in reversing or halting the slide in growth of income per capita toward zero.

Let us do more formal statistical testing. Long and inconclusive literature on aid and economic growth was produced in the 1960s, 1970s, and 1980s, which was hampered by the limited data availability and inconclusive debate about the mechanisms by which aid would affect growth. The possible reverse causality made conclusions difficult: if donors gave greater aid in response to slower growth, then interpreting how aid flow affected growth could be difficult. The literature got new life in 1996 with a paper by London School of Economics economist Peter Boone, who found that aid financed consumption rather than investment. (Financing consumption of a few poor people is not so bad, but the Big Push hoped for the society-wide transformation that would come from aid financing investment and growth.) Boone addressed the problem of reverse causality by using political factors to predict which countries got aid—usually rich countries gave aid to poor countries that were their political allies, or with which they had a colonial association. When aid is predicted by political factors that are themselves unrelated to growth outcomes, you can examine whether the predicted values of aid caused higher growth. Even controlling for possible reverse causality, Boone found aid to have zero effect on investment. Similarly, controlling for reverse causality, he found aid to have zero effect on growth. *The Economist* publicized Boone's research, and it was widely known in the aid policymaking community.

Boone's research created a terrible disjunction: aid policy was based on the premise that aid raises growth, but now the best study of the question was saying that this premise was false. Soon a study appeared to fill the vacuum between policy and research,[7] an academic study by World Bank economists Craig Burnside and David Dollar.[8] I am not saying that Burnside and Dollar consciously set out to reach a predetermined conclusion, which would obviously have been bad science. Rather, theirs was a serious scientific study; there were also other equally serious studies that found different results. The point is, the policy community chose to believe the finding that was most favorable to the aid policies it wanted to implement.

Burnside and Dollar related growth rates in developing countries to foreign aid received, as figure 2 does for Africa. However, their new twist distinguished between aid recipients who had "good" policies (measured by things such as low budget deficits, low inflation, and free trade) and those with "bad" policies. Their hypothesis was that good policy increased the payoff to aid, so growth should be related to aid among countries with good policy. This was intuitively appealing, because it recognized that bad government could be the problem, as discussed in the previous section. If poor countries had good governments, then perhaps aid would increase growth after all.

Their sample consisted of six four-year time periods running from 1970–1973 to 1990–1993. In many of their tests, they found that when a country both got more foreign aid and had good policy, growth went up. They summarized: "We find that aid has a positive impact on growth in developing countries with good fiscal, monetary, and trade policies but has little effect in the presence of poor policies" (p. 847).

Their paper reinforced the hope that aid could accomplish great deeds, which fed a policy recommendation to increase foreign aid to a country only if that country's policies were good. In early 2002, *The Economist* rebuked then U.S. Treasury secretary Paul O'Neill for his skepticism about foreign aid on the grounds that "there is now a strong body of evidence, led by the research of David Dollar, Craig Burnside[,] ... economists at the World Bank, that aid does boost growth when countries have reasonable economic policies." An article in the *New Yorker* in 2002 chimed in that "aid can be effective in any country where it is accompanied by sensible economic policies," based on the Dollar and Burnside study.

President George W. Bush was apparently reading the *American Economic Review* as well. On March 14, 2002 (any coincidence in timing with the war on terror is purely intentional), he announced a five-billion-dollar increase in U.S. foreign assistance, about a 50 percent increase.[9]

The White House followed up on November 26, 2002, with the creation of the Millennium Challenge Corporation (MCC), whose job is to administer the five-billion-dollar increment in foreign aid. Arguing that aid works only with good policies, the administration announced sixteen indicators of country performance to guide the selection of countries to receive MCC aid—three of the indicators were versions of the Burnside and Dollar policy measures (most of the rest were measures of quality of institutions). On its Web site, the White House said that the new aid was motivated by the idea that "economic development assistance can be successful only if it is linked to sound policies in developing countries."[10]

In May 2004, the Millennium Challenge Corporation announced the selection of sixteen "good policy" countries eligible to apply for its aid grants from fiscal year 2004 funds.[11] In March 2005, the MCC reached its first agreement with a "good policy" country, a Millennium Challenge Compact with Madagascar.

How much can we rely on the original study that sent this freight train down the tracks? A study I did with Ross Levine (Brown University), and David Roodman (Center for Global Development) used the exact same techniques and specifications as Burnside and Dollar, but added new data that had become available since Burnside and Dollar did their study. We also hunted for more data in their original sample period (1970–1993). We found more data even over their sample period by consulting the original sources rather than secondary sources. Using updated data, we did the same statistical exercise with four-year averages with the same control variables, including terms for aid/GDP, and their policy index (a weighted average of budget deficits/GDP, inflation, and an index of openness to trade). We found no evidence that aid raised growth among countries with good policies, indicating no support for the conclusion that "aid works in a good policy environment." Our study was published as a comment on Burnside and Dollar in the *American Economic Review*.

The original researchers and other researchers may have tried many different statistical exercises, but the aid policy community is tempted to select the study that confirms its prior beliefs (known as "confirmation bias")—even though other statistical exercises may have found no evidence for it. Applying new data to the old statistical exercise is a good test of whether the original result really holds and is not just confirmation bias. The statistical exercise with the new data is constrained by the old statistical exercise, so you are not searching among many different exercises for the one confirming prior beliefs. Even good first-round research can suffer from confirmation bias.[12]

The cycle is now starting all over again. After my co-authors and I found no evidence for the "aid works in a good policy environment" conclusion, a new study came out by Michael Clemens, Steven Radelet, and Rikhil Bhavnani (hereafter denoted CRB) of the Center for Global Development. I respect these authors a lot and think they were following high academic standards. Their new twist on the statistical exercise was to separate aid that could be expected to have an impact on growth in the short run from aid that had either a humanitarian purpose or could work only in the long run, such as health or education aid. They found a strong growth effect for their preferred category of aid ("short-impact aid")—and not only when there was good policy in the recipient country.

Again, the original research was scientific; the use of it was less so. Aid advocates once again regarded the new finding as supporting their recommendations. The UN Millennium Project Report in January 2005 cited the CRB study as providing support for the project's proposal of massive increases in aid.[13] The Blair Commission for Africa, in March 2005, recommended an immediate doubling of aid to Africa, and cited the CRB findings as support for its recommendations.[14]

Unfortunately for these recommendations, researchers again subjected the positive aid findings to further scrutiny and found them wanting. The chief economist of the International Monetary Fund, Raghuram Rajan, and IMF researcher Arvind Subramanian subjected the CRB finding to statistical testing. They used the simplest specification to control for possible reverse causality from adverse country characteristics to aid receipts, and a standard specification for the determinants of growth. In their May 2005 study, Rajan and Subramanian found no evidence that either "short-impact aid" or any other type of aid had a positive effect on growth.[15] For good measure, they also tested the Burnside-Dollar hypothesis yet again, and found no evidence that "aid works in a good policy environment."

They also considered some alternative explanations as to why foreign aid does *not* raise growth. One well-justified complaint about aid is that it is often tied to the purchase of goods and consultants from the donor country, which may prevent the aid from bringing much growth to the recipient country. Another possibility is that the donor country gives the aid for political reasons, which again may limit the aid's effectiveness. There is one simple test of these explanations—only aid from national aid agencies (bilateral aid) is tied, while aid from the World Bank and regional development banks (multilateral aid) is not. Similarly, bilateral aid is far more politicized than multilateral aid. Rajan and Subramanian found, however, that there was no difference between the effects of bilateral and multilateral aid on growth. Another test they did was to see if having a high share of aid coming from Scandinavian countries (which are less motivated by political alliances and do less aid tying) was associated with faster growth—they found it was not.

With so little light shed by statistical studies of growth, the big picture is perhaps still useful in evaluating the aid and growth relationship. Do we believe that African growth would have declined even more sharply from the mid-seventies to the present but for the tripling of aid as a percentage of income?

There is another aspect to both the Burnside-Dollar and CRB studies that aid agencies and advocates have chosen to emphasize much less. To the extent that they found any growth effect at all, both Burnside-Dollar and CRB found that the larger the aid already was, the smaller was the additional growth benefit from that additional injection of aid. In the CRB study, their category of aid had a *zero* effect on growth when it reached 8 percent of the recipient's GDP, and after that the additional aid had a *negative* effect on growth. This feature of their results directly contradicts the Big Push reasoning, which is that small sums don't help because you need a sufficiently *large* mobilization of aid to fix all the big problems simultaneously (that's why it had to be a *Big* Push). This theory implies that the larger the aid is already, the larger the additional growth benefit from an additional injection of aid. This is contrary to CRB. There are already twenty-seven countries with aid receipts over the 8 percent of GDP at which the CRB-estimated effect of additional aid turned negative; if the donors adopt the current Big Push proposals, virtually all low-income countries (forty-seven of them) will be far above that level.[16] Unfortunately, the Blair report and the Millennium Project report select research results to support a Big Push idea that is contradicted even by the selected studies themselves.

We can also check on some of the intermediate steps in the aid and growth story. Jeffrey Sachs and co-authors previously predicted that large aid increases would finance "a 'big push' in public investments to produce a rapid 'step' increase in Africa's underlying productivity, both rural and urban."[17] Alas, we have already seen this movie, and it doesn't have a happy ending. There is good data on public investment for twenty-two

African countries over the 1970–1994 period. These countries' governments spent \$342 billion on public investment. The donors gave these same countries' governments \$187 billion in aid over that period. Unfortunately, the corresponding "step" increase in productivity, measured as production per person, was *zero*. Perhaps part of the reason for this was such disasters as the five billion dollars spent on the publicly owned Ajaokuta steel mill in Nigeria, begun in 1979, which has yet to produce a bar of steel.[18]

What about the elusive "takeoff" into self-sustained growth? If we define "takeoff" as a one-time shift from zero growth to sustained positive growth, there are surprisingly few countries whose development experiences fit this description. Most countries that escaped from extreme poverty did so with gradually accelerating growth, sometimes punctuated by crises of zero or negative growth. Japan is the only rich country that became rich by means of a takeoff. In more recent data, there are only eight countries (all in South and East Asia) that had a takeoff in the period 1950–1975: China, Hong Kong, India, Indonesia, Singapore, South Korea, Taiwan, and Thailand. Three of the eight countries had aid-to-GDP ratios above the norm: Indonesia, South Korea, and Taiwan; in the others, aid did not play an important role in their takeoff. Moreover, other countries got high foreign aid over this period and did not take off. Statistically, countries with high aid are no more likely to take off than are those with low aid—contrary to the Big Push idea.

So the aid Planners keep pouring in aid resources with the fixed objective of stimulating higher growth, although evidence does not support an effect of aid on growth.

The Problem of Evaluating the White Man's Burden

One thing that makes the aid debate so contentious is that it is not easy to evaluate the effect of Big Pushes. Actually, one argument *against* Big Push programs is that they are so hard to evaluate. All of the major interventions of the White Man's Burden have similar evaluation difficulties.

My daughter Grace asked me several years ago as we were driving on the Washington Beltway, "Daddy, why do ambulances make so many accidents?" Of course, now that she is nine, Grace knows that the presence of an ambulance at every accident is a consequence rather than a cause of the accident. The presence of the IMF and World Bank and aid agencies at country crises is surely a consequence rather than as a cause of the accident. This is the selection effect—ambulances show up at car wrecks, not at tailgate parties.

This is the same as the reverse causality problem just mentioned about foreign aid. Once you control for the selection effect, you find that things could have been even worse without the aid. This is what is called the counterfactual question: How does what happened with the White Man's Burden compare to what would have happened *without* the White Man's Burden?

There are several approaches that can partially (but not completely) resolve the selection problem and address the counterfactual question for the big programs of the White Man's Burden. One is to find factors that are *not* themselves determined by an economic crisis and to ask if the variation in the White Man's Burden programs associated with those factors had positive or negative effects. If some ambulances just patrolled a neighborhood because the mayor lived there, we could evaluate the effect of the ambulance patrol on survival from heart attacks by comparing what happened to the heart attack victims who lived next door to the mayor with what happened to victims elsewhere. All the statements I make earlier about "controlling for reverse causality" are based on some method like this. The method is never perfect. For example, it won't work if being the mayor's neighbor has a direct effect on your survival fitness that has nothing to do with the ambulance patrol—that would contaminate the comparison between the mayor's neighbors and others.

Another is to analyze cases where there were repeated White Man's Burden efforts. If ambulances keep showing up at the accident, but the injured still do not get any help for their injuries, you would question how good the ambulance service is. Unfortunately, these methods are not always available, but we still need some way of judging real-world programs that are going ahead anyway. The last resort, which is far from perfect but still provides insight, is simply to describe the results of a program or intervention. If a program is associated with a disastrous outcome, you need to believe that things would have been even more disastrous without the program. If all the ambulance patients are always DOA at the hospital, it's hard to believe that the ambulances are doing any good. This book will use all of these methods.

Alternative to the Legend of Development

Fortunately, there are some people who work on aid and poverty who do have a more neutral, modest mind-set. These are mainly academic economists, who are woefully short of a plan to eradicate poverty or achieve world peace. They are not good visionaries and are terrible at public relations. They experiment and come up with smaller but more useful things that outsiders can do to help the poor, which they subject to ruthless testing to see if they really work.

With smaller interventions, more rigorous evaluation is available to address the counterfactual question. One scientific method used is the controlled experiment. The control group represents what would have happened to the treatment group without the treatment. The difference between the two groups is the effect of the treatment.

The researcher must choose both groups randomly—say, a lottery determines who is in the treatment group and who is in the control group. If you assign people based on some other criteria, then the difference between the treatment and the control groups could reflect the selection criteria rather than the treatment. For example, if you assigned people with more severe problems to the treatment group, then you could get a spurious negative effect of treatment. (You don't want to test the effect of ambulances on health by comparing the health of ambulance patients to that of the man on the street.) Conversely, if you assigned those with the most potential to benefit from the treatment to the treatment group, then you would get an overestimate of the treatment effect.

The U.S. Food and Drug Administration (FDA) follows this approach when it decides if new drugs work. It first does randomized treatment and control groups. If the drug works for the treatment group compared with the control group, then everyone gets the drug.[19] The FDA may feel a stronger incentive to use scientific methods than aid agencies because it is democratically accountable to voters, who are the same group that will be using FDA-approved drugs. If the drugs do not actually work among the general population, or if they generate side effects that kill off the patients, the new drug users (or their survivors) will complain to the politicians. The politicians will put the heat on the FDA, which will then take more care to test scientifically what really works but does not include bad side effects. The intended beneficiaries of the aid agencies—the poorest people in the poor countries—don't have a similar way to put heat on the agencies.

The Dutch aid organization International Christian Support Fund (ICS) distributed deworming drugs to schoolchildren in southern Busia district, Kenya, where 92 percent of children were infected with intestinal worms that caused listlessness, malnutrition, and pain. Economists Michael Kremer of Harvard and Edward Miguel of Berkeley took the randomized approach in assessing the effects of deworming drugs. Kremer and Miguel studied programs that administered drugs and that conducted worm-prevention education for schools in Busia district, Kenya. The ICS project phased in the programs over three years, so there were three groups for Kremer and

Miguel to study. In the first phase, phase I schools could be compared to phase II and III schools. In the second phase, phase I and II schools could be compared to phase III schools. Kremer and Miguel were able to identify a positive effect of deworming drugs on school attendance and a zero effect of deworming education on worm infection rates. The deworming drugs decreased school absenteeism by one quarter. "Pupils who had been miserable now became active and lifeful," said schoolteacher Wiafred Mujema.[20]

Kremer and Miguel's practical scientific approach identified a way to help children stay in school (give them deworming drugs) and also identified other methods that didn't work (educate children on behavior to prevent worm infection). After the results came in, ICS expanded its deworming program; it now covers all of Busia district plus neighboring Teso district. Other aid organizations have imitated the deworming program around the world. If this practical, critical approach spreads, much more of the foreign aid dollars available could actually reach the poor! And then maybe aid advocates could make the case for more foreign aid.

Not all scientific work is on randomized trials of individual interventions; some is on statistical analysis of aggregate data. And not all findings are positive; some tell policymakers and aid officials what *not* to do. Researchers Thorsten Beck, Asli Demirgüç-Kunt (both at the World Bank), and Ross Levine (Brown University) studied whether small and medium enterprises (SMEs) were catalysts for poverty reduction. The aid community believes in SMEs' catalytic role, with the World Bank having lent $10 billion to support SMEs over the last five years.[21] USAID spends about $170 million a year on micro-enterprise promotion.[22]

Unfortunately, in a thorough review of both firm-level and macroeconomic data, Beck, Demirgüç-Kunt, and Levine found no evidence that SME promotion created economic growth or poverty reduction. They sensibly point out that there is nothing sacred about small firms. Firm size reflects many things, such as whether it is more efficient to handle transactions in the marketplace or inside the firm or whether a given technology is more productive at a large or small scale. Some countries and sectors may be more competitive with small firms; others with large firms. There is no reason that aid Planners should try to artificially promote one size firm versus a different size firm.

This skeptical paper caused panic in the pro-SME aid community. I myself got an e-mail from a contractor for an aid agency asking me to write a paper refuting Beck, Demirgüç-Kunt, and Levine. I declined, explaining that academic researchers usually don't first find the defendant guilty, and then afterward hold a trial.

Other development researchers study many aspects of economic policy, institutions, and politics of poor countries to identify things that seem to contribute to development, based on statistical evidence from household-level, firm-level, and country-level data. These studies point to piecemeal ways to move toward prosperity, such as keeping roads in good condition or pursuing good monetary policies to keep inflation low—not big answers or comprehensive reforms.

Unfortunately, the stubborn survival of the legend of the Big Push, despite evidence of its failure, has continued to foster the planning approach to development. The Planners' response to failure of previous interventions was to do even more intensive and comprehensive interventions. The next two chapters examine some more of the economic and political complexity that makes these top-down plans fail.

Teenage Paramedic

The death of mothers during childbirth is virtually unknown in rich countries, but it is tragically common in poor countries. Instead of the new life with childbirth that many of us in rich countries count as the most supreme moment in a lifetime, a family in a poor country must too frequently confront the death of the wife and mother (and often of the newborn baby as well). The woman herself dies in agony due to such causes as the seizures and severe agitation of eclampsia. Eclampsia (and other causes of death in childbirth) can be prevented with prenatal care that recognizes the warning signs and gets the woman to the hospital once she displays those signs. Providing such prenatal care is a major challenge in poor countries.

Feroza Yasmin Shahida is a nineteen-year-old Bangladeshi girl from a poor peasant family. She got a scholarship from a program run by USAID and the World Bank to finish secondary school. Now she is a bicycle paramedic responsible for 515 families in the countryside around Savar, Bangladesh. She is the only health worker these 515 families have. She earns twenty-five dollars a month working for Gonoshasthaya Kendra (GK), the "People's Health Center."

GK is the brainchild of Dr. Zafrullah Chowdhury (affectionately called Dr. Zaf), a Bangladeshi doctor who returned from Britain after Bangladesh won its independence in 1971. Dr. Zaf trained teenage girls to treat common ailments, deliver prenatal and post-natal care to pregnant women, and refer any emergencies to the hospital that he built. Foreign donors and the Bangladeshi government gave Dr. Zaf money, but he also charged his poor patients modest fees to expand services further. He found that even the poor were willing to pay for good service. Charging the poor modest fees for health care—a notion that outrages Planners and anti-globalization activists—is a way to increase accountability for delivering health services. If the villagers don't get good service after they have sacrificed to pay for it, they loudly complain. Dr. Zaf says, "If a woman dies, the worker has to face the village. Accountability is here." GK has been successful in lowering maternal deaths in childbirth, infant mortality, and also the number of children that women choose to have. Maternal mortality in the area covered by GK is one fourth of the national average.

If Feroza continues to be one of Dr. Zaf's best paramedics, she will be promoted to supervisor, with a raise to one hundred dollars a month and a scooter instead of a bicycle. Dr. Zaf searched for and found a piecemeal way to improve the lot of the Bangladeshi poor.

The Secret History of Grameen Bank

Mohammad Yunus of Bangladesh, the founder of the Grameen Bank and the main inventor of microcredit schemes, didn't start off with the goal of giving poor people credit. As Columbia University Business School professor Bill Duggan tells the story in a great book about people who find things that work, *Napoleon's Glance,* Yunus started off with the conviction that the Green Revolution, and irrigation, was the answer to poverty in Bangladesh. His doctoral dissertation at Vanderbilt University was titled "Optimal Allocation of Multi-Purpose Reservoir Water: A Dynamic Programming Model." His first attempt to help the poor was to sponsor tube wells for irrigation during the dry season so farmers could grow two crops a year. Yunus gave the farmers a loan out of his own money to finance the scheme. The farmers reaped a good harvest. Ironically for the founder of the idea that the poor can be a good credit risk, the farmers didn't fully repay Yunus, and he lost money. But he persisted, with the city boy visiting as many rural villages as possible to try to understand how to help. He encountered a woman named Sufiya Begum making a bamboo stool. Begum made a pitiful two cents on every stool, mainly because a moneylender charged her a very high interest rate (around 120 percent per year) to advance her the bamboo. Yunus realized that very small loans to very poor people could make a big difference in their lives. Contrary to conventional wisdom at the time, he realized that the poor had a huge untapped demand for credit. He experimented, and found that microcredit borrowers would repay the loan in order to get access to future loans and also because of peer pressure from other microcredit borrowers. His first loan was to Sufiya Begum, who started a successful peddling business with the money, instead of making more bamboo stools. There was a huge demand for such loans, and Grameen Bank became the legend that it is today, with imitators from all over the world. Yunus was a Searcher.

Microcredit is not a panacea for poverty reduction that some made it out to be after Yunus's discovery. Some disillusionment with microcredit has already come in response to these blown-up expectations. Microcredit didn't solve everything; it just solved one particular problem under one particular set of circumstances—the poor's lack of access to credit except at usurious rates from moneylenders.

CHAPTER THREE

You Can't Plan
a Market

The nature of man is intricate;
the objects of society are of the greatest complexity:
and therefore no simple disposition
or direction of power can be suitable
either to man's nature
or to the quality of his affairs.

Edmund Burke, "Reflections on the
Revolution in France," 1790[1]

The failure of the Big Push led to some soul-searching among foreign aid agencies, beginning in the 1980s. Maybe the failure was due to poor countries' interference with free markets. After all, if one of the secrets of Western prosperity was the feedback and accountability of free markets, the most obvious thing the West could do to transform the Rest was to introduce free markets.

The next step in escalation of the White Man's Burden was to condition aid on the Rest's adopting a rapid transition to markets. There is usually a sharp division between those who favor free markets and those who don't, with each camp fearful of ceding any ground to the other. This book arrives at a paradoxical finding: free markets work, but free-market reforms often don't.

To explain this paradox, this chapter will discuss how introducing free markets from the top down is not so simple. It overlooks the long sequence of choices, institutions, and innovations that have allowed free markets to develop in the rich Western economies. It also overlooks the bottom-up perspective on how markets often *don't* function well in the low-income societies of Africa, Latin America, Asia, and the former Communist bloc. Markets everywhere emerge in an unplanned, spontaneous way, adapting to local traditions and circumstances, and not through reforms designed by outsiders. The free market depends on the bottom-up emergence of complex institutions and social norms that are difficult for outsiders to understand, much less change.

Paradoxically, the West tried to *plan* how to achieve a *market*. Even after evidence accumulated that these outsider-imposed free markets were not working, unfortunately, the interests of the poor did not have enough weight to force a change in Western policy. Planners underestimated how difficult it is to get markets working in a socially beneficial way. People everywhere have to explore with piecemeal, experimental steps how to move toward free markets.

Russian Nights

Russia became a free-market economy on January 1, 1992. At least that's what the West told the Russians they were becoming when the Russians removed controls on prices and soon after privatized state enterprises, with advice from us hubris-laden Western experts. Western economists wrote a prominent article in 1992 promising Russians that "enormous scope exists for increases in average living standards within a few years."[2] The same economists said in December 1991 that the Russian "shock therapy" plan (the top-down imposition of markets) contained "all the essential elements necessary for rapid transition to the market."[3]

Russia received thirteen structural adjustment loans in the 1990s alone. Thousands of percent inflation and a decade of production collapse later, we outside experts had to admit that the market had not created "enormous scope . . . for increases in average living standards within a few years." Overnight transformation to a market economy had joined the list of failed utopian schemes.

Economists like me were slow on the uptake, in that it took us a decade of failure to convince us that top-down imposition of markets did not work. With the World Bank, I was intermittently working on Russia in 1990–1995, and I confess I believed in shock therapy. Like many other Western economists flooding Moscow at the time, I had only the most superficial knowledge of Russian institutions and history. Economists more familiar with the pre-reform Soviet Union were much more prescient. University of Maryland economist Peter Murrell—a longtime student of centrally planned economies—wrote a series of articles in 1991–1993 arguing against shock therapy as utopian social engineering. At the time, he lost the argument. He wrote to me recently that to try to convince other economists of his views was itself a "utopian" project, and he turned his attention to other subjects after 1993. History vindicated Murrell's scathing description of shock therapy: "There is complete disdain for all that exists. . . . History, society, and the economics of present institutions are all minor issues in choosing a reform program. . . . Establishment of a market economy is seen as mostly involving destruction . . . shock therapists assume that technocratic solutions are fairly easy to implement. . . . One must reject all existing arrangements."[4]

Murrell was quick to realize the relevance of Burke and Popper for events in Russia. His quote of Popper in 1992 is a perfect prediction of how Russian reform would fail: "It is not reasonable to assume that a complete reconstruction of our social system would lead at once to a workable system."[5]

Economists Clifford Gaddy and Barry Ickes, also longtime Soviet experts, closely followed the response of the old Soviet enterprises to the new environment of markets. Shock therapy predicted that those enterprises that were most competitive at the new market–determined prices would expand, while inefficient dinosaurs would go extinct. That is not what happened, according to Gaddy and Ickes. The Soviet plant managers had had a network of relationships with state bureaucrats and other plant managers that enabled the managers to survive. Using the barter and delivery of goods to offset tax liabilities, they managed to keep producing goods nobody wanted in a "virtual economy" that had no resemblance to the fantasies of shock therapists. The share of Russian enterprises that were running losses actually increased in the early years of shock therapy, to 40 percent, and has since remained stable.[6]

In one illustrative example, the Middle Volga Chemicals Plant in Samara Oblast managed to find a "market" for ten tons of toxic chemicals. It passed these along to the Samara Oblast government in lieu of obligations to pay into the unemployment fund. The Samara government in turn used these chemicals to satisfy its obligation as a relatively rich region to make transfer payments to poor regions. It did so by agreeing with the Russian Ministry of Labor that Samara would ship goods to the unemployment compensation fund in the poor republic of Mari-El. So the ten tons of toxic chemicals wound up in Yoshkar-Ola, the capital of Mari-El. What the unemployed workers in Mari-El did with ten tons of toxic chemicals is not known.[7]

As this example suggests, some Soviet enterprises were surviving even though they were using up valuable inputs to produce worthless outputs. They got subsidized electricity and gas from the state electricity and gas monopolies. The latter, Gazprom, was sitting on huge deposits of natural gas, and was one of the few sources of genuine value creation in the economy. Many other enterprises were actually destroying value rather than creating it. They could sustain the demand for their worthless output by using their Soviet-era relationships with other worthless firms. For example, enterprise A could produce some crap that enterprise B would accept as an input to produce its own crap, which B in turn would pass along to enterprise C, who would close the loop by selling its crap as an input back to enterprise A. Meanwhile, A, B, and C were all using up valuable gas and electricity. The Soviet-trained plant managers at the bottom outwitted the shock therapists at the top. The local and often the federal authorities went along with the game because they did not want to face large-scale unemployment.

As far as companies that were actually producing value were concerned, they were the target more of private looting than of private entrepreneurial activity. The Russian "free-market reforms" included privatization of former state enterprises. The reforms followed the disastrous sequence of free markets and privatization without first creating the rules that make profit-seeking behavior beneficial to society. Searchers in markets need rules or else they become opportunists who benefit at others' expense. In 1995, in return for support of the "pro-market reformer" Boris Yeltsin, for example, Russian tycoons snatched up the valuable firms at bargain-basement prices. At the auction of the prize oil company Yukos, the Yeltsin government excluded bids from foreign buyers, eliminating most deep-pocket competitors. The Yeltsin government also allowed the banks running the auction to bid on the properties they themselves were auctioning. So Mikhail Khodorkovsky could bid on the auction of Yukos, even though he owned the bank running the auction, Menatep. Russian privatization chief Alfred Kokh alleged that Khodorkovsky used the money of Yukos itself to bid for Yukos, perhaps by pledging future oil deliveries in return for loans. He managed to buy 77 percent of Yukos shares for $309 million in December 1995.[8] This was a pretty good deal for a company that by 2003 reached a market valuation of $30 billion.[9] Khodorkovsky joined the top ranks on *Forbes*'s annual billionaires list.

Thirteen years after the official crusade to remake Russia in the image of the United States began, the patient is ailing. This is not just a metaphor: the Russians are dying at alarming rates. After the collapse of communism, the Russian suicide rate increased by 50 percent. Life expectancy increased almost everywhere else except for AIDS-crisis countries, but it declined in Russia, especially for men (see figure 3). This trend began in the latter decades of the Soviet Union, and has continued in post-Soviet Russia.[10]

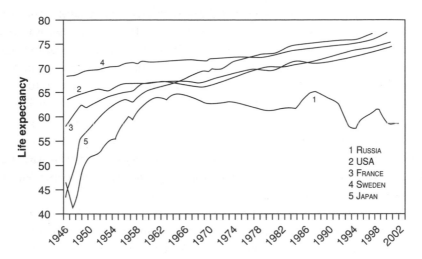

Fig. 3. Life Expectancy for Men in Russia and Developed Countries, from UNDP Russia Human Development Report

After the Western illusion of supporting "democratic reformers" such as Yeltsin, Yeltsin's anointed successor, Vladimir Putin, stamped out much of the little democracy Yeltsin had left behind. In 2004, Freedom House downgraded Russia from "partly free" to "not free." Putin went after Mikhail Khodorkovsky for alleged nonpayment of taxes (a crime that would apply to most of the Russian population). A court convicted Khodorkovsky in May 2005 and sentenced him to nine years in prison.

The Russian economy has registered strong growth since the crisis of 1998, but this is only partial recovery from a deep trough. Russian per capita income in 2004 was still 17 percent below the Soviet peak in 1989. The public is underwhelmed: in a survey in December 2004, 41 percent of the population viewed the economy's performance as "poor," while a more sanguine 46 percent described it as "mediocre." After seven years of "transition," 70 percent of the Russian population in 1999 thought the country was headed in the "wrong direction." After partial economic recovery, Russians cheered up enough that only 56 percent thought it was still going in the wrong direction in January 2005.[11]

The Flight of Icarus

Shock therapy was the application to Russia of what the World Bank and the IMF called "structural adjustment," which in turn was heir to the Big Push.

Structural adjustment loans were the brainchild of World Bank president Robert McNamara and his deputy, Ernest Stern, who sketched out the idea on a flight the two took together to the World Bank/IMF Annual Meeting in Belgrade in late September 1979. Structural adjustment loans were given to finance imports, and were conditional upon countries adopting free markets. The IMF, which had already been doing conditional loans for a long time, signed on to the new idea. What was the inspiration for what turned out to be a historic World Bank mistake of financing comprehensive reforms instead of financing piecemeal improvements? The idea was that developing countries needed the big reforms in order for individual projects to be productive, hence the escalation of World Bank intervention.

This reasoning was appealing. I used to believe in shock therapy and structural adjustment. We proponents of such comprehensive reforms convinced ourselves at the time that partial reform would not work unless all of the complementary reforms happened quickly and simultaneously. Sometimes we clinched the argument with a metaphor like "You can't cross a chasm in two leaps." It seemed plausible that the returns on small interventions would be low if the whole economic and political system was messed up—hence the attempt to remake the system in one fell swoop.

What we shock therapists didn't realize was that *all* reforms are partial; it is impossible to do everything at once, and no policymaker has enough information even to know what "everything" is. The choice is between large-scale partial reforms (which shock therapy mislabels as comprehensive reforms) and small-scale partial reforms. Either large-scale or small-scale partial reforms could backfire, but it is much easier to correct the small mistakes than the large mistakes. The "unintended consequences" problem is greater with a large-scale reform than with a smaller one. The attempted changes at the top are out of touch with the complexity at the bottom, as we will see in this chapter. To make a long story short, the shock therapy often ran afoul of poor institutions that failed to prevent public corruption and private looting. The overambitious reforms of shock therapy and structural adjustment were the flight of Icarus for the World Bank and the IMF. Aiming for the sun, they instead descended into a sea of failure.

The World Bank and the IMF gave Côte d'Ivoire twenty-six structural adjustment loans in the 1980s and 1990s. Per capita income in the country plunged throughout the period in one of the worst and longest depressions in economic history. Today, Côte d'Ivoire is mired in civil war. Indeed, it's a little unnerving that almost all recent cases of collapses into anarchy were preceded by heavy World Bank and IMF involvement. Although I don't think the IMF and the World Bank caused the Ivorian collapse into anarchy, it would be hard to argue that their involvement in the country had a *positive* long-run effect.

I have picked out the African countries that were in the top twenty worldwide in the number of structural adjustment loans received from the World Bank and the IMF. Most African countries that received intensive treatment from structural adjustment have had negative or zero growth. I have also listed the top ten recipients of structural adjustment loans in the ex-Communist countries. Most ex-Communist countries that received shock therapy and many structural adjustment loans have had sharply negative growth and high inflation (see table 2).

Table 2. Structural Adjustment Loans, Growth, and Inflation in Poor Countries with most Structural Adjustment Loans Received

	Number of IMF and World Bank adjustment loans 1980–1999	Annual per capita growth rate from the date of first structural adjustment loan (%)	Annual inflation rate from first adjustment loan to 1999 (%)
African Countries That Were in the World's Top Twenty of Structural Adjustment Loans Received 1980–1999			
Niger	14	−2.30	2
Zambia	18	−2.10	58
Madagascar	17	−1.80	17
Togo	15	−1.60	5
Côte d'Ivoire	26	−1.40	6
Malawi	18	−0.20	23
Mali	15	−0.10	4
Mauritania	16	0.10	7
Senegal	21	0.10	5
Kenya	19	0.10	14
Ghana	26	1.20	32
Uganda	20	2.30	50
Top Ten Recipients of Structural Adjustment Loans over 1990–1999 Among Ex-Communist Countries (Growth and Inflation Measured from First Adjustment Loan to 1999)			
Ukraine	10	−8.4	215
Russian Federation	13	−5.7	141
Kyrgyz Republic	10	−4.4	25
Kazakhstan	9	−3.1	117
Bulgaria	13	−2.2	124
Romania	11	−1.2	114
Hungary	14	1.0	16
Poland	9	3.4	52
Albania	8	4.4	40
Georgia	7	6.4	37

On balance, the outcomes associated with frequent structural adjustment lending are poor. Using the methods of evaluation mentioned earlier, one finds that, first, things were so bad in so many countries that were recipients of structural adjustment loans that it stretches belief that the loans had a strong *positive* effect. Second, since structural adjustment loans were repeated year after year, one wonders why the patient did not improve after repeated doses of the medicine. Finally, formal statistical methods to control for possible reverse causality from crisis to treatment still found that structural adjustment lending has had a zero or negative effect on economic growth.[12] Another influential recent study by Adam Przeworski of New York University and James Vreeland of Yale found that the effect of IMF programs on growth was negative, even when the study controlled for the adverse-selection effect. Another piece of evidence: as we see in a later chapter, African countries (even the "success stories") couldn't pay back zero-interest structural adjustment loans, and the World Bank and IMF had to forgive the debts. The White Man's Burden was deployed in other ex-Communist countries of Eastern Europe and the former Soviet Union besides Russia. These countries themselves technically had white people, but the Western whites were convinced they had missionary gifts for their Eastern counterparts. Unfortunately, the attempted leap across the chasm fell a little short of the other side, as shown in figure 4, aside from the Polish success story. It's hard to know how to attribute blame for this disaster, but clearly the high expectations of the Western reformers were not realized.

Another region where there was great hope for comprehensive reform was Latin America, which had followed a regime of state intervention and restrictions on free trade from the 1950s through the 1970s. After the debt crisis of the early 1980s, in which Latin American countries were cut off from access to new loans from international private banks, the countries started moving toward free markets. As usual, structural adjustment loans from the World Bank and IMF supported these comprehensive reforms. One widely used index shows increasing economic freedom from 1985 to 2000 on average in Latin America (see figure 5).

Unfortunately, the comprehensive reform in Latin America has not been accompanied by economic growth. Ironically for structural adjustment proponents, the best period for Latin American growth was in the period of state intervention, 1950–1980. If that growth had continued, income in Latin America would now be three times higher than it was in 1950. Instead, in 2003, income there was barely twice the level of a half century earlier, with little progress made over 1980–2003 (see figure 6). The backlash against free

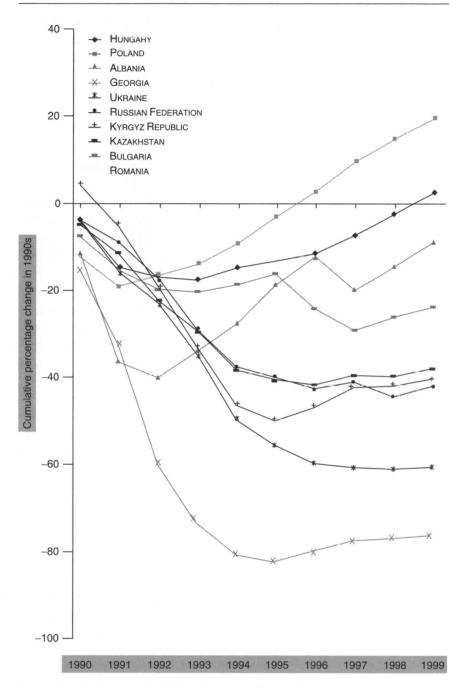

Fig. 4. Growth Trajectory in 1990s of Intensive Structural-Adjustment-Lending Ex-Communist Cases

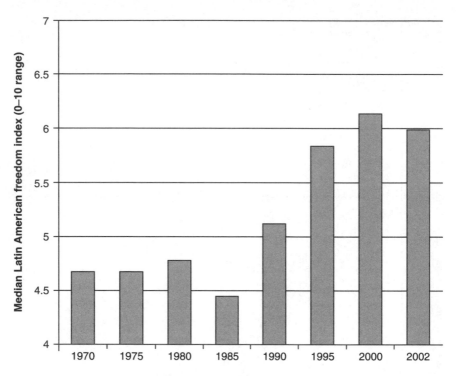

Fig. 5. Economic Freedom Index in Latin America

markets is unfortunately now gaining strength in Latin America, with free markets tarnished by the utopian expectations of structural adjustment.

So we have three regions where there were great hopes for structural adjustment and shock therapy—Africa, the former Communist countries, and Latin America—and three regions where those hopes were dashed. What was the West's response?

The response to failure was to do more of the same. The IMF and World Bank kept on giving out structural adjustment loans for more than two decades, despite their record of failure. Today, they are still doing those loans; they have just changed their name to "poverty reduction loans." This is the fixation-on-a-big-goal characteristic of Planners, despite repeated failures to reach the goal.

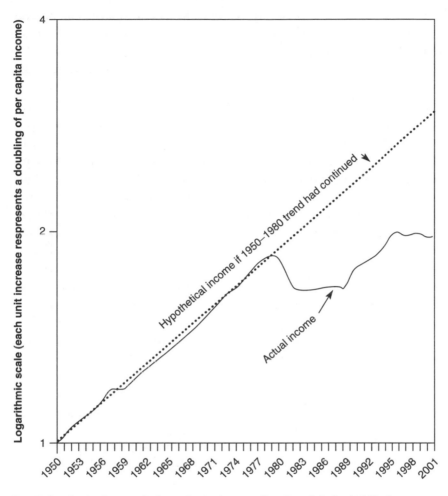

Fig. 6. Per Capita Income Index in Latin America (Log Base 2 Scale, *1950=1):
Actual and Trend, 1950–2003

I'm Hungry—Let's Invent Free Markets

The free market *is* a universally useful system. Economic freedom is one of
mankind's most underrated inventions, much less publicized than its cousin
political freedom. Economic freedom just means unrestricted rights to
produce, buy, and sell. Each of us can choose the things we want and not
have somebody else decide what is best for us. We can also freely choose
what we are going to sell and what occupation to choose, based on our
inside knowledge of what we are best at and most like doing.

This freedom of choice and of personal knowledge makes possible the great gains that come from specialization. If I were limited to my consuming only what I could make or do myself, the results would not be pretty. My cooking skills are limited, for example, as my kids will attest. Rachel, Caleb, and Grace long ago got tired of my staple menu items of boiled spaghetti, macaroni and cheese, and rice and beans. Hence, we rely on the historic market innovation of takeout, which opens up to us a wonderful world of bagels, pizza, and rich cuisines from cultures such as China, Ethiopia, Japan, Thailand, Vietnam, and Tex-Mexico. Even when we are stuck with my cooking repertoire, this still depends on my purchasing pasta, cheese, rice, and beans from supermarkets. Without markets, I would be forced to grow the wheat, beans, and rice myself, milk the cow, process the grains and beans into edible form, and make the cheese and pasta. (I have no clue how to do any of the above.) Instead, I trade on the free market my economist services (which inexplicably find some buyers at New York University) and get money in return. I use this money to select home cooking items and to order takeout.

Adam Smith celebrated specialization in *The Wealth of Nations* in 1776. Each of us has some innate advantages in doing some things and innate disadvantages in doing others. Market exchange makes it possible for us to determine what we are good at, to specialize in producing it, and to trade it for other things produced by people good at producing those things. This applies to nations as well as individuals, which is part of the intellectual case for free trade. As an old joke has it, heaven is where the chefs are French, the police are British, the lovers are Italian, and the car mechanics are German—and it is all organized by the Swiss. Hell is where the chefs are British, the police are German, the lovers are Swiss, and the car mechanics are French—and it is all organized by the Italians.

Specialization doesn't necessarily involve innate abilities. This awful joke became an awful joke because we see some national differences (although I can't necessarily verify the ones implied above), but don't really believe these differences are innate. The French don't have any gene that makes them wonderful cooks or lousy car mechanics; but they have refined their culinary tradition from one generation to the next. This also applies to individuals. You learn by doing. As each person does a task repeatedly, practice makes perfect, no matter whether that task is playing Mozart sonatas or nailing shingles to a roof. As each of us specializes and then trades our final products with one another, we all become better off.

The other great accomplishment of markets is that they reconcile the choices people make for themselves with the choices other people are making. Back at the dinner table we find that no Planner is necessary to process the enormous amount of information required to decide how much pasta, rice, cheese, and takeout cuisines of various cultures to supply to the people of New York. This great achievement of markets is achieved through Searchers. The suppliers search for customers, the customers search for suppliers, and the price adjusts up or down to equate supply and demand. So the market determines prices and quantities to reconcile the needs and abilities of suppliers and consumers. The price reflects both the additional cost that the supplier incurs to supply an additional item and the additional benefit that the consumer gets from purchasing one more of each item. Hence, the market matches the additional cost to society of producing each item to the additional benefit to society of consuming that item. The market comes up with a basket of commodities produced at the lowest possible price for the highest possible benefit. Economists have mathematical proofs that show that, under certain conditions, free markets lead to the best possible allocation of the economy's resources for everyone—given each person's initial stock of possessions. (Of course, it is disturbing that some people have tinier endowments than others; I will get to that later.) Adam Smith celebrated the social good achieved in this system, even though each of us is operating out of self-interest.

The West often awards itself credit for having invented the market. This is nonsense. Any visit to an outdoor market in Africa, Asia, the Middle East, or Latin America will quickly convince you that markets are vibrant in poor countries. Historical anecdotes suggest that these markets predated Western contact.

And market instincts are hardwired into human nature. As any parent knows, children understand the concept of gains from trade early on. The first thing that Rachel, Caleb, and Grace did after the neighborhood Easter egg hunt when they were young was empty out their candy and start trading—Rachel likes dark chocolate, Grace likes milk chocolate, and Caleb likes peanut butter cups. When Tom Sawyer traded Huck Finn a pinch bug for a tooth, he was acting out of instinct, not MBA training.[13]

For some goods, the price the suppliers want is too high relative to what the consumers are willing to pay, and therefore suppliers don't produce. There is no takeout market in New York for the Jell-O mixed with fruit cocktail and topped with marshmallows that my mother made when I was growing up in Bowling Green, Ohio. Unlike bagels, Jell-O doesn't meet the market test that consumers are willing to pay a high enough price to cover the suppliers' costs, and so we have bagel shops and no Jell-O shops.

Markets have potential for mutually beneficial trades. If an Ohioan has more bagels than he wants, and a New Yorker has more Jell-O than he wants, they are both better off if they trade bagels for Jell-O. The intensities of their desire for bagels and Jell-O and their holdings of bagels and Jell-O determined the terms of trade. Many critics of free markets miss this point—that any voluntary exchange makes *both* parties better off, although not necessarily to the same degree. Our sense of fairness is offended if the price seems too high for one party or the other—if a New Yorker has a lot of unwanted Jell-O and a high demand for bagels, then an Ohioan can drive what will look like a great bargain in getting a lot of Jell-O for his bagels. Still, even if the Ohioan benefits more than the New Yorker, they are both better off making the trade.

Consumer Searchers are always on the lookout for beneficial trades. Supplier Searchers are on the lookout for profitable products to supply. The market has no use for the Millennium Jell-O Plan.

Financial Markets Are Good, Too

How does the financial market come in to all this? Financial markets refute the common perception that what you can invest in the future is limited to your own funds. You can borrow to buy land or start a small business (this works less often than it should, but much more often than if financial markets didn't exist). The beauty of financial markets is that they make high return investments available to everyone. This idea motivates the enthusiasm for microcredit schemes that reach destitute people, such as that of the Grameen Bank in Bangladesh.

Given that everyone can enter, financial markets equalize the returns (i.e., the percentage you get over and above repaying the cost of the original investment) to various types of investments across the economy. Anyone can enter any industry. If bagel stores have a high return, then many people will enter bagel retailing until they drive down the returns to normal levels. Any economy in which people do not equalize returns across all types of activities (getting an education, buying land, starting a small business, etc.) is not a free-market economy. It is also not making the most out of its stock of savings. You can see this by asking what would happen if you took money out of a low-return activity (Jell-O stores) and put it in a high-return activity (bagel stores). The value of output would go down by less in the Jell-O takeout industry than it would go up in bagels, and so the economy would produce more out of the same stock of savings. Anytime returns are unequal, such free gains in output are possible. Wall Street wizards, entrepreneurs, or Bill Gates search out any unusually high-return activities, and by investing in them, drive down their returns, while ruthlessly taking capital away from low-return activities. Again, no central bureau is in charge of investments—just myriad Searchers such as financial firms. Planners would do an awful job allocating money across sectors in the financial markets because they have no way of getting information on which sectors have high payoffs. There are many savers and investors, and financial firms play middlemen between the two.

So the bottom line is that financial markets (1) are a great source of free-market efficiency, and (2) create opportunities for anyone to get rich by borrowing and investing.

If we combine the virtues of goods markets and financial markets, we get a positive-feedback loop for any successful search to meet the needs of our fellow citizens. If we supply a product in high demand, we will reap high profits. Profits induce us to expand production, pulling workers and raw materials away from other products in less demand to produce the high-demand product. Outside investors want to share in the high returns, giving us more financing to expand our scale even more. An equally powerful incentive exists to *invent* a brand-new product to meet consumer needs. The positive-feedback loop to searching for solutions to customers' problems has made the market the greatest bottom-up system in history for meeting people's needs. (If only foreign aid could work like this!)

Not only that, but the common thread in the success stories of the last few decades—Hong Kong, Korea, Singapore, Taiwan, China, India, Chile, Botswana, etc.—is that the Searchers for success in each of these countries (which were often far from laissez-faire market economies) subjected their efforts to a market test, often through international markets. Would private foreign investors invest? Would the rest of the world buy what they were producing? The answer was yes, which gave the Searchers feedback to move in the direction of prosperity, although their paths toward market successes varied from the simplistic visions of shock therapy.

Bottom-up Problems with Markets

With this paean to the glories of the market, the question becomes why markets don't make all societies rich. This book is *not* suggesting a simple recipe for national success; the point of this chapter is the opposite: no recipe exists, only a confusing welter of bottom-up social institutions and norms essential for markets. These evolve slowly on their own from the actions of many agents; the Western outsiders and Planners don't have a clue how to create these norms and institutions.

Nor are markets of much help to those who are now very poor—after all, the poor have no money to motivate any market Searchers to meet their needs. The hope for the poor depends on the same dual forces this book emphasizes throughout: (1) homegrown, market-based development that will lift up both rich and poor (which this chapter further argues is way too complex a task for Western assistance); and (2) Western assistance for meeting the most desperate needs of the poor until homegrown market-based development reaches them. (Western assistance could also borrow some ideas from markets, such as eliciting feedback from customers.)

The quest for helping the poor gets more complex the more you study it, but please don't give up! There is hope once you give up the Planner's ambition of universally imposing a free market from the top down. I point out in this chapter some of the universal problems with markets for poor countries, but the solutions are as varied as the countries and their complex histories.

The problem with praise of markets is that it overlooked all the bottom-up searches necessary to make markets work well. One of the main things that social institutions and norms must do is find ways to prevent market participants from "opportunistic behavior," more commonly known as "cheating." While the theory of the invisible hand celebrates self-interest as socially beneficial, this is true only if there are norms that make possible mutually beneficial transactions between parties. Lack of checks and balances on greed can prevent economic development just as a lack of markets can.

One type of cheating occurs when you cannot observe the quality of the good I am offering you. I could cheat you by running a taquería in Mexico City and selling you tacos made under unsanitary conditions. (I will spare you the details—let's just say I don't wash my hands frequently.) When you later get sick, you realize you paid more than you would have had you known how unsanitary the tacos were. The quality problem is ubiquitous, and even the simplest kind of exchange has problems. If you had known the tacos might be unsanitary, you would have offered a lower price. If I adopted costly but safe food handling methods and sold you healthy tacos, but you couldn't observe my safe handling and still offered the low price, then I would be the one who lost out in the exchange. So I would not bother with safe food handling, selling you the lousy tacos you expected. I could even keep all the best taco ingredients and safest procedures for tacos consumed by my own family, and sell you the tacos made with shoddy ingredients and food safety procedures. So the market does not supply healthy tacos! The economist George Akerlof of Berkeley won the Nobel Prize for this kind of insight, applied to sales of used cars.[14] Even slightly used cars sell for far less than new cars because buyers have no information on the cars' quality (and used car sellers have a tendency to sell lemons).

Many other types of cheating exist. For many transactions, payment at the time we get the service is not efficient. Either the service comes first, or the payment comes first. So, whoever acts second can renege on the contract— by not paying or by not delivering the service. I can arrange to have fresh meat, tomatoes, chilies, cilantro, and onions delivered to my taquería by farmers. It has to be worth the trip for them to deliver the produce, so they will demand payment in advance. Now they might not show up, disappearing with my advance payment. Credit markets have this problem in spades—the borrower has no incentive to pay back the loan unless the lender can enforce repayment.

Another trick by the supplier could be to appear before the lunchtime peak and demand extra payment above what I have already paid, knowing he has me in a tight spot—it being too late for me to find another supplier. This is the "hold-up" problem—often at a point in a transaction, one party has a stranglehold on the other and can extort additional payment. A contemporary of Julius Caesar's, Crassus, made a fortune in early Rome with a private fire company that would negotiate a price for extinguishing a fire as it was raging.[15]

Can I Trust You?

There are solutions to cheating on market transactions. Maybe you and I are very honest, and we don't cheat each other. Some honesty and fairness seems biologically hardwired into us as Homo sapiens, which makes possible more trade than pure self-interest would predict.[16] Over and above this biological minimum, there are variations in trust across people and groups. Some who emphasize culture say some ethnic groups have evolved norms of honesty. Others argue that political, social, and economic incentives determine honesty.

Different societies have different amounts of "social capital" or "trust," that is, how much people follow rules without any coercion. Trust measures the confidence we have in perfect strangers. If each of us trusts the other, even a stranger, then the cheating problem does not arise. World Bank economists Steve Knack and Phil Keefer examined the effects of trust by using the results of surveys that asked people from different nations, "Generally speaking, would you say that most people can be trusted, or that you can't be too careful in dealing with people?" Knack and Keefer measured "trust" as the percentage of people who chose the first answer. They found that low-income societies have less trust than rich societies, and societies with less trust have less rapid economic growth.[17] Figure 7 shows the strong positive association between trust and income. If we order the survey sample into four equal size groups, going from low trust to high trust, per capita income is a lot higher in the high-trust group than in the low-trust group. In rich Denmark, where trust is so high that mothers leave babies unattended on the street while they shop, 58 percent say they can trust people. In the poor Philippines, only 5 percent are trusting.

Note that what is important here is whether you trust *strangers*. Almost every society has cooperative relationships between kinfolk. What is important is the radius of trust. Do you trust only the members of your immediate family? Or does the circle widen to include your extended family, or your clan, or your village, or your ethnic group, or all the way to strangers? In a low-trust society, you trust your friends and family, but nobody else. As a Filipino businessman lamented, "We have no institutional loyalty, only personal loyalty."[18]

Trust is also associated with unforced good behavior toward strangers. *Reader's Digest* did a survey of American and European cities in which wallets containing money were randomly dropped on the street. The survey then counted how many wallets were returned with the money intact. The percentage of returned wallets is strongly associated with the percentage

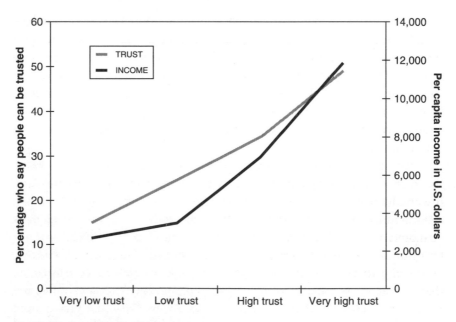

Fig. 7. Trust and Per Capita Income

answering yes to the trust survey question. Denmark performed well on returned wallets (almost *all* of them were returned), just as it did on trusting strangers. Casual observation suggests that trust is higher in small towns than in impersonal cities. In Bowling Green, Ohio, you buy a movie ticket from a girl in the window out in front of the cinema. You then walk into the cinema lobby, through an entrance anyone could enter, without anyone's checking to see whether you've bought a ticket!

The larger the radius of trust, the less you worry about cheating in business transactions. A low-trust society such as Mexico features a strong insider/outsider mentality. The slang term for your buddies is *cuates* (your twins). You would do anything for your *cuates*, but ripping off a stranger is okay. You are amazingly courteous to a social acquaintance, but anonymous interactions tend to be rude. So you leap to hold the door open for a lady in a social situation, but later shove some ladies aside to get into a subway car.

Trust affects virtually every dimension of doing business. Malagasy grain traders carry out inspections of each lot of grain in person because they don't trust employees. One third of the traders say they don't hire more workers because of fear of theft by them. This limits the grain traders' firm size, cutting short a trader's potential success.[19] In many countries, companies tend to be family enterprises because family members are the only ones felt trustworthy. So the size of the company is then limited by the size of the family.

Other Solutions for Cheaters

Even if we don't trust one another, there are other bottom-up solutions to opportunism. As far as not delivering products or not repaying debts, there are credit reporting agencies and Better Business Bureaus that can handle these problems. Warranties protect the consumer against product defects.

A poor country cannot use these solutions as much as a rich one. The transactions are not large enough, and communications are too costly for credit reporting agencies or Better Business Bureaus. The supplier can abscond by not honoring a warranty just as it can default on a debt.

Don't jump to the conclusion that courts are a simple answer. The costs of legal action are not worth it with tiny transactions. One study found that African manufacturers seldom used courts to settle disputes. As predicted, the use of courts was less likely the smaller the size of the firm.[20] Institutions such as courts are usually not reliable in poor countries anyway. They are more corruptible—the richer or stronger party will pay bribes or intimidate the judge into seeing things their way.

Credit reporting agencies also work less well in poor societies—tracking down con artists is hard because they leave no paper trail. You don't have too many driver's licenses if few people drive. Formal addresses are seldom clear in shantytowns. You don't have phone numbers if you don't have phones. The lack of formal or private institutions to prevent cheating means that quality will be low (e.g., food establishments sell poor and unhealthy food). Most transactions in poor countries will be anonymous cash-and-carry transactions trading poor-quality goods for money. The closest approximation in the rich countries might be flea markets or garage sales. The economist Marcel Fafchamps (on whose work this chapter bases some of its exposition) quips that Africa has a flea-market economy rather than a free-market economy.

It's Whom You Know...

Nevertheless, poor people are inventive in searching for solutions to cheating. In West Africa, the age group is an association of all men in a tribe who come of age at the same time. In Nigeria, according to the district head of Owokwu, "Age-groups are ... generally self-development oriented. They ... act as thrift and credit associations, procure farms for their members. ... People of the same age have to qualify to be members of the group by being upright members of the community. They also have to be hardworking, of sane mind, and not convicted of any crime."[21] The age group prevents opportunistic behavior by its members.

Another solution is to have an ongoing relationship of trading, so one of us will not cheat the other and risk losing all future trade. Potential business partners stay on probation for a while until you trust them. Marcel Fafchamps reports that Malagasy grain traders don't grant a client trade credit until after they have done about ten cash transactions with him. African manufacturers report that they require six to twelve months of repeated interaction with a client until they grant trade credits.[22] Once businessmen form a trusting relationship, they continue it to save on the costs of starting up a new one. One survey found that the average business relationship in Africa lasted seven years.

We could also belong to a multimember network of businesses that sanctioned our behavior and issued referrals to third parties—other taquería owners could form a business association that shared information on who were the reliable suppliers. A supplier cheating one taquería would risk losing the whole market.

These networks form at lowest cost among people who interact for other reasons. Economic historians Nathan Rosenberg and L. E. Birdzell relate how many financiers and entrepreneurs behind America's nineteenth-century industrialization learned to trust one another by serving together in the Civil War.[23] A more common setting for social interaction is the family or ethnic group, whose members develop trust in one another through encounters such as those at weddings, funerals, birthday parties, and ethnic festivals. A web forms of socially linked businessmen who trust one another enough to extend credit, to recommend suppliers or buyers, and to not engage in hold-ups. One ethnic group is usually prominent in business in a poor society. In pre-industrial Europe, it was the Jews. In East Africa, it's the Indians. (Indians own almost all businesses in Kenya, although they make up only 1 percent of the population.) In West Africa, it is the Lebanese. In southern Africa, it is whites and Indians. Among indigenous African groups, often one dominates trading—the Bamileke in Cameroon, the Luba in the Democratic Republic of the Congo, the Hausa in West Africa, the Igbo in Nigeria, and the Serahule in the Gambia. In Southeast Asia, the overseas Chinese (the "bamboo network") play this role. Often there are subgroups— for example, the overseas Chinese came largely from the coastal enclaves stretching from Canton to Fuzhou (the same region leads the boom in China itself today).[24]

These ethnic networks solve many of the cheating problems. As one observer of the "bamboo network" noted, if a Chinese businessman reneges on an agreement, he goes on the blacklist. Since the overseas Chinese straddle many international boundaries, they promote international and domestic benefits from trade. The economist James Rauch found that international trade is unusually high between any two countries that both have large minorities of overseas Chinese.

Other ethnic networks have evolved other strategies to enforce good behavior. The Hausa in Ibadan, Nigeria, both own houses and broker long-distance trade in cattle and kola nuts. If the brokers cheat their business partners and then disappear from Ibadan, their problem is that they leave behind valuable houses as hostages. The chief of the Hausa quarter will prevent these cheaters from selling their houses when they go on the lam.

The economist Avner Greif describes a "multilateral punishment strategy" that keeps agents from cheating a network of merchants. He argues that the higher the probability that merchants will hire an agent again even after he cheats, the more likely he is to cheat. If an individual merchant blacklists an agent who cheated him, other merchants could hire the agent—so bilateral punishment doesn't work as well as multilateral punishment. If everybody in the network agrees that they will never hire an agent who has ever cheated any of them, that destroys the employment prospects of a cheating agent. The network consists of merchants who interact frequently enough to convey information about cheating agents. Hence, with multilateral punishment, merchants can trust agents not to cheat. Greif applied this idea to the eleventh-century Maghribi traders (Jewish merchants based in Cairo), who operated around the Mediterranean using agents, even in the absence of any courts.[25]

The ethnic networks also work as referral services for finding new business. The bamboo network gathers information on who needs what supply components, subassembly plants, financing, and so on. The people involved know one another, and can pass this information on to third parties in the network who do not know their potential business partner. The network expels anyone who misbehaves, who then loses all access to information.[26]

The Market Net

I am in Addis Ababa's city market, the largest open-air market in Africa. No shortage of markets here. I go to buy handicrafts and gifts for the kids. The taxi driver recommends a particular shop, and I make a number of purchases there. Afterward, the shop owner takes me to see other shops in the market. We talk as we stride along, and he tells me he is a Gurage, Ethiopia's entrepreneurial minority. The Gurage make up only 4 percent of Addis Ababa's labor force but own 34 percent of the businesses. He takes me to other Gurage businesses in the market, where he bargains on my behalf (getting me better bargains than I got in his shop). His referrals to other Gurage shops created the opportunity for their owners and me to do deals.

These ethnic specializations can become self-perpetuating. The Luo tribes-people in Kenya, who live next to Lake Victoria, are fish traders. Such is their reputation for fish trading that the Luo entered the business of fish trading in Mombasa, far from Lake Victoria, on the coast of the Indian Ocean. If Kenyans think of the Luo as having a network that ensures high-quality fish, then they will prefer to buy fish from Luo traders rather than from other ethnic groups. The Luo will drive other ethnic groups out of the fish-trading business, but the other groups may find another niche—for example, the Indians, with their network of retail businesses in Nairobi. Kenyans now would not buy retail products from a Luo retail shop in Nairobi, just as they would not buy fish from an Indian fish trader.

The next generation of Luo will find it more rewarding to become fish traders than shop owners, just as the next generation of Indians will make the reverse decision.

Ethnic specialization is widespread. Even in market-rich New York City, there are ethnic concentrations by occupation. Hasidic Jews famously dominate the diamond trade on Forty-seventh Street in Manhattan. Studies find that a remarkably high share of all nail salons in many American cities are Vietnamese owned and operated. These patterns may reflect the same ethnic "brand-name" effects as in Kenya. Fafchamps speculates that the caste system in India, with its rigidity of hereditary occupations by caste, may be the result of such a process. Since some occupations are more rewarding or high skilled than others, this is a recipe for persistent ethnic (or caste) income inequality.

However, ethnic specialization is not as ubiquitous in rich countries as in poor countries because there is an impersonal solution in rich countries to establishing a reputation for quality and fair dealing: creating a large corporation. The corporation spends a large upfront amount to create a brand-name reputation and has a lot to lose if it cheats. The size of transactions is too small in poor countries to make the corporate solution work.

The ethnic differentials also persist because the networks freeze out the outsiders. In Zimbabwe, whites and Asians own most of the business firms, which seldom deal with indigenous African-owned firms.[27] Refusing to deal with outsiders limits entry into particular sectors, limiting competition and giving above-normal profits to the established well-connected firms. Those in the networks also may have a competitive advantage over outsiders because they share technical knowledge with one another. Economists Tim Conley and Chris Udry found that Ghanaian farmers shared technical knowledge within their social network about a new opportunity to grow pineapples for export to Europe, such as how much fertilizer to use.

However, networks are far from a perfect solution to making markets work. The networks exclude as well as include, missing many entrepreneurs and suppliers when they limit trade to a minority. The gains from trade through personalized exchange are much less than through the impersonal exchange made possible by formal institutions.[28]

Also, if business networks form among minority ethnic groups, this situation can breed ethnic hostility to markets among the majority population. Resistance to market reform in Russia is bound up with anti-Semitism and other prejudices, because some perceive that Jews, ethnic groups from the Caucasus, and other ethnic minorities have disproportionately benefited from free markets.

The well-connected people advance rather than the well qualified. Firms in poor countries are very often family firms. As a trading friend says, the firm does better to hire the family idiot rather than the village genius—the former at least can be trusted not to cheat them. When formal institutions establish the rules of the game, the market finds the village genius and uses him according to his merits. The social networks may retard formal institutions, as network members will out-compete the formal institutions until the latter reach some critical mass.

Old-school networks do connect businessmen in rich countries. However, because formal institutions work better in rich countries, these networks recruit their members more according to merit than in poor countries—the old-school ties will be valuable only if it was a good school.

Feeling confused? You are not yet confused enough. How can top-down Planners make markets work when it requires understanding not just free markets but also the bottom-up search for the social norms, producer and consumer networks, and kin relationships that facilitate exchange? Whether you and I can become better off through markets depends now on more than our individual choices. All in a society must develop the informal social ties that make our individual market choices possible. The chances are low that the international jet set will understand us enough to make markets work for us. The quest to help the poor has put far too little effort into learning about their informal social arrangements.

Showdown at Predators' Pass

Another problem society must solve is protection of property and person. High-value property magnifies the need for protection. Without rules to protect us, you and I play a disastrous game of threat and self-protection. Suppose each of us has the same amount of money but only two choices as to what to do with it—devote all our funds to producing new goods, thus increasing our funds, or spend some of our resources on guns, which enable us to protect our own property and also seize our neighbors' property at gunpoint. If you buy a gun and I don't, then you get my money and your original money less the cost of the gun, and I end up with nothing. If I buy a gun and you don't, then the opposite is true. If we both buy guns, then we have a predators' equilibrium, neither of us produces anything, and we each just keep our original money.

We would both be better off by not buying guns and just producing. Yet in a lawless world, that would never occur. Each one of us can always do better by buying a gun, whatever the other one does. If you don't buy a gun, I can seize your property and increase my funds more than by production. If you do buy a gun, I can at least defend my property against you. So buying a gun is always my best move; the same holds for you, and so we both wind up with less money than if we had both been peaceful. In terms of game theory, this game is the classic prisoner's dilemma.

This assumes that buying guns is legal. In the United States, where you can buy assault weapons on the airport highway but where airport security scrutinizes your nail clippers, this may be a good assumption. One way to avoid the predators' equilibrium is to allow only honest policemen to have guns.

But predation doesn't happen as often as this theory predicts, even without a policeman looking over your shoulder. Many opportunities for pilfering go unrealized. The social norm that stealing is disgraceful is a sanction against predation. Most kinds of social conflict resolution don't involve armed coercion. Academic seminars can be intellectually violent, but, fortunately, professors don't pack semiautomatic weapons.

These social norms are more effective in communities with face-to-face interactions as opposed to situations with anonymous social interactions—one reason why small towns have less crime per capita than the big cities. Social norms also seem to be stronger among rich people than among poor people, as a rich person loses more economic opportunities and income from social disgrace. This is why you can usually be sure an executive in a suit will not mug you.

Social norms against predation don't work so well in many poor communities today. In a Brazilian urban slum, young men and women said it was every person for himself: "People are like a dog...only protect their house...if outside the house someone is robbed or dead...nobody cares."[29] In the slums of Dhaka and Chittagong in Bangladesh, "musclemen" kidnap and rape young girls. They demand protection money from slum dwellers on the threat of burning down their houses.[30] A formerly prosperous woman named Nasibeko of Kuphera village, Malawi, reports, "Our life was fine until one day when our cattle were stolen. After that, our lives became miserable." Farmers in Mtamba, Malawi, say, "We can't grow cassava these days to support us when the maize is finished because thieves will come to steal it."[31]

Responding to ineffective social norms, poor communities often form their own self-protection groups. In their more benign form, such groups provide community safety. In some villages in Tanzania, self-protection groups called *sungusungu* deter cattle theft. The young men of the community take turns participating, and the women provide food for them as implicit payment. Nigerian age groups also help provide law and order in local communities. And in Phwetekere, Malawi, villagers started a neighborhood watch to discourage crime.

Unfortunately, self-protection groups can get out of hand. In a less benign form, vigilante bands capriciously respond to rumor and innuendo, playing the role of judge, jury, and executioner. A villager in Phwetekere, Malawi, reported to an interviewer that the village had burned a thief to death the week before the interview.[32] I once witnessed a mob in Nairobi, Kenya, strip an accused thief naked and haul him down the street in a cart, while beating him.

An even less savory possibility for controlling predation (as well as cheating) is a Mafia-like organization. The Chinese in Southeast Asia are famous not only for trade but also for triads, Mafia-like gangs. If someone cheats a triad member, he has a violent way to persuade the cheater to pay. Although any such information is speculative, one study of Hong Kong businesses estimated that 40 percent of them had triad members on their boards of directors.[33]

Drug lords dispense justice in slums in Jamaica.[34] The Mafia was omnipresent in Russia after the Soviet collapse Even a murderous Mafia can meet a genuine social need when law and order collapses (as it did in Russia, or earlier in Sicily in the nineteenth century). The Mafia can prevent anyone from robbing anybody else in their territory with just the threat of violence to deter the robber. The problem is that there is no good way to exit from the Mafia's protection, which means the organization almost always overstays its welcome.[35]

Elsewhere around the world, warlords, clan leaders, semi-feudal landholders, tribal chiefs, and village headmen often dispense justice in many poor societies. Villagers in Malawi report high satisfaction with dispute resolution by village headmen.[36] Mafia dons, warlords, and feudal landlords probably do not achieve as much client satisfaction. These examples show that bottom-up solutions don't always lead to attractive outcomes. Yet the Western world evolved gradually through such bottom-up mechanisms, some combination of benevolent social norms, self-protection societies, and local strong men. Perhaps the story of the Western state is just that warlords sorted themselves out, as the strongest warlord put down the rest and gradually evolved into a more benevolent, accountable government. Some scholars have speculated that the benevolent outcome came about in part because Europeans could often simply move from a bad jurisdiction to a better one.

This is of course a vast oversimplification. Western social scientists don't begin to comprehend fully the complex process of state formation and rule of law in the West, so they shouldn't be too quick to predict how it will work anywhere else.

Property Rights

Property rights also determine whether markets work. Do I have title to the land, building, and equipment making up my taco stand? Hernando de Soto noted in his great book *The Mystery of Capital* that the majority of land occupied by the poor urban majorities in the developing world does not have legal title—*nobody* owns it. Only if I felt secure that I would keep my taco stand would I invest in more sanitary food-processing equipment. I can borrow from a bank to purchase such equipment only if I have title to the property to put down as collateral. Only then will the bank feel secure that I will not abscond with the loan. Even then, the loans will be available only if the laws allow the bank to take my taquería if I default on the loan. Property rights are also critical if I opt for incorporation. Lenders and shareholders need to feel secure that they really do have a claim on corporate property.

Property rights are an incentive to accumulate assets over time and across generations, which is often necessary to have the productive capacity to meet consumer needs. When I sacrifice consumption to buy land, factories, or other assets, I don't want someone else seizing the assets. For example, a man in Isla Trinitaria, Ecuador, cut back even on food and clothing to save enough to build up a small shellfish business. But he lost it all when the mayor seized the land.[37]

What determines property rights? Alas, property rights are more complicated than the state enforcing them from the top down (and the state itself may be a thief, as the next chapter discusses). Property arises from a decentralized searching for solutions, just like the other complexities of markets. Your right to your property is only as strong as those around you are willing to acknowledge.

Stronger ethnic groups often seize land from weaker ones. In India, Hindu settlers push the tribal Adivasi population into the degraded forests and eroded hill slopes, scrubland, and rocky soil.[38] (White people are not the only ones to push others around.)

Even countries with strong property rights today had those rights emerge gradually from the bottom up. American property rights did not spring full- blown from the minds of the Founding Fathers, and even then the rights applied differently to different groups.

George Washington Slept Here

Those of you unwise enough to have read my first book have already met my disreputable frontier ancestor, Thomas Cresap. Dragging my relatives in at every opportunity, let me tell you about his son, Michael. In 1774, Michael (my great-great-great-great-great grandfather) was in the Ohio River country near today's Wheeling, West Virginia. Michael Cresap was interested in the Ohio River area downstream from Wheeling, since he claimed some riverfront land there. Two tracts of choice river bottomland he claimed were "Cresap's Bottom" and "Round Bottom." Michael's methods of establishing title to the land were relaxed.

One who disputed his methods was Mr. Founding Father himself. George Washington was speculating in Ohio River land to supplement his army and plantation income. Both Michael and George claimed the piece of land called the Round Bottom. George Washington, in a rare burst of humor, said that Michael's "claim to the round bottom & other lands on the Ohio River for 30 miles is equally well founded." That is, George said, Michael founded his claims on nothing. Michael's method, George derided, was claiming "every good bottom upon the river; building a cabbin thereon to keep off others; & then selling them, and going on to possess other lands in the same manner."

Other title methods on the American frontier made Michael's methods look like a formal court hearing. Another technique was to slash trees along the boundary line of the land you were claiming. Squatters' right to land is an old tradition. Congress later willy-nilly appropriated some of the same frontier land for Revolutionary War veterans. Many pieces of land on the frontier thus came to have multiple claimants. The only thing the whites, who squabbled about one another's land rights, could agree upon was that the real owners of the land—the Native Americans—had no rights at all.

The federal government after 1790 tried to sort out the land chaos for the whites, if not for the natives. More than twenty acts of Congress addressed the land issue between 1799 and 1830, along with numerous state-by-state legislative acts. The tug of war between squatters' rights and more formal legal titling continued. Lax enforcement made for inconsistency on the ground. A "preemption" right was finally recognized by Congress in 1830 (and made permanent in 1841), essentially legalizing squatters' rights.[39]

The Homestead Act during the Civil War formalized acquiring legal title by settlement on federally owned land.

Michael Cresap died in 1775 fighting under Washington in the Revolutionary War, leaving his heirs to litigate about land titles. The Round Bottom dispute between the Cresaps and the Washingtons that dated back to 1773 was finally settled in a Richmond, Virginia, courthouse in 1834, in favor of the Washingtons (big surprise).

Michael's claim to Cresap's Bottom, on the other hand, endured. His son, Michael, Jr., farmed the fertile land. My grandmother told me about her childhood visits to the old Ohio River homestead where her mother, Hannah Cresap, grew up. The land remained in the Cresap family until the twentieth century, when the family sold it to coal companies at a handsome profit. Today a huge power plant and a coal mine occupy Cresap's Bottom, whose owners would quickly chase away squatters with court orders. When Hannah Cresap died, my mother bought a lime green couch with the proceeds from her inheritance. I grew up reading books on a lime green couch financed by the property rights established over two centuries ago on Cresap's Bottom.

To Title or Not to Title?

Legal title is not worthwhile when the assets are not valuable. It is not worth it with a rustic cabin. The costs of litigating over title to property can be more than the value of the property itself (as my ex-wife and I found out through our divorce lawyers' bills). Top-down titling of land requires a substantial investment in surveying, mapping, defining boundaries, and maintaining land records. Titling requires a long-standing written tradition. Then you can search court records for any other (perhaps long-forgotten) party with a legal claim to the property.[10] The large fixed cost is not worth it unless the value of the asset is high.[41] It *is* worth it today in Cresap's Bottom to protect a power plant.

Property law in the United States, as with many other kinds of law, evolved as piecemeal solutions to deal with particular problems as they arose. California miners during the 1849 gold rush agreed among themselves to the division of mining claims, enforced by a committee elected in each mining camp. The miners had no advance information about which claims would strike it rich, and it was in all of their interests to avoid a violent free-for-all. Hence they just agreed beforehand to split up the land, and then let each miner keep whatever he found on his land. California state law later retroactively recognized the informal claims the miners had devised themselves.[42] The collection of past practical solutions gradually determines a legal norm.

Custom and Law

We see the same process in developing societies. Titling is even more complicated if the land is used for different purposes by different parties (for example, for grazing by pastoralists and for growing crops by farmers). Poorer societies define land ownership more by oral tradition, customary arrangements, or informal community agreement than by formal titles. An expensive system of land titling under such circumstances is senseless (the Planners don't investigate local custom enough to get this, as when aid agencies recommend computerized databases of land titles).

Customary arrangements can also deal with property owned by the community, like common pastureland on which all can graze their cows. Common property is subject to the "tragedy of the commons" problem, in which each herdsman overgrazes the pasture because the costs are borne by the community rather than by the herdsman. (I want my cow to eat the grass before your cow does.) However, if population density is low and land abundant, the tragedy of the commons does not arise, and community ownership works fine. Even when pressure on the land tightens up, informal community arrangements can still control overgrazing (say the village elders decide that you and I may let our cows into the pasture on alternating days).

NYU professor Leonard Wantchekon offered this account of how his village in Benin managed a common property resource, the fishing pond (overfishing is a classic example used for the tragedy of the commons), when he was growing up: To open the fishing season, elders performed ritual tests at Amlé, a lake fifteen kilometers from the village. If the fish were large enough, fishing was allowed for two or three days. If they were too small, all fishing was forbidden, and anyone who secretly fished the lake at this time was outcast, excluded from the formal and informal groups that formed the village's social structure. Those who committed this breach of trust were often shunned by the whole community; no one would speak to the offender, or even acknowledge his existence for a year or more.

When the value of the land increases, formal titles are worth the transaction costs—in return for greater ownership security. Now loose customary arrangements will not hold up; ignoring custom pays too well. Hence, a growing economy moves from customary law to formal law, but outsiders cannot know enough to engineer such a transition.

One example of how *not* to do it is having Western lawyers and accountants rewrite the legal code overnight from the top down, as the West tried in Eastern Europe after 1990. In Eastern Europe, chief recipients of foreign aid were the Big Six accounting firms in the West,[43] who drafted new laws for Eastern Europe and trained thousands of locals in Western law. Eastern European legislatures passed the Western-drafted laws, satisfying aid conditions for the West, but the new laws on paper had little effect on actual rules of conduct. At the behest of donors, Albania dutifully passed a bankruptcy law in 1994, one of the elements of property rights. Only one bankruptcy case ever made it to the Albanian courts, even after a national pyramid scheme in the mid 1990s led to losses for investors amounting to 60 percent of the GDP.[44]

As legal practitioner Wade Channell summarized the legal reform experience of Eastern Europe after 1990: "It is hard to imagine any rule of law aid specialist pursuing law reform in his or her own country in this fashion. If I assembled half a dozen recognized European or U.S. specialists to redraft the U.S. Code of Judicial Ethics and then tried to get it passed by the U.S. Congress with little or no input on the proposed draft from congressional committees, the judiciary, the bar, business interests, law schools, or other stakeholders, I would be looking for a new career rather quickly. Based on many current practices, however, that career could easily be found abroad 'helping' transition countries with the same process."[45]

Titling Toward Confusion in Kenya

Lord Lugard, the architect of British colonial rule in Africa, said land tenure follows "a steady evolution, side by side with the evolution of social progress." This "natural evolution" leads to "individual ownership." The Native Land Tenure Rules of 1956 privatized land in Kenya, advertising it as "a normal step in the evolution of a country," under which "energetic or rich Africans will be able to acquire more land."

The anthropologist Parker Shipton, one of the few outsiders who bothered studying the region in detail, looked at the consequences of land titling for the Luo tribe in western Kenya in the early 1980s.[46] The traditional system among the Luo was a complicated maze of swapping plots among kin and seasonal exchanges of land for labor and livestock. There were both individual and family rights in cultivated fields and free-grazing rights for the community after the harvest. Each household's claim to land included many plots of different soils and terrains, on which many different crops grew—not a bad system with which to diversify risk in an uncertain climate. The traditional land patron (*weg lowo*) would often give temporary land rights to the client (*jodak*). There were seasonal exchanges of plows and draft animals for land, or land for labor.

Land titling brought many uncertainties into this complex system. Would the government give the titles to the *weg lowo* or to the *jodak*? The system inclined toward the latter, fostering bitter conflict between the two groups. Sometimes the former *weg lowo* would wind up as the *jodak* of his former *jodak*. An unpaid adjudication committee, who expected both parties to provide a feast for them, made the decisions. The system favored whoever could bring more goats to the feast. Often claimants would not bother with adjudication as the costs of the feast exceeded the value of the property.

Although land sales increased after formal registration, neither the buyers nor the sellers wanted the high fees or red tape associated with registering the sales. The system of formal titles thus gradually lost correspondence with those who the locals knew owned the land. An increasing number of formal titleholders resided in the local graveyard.

The opportunistic behavior that bedevils market transactions also plagued land sales in Kenya. Sellers who had earlier pledged their land as collateral for a loan would fail to inform the buyer of this claim on the land. Banks found it politically difficult to auction off the collateral land after loan default, since land owned by kin of the defaulter surrounded it. Some sellers sold to several buyers at once, using different elders as witnesses.

The adjudication committees required that sellers retain enough land for the subsistence of their own families. Sellers sometimes exploited this rule by selling "too much" land, gambling that the land-control board would give back some of their land while the buyers would not recover the purchase price.

Ocholla Ogweng of Kanyamkago got a loan of thirty thousand Kenyan shillings from Barclay's Bank in 1979. To raise collateral, he asked the help of his wife's father, Ogwok Nyayal. Mr. Nyayal arranged with his sister's husband, Mr. Alloyce Ohero, to pledge his land as collateral for Mr. Ogweng's loan. Alloyce Ohero then sold part of his land to two strangers, without informing them of the Barclay's Bank lien, and they settled on the land. Mr. Ohero died in 1981, and Mr. Ogweng defaulted on his loan. The two sons of Alloyce Ohero expected to inherit the unsold part of his land, equally unaware of the Barclay's Bank claim. By 1982, a court broker prepared to auction off all of Mr. Ohero's former land on behalf of Barclay's, to the consternation of everyone involved. The two strangers blamed Mr. Ohero's sons, who blamed their uncle Ogwok Nyayal, who blamed Alloyce Ohero, who, if he had been alive, would have blamed Ocholla Ogweng. Here was a deal with nothing for everyone.

What looks like opportunistic behavior could be the mingling of private property with traditional values, which place obligations to kin above those to strangers or banks. By imposing land titling on such complex social customs, "private property rights" may actually increase the insecurity of land tenure rather than decrease it.

Perhaps chastened by these experiences, formal land law in Kenya is now moving back toward recognizing customary rights. The government is allowing the paper titles to lapse.[47] Reformers who want to increase the security of property rights have to search for what works in each locality. A more likely way forward for formal law would be building on the customary law rather than contradicting it.

Bottom-up Legal Evolution

Researchers have accumulated evidence that the bottom-up approach to law has proven to be superior for economic development to more top-down approaches. A series of studies compare development outcomes in countries with a common-law tradition to those with a civil-law tradition. The common-law tradition originated in England and spread to British colonies. In this tradition, judges are independent professionals who make rulings on cases based on precedents from similar cases. The principles of the law evolve in response to practical realities, and can be adapted to new situations as they arise. As the great American jurist Oliver Wendell Holmes said, "It is the merit of the common law that it decides the case first and determines the principles afterwards."[48]

The modern civil-law tradition originated under Napoleon, in France, and spread to French and Spanish colonies. (Spain was under the control of Napoleon at the time.) In this tradition, laws are written from the top down by the legislature to cover every possible situation. Judges are glorified clerks just applying the written law. This system of law lacks bottom-up feedback of the common law that comes from having cases determine law. As a result, the law is less well adapted to reality on the ground and has trouble adapting to new situations as technology and society change. Ironically, France itself proved more flexible in applying the civil law than French or Spanish colonies, who have followed a judicial formalism that was slow as well as poorly adapted to changing circumstances.

The differences show up in institutions (see figure 8). Systems that rely on case law have a positive-feedback loop between the law and the arrangements that economic actors need to facilitate markets. Case law countries thus wind up with a wider variety of formal institutions more supportive of prosperity—property rights, contract enforcement, rule of law, and even corporate accountability—than do civil-law countries. Australia, Canada, New Zealand, Pakistan, Uganda, and the United States are examples of former British colonies that have well-developed property rights protection for their level of income. Algeria, Colombia, Haiti, and Nicaragua are examples of former French or Spanish colonies that have poor property rights protection for their level of income.

The search process of the common law was particularly important in supporting financial markets. Finance requires more complicated arrangements, such as legal protection of shareholders in companies and bankruptcy proceedings to give creditors their money. Indeed, it turns out that countries with British legal origins have better legal protections for

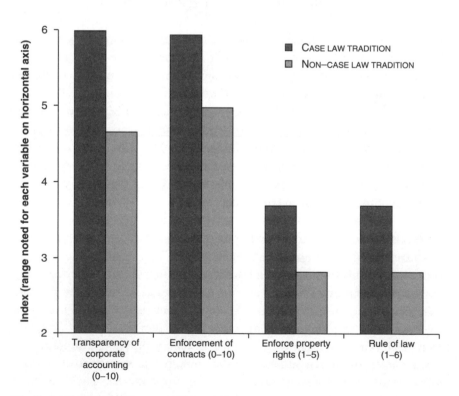

Fig. 8. Institutional Outcomes and Legal Traditions
Source: Back and Levine 2004[49]

shareholders and creditors than countries with French legal origins. The result is that case law countries have much more developed financial markets, as measured by indicators such as the share of private credit in GDP, and stock market capitalization and liquidity.

Finance Without Good Laws

Mexico is a civil-law state that has failed to evolve good financial laws. Take the example of privatization of Mexican state banks beginning in 1991. Privatization is one of the staples of free-market reform urged by the World Bank and the IMF. But in the case of Mexico, things did not go according to plan. The problem began with the privatization program itself, in which buyers of the banks could use loans from the banks they were buying to purchase the banks. One buyer covered 75 percent of the purchase price with this trick. Normally, savers would not want to deposit in banks with such shaky financing, but savers had deposit insurance from the Mexican government. The newly privatized banks thus expanded credit rapidly, with little regard for risk. Lax banking regulations allowed them to roll over loans that borrowers did not repay without even having to declare the loans in default. Bank credit grew by more than 20 percent per year in real terms from 1991 to 1994, while past-due loans grew by more than 40 percent per year.[50] If the banks did try to collect from borrowers, they ran into Mexico's torturous (civil-law) bankruptcy laws, in which it took between three and seven years for banks to recover collateral from borrowers. The reckless credit expansion contributed to the collapse of the peso beginning in December 1994, in which the currency lost half of its value, and Mexico had a severe recession.

In the aftermath of the peso crisis, the government designed a bailout of the banking system's bad loans. Unfortunately, the government (with World Bank and IMF acquiescence) dragged its feet on the bailout. With an anticipated bailout, the banks' owners had incentives to lend to themselves and then default. During 1995–1998, the banks gave 20 percent of large loans to individuals on their own boards of directors. The looting of the banks raised the cost of the bailout to the government, which in the end amounted to 15 percent of the Mexican GDP.

Since 1998, regulation of banks has been much tougher, and the government has allowed foreign banks to enter in order to put competitive pressure on Mexican banks. The bad loan problem has finally been solved, but mainly because banks lend less to the private sector. Because of the still-shaky bankruptcy laws, banks are now extremely cautious about private borrowers—the share of private loans in bank assets declined from 49 percent in 1997 to 30 percent in 2003. Mexico has still not solved the problem of making financial markets work because of the difficulty in getting the bottom-up rules and incentives right.[51] This story may give some insight into why the payoff to Latin America's "free-market" reforms was disappointing.

Top-down Dreams

So the West cannot design a comprehensive reform for a poor country that creates benevolent laws and good institutions to make markets work. We have seen that the rules that make markets work reflect a complex bottom-up search for social norms, networks of relationships, and formal laws and institutions that have the most payoff. To make things worse, these norms, networks, and institutions change in response to changed circumstances and their own past history. Political philosophers such as Burke, Popper, and Hayek had the key insight that this social interplay was so complex that a top-down reform that tried to change all the rules at once could make things worse rather than better.

Economic theorist Avinash Dixit has a more recent example of why top-down reform may have unintended consequences. Suppose a society is facilitating market transactions mainly through networks. We have seen that such networks are self-enforcing in that any cheater can be expelled from the network and thus lose all future business opportunities. Now suppose that the World Bank twists the arm of a government to set up a system with formal rules overseen by courts. Suppose such a parallel system is at least partially effective, making some business opportunities possible through the formal rules. Some of the participants in the informal networks can cheat their partners, exit the network, and begin operating in the formal system. A society could get caught in a disastrous in-between situation in which the networks break down, disrupting the previous trades, but the formal system still operates imperfectly, limiting the scope for new trades. Having two sets of rules is often worse than having only one. A reform where the gradual introduction of formal rules *reinforced* the existing networks would work better than one that tried to replace them. A plausible story for the evolution of institutions in the West is that informal relationships and norms in networks gradually hardened into formal rules (which are still supported by informal relationships and norms).[52]

This is armchair speculation, but Dixit's story may help explain why the transition from communism to capitalism in the former Soviet Union was such a disaster, and why market reforms in Latin America and Africa were disappointing. Even with severely distorted markets, the participants had formed networks of mutual trades and obligations that made the system functional at some level. Trying to change the rules all at once with the rapid introduction of free markets disrupted the old ties, while the new formal institutions were still too weak to make free markets work well. Gradual movement to freer markets would have given the participants more time to adjust their relationships and trades.

The main moral of the story is that free-market opportunity depends on bottom-up social choices that Planners usually don't begin (or try) to understand. When researchers try a little harder (as did many of the hardworking researchers on whose work this chapter draws), there is hope for gradual, piecemeal reform and spontaneous efforts by Searchers among poor people themselves.

And things are not so impossibly complex that policymakers should just throw their hands up and say it's hopeless. Poor people are resourceful despite the screw-ups by Planners.

Stagnant Economies, Dynamic Individuals

In fact, there have been positive bottom-up market trends in Africa, Latin America, and the ex-Communist countries, even though top-down structural adjustment and shock therapy failed. The younger generation is seizing opportunities to expand its horizons, with many more people getting advanced degrees both at home and in the West (which is part of the India and China success stories). Children in the new generation are coming of age knowing only markets, and there is hope that they will make markets work better than their parents did. New electronic technologies are spreading rapidly, such as computers, Internet access, cell phones, VCRs, and DVDs.

In 1992, Nigerian moviemaker Ken Nnebue released a film called *Living in Bondage*, a melodrama about a man who joins a secret sect that promises him great wealth if he sacrifices his wife. The film's dialogue is in Igbo, with subtitles in English. Rather than showing the movie in theaters, which many Nigerians could not have afforded, Nnebue released the film directly to video. Thus was born the Nigerian movie industry, known as Nollywood, sometimes called the third most vibrant movie industry in the world after Hollywood and Bollywood. Shooting with a very low budget and a tight schedule, Nigerian moviemakers churn out thousands of titles affordable to poor Africans. The industry reaches the African mass market by emphasizing local cultures and themes most relevant to Africans. People in Nigerian video stores often pass up the latest Hollywood release in favor of one from Nollywood.[53]

Despite Africa's economic stagnation, this is not to say that life is unchanging. New technologies have been spreading, giving Africans more information, more entertainment, more choices. The number of TV sets on which to watch Nollywood films has skyrocketed, following the previous explosion of radios. (See figure 9.)

There is another interesting indicator of the growth of bottom-up markets. I noticed sometime in the late 1990s the remarkable prevalence of cell phones almost everywhere, from Moscow to Prague to Accra to Soweto to La Paz. Sometimes it seemed to me there were more people walking on the street with cell phones in these places than in much richer places, such as the United States. Figure 10 shows the growth of cell phone density in Africa, Latin America, and the ex-Communist countries (each unit increase

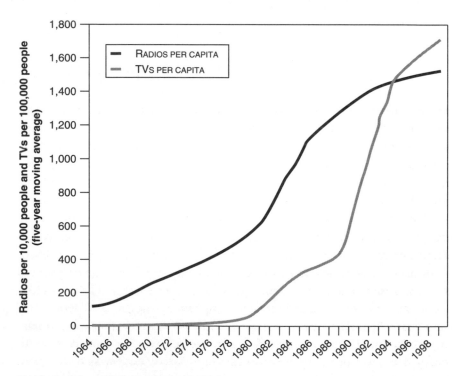

Fig. 9. Radios and TVs Per Capita in Africa

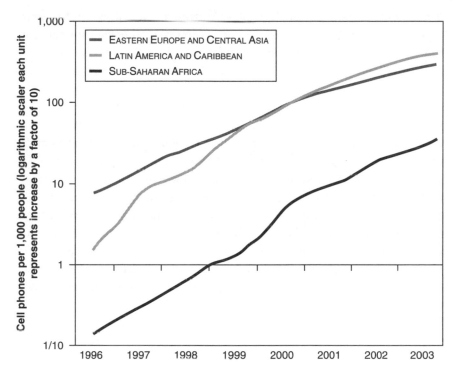

Fig. 10. Cell Phones Per Thousand People

on the graph represents an increase of tenfold in the number of cell phones per thousand people).

In Africa since 1996, the number of cell phones has been increasing by a factor of ten every three years. The explosion of cell phones shows just how much poor people search for new technological opportunities, with no state intervention, with no structural adjustment or shock therapy to promote cell phones. These are not just consumer pleasures. Cell phones help farmers, fishers, and entrepreneurs check out prices, suppliers, and consumers; arrange meetings; transfer funds; and lots of other things that are logistical nightmares in societies without good landline phones, functional postal services, or adequate roads.[54]

Entrepreneur Alieu Conteh started building a cellular network in the Democratic Republic of the Congo (formerly Zaire) when it was still in the midst of its civil war in the 1990s. He couldn't get a foreign manufacturer to ship cellular towers into the country with rebel soldiers around, so he got local men to weld scrap metal into a makeshift tower. Demand exploded for Conteh's phones, and in 2001 he formed a joint venture with the South

African firm Vodacom. One illiterate fisherwoman who lives on the Congo River without electricity relies on her cell phone to sell her fish. She can't put the fish in a freezer, so she keeps them live on a line in the river until customers call to place an order. Vodacom Congo now has 1.1 million subscribers and is adding more than a thousand a day.[55]

There has been a similar explosive growth in Internet users in Eastern Europe, Latin America, and Africa (see figure 11). On my first World Bank trip to Ghana in 1985, I had to make an emergency call to the States at the only working overseas phone line in Accra—through a pre–World War II switchboard in the basement of a hotel. Now there is a Wi-Fi Internet connection in my hotel room, where I can communicate back home every day. Whereas in 1996 the typical African country had only one Internet user for every 27,000 people, in 2003 there was one for every 138 people, and it is still climbing rapidly. Although the ex-Communist countries also started with virtually no Internet users in 1996, the rate of adoption has climbed steeply there and now surpasses Latin America and the Caribbean (even though the latter region has also had rapid Internet expansion).

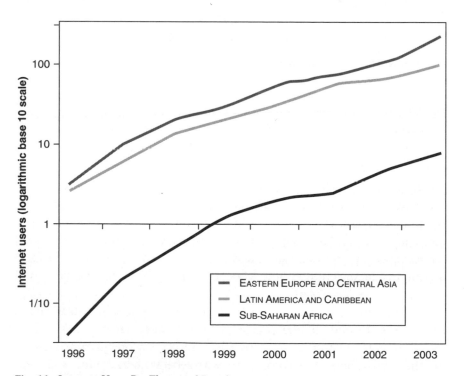

Fig. 11. Internet Users Per Thousand People

Even when the economy-wide story is disappointing growth, some individuals buck the trend. A forty-year-old woman named Ayorkor in Teshie, a town near Accra, Ghana, tells her story:

> I managed to save a little and feed my children at the same time. When I managed to save enough, I started selling cooked yam, and here I made more money and managed to save. I was lucky to meet a friend who gave me secondhand clothes on credit to sell. This I did very well and started building my capital. Now I am trading with my own money. My first two children are in the secondary school and my last child, who is eighteen months old, is in a crèche [day-care center]. I managed to get out of poverty because I was not ready to give up, and so I fought hard, and with the help of a friend I succeeded.

A seventy-six-year-old man named Udo from Ikot-Idem, Nigeria—a man with two wives and thirteen children—tells a similar story of climbing out of poverty:

> When I grew up to fend for myself, I decided to trade soap. My initial capital came from picking and selling palm fruits, and saving the proceeds. My initial capital of two manilla [traditional currency] was wisely invested and yielded good dividends. When I had saved twenty manilla, I bought an initial stock of hens for three manilla. After toiling for many years, I was able to marry. Following marriage, I became poor again. But I continued harvesting palm fruits and tapping palm wine until I saved enough money to stand financially. When I saved fifteen shillings, I bought some kernel, which I carried on my head to sell in Azumini. By so doing we successfully combined soap trade with a palm kernel business. I saved up to twenty pounds to buy a new bicycle, which enabled me to ply my trade on a larger scale. My wife and I became adequately clothed. We bought additional farmland and intensified food production. Having acquired enough land, I proceeded to plant palms, which I obtained from the government. These plants I nursed, and with the subsidy received from the government for fertilizer and farm implements, I established my plantation. The palm estate has enabled me to build a house for myself and to feed my family.

These examples of dynamism at the bottom have not yet propelled the societies as a whole into sustained growth, for all the reasons given in this chapter and the next. Individuals are dynamic, yet the complex interactions of individuals in society can cause stagnant economies. Still, the dynamism of the poor at the bottom can sometimes lead to emergence out of stagnation of the wider society.

Miracle in Xiaogang

In the tiny village of Xiaogang, Anhui province—the heart of China's rice-growing region—twenty families held a secret meeting in 1978. The villagers were desperate because they were starving. As Stanford economist

John McMillan tells the story, the commune system that the Communists had in place all over China was leading to a breakdown in food production. Under this system, everybody was collectively responsible for tilling the land, and everybody had a share in the land's output. You got your rice share whether you worked hard or not, and as a result people hardly worked. The villagers of Xiaogang reached an agreement: they would divide up the land and farm it individually, with each person keeping the output of his own land. They kept their agreement a secret out of fear of the Communist authorities. Rice production in Xiaogang shot up. The results were too spectacular to stay secret for long. Neighboring villages wanted to know how Xiaogang had increased its rice production so much. Other villages also put into place individual farming.

Before long, the Communist authorities got wind of the spontaneous outbreak of property rights in the countryside. The news arrived at a propitious moment, when reformers in the party were seeking to get rid of the doctrinaire Maoists. Confronted with the evidence that food production increased dramatically with individual farming, the provincial Communist Party officials gave their blessing and reported the developments to authorities in Beijing. By 1982, a Communist Party conference ratified what had already happened in the countryside, approving individual farming. By 1984, there were no communes left.[56] This was just one pebble that started the landslide of the Chinese economic miracle. Gradualist, homegrown reform in China did much better than did outsiders' fantasies of shock therapy in Russia.

Piecemeal reformers, foreign and domestic, can try to move toward better systems that are sensitive to local conditions and that unshackle the dynamism of individuals everywhere. The dynamism of the poor at the bottom has much more potential than plans at the top.

The Shell Foundation's Businesslike Approach to Poverty

One of the least known problems of poverty is indoor smoke from cooking. During a recent trip to Africa, I saw a young girl cooking in an unventilated hut all day long, in smoke so thick I could not stand to stay in the hut for more than a few seconds. This scene is common in homes throughout Africa, multiplying many times children's chances of dying from respiratory infections. The World Health Organization estimates that indoor air pollution in a smoky hut exceeds by a factor of sixty the European Union's standard maximum for outdoor air pollution.[57]

The sufferings from acute respiratory infections are hard to convey to people in rich societies, who no longer experience them. The lungs fill with pus, some of which the patient coughs out. The infection causes chills, fever, shaking, sharp pains in the chest, nausea, and vomiting. Death follows when the infection goes untreated. This is how indoor smoke kills. The death toll is around 1.8 million a year worldwide.

The Shell Group is one of those large multinational corporations that are so feared by globalization protesters. Many of these corporations are responding to this social pressure by setting up charitable foundations. They bring to the table their own unique business skills, which makes them think more like Searchers than like Planners. The Shell Group's charitable wing, the Shell Foundation, explains its philanthropic approach:

> Our partners need to be adept at applying business thinking and business principles to how they operate and to the interventions they propose.... [We stimulate] the deployment by our partners of the same set of skills and entrepreneurial instincts... that business people everywhere use to identify and assess business opportunities and then overcome the problems that must be solved en route to setting up and operating an enterprise. These include understanding the market and knowing who your customer is, what they want and will pay for... Our partners usually... will be particularly enterprising as they search for solutions.

For example, the Shell Foundation is tackling the problem of indoor smoke. Traditional aid approaches have not made much headway on this problem. Official donor agencies tried to force technical fixes—such as stoves designed to reduce smoke—on the poor without consulting them on what kind of stoves they wanted and would use. The utilization rate of these new stoves turned out to be a big disappointment. The aid Planners were not thinking like business-men—that is, giving the customers what they wanted at a reasonable cost. The Shell Foundation is experimenting with a market-based approach, in which dozens or even hundreds of microenterprises produce and distribute stoves, adapting them to local consumer wants. The approach is pragmatic: a combination of cash sales to consumers, sales to NGOs and to public institutions that use their own social distribution networks, experimentation with microcredit to finance stove purchases, and accepting payments in goods rather than cash.

Corporate charity cannot replace official foreign aid, but its mar-ketlike approach is a good model of what it's like to be a Searcher.

Improvements to Doing Business

Not all piecemeal improvements are tangible projects. Simeon Djankov at the World Bank, with many collaborators, has started a promising initiative to reduce obstacles to doing business in poor countries. He has found in his research that countries that require more red tape to start a new business have higher corruption and large informal sectors operating outside the law. Business is also shackled in poor countries by cumbersome procedures to collect debts, enforce contracts, register property, and collect from bankrupt business partners;[58] "It takes 153 days to start a business in Maputo, but 2 days in Toronto. It costs $2,042 or 126% of the debt value to enforce a contract in Jakarta, but $1,300 or 5.4% of the debt value to do so in Seoul. It takes 21 procedures to register commercial property in Abuja, but 3 procedures in Helsinki. If a debtor becomes insolvent and enters bankruptcy, creditors would get 13 cents on the dollar in Mumbai, but more than 90 cents in Tokyo.[59]

Djankov and his collaborators have shined a bright light on this issue by compiling indicators of costs of doing business for as many countries around the world as possible. Every year, they issue a report highlighting the countries that have improved the most and those that failed to improve. This honest reporting affects a country's ability to attract capital and so creates incentives for piecemeal changes to cumbersome regulations.

CHAPTER FOUR

Planners and Gangsters

No one's life, liberty, or property is safe
While the legislature is in session.

Corollary of Murphy's Law

Upon leaving for exile in 1828, after ruling for three years, Antonio José de Sucre Alcalá, the first president of independent Bolivia, summed up his country's situation. Sucre said, "The solution was impossible."[1] One hundred and ninety-five presidents later, Bolivian president Carlos Mesa maybe had similar thoughts when he resigned under pressure in June 2005.

In the sixteenth century, Bolivia (then known as Upper Peru) was among the richest provinces in the Spanish American empire. Today it is among the poorest countries in Spanish-speaking America.

What makes Bolivia so poor and ungovernable? Maybe 450 years of a white elite ruling a majority Indian nation has something to do with it. As late as 1997, representatives of indigenous parties made up less than 1 percent of Congress. The Bolivian government was ranked with the worst quarter of governments rated on corruption.

In 1545, Spaniards discovered the Americas' richest vein of silver at Potosí.[2] From then until the 1650s, Potosí was the largest silver mine in the world, generating Bolivia's first economic boom. Potosí was the largest city in the Western Hemisphere at that point.[3] The European mineowners reinstated a forced labor system that had existed under the Inca empire, called the *mita*, drafting indigenous people to do the unpleasant work in the mines.

The boom spilled over into profits for European farmers growing maize, wheat, and coca leaf for mine workers. Under the *encomienda* system, well-connected conquistadores got large grants of land with rights to the labor and produce of the Indians who lived on them.

Indian mortality from European diseases broke up traditional communities and freed up land, which the wealthiest Europeans absorbed into the former *encomiendas*, now known as haciendas. Hacendados used Indian labor from those stranded by the decline of traditional communities.[4]

The rest of the Indians lived in their own communities, subject to a tribute tax for the crown.

Bolivia was the last Spanish colony in America to become independent, in 1825. The independent state was not so different from the colony. Haciendas only grew in importance. In 1846, about 5,135 hacendados managed a labor force of 400,000 Indian peasants. Six hundred twenty thousand Indians lived in autonomous communities. Another 200,000 were small-time landowners or rented land from haciendas or free communities.[5] The 1880–1930 tin boom created even more rapacious demands by landowners. The government broke up free Indian communities by introducing individual titles to lands. The haciendas acquired land through small purchases in each community to break the community's cohesion, then used fraud and force as well as straight purchase to acquire Indian lands. Free communities saw their share of land fall from half in 1880 to less than a third by 1930. This third was the most unarable land.[6]

Not that the Indians could do much to protest. The elite showed little interest in the education of the majority. In the middle of the nineteenth century, only about 20 percent of the population could speak Spanish.[7] Only 10 percent of school-age children were in school.[8] Literacy requirements then restricted voting to the white population. The electorate was only about thirty to forty thousand in 1900.[9] In the 1900 census, 13 percent of Bolivians were white. Indians worked on haciendas in return for use of usufruct land. They performed the hated *pongo* service for landowners, attending to the personal needs of the hacendado family. The Indians had to do *pongo* service even if the landowner lived in a faraway city, with the Indian bearing the transport costs.

The 1952 revolution failed to help poor Bolivians get out of poverty. Instead, the revolution took a conservative turn, in which the white elite soon regained ascendancy. After unstable civilian governments, unstable military governments took over. The military ruled from 1964 until 1982. There were eight coups from 1964 to 1981. Bolivia returned to democracy in 1982, but the transition was not smooth. Under the first democratic government, financial mismanagement caused hyperinflation to peak at 25,000 percent in 1985.[10]

After 1985, the donors got heavily involved. The government brought inflation down and pursued free-market reforms at the behest of the IMF and the World Bank, but economic growth did not revive.

After all the to-and-fro of Bolivian history, the Indians are still on the margins of the national society. Representation of indigenous parties in Congress was still only around 1 to 2 percent in the new democratic period of 1982–1997. The incidence of extreme poverty among the indigenous was 52 percent against 27 percent for non-indigenous in 2002.

Institutions remain enfeebled after Bolivia's chaotic history of European minority rule. There were sixteen massive purges of the judicial system between 1931 and 1982, making courts subservient to political interests.[11] A survey rated Bolivia's Customs Agency and its Internal Revenue Agency as the most politicized and corrupt government agencies. Enterprise surveys cite Bolivia as near the top in the world in the percentage of firms who cite corruption and the dishonesty of courts and police as obstacles to doing business there.[12]

Increased demands for representation by indigenous groups provoked the current political crisis. The American-imposed war against cocaine trafficking alienated coca leaf growers (also mainly indigenous). IMF structural adjustment conditions were unpopular. After seeing little benefit from previous silver and tin booms, indigenous groups are suspicious about an incipient natural gas boom driven by foreign companies. Violent uprisings occurred in April 2000, September/October 2000, January 2002, and February 2003, before an October 2003 uprising forced out President Gonzalo Sánchez de Lozada.[13] His successor, Carlos Mesa, similarly resigned in June 2005. Mesa was unable to deal with another uprising of indigenous protesters, who blockaded roads to La Paz, demanding nationalization of the gas industry.[14]

Planners and Politics

One gut instinct that many people have about the poverty of nations is probably close to the target: it's all politics. As if the problems with markets were not enough, poor countries have bad governments. A good government might resolve some of the problems with markets discussed earlier.

Planners opt for one of two camps about bad government. One camp (associated with the U.S. government, the World Bank, and the IMF) says that poor-country governments are awful and the West should get tough with the bad governments—force them to change in return for aid. The other camp (associated with the United Nations and Jeffrey Sachs) says that poor-country governments are not so bad and that countries should be free to determine their own development strategies. However, this artificially restricts the debate. It may be true that poor-country governments are bad, and it may be just as true that Western attempts to change them have been fruitless. Continuing my subliminal quest for the most politically unappealing truths, this chapter considers what to do if both statements are true.

I feel awfully undiplomatic pointing out bad government in other countries. In the spirit of the rest of this book, outsiders like me need a lot of humility when they pass judgment on another society's government. Certainly my own government is no paragon when it goes around invading other countries for unconvincing reasons, violating human rights of prisoners in the war on terror, and financing political campaigns with corporate payola. I will *not* advocate some banana-republic stereotype of bad government everywhere in developing countries. There is a lot of variation both across developing countries and *within* governments as to quality of government officials. There is a layer of capable, honest, well-meaning technocrats in almost every government, who themselves are a promising group of Searchers looking for a way to increase opportunities for poor people. Over a couple of decades working on developing countries, I have met outstanding government officials from every continent, whom I admire greatly. These officials complain more knowledgeably about bad politics and corruption in their own countries than outsiders can.

We must face reality—decades of research by social scientists, not to mention everyday observation, show just how dysfunctional government can get in many countries of the Rest. We don't do the poor any favors by tenderly respecting the sensitivities of bad rulers who oppress their own people.

The theme of this chapter is similar to the last one on free markets: democracy works, but imposing democracy from the outside doesn't. First the chapter sketches a Civics 101 story of how good government might work through democracy. The chapter doesn't claim to resolve the many complicated issues of how and whether democracy works. It just gives one angle on democracy that throws it into sharp relief compared with Western assistance—democracy features feedback and accountability, rewarding Searchers, while foreign aid (or, in a later chapter, military intervention) does not.

But Planners with no feedback and accountability cannot impose a system of feedback and accountability! The chapter makes this more explicit by torturing you with many of the complexities that make attaining effective democracy and good government so difficult, even for insiders, and much more so for outsiders. Finally, the chapter goes through some of the evidence on how donors respond to bad government.

After the failure of free-market reforms, the next step in the escalation of the White Man's Burden (mainly in the nineties) was the attempt to foster "good institutions." With their Sisyphean efforts to transform bad governments into good ones, donors wind up unable to screen out gangsters. We have yet another example of Planners aiming at the impossible, instead of letting Searchers work on the possible. (In two later chapters, we examine how outside Planners try to impose good government through "postmodern" trusteeships and military invasion.)

Can the State Build the Good Society?

Government institutions such as courts, judges, and police could solve some of the problems we saw with market transactions in the previous chapter. Impartial courts and police help make the market work in rich countries by enforcing contracts, protecting property rights, providing security against predators, and punishing lawbreakers.

The Achilles' heel is that any government that is powerful enough to protect citizens against predators is also powerful enough to be a predator itself. There is an old Latin saying that goes, *"Quis custodiet ipsos custodes?"*—which translates freely as "Why would you trust a government official any more than you would a shoplifting serial killer?"

Democracy's answer to "Who will watch the watchers?" (the more conventional translation of the above) is everyone. The other great invention of human society besides free markets is political freedom. According to the simplest view of democracy, an open society with a free press, free speech, freedom of assembly, and political rights for dissidents is a way to ensure good government. Free individuals will expose any predatory behavior by bad governments, and vote them out of office. Voters will reward with longer terms of office those politicians who find ways to deliver more honest courts, judges, and police. Political parties will compete to please the voters, just as firms compete to please their customers. The next generation of politicians will do better at delivering these services. Of course, no real democracy works anywhere close to this ideal, but there are some that come close enough to make development possible.[15]

Assuming good institutions are in place, markets work for private goods, the kind consumed in private, that affect only their individual consumer and nobody else. What about public goods such as roads and water? Another potential achievement of democracy is to provide feedback from the voters on how much and what kind of public good they need. If the voters see a shortage of roads in a particular location, they lobby and vote for politicians who offer increased government road building and road maintenance, financed by taxes on the voters. Political Searchers respond to these needs in return for the political support of the voters, akin to the way that private Searchers respond to consumer demands. The voters will reject a government that allows moon crater–size potholes to develop on major traffic arteries. The existence of little problems such as traffic jams in large cities shows that this does not work perfectly, but it works well enough to make road transport possible on a large scale in rich societies.

The stylized facts in the data support the idea that democracies do a good job of providing public services. Some World Bank researchers have collected surveys of many different attributes of government around the world. The two that are most relevant here are their measure of "voice and accountability" (democracy) and "government effectiveness" (whether the government fixes your potholes). Of course, these are highly correlated because they both go up with per capita income (which is probably both cause and effect). However, even after removing the effect of per capita income on each outcome, democracy is highly correlated with government effectiveness on delivering public services. Figure 12 shows the parts of democracy and

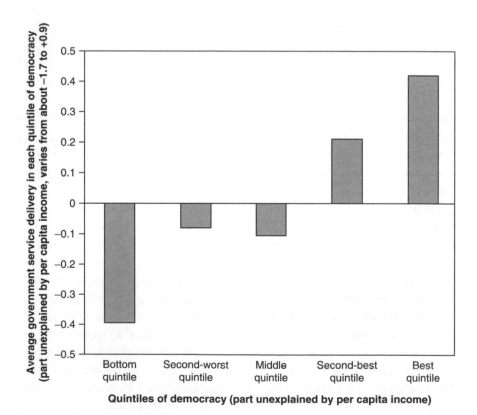

Fig. 12. Democracy and Government Service Delivery

government effectiveness that are *not* explained by per capita income; the unexplained part of democracy is strongly associated with the unexplained part of the quality of government service delivery.

Democracy is a bottom-up system that rewards local, specialized knowledge in a similar way to free markets. In a democracy, the squeaky wheel gets the grease. Whoever complains most vociferously about their local problems, which usually is related to how severe the problem is, will attract the attention of politicians and get a remedy. Democratically elected politicians at the national level will craft solutions to national problems that are more sensitive to the peculiarities of local cultures, social norms, and circumstances than those that outside benefactors would impose. Harvard economist Dani Rodrik calls democracy a "meta-institution" that uses locally specific knowledge to choose all the other appropriate institutions for making a society work.[16]

Why Democracy Is Not So Simple

Alas, democracy is not a quick fix for poor countries, just as free markets are not a quick fix. The road to a stable democracy is even more tortuous than that to efficient markets. Just like markets, the functioning of democracy depends on the slow and bottom-up evolution of rules of fair play. You can cheat at elections just as you can cheat your market customers, as a sorry history of rigged elections around the world illustrates. How to prevent cheating? Just to cite one problem, judges could referee what is fair political competition, but who appoints the electoral judges?

Even aside from cheating, democracy is an intricate set of arrangements that is far more than just holding elections. Another problem with democracy is that of the tyranny of the majority. If a majority of the society hates a minority, they may decide to abuse that minority. If the majority hates some minority viewpoint, they may vote to censor dissidents. This would limit the free speech and debate that is one of the virtues of democracy. These points are far from hypothetical in poor-country democracies, which are often polarized along ethnic and class lines and where the winners sometimes abuse the losers.

This is why a complete definition of democracy involves some protection for individual rights and freedom of dissent as well as majority rule. To see why democracy doesn't work well without these, consider what is known as the paradox of democracy. The paradox is that the majority may vote to abolish democracy.

To see one way in which this could happen, suppose that the majority wanted to make sure that its preferred policies were followed forever after. They could simply vote to deny the minority the right to vote in future elections. For example, the red states in the United States, which had a slight majority in the 2004 election, might want to make sure that the American government from now on consisted of god-fearing gun owners rather than married gay couples having abortions. So they could pass an electoral reform that denied citizens of blue states the right to vote. Then the majority of the most zealous remaining voters could vote to disenfranchise a less-zealous minority. So now the electorate is down to a little over 25 percent of the citizens. This could keep going indefinitely, until only television evangelists were voting.

Fortunately, the U.S. Constitution and its amendments guarantee every citizen basic rights such as voting and freedom of speech; usually honest Supreme Court justices enforce the Constitution; and the social norms that would protest such a violation of the blue states' rights are strong. American democracy is not utopia; it is just a system that has worked pretty well to search for good economic results for most people. Social norms may be the most difficult part of building a democracy—many poor countries are far from such norms. A staple of elections in many poor countries is to harass and intimidate the opposition so that they don't vote.

Minority rights are even more important in ethnically more heterogeneous poor countries. Unfortunately, the same ethnic heterogeneity makes it less likely that a minority-protecting democracy will evolve, as Philippe Aghion, Alberto Alesina, and Francesco Trebbi of Harvard have recently pointed out. The people who make the rules are going to be those who belong to the majority ethnic group, and they are unlikely to write rules that give away some of their power to a minority group (as Iraqi Sunnis today could testify). Aghion, Alesina, and Trebbi found that checks on the majority's executive power (and even democracy in general) were statistically less likely with higher ethnic heterogeneity.[17] In fact, a recent study found that democracy, as usually defined by Polity IV, does *not* lower the probability of the most extreme violation of minority rights of all: state-sponsored mass killings (even genocide) of political or ethnic victims.[18] A more complete definition of a democracy would include protections for minorities.

Property Rights and Democracy

Another form of violation of individual rights could come about if the majority decided to redistribute the income of a minority. This could prove politically appealing if the majority were poor and the minority were rich. Democracy for a long time was viewed as a threat to private property for just this reason. James Madison and Alexander Hamilton worried a lot about this in writing the U.S. Constitution, and they sought to build in checks—such as the Senate and the Supreme Court—against a populist majority. The Fifth Amendment to the Constitution (the same amendment that protects you against self-incrimination) rammed home the rule that nobody could "be deprived of . . . property, without due process of law; nor shall private property be taken for public use, without just compensation." But a populist majority could still vote for high taxes on the rich, stunting future development prospects.

An oligarchy (rule by the rich few) could thus have decent economic growth (even if abysmal justice) compared with a democracy, at least for a while. In a recent paper, economist Daron Acemoglu of MIT talks about the tradeoff between oligarchy and democracy for economic growth.[19] The oligarchy has the advantage of eliminating the democratic threat to property rights. This could make economic growth quite high for a while as the elite invested in what they were good at doing, secure that they would get to keep the returns. However, an oligarchy is not a good system for Searchers. The elite protect only the rich who are incumbents, and erect barriers to the entry of newcomers. Acemoglu points out that in the dynamic world economy, the payoff to any particular economic activity is always changing, as old sectors decline and new sectors emerge. A democracy with equal rights for everyone will do better giving opportunities to the Searchers, whom we need to get the new sectors to emerge.

To make things concrete, Acemoglu gives the example of the Caribbean versus New England in the eighteenth and nineteenth centuries. In the early eighteenth century, the Caribbean was much richer thanks to profitable sugar plantations worked by African slaves and owned by European settlers. The white Caribbean oligarchy invested a lot in the profitable sugar economy, secure in their own brutally enforced property rights over their human and real property. The New Englanders had more democracy, but only modest incomes from family wheat farms, fishing, and the shipping trade. However, New England was able to take advantage of the new technologies emerging out of the industrial revolution, with opportunities for new entrepreneurs to emerge from humble origins. The Caribbean oligarchs just kept on doing sugar, even though sugar's fortunes declined in the nineteenth century. By the end of the nineteenth century, New England was much richer than the Caribbean.

Oligarchy, Democracy, and Revolution

Acemoglu and political scientist James A. Robinson of Harvard also discuss the role of the oligarchy in a fascinating new book, *Economic Origins of Dictatorship and Democracy*. They see democracy emerging out of a strategic face-off between the rich minority and the poor majority.[20] The rich prefer not to have democracy because of the threat of redistribution. However, an even worse threat to the elite is total revolution by the poor, which would destroy the elite altogether. The poor can threaten revolution in order to try to extract democratic concessions from the rich. Often there is only a temporary revolutionary window of opportunity, such as during a war or a major economic crisis. (Although Acemoglu and Robinson had in mind a traditional elite, the rich minority could just as well be a recently created group of political insiders who fed off state revenues.)

Why don't the rich just defuse the temporary crisis by promising some redistribution toward the poor, instead of agreeing to democracy? Or why don't they just repress the poor with military force? Acemoglu and Robinson show that the first option doesn't work because the poor are not stupid—they know that the autocratic elite can reverse the redistributive policies after the revolutionary crisis passes. Only a permanent institutional change toward democracy assures the poor that they will remain in charge and will permanently benefit from some redistribution.

Repression could work with a poor, disorganized population, but it gets more and more costly (and less likely to succeed) as the majority gets more educated and has more politically active Searchers (a point that is not lost on the oligarchy, who often block mass education). Under these circumstances, the elite agree to a transition to democracy. Acemoglu and Robinson cite the gradual movement toward universal suffrage in Britain in the nineteenth century as an example. As Prime Minister Earl Grey explained in 1831, well before he launched his world-class brand of tea: "There is no-one more decided against annual parliaments, universal suffrage and the ballot, than I am. My object is not to favour, but to put an end to such hopes and projects.... The principle of my reform is, to prevent the necessity of revolution ... reforming to preserve and not to overthrow."[21]

The rich gave in more easily to democracy in Britain and America because the design of the new democratic system had some checks against the redistributive powers of the majority. A two-chamber legislature had the upper chamber less under the sway of the majority. A system of winner-take-all elections for legislative representatives (as opposed to holding plebiscites on how much to tax the rich) made the more radical redistributionists unelectable.

The rich also find it reassuring that they can spend their money lobbying against redistribution. You need just the right amount of protection for the rich under democracy: too little, and the elite won't want to agree to democracy; too much, and the poor will go ahead and have the revolution anyway. A more recent example is the Chilean military oligarchy agreeing to democracy in 1990, conditional on giving the military enough remaining power to protect the free-market and private-property reforms they had introduced during their bloody tenure from 1973 to 1990.

In natural-resource producers, or in very unequal societies (these two categories heavily overlap, as we discuss), things will not work out so well. In these societies, the assets of the rich are in land or natural resources, which are much easier to tax than machinery or human skills. The rich thus have much more to lose from a democratic majority deciding on taxes. The poor will choose a higher tax rate, the higher the inequality. (They have more to gain from redistribution if the gap between rich and poor is large, and they have less future income to lose if tax rates penalize income growth.) Poor peasants are also much easier to repress with force than richer industrial workers. Thus perpetual oligarchy is more likely in unequal agrarian or mineral societies than in more equal industrial societies, as Latin America demonstrated for most of the nineteenth and twentieth centuries. Cross-country studies have indeed found the incidence of democracy to be higher in more societies with a higher share of income going to the middle class—even when addressing possible reverse causality from democracy to the size of the middle class (see figure 13).[22]

What has determined different-size middle classes in different countries? Many authors have pointed to natural-resource endowments. Economic historians Stanley Engerman and Kenneth Sokoloff have highlighted the role of sugar plantations and silver mines in contributing to Latin America and the Caribbean's high inequality (which adds another angle on Caribbean stagnation to that given earlier). The plantations and mines had to be operated on a large scale, and wound up in the hands of a few, and the planters relied on slavery to work the sugar plantations—an extreme form of inequality. You couldn't grow sugar in North America; wheat was the crop

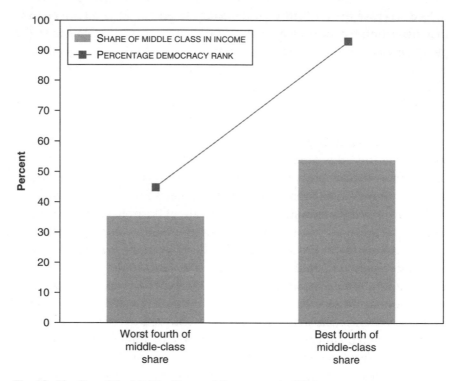

Fig. 13. The Size of the Middle Class and Democracy in 2004

of choice. Wheat could be produced on a small scale, hence a middle class was formed made up of family farmers in the United States and Canada. Heavy reliance on tropical commodities and minerals was also associated with inequality elsewhere in the world.

In unequal societies, the violent repression of the poor by the rich creates grievances among the victims of that repression. Violence begets more violence, so violent revolution is also more likely (as opposed to the happy democratic compromise described earlier). Hence, in Latin America, we have seen successful violent revolutions such as that in Mexico early in the twentieth century and in Bolivia (at least an incomplete revolution), Cuba, and Nicaragua; and attempted revolutions such as those in El Salvador, Guatemala, and Colombia. The big successful Communist revolutions occurred in poor agrarian societies—Russia in 1917 and China in 1949—not in industrialized societies, as Marx had predicted. Democracy in unequal agrarian societies tends not to last, as it alternates between populist demagogues attempting redistribution and the rich striking back with military coups. Democracy is indeed negatively associated with the share of agriculture in the economy in cross-country data (although the share of agriculture could just be a proxy for income), controlling for the size of the middle class (which remains an important statistical predictor of democracy).

A natural-resource oligarchy is particularly inimical to democracy. Oil is infamous for undermining or preventing democracy. Oil revenues are very easy to redistribute, so wealthy and well-connected insiders who benefit from oil controlled by a dictatorship have a lot to lose from a democracy that would surely result in redistribution. Hence we get oil societies desperate to prevent democracy, ranging from the oil-rich Middle East to Africa. NYU politics professor Leonard Wantchekon documented systematically the association of resource wealth with autocracy in Africa, as others did using worldwide patterns.[23] Wantchekon shows that new democracies have succeeded in Africa mainly in resource-poor places such as Benin, Madagascar, and Mali, while oil-rich states such as Algeria, Cameroon, Gabon, and Libya still have dictators. Worldwide, oil producers were on average in the worst fourth of the world's countries in democracy in 2004, as democracy was measured by three World Bank researchers.[24] (Unfortunately, foreign aid can be a lot like oil revenues in its negative effect on incentives for democratization, as we see later.)

The negative effect of oil on democracy could be one of the main mechanisms for the "natural resource curse," in which windfalls of natural resources, even though boosting income directly, have a negative effect on subsequent economic growth.

European Minority States[25]

There is one big historical experiment with oligarchy that confirms the Acemoglu predictions, which happens to be indirectly related to one unsavory side of the West's interaction with the Rest. This was the settlement of relatively rich Europeans as a minority group among poor indigenous people in the Americas and some places scattered throughout Africa. Places of minority European settlement included most of Latin America and the Caribbean, Algeria, Angola, Kenya, Rhodesia, and South Africa. The rich Europeans in Latin America, the Caribbean, and African settler colonies typically awarded themselves a monopoly of political power and privileged access to land and education (albeit to a more extreme degree in Africa than in Latin America, since Latin American racial distinctions were not as sharp). Hence the whites fit almost perfectly the definition and predicted behavior of an "oligarchy." Although the white

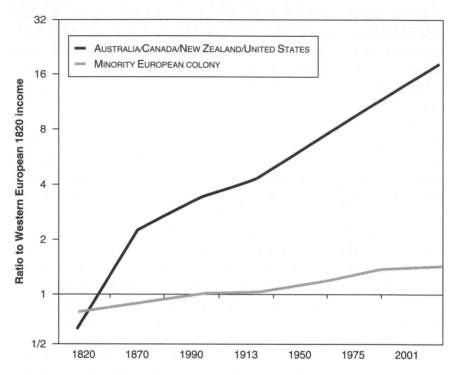

Fig. 14. Minority European Versus Mostly European Colonies

minority societies account for only a small part of poor countries today, they illustrate a general problem of oligarchy that is far more widespread.

Figure 14 above shows indeed that the minority European settlements were richer than the average of Australia, Canada, New Zealand, and the United States in 1820; the latter were democratic places with a large majority of the population European. However, these democratic countries dramatically outperformed the economies of oligarchy over the next two centuries. As Acemoglu predicted, oligarchy can perform well for a while, but tends to stagnate eventually. The Bolivian example given at the beginning of this chapter fits the pattern of oligarchy and stagnation.

Illiberal Democracy

Fareed Zakaria, in his 2003 book, *The Future of Freedom,* has brought to wide attention the idea of "illiberal democracy." Why do democracies sometimes produce awful government despite free elections?

A big problem with democracy and development, particularly with uneducated voters, is that the politicians could appeal to voters' gut instincts of hatred, fear, nationalism, or racism to win elections. Edward Glaeser of Harvard had the insight that politicians will promote hatred when it helps achieve other unrelated political goals.[26] A politician who wants to avoid redistribution to the poor will preach ethnic hatred toward a poor minority that happens to be ethnically distinct. Thus, for example, rich white leaders in the American South defeated populism in the late nineteenth century by persuading poor whites to hate poor blacks. (This is one way that an oligarchy can keep power even in a democracy.) Unfortunately, the political entrepreneurs can pander to the majority's hatreds as well as (or instead of) to the majority's need for public services.

Without protections for minority rights such as those discussed earlier, majority ethnic groups in a democracy can exploit minority ones. In many ethnically divided countries today, politicians often exploit ethnic animosities to build a coalition that seeks to redistribute income to "us" from "them." The perpetual distributive contests among ethnic groups in Africa, for example, have complicated African democracy and made it difficult to achieve long-run development there. Even if patronage is not so overt, voters may simply not trust a leader from another ethnic group to act in their interest. Different ethnic groups may have conflicting interests in public services: group A wants a road in their region, while group B wants a road in *their* region; the more segregated ethnic groups are, the less likely group B voters are to use, or care about, the road in group A's region. This may cause voters to choose a lower level of public services overall. Researchers have documented links between ethnic divisions and poor schooling and infrastructure, between ethnic divisions and poor-quality government, and between ethnic divisions and lower spending on public services.[27]

Ethnic hatreds are at work even when politics are not democratic. For example, Arab leaders may preach incessant hatred of Israel because that hatred justifies a powerful army, which also comes in handy to suppress political dissidents and preserve the autocrats' hold on power. Pakistani leaders may have preached hatred of India and kept alive the Kashmir dispute for similar reasons. Nationalism may be even more of a popular political platform in poor countries, where the masses have less accumulated wealth at stake when they fight ethnic wars. This is not to deny that many nationalist grievances are genuine; it is just that nationalist leaders seem to pursue such grievances at the expense of future economic development.

Another problem with the ideal vision of democracy is corruption. Competitive elections are no guarantee against corruption. Politicians can buy votes instead of earning them with good government. They can steal from state coffers to fund payoffs for their supporters. Corrupt politics merge with ethnic politics as parties compete to win resources for their own ethnic group. Politicians can buy off journalists or dissidents who might expose their peccadilloes. Even democratically elected politicians can buy favors from the army and the police to intimidate the opposition in future elections. It could turn out that all political parties are corrupt and that it is just the better-organized machine that wins the election. For example, Pakistani democracy in the 1990s was dominated by two rival political machines led by Benazir Bhutto and Nawaz Sharif, who were both corrupt. The president of Pakistan, Farooq Leghari, even accused Prime Minister Bhutto's government of complicity in killings of political opponents. (Bhutto denies the charges against her.) Overturning corrupt democracy often takes freedom of speech and freedom of the press, which in turn require many independent sources of power that cannot all be bought off by corrupt politicians.

Are you worn out by all this to-and-fro about whether free elections will come about, and whether they will work if they do? I hope you are now so worn out that you won't impose a simplistic democratic blueprint on poor countries! I have not even gotten close to an exhaustive survey of what makes democracy possible or impossible, work well or work badly. But even this superficial sketch of democracy and its vulnerabilities has uncovered several reasons why good government may not take hold—elite manipulation of the rules of the political game, weak social norms, landed wealth, natural resources, high inequality, corruption, and ethnic nationalism and hatreds.

Unfortunately, the aid agencies have had little idea how to fix these problems from the outside when they have tried to change bad governments into good governments. In fact, we will see in later chapters that during the previous history of Europe's attempted transformation of the Rest—colonization, European-imposed borders, decolonization, and military intervention—the West often made things worse rather than better on many of these dimensions.

Problem Governments

Many countries of the Rest have conditions unfavorable to democracy and good government: they are producers of natural resources such as oil, and/or are unequal agrarian societies, and/or are just unequal, and/or have a lot of ethnic conflict. So many countries of the Rest have corrupt and undemocratic governments. Badly governed countries are poor countries.

We see an association between democracy and income (see figure 15). The graph is logarithmic, meaning that every unit increase on the graph represents a doubling of per capita income. As one moves from the least democratic to the most democratic countries, income increases by a factor of ten.

Correlation is not causality—it could be that rich people demand more political rights and, in general, good government. Democracy could also be standing in for some other aspect of good government. However, to deal with the first problem, since researchers know a little bit about the determinants of bad government, studies can explore whether bad government *causes* poverty, rather than (mainly) the other way around. We can take the part of bad government induced by the factors mentioned earlier—such as commodity and natural-resource endowments—and see if it is associated with poverty. If it is, that would suggest that bad government caused poverty. We can also test whether these noneconomic factors affect poverty

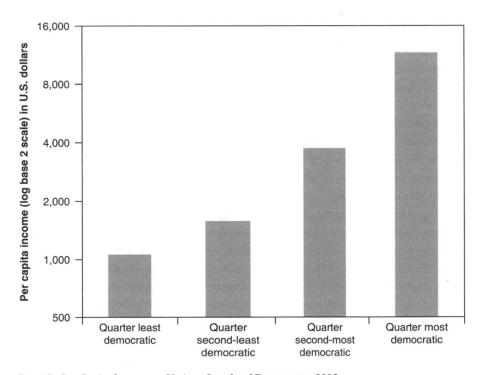

Fig. 15. Per Capita Income at Various Levels of Democracy, 2002

directly or only through bad government. Most of the research that takes this line finds that bad government does indeed cause poverty, and that the influence of the noneconomic factors is only through bad government, not directly on poverty.[28]

The research is less successful at identifying which aspect of bad government matters, such as democracy versus corruption. Different dimensions of good government tend to come together in packages, so it is hard to tell which one is causing economic development.

We have already seen that bad government has a lot to do with the low growth of poor countries that were allegedly in "poverty traps." Now we see some evidence that bad government has a lot to do with their being poor in the first place.

Along with these formal data, we have plenty of anecdotes of what a poor job the state does in poor countries in enforcing contracts and protecting property and persons. In one poor neighborhood in Thailand, the police were so ineffective that parents reported keeping children out of school to guard the family homes against break-ins.[29] Police in Mtamba, Malawi, gave crime victims the unwelcome assignment of catching the thief or murderer and delivering him to the police station.[30] Far from enforcing property rights, the police themselves often seize property to extort bribes. The police grabbed the tea shop of Ali Ahmad in Patna, India, and detained him. He bribed the policeman 920 rupees to get his shop back, which his wife borrowed from a neighbor at a high interest rate. In Patna, the police and criminals collaborate in blackmail, harassment, and extortion from shop owners and vegetable sellers.[31]

Likewise, traders in food crops in Cameroon describe soldiers and police setting up roadblocks to demand bribes, which the traders must pay or risk seizure of their goods. Not exactly the kind of strong property rights that would facilitate trade.[32]

The rich can often count on better treatment from the police than the poor can; the police will back the rich in any dispute between the two. Some poor people in Dangara, Uzbekistan, said, "The police have become the rich people's stick used against common people."[33] Villagers in Bangladesh told interviewers, "Poor people have no access to the police station, government offices, and the judge of the village court. The rich people dominate these institutions." Illiterate poor people have difficulty with written documents and formal bureaucratic procedures to prove claims to property.

Reporting a crime to the police is often counterproductive, as the police themselves rob the poor or are in cahoots with the criminals. In Ozerny, Russia, a robbery victim identified the perpetrator and filed a statement with police. The victim was understandably distressed later to see "the policeman drinking with the guy who robbed me."[34]

Dealing with Bad Governments

The foreign aid Planners in the West have never figured out how to deal with bad government in the Rest. We donors are reluctant to admit publicly that some bad governments have deep historical roots, as sketched in the first half of this chapter, even if we know it privately.

The donor agencies are dealing with a difficult problem: they want to give aid to poor countries, not to rich countries. The rich countries have decided that the donor agencies have to give mostly to the government in the recipient country. For example, the writers of the original charters of the IMF and the World Bank—mainly the United States and the United Kingdom—decided that they could operate only through governments in the recipient countries. If virtually all poor countries have bad governments, then the donor agencies will give aid to countries with bad governments.

Another problem is that foreign aid is used as a political reward to allied governments, no matter how unsavory they are. U.S. military aid to a poor country, presumably a measure of strategic importance to the United States, helped predict whether that country received IMF and World Bank structural adjustment loans. However, strategic geopolitics explains only a small portion of the variation in aid receipts across countries; many bad governments of no strategic importance whatsoever still get a lot of aid.

So we had the world's twenty-five most undemocratic government rulers (out of 199 countries the World Bank rated on democracy) get a sum of $9 billion in foreign aid in 2002. Similarly, the world's twenty-five most corrupt countries got $9.4 billion in foreign aid in 2002. The top fifteen recipients of foreign aid in 2002, who each got more than $1 billion each, have a median ranking as the worst fourth of all governments everywhere in 2002 (ranked by democracy, corruption, etc.). It would be good to get aid from the rich of rich countries to the poor of poor countries, but what we see happening is that aid shifts money from being spent by the best governments in the world to being spent by the worst. What are the chances that these billions are going to reach poor people?

Despite these sorry numbers, donors now aim at transforming government. Ten years ago, the aid donors, the World Bank, and the IMF seldom discussed corruption or dictatorship. Since then, donor talk radio has been full of chatter about "good governance." However, donors have still not figured out what to do to make good governance happen, or how to be selective about whom they give their money. As the figures just cited show, the gangsters are still getting plenty of aid.

More systematically, Alberto Alesina of Harvard and Beatrice Weder of the University of Mainz have found no evidence that aid donors give less aid to corrupt countries; in fact, in some of their statistical analyses it was found that donors gave these countries more aid.[35] Have things changed over the past few years? In 1996, there was no association between how much aid per capita a developing country received and its rating on the World Bank measure of corruption (controlling for other determinants of aid per capita, such as per capita income and population size). Six years later, in 2002, after oceans of ink on corruption, there was still no association between aid given to a country and how corrupt that country was.[36] Similarly, there was no association between aid given to a country and how democratic it was, either in 1996 or 2002, controlling for per capita income and population size.

So donor bureaucracies remain stuck with the recipient government bureaucracy when they try to implement their aid projects, even when that bureaucracy is not customer-friendly to the poor. World Bank economists Deon Filmer and Lant Pritchett report on the results of a survey at government health centers in the Mutasa district of Tanzania. In the survey, new mothers reported what they least liked about their birthing experiences assisted by government nurses. The poor mothers-to-be were "ridiculed by nurses for not having baby clothes (22 percent)...and nurses hit mothers during delivery (13 percent)."[37]

Good Government in the Tropics

There have been *some* cases of foreign aid supporting reform and good government. One happy example is with the aforementioned Botswana. Before independence, Seretse Khama was heir to the most prominent traditional chiefdom. He shocked the neighboring white South Africans by marrying a white woman, which caused the British colonialists to ban him from Botswana until he gave up his chiefdom. Khama became Botswana's leader anyway upon independence in 1966.

Prospects at independence were not great for a country that was mostly desert. Faced with a crippling drought, Botswana accepted large amounts of foreign aid, especially from the altruistic Scandinavians. In the 1960s and 1970s, aid averaged about 16 percent of Botswana's income.

After discovering large amounts of diamonds in the late 1960s, the Khama government managed to avoid the curse discussed earlier that had plagued other mineral-rich nations, such as Angola, Nigeria, Sierra Leone, and Zaire. The government managed both aid and diamond revenues wisely enough to foster economic growth, with the result that the economy expanded at 10 percent every year.

Rapid growth continued under Khama's democratic successor, Ketumile Masire, who took over in 1980 and governed until 1998. Masire's government prevented a famine in 1981–1987 when drought devastated crop production. The government expanded rural villages' access to clean water, health clinics, and good roads. It decentralized government functions to local authorities to increase democratic accountability.[38] The government was not perfect—it failed to prevent one of the world's worst AIDS crises—but its accomplishments give a hint of how much development was possible in Africa with good government.

There are other cases of good government breaking out even without much donor involvement. Aid researcher Judith Tendler at MIT wrote a great book called *Good Government in the Tropics*, about the success story of the Ceará state government in northeastern Brazil. Traditionally one of the most corrupt and backward states in Brazil, Ceará had two reformist governors alternating in power from 1987 to 2001—Tasso Jereissati and Ciro Gomes. They had the State Department of Health do a new preventive health program using community health workers. Only a few years after the beginning of the program, vaccination rates for measles and polio had increased from 25 percent to 90 percent. Infant mortality in Ceará fell by one third.[39]

It would be too simplistic to attribute these success stories just to governors Jereissati and Gomes. Part of the success of the Ceará programs was the way they built in feedback from the poor. The state publicized the new programs, leading the local communities to expect more from (and to monitor) the government workers, such as the new health workers. The health workers themselves felt motivated by community approval when they got good results, and they got rewarded for such approval. The Ceará story shows that good government can happen in the tropics, and that it can happen for homegrown reasons.

Could Aid Make Government Worse?

We can turn to cross-country data to see which is most typical—aid promoting good government, aid not affecting government at all, or possibly even aid promoting bad government. Earlier, this chapter talks about how oil makes democracy and good government less likely—the "natural-resource curse." More recent studies have found that there is also an "aid curse"— probably for the same reasons as the oil curse. High aid revenues going to the national government benefit political insiders, often corrupt insiders, who will vigorously oppose democracy that would lead to more equal distribution of aid. Systematic evidence in a couple of recent studies suggests that aid actually decreases democracy and makes government worse. Steve Knack of the World Bank finds that higher aid worsens bureaucratic quality and leads to violation of the law with more impunity and to more corruption. Maybe bad government attracts donors who want to reform it just as sinners attract televangelists. However, even if you control for this effect, donors make government worse.[40]

Simeon Djankov (of the World Bank), Jose Montalvo (of Pompeu Fabra University in Barcelona), and Marta Reynal-Querol (World Bank) similarly found that high aid caused setbacks to democracy over 1960–1999.[41] They found aid's effect on democracy to be worse than the effect of *oil* on democracy.

Social Action Programs for Lending

Bad governments can sabotage even the most well-intentioned aid programs. Another critical government input for development is good public services. Governments in poor countries often fail at delivering basic health and education services. One egregious case that donors tried to remedy is Pakistan, which has poor health and education even when compared with other poor countries at its level of income. Pakistan has 36 percent lower births attended by trained personnel. It has 11 percent more babies born with low birth weight, 42 percent lower health spending per capita, 1.6 percent less GDP in public health spending, twenty-seven excess infant deaths per thousand, nineteen excess child deaths per thousand, and 23 percentage points lower share of the population with access to sanitation. Relative to children in other countries at Pakistan's level of income, 20 percent fewer Pakistani elementary school–age children are enrolled in primary school. This gap is explained entirely by the 40 percent fewer elementary school–age girls who attend primary school. The 14 percent shortfall in secondary enrollment compared with other countries at Pakistan's income level is explained mainly by a 20 percent shortfall for females. Twenty-four percent more of Pakistan's population is illiterate than is normal for a country of its income level, reflecting excess illiteracy of 32 percent for females and 16 percent for males.

The World Bank in 1993 tried to repair this social train wreck by supporting a "social action program" in Pakistan, which aimed to "improve the coverage and quality of basic social services." An independent analyst, Dr. Nancy Birdsall of the Center for Global Development, later concluded that aside from a few modest successes, the period during which the SAP was implemented witnessed stagnation, marginal improvement, and—in some cases—even a decline in social indicators. For example, aggregate education enrollment rates stagnated during the 1990s, with enrollments for children from public schools registering a modest decline.[42]

World Bank staff recognized the first phase of the project, SAP I, as a failure. Therefore, World Bank management approved a second phase, SAP II. Deep into the project, in 2000, a World Bank review concurred: "Improvements in service delivery are either not happening, or occurring at a very slow pace." After nearly a decade of failure, the SAP was finally abandoned in June 2002.

Dr. Birdsall asked, "Why did a sound idea turn into a practical disaster?" She said that "implementation failures were rampant—manifested in non-merit recruitment of staff, absenteeism of teachers and doctors, and frequent transfers of essential staff.... [P]oliticians used staff recruitment, construction contracts, and site selection for schools and clinics to enrich their kith and kin." A Pakistani economist gave the deeper reason for failure in 2003: "[T]he poor face markets, state institutions and local structures of power that discriminate against [them].... [They are] unable to access public entitlements like... goods and services." Foreign aid could not deal with the deep roots of bad government in Pakistan, such as a powerful agrarian elite and sharp ethnic divisions.

The Selling of Bad Governments

Since donors understandably don't want to admit they are dealing with bad governments, diplomatic language in aid agencies becomes an art form. A war is a "conflict-related reallocation of resources."[43] Aid efforts to deal with homicidal warlords are "difficult partnerships."[44] Countries whose presidents loot the treasury experience "governance issues." Miserable performance is "progress [that] has not been as fast and comprehensive as envisioned in the PRSP."[45] When government officials want to steal while the aid agency wants development, there are "differences in priorities and approaches [that] ... need to be reconciled." If debt-relief dollars disappear before reaching the poor, then "continued progress on the Expenditure Management and Control Program will be needed to maximize the benefits from the HIPC [Heavily Indebted Poor Country] Initiative."[46]

Diplomatic donors also put a positive spin on awful recipient governments by asserting that while things are bad, they are getting better. The use of gerunds indicating progress is ubiquitous in aid documents, such as "developing," "emerging," and "improving." This language infects even scorecards that are supposed to hold governments accountable for poor results. The aid agencies recently evaluated the "supportive environment" for achieving the Millennium Development Goals created by Cameroon's autocratic and corrupt ruler Paul Biya (in power since 1982).[47] The aid agencies' possible evaluations were "strong," "fair," and "weak." They opted for "weak but improving."

The "weak but improving" line is popular among aid agencies in Africa. The World Bank produced a stream of progress reports on Africa over the last two decades. It first described the poor state of African government: "Domestic policy inadequacies ... trade and exchange rate policies have overprotected industry, held back agriculture" (World Bank, 1981). "Unless [there are] major changes in African programs ... no amount of external assistance can generate rising levels of income" (World Bank, 1984). "Weak public sector management has resulted in loss-making public enterprises, poor investment choices, costly and unreliable infrastructure, price distortions" (World Bank, 1989). "Most African countries still lack policies that are sound" (World Bank, 1994). "The adjustment decades also saw a substantial deterioration in the quality of public institutions, a demoralization of public servants, and a decline in the effectiveness of service delivery in many countries" (World Bank, 2000). Africa "remains the world's foremost development challenge. Many countries continue to be held back by weak institutions, civil strife ... " (World Bank, 2004).[48]

Donors then responded to these disasters with perpetual promises of a change for the better, sometimes detecting a nascent trend toward improvement: "many African governments are more clearly aware of the need to ... improve the efficiency ... of their economies" (World Bank, 1983). "African leaders increasingly recognize the need to revise their development strategies. ... [S]ome countries are introducing policy and institutional reforms" (World Bank, 1984). "Progress is clearly under way. Especially in the past two years, more countries have started to act, and the changes they are making go deeper than before" (World Bank, 1986). "Since the mid-1980s Africa has seen important changes in policies and in economic performance" (World Bank, 1989). "African countries have made great strides in improving policies and restoring growth" (World Bank, 1994). "Since the mid-1990s, there have been signs that better economic management has started to pay off" (World Bank, 2000). "Africa's leaders... have recognized the need to improve their policies, spelled out in the New Partnership for African Development [NEPAD].... [They] have pledged to pursue a compact of good governance with their people" (World Bank, 2002). There has been "remarkable progress in several African countries over the past year" (World Bank, 2004).

The contradiction between "weak institutions" and "remarkable progress" calls to mind Japanese government propaganda during World War II, which to the very end of the war celebrated every battle as a triumph. The long-suffering Japanese people could track the war's progress only by noting that the glorious victories of the emperor's forces were moving them ever closer back to Japan.

Differences in Government Performance Across Countries and Sectors

Some blame the perception of bad government in Africa on racism—an insult to the many courageous Africans who have resisted tyrannical rulers at risk of their lives and safety. It is a mistake to go to either extreme—overlooking bad government in Africa or embracing a stereotype of African government as *always* bad or ineffective.

The aforementioned Botswana is a long-standing African democracy. Countries such as Benin, Ghana, and Mali now have democratic governments after decades of autocracy (see figure 16). Other countries such as Kenya and Nigeria now have more turbulent democracies that are still an improvement over the dictators who used to hold power. A rating of democracy (again from Polity IV) shows a rise in democracy in Africa since the early 1990s, although still far short of a high rating (such as Botswana achieves).

Moreover, governments—together with foreign aid—do not have a universal record of failure in Africa. One success was the steady expansion of education, represented by the huge leap in adult literacy rates from 1970 to 2000. Another accomplishment has been in reaching girls for education, as the ratio of female-to-male literacy has climbed steadily over the last thirty years (see figure 17). The higher literacy of men and women has so far not translated into increases in earnings, but education is both a worthy end in itself and a contribution to many other good development outcomes.

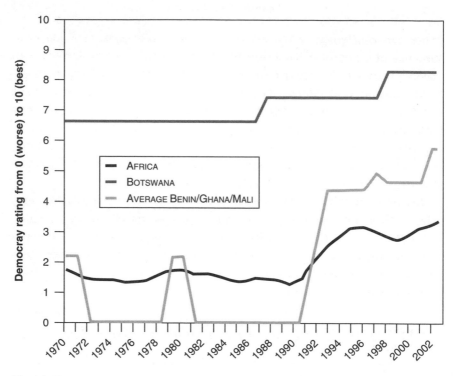

Fig. 16. Democracy in Botswana and Average for Africa

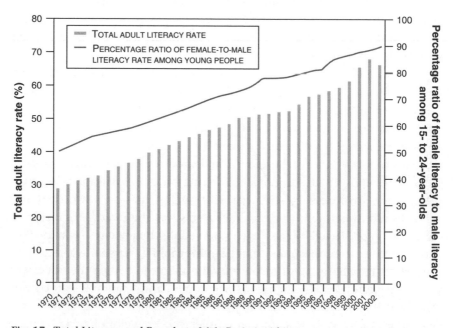

Fig. 17. Total Literacy and Female-to-Male Ratio in Africa

There are some quality problems, such as poorly motivated teachers and the absence of textbooks, not to mention inadequate utilization of educated people because of other distortions in African economies—which may be why education has not translated into rising incomes.

There were also upward trends in electrification (provided by state-owned utilities) until 1990, although this stagnated afterward. Electric production per person increased by 50 percent from 1973 to 1990. Again, there are some quality problems, with power outages common, but the increased quantity indicates that some progress is being made (see figure 18).

In a more general area where effort is less visible—corruption—there are so far no signs of progress (see figure 19, which has two different measures of corruption). Some democratic governments in Africa have turned out to be as corrupt as some autocratic ones. As the great Alfred E. Newman once said, "Crime does not pay...as well as politics."

Some progress in government performance in Africa is taking place—from which donors might have learned more if they had not patronizingly claimed progress in places where and when there was none. These examples also show that governments and donors working together do sometimes achieve something—again, it seems that piecemeal interventions with visible outputs, such as education and electricity production, show more progress than more general programs where effort is less measurable, such as controlling corruption or stimulating economic growth. Donors are more accountable

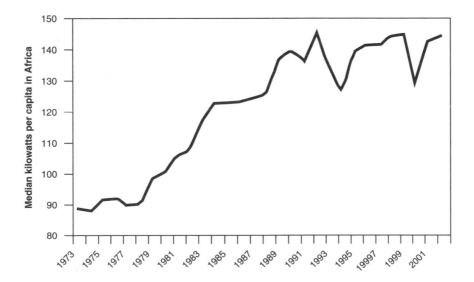

Fig. 18. Electricity Production Per Capita in Africa

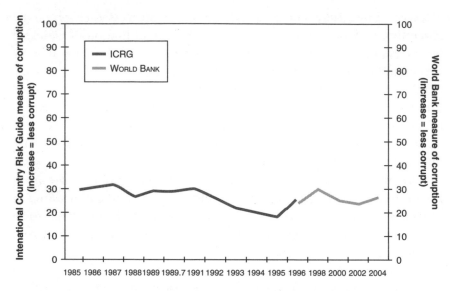

Fig. 19. Percentage Ranking on Corruption of Typical African Country, 1985–2004

for visible, piecemeal improvements. Governments, even nondemocratic ones, could also be more accountable for these hotly demanded and visible services. The interaction between the donors and African governments led to happier outcomes in these areas—perhaps because the greater account-ability of the donors forced them to work out a pragmatic way to deal with the governments, or the governments were more accountable in these areas to deal with donors and the public, which facilitated the outcome.

The trend toward increased democracy in Africa (noted in figure 16) may be an exception where donors contributed to progress on a general goal of transforming government. However, this chapter has mentioned two find-ings that are evidence against this: (1) who got aid was unrelated to democ-racy, so it is unclear how the donors applied pressure; and (2) the formal statistical findings suggest that aid makes democracy worse, not better. Maybe Africans should get some credit for increased democracy for themselves?

Power to the People

The World Bank and the IMF are certainly aware of the problems of dealing with gangsters in trying to deliver foreign aid. They have recently emphasized consultation with nongovernmental think tanks and philanthropic organizations (the so-called "civil society"), seeking to have ordinary people participate in designing economic policy by getting their input on a "Poverty Reduction Strategy Paper" (PRSP). This is a positive step for the World Bank and IMF, to talk to people outside government.

However, as a device to get good government, this falls a few valleys short of the mountaintop. A PRSP is no substitute for democracy. Even if civil society prepared the PRSP with participation by everyone and his cousin, it is unclear how we bureaucrats could redistribute power from those who had it to those who did not. For example, in April 2002, the World Bank and the IMF awarded a second round of debt relief to Burkina Faso, based upon the country's satisfactory completion of a participatory PRSP.[49] Burkina Faso is run by the same ruler who has been in power since 1987, who was among the worst fifth in the world in corruption in 2001, and who supported rebel warlords who perpetrated atrocities in Angola, Liberia, and Sierra Leone.

To the aid agencies, participation is an apolitical technical process of consulting the poor. As Daniel Patrick Moynihan said about a similar participation idea in the 1960s: "The socially concerned intellectuals... seemed repeatedly to assume that those who had power would let it be taken away a lot easier than could possibly be the case if what was involved was *power*."[50]

The participation chapter of the IMF and World Bank's PRSP Sourcebook advocates consultation of the poor "stakeholders." The Sourcebook does not address how aid deals with tyranny and political conflict—if "stakeholders" disagree with a dictator, as seems likely, who does the IMF and World Bank listen to? What if stakeholders disagree with one another? It is hard to think of how the IMF and World Bank are in a position to do anything constructive to referee political conflict and opposition to tyranny.

Often society and politics fracture along regional or ethnic lines, and foreign aid maintains neutrality with difficulty. For example, a study of the Mahaweli irrigation project in Sri Lanka showed that aid biased toward Sinhalese areas exacerbated the Tamil-Sinhalese hatred during the ongoing civil war.[51] Even humanitarian aid can make political conflict worse rather than better. In the worst-case scenario of Somalia in the early 1990s, food aid increased violence among rival clan militias, who fought to steal the food. The warlords may even have provoked starvation to get more food relief. This was not typical—most poor-country government leaders are better than Somalian warlords (rather faint praise).

Ironically, the way the donors implement "participation" sometimes contradicts existing democratic mechanisms. In Tanzania, the democratically elected government had already devised a National Poverty Eradication Strategy in consultation with its parliament, but the IMF and World Bank insisted upon a new process for the Poverty Reduction Strategy Paper anyway. Because of "the urgency with which they wanted to secure HIPC relief, the Tanzanians initially acquiesced in the World Bank writing the I-PRSP for them."[52]

The IMF and the World Bank don't show a ton of respect for democracy when it starts to take hold. As Yale Professor of political science and anthropology James C. Scott points out, there is an inherent contradiction between planning (what he calls "high modernism") and democratic politics: "Political interests can only frustrate the social solutions devised by specialists with scientific tools adequate to their analysis. As individuals, high modernists might well hold democratic views about popular sovereignty . . . but such convictions are external to, and often at war with their high-modernist convictions."[53]

The head of the IMF, Michel Camdessus, told the Haitian parliament during the 1990s that if it rejected privatization of state enterprises, it "would mean that the people are rejecting the support that they need, [support] the international community sees as necessary for Haiti. It will mean that Parliament rejects those policies and this support at a very heavy cost."[54] Similarly, one of the main World Bank goals for Bolivia in 2004 was that "Bolivia opts for a 'Yes' vote in the Referendum" on gas exports.[55]

This is not to automatically canonize democratically elected governments. They, too, can make terrible choices—this reinforces the main point of this chapter: it is awfully hard to get democracy working well. And the IMF and World Bank could conceivably take a stand for unpopular positions that are the best thing for the country. Yet outside interference doesn't have a great record on improving matters, on making governments do the "right" thing.

Ventriloquism

The Planners are aware that it looks bad to boss around poor-country governments, and increasingly they deny that they do so. At the same time, the IMF and World Bank want to put conditions on aid and loans to ensure that the governments use the money well. The Planners tie themselves up in rhetorical knots as they try to resolve the unresolvable contradiction between conditions and sovereignty. In 2001, the World Bank described the Poverty Reduction Strategy Paper as a means to resolve the contradiction:

"the PRSP... was a crucial step towards greater national ownership of development programs which is essential for increased effectiveness of external assistance."[56] The IMF agreed: "The broadest and most fundamental changes to the work of the IMF arise from the fact that the targets and policies embodied in [IMF]-supported programs will emerge directly from the country's own poverty reduction strategy."[57] (The "country" here means the government, as it almost always does in foreign aid.)

Cornell political scientist Nicolas Van de Walle describes the PRSP process as one of "ventriloquism" by the IMF and World Bank.[58] The IMF and World Bank have allegedly given up on telling governments what to do. So, instead, they want a government to tell them what it will do in order to get a loan. Of course, the IMF and World Bank will approve only acceptable actions in return for infusions of cash. So the poor-country governments, instead of being told what to do, are now trying to guess what the international agencies will approve their doing. The PRSP plans are similar to the long lists of conditions that the IMF and the World Bank impose on the poor countries. If the government doesn't guess the right answer the first time, the IMF and World Bank prepare a "joint staff assessment" of each PRSP.

Peer Review

Another device by which donors try to get "local ownership" of good government reforms is "peer review" of some African rulers by others. This is part of what is called the New Partnership for African Development (NEPAD), which is supposed to have African rulers enforcing standards of good governance on one another. It is a little mysterious why the donors embrace a mechanism of accountability for African governments that they would never apply to their own countries. (Would the American government submit to peer review by the Canadians?) Anyway, "peer review" misses the whole point of democracy, which is government accountability to its own citizens—not to some other government.

The International Monetary Fund and the Gangsters

The IMF's charter bans it from considering domestic politics. Sometimes this approach leads to happy outcomes. Over the last decade, Mexico has made a transition to democracy and has pursued pro-market reforms and macroeconomic stabilization. It did this with the support of IMF lending (short-term crisis loans called standbys), although corruption, drug trafficking, and violence remain problems. The IMF tactfully overlooked Mexico's previous autocratic government.

But a problem with the apolitical approach is that it is not apolitical. Supporting a sitting government with funds is unavoidably a political act. Such an approach doesn't have much of a safeguard against the IMF enabling some really awful rulers. To see some of the consequences, answer the following trivia question: Who got the most standbys from the IMF over the last half century? The answer is Haiti, with twenty-two. And not just Haiti, but the Duvalier family (Papa Doc and Baby Doc), under whom Haiti got twenty of the twenty-two standbys from 1957 to 1986.

The politics were bad, but the Duvaliers made up for it with even worse economics. The income of the average Haitian was lower at the end of the Duvalier era than at the beginning. Half of all children did not go to elementary school when Papa Doc came to power; half of all children were still out of school when Baby Doc left power.

The Duvalier dynasty was only the latest installment in a toxic history. Haiti has known some degree of democracy for only five recent years out of its two hundred-year history (1990, 1994–1998); for most of that history it had the worst possible democratic rating on a scale of zero to ten.[59] After almost two hundred coups, revolutions, insurrections, and civil wars since independence, Haiti today still has one of the world's most undemocratic, corrupt, violent, and unstable governments.[60] The IMF didn't check the history: how much could it help a state that had been dysfunctional for two centuries?

The dysfunctional state reflects in part the legacy of minority European settlement of the worst kind. In 1789, Haiti (then known as Saint-Domingue) was one of the richest places in the world, and the most unequal. A population of 40,000 whites, 30,000 freed mulattoes (the offspring of slave owner wenching), and 450,000 slaves produced $800 million in exports in today's dollars. These exports included sugarcane, coffee, cotton, indigo, and cocoa.[61] Saint-Domingue provided 60 percent of the world's coffee and 40 percent of the sugar imports of France and England.[62] The value of production per worker was far higher than that in the United States.[63]

Today, Haiti is the poorest country in the Western Hemisphere and among the poorest tenth of countries worldwide. Its population of 8.3 million produces $463 million in exports of goods and services. Exports per person were thirty-one times higher in 1789 than in 2002.

A slave regime produced the 1789 exports. The legacy of slavery has something to do with Haiti's failure at political and economic development.

The exports of 1789 showed just how much potential the land of Haiti had; the exports of 2002 show how two centuries have passed moving the country ever further away from that potential.

The Haitian Revolution of 1791–1804 overthrew the hated slave owners. However, the mulattoes and their descendants took the whites' place as the oligarchy, which dominates to this day, and the black majority transferred its hatred of the white slave owners to the mulatto elite. Much of Haiti's history consists of struggles between the mulatto elite and the black military elite (who originated in the leaders of the war of independence), with all possible permutations of alliances, betrayals, and divisions making any stability or prosperity a distant dream.

Throughout the nineteenth century, blacks and mulattoes in Haiti alternated in power. Of the thirty-four signers of the Haitian declaration of independence, only five died a natural death. Only one Haitian ruler finished his constitutional term alive.[64] In the second half of the century, political life was polarized between a mulatto Liberal Party and a black National Party.[65]

For example, the mulatto leader Jean-Pierre Boyer ruled from 1818 to 1843, with all important political posts filled by mulattoes.[66] Emulating French colonial policy, he founded schools for mulattoes but none for blacks. An Englishman observed at the time, "The present government seems to consider the poverty and ignorance of the people as the best safeguards of the security and permanence of their own property and power."[67] The illiteracy and powerlessness of the majority of the population had condemned Haiti to underdevelopment long before the Duvaliers and the IMF arrived, and it still does today. The IMF giving Haiti credit after credit did nothing to address the centuries-old political roots of macroeconomic instability, not to mention the country's underdevelopment.

The International Financial Institutions Get Taken Again

One test of how donor agencies deal with government is to see how they respond to some of the worst cases. Haiti is not the only failed state getting IMF credits. Another notorious case is Mobutu's Zaire. The IMF gave Mobutu eleven bailout loans during his tenure. It was not that his thefts were a secret. The IMF had sent a German banker named Erwin Blumenthal to the Central Bank of Zaire in 1978–1979. He carefully documented how much Mobutu was stealing, and reported back to the IMF and the World Bank.

Mobutu could use thuggery as well as bribery: In the late 1970s, a Zairean army unit attacked an uncooperative resident representative of the IMF and the World Bank. The soldiers beat him up and raped his wife and daughters, with strong signs of Mobutu's complicity.[68]

The two institutions nevertheless kept on lending. Zaire spent 74 percent of the time during the years 1976–1989 in an IMF program. The fund thought giving Mobutu a carrot to reform would help the country's people. The IMF and World Bank finally cut him off in 1990, twenty-five years into his misrule. Altogether, the country had received twenty billion dollars in foreign aid during Mobutu's tenure.[69] Of course, Mobutu was a cold war protégé of the West, but the IMF and World Bank claim to be apolitical.

An even more extreme example of what the apolitical approach can yield comes from the period just before the Rwandan genocide that began on April 7, 1994. In fairness to the international financial institutions (IFIs), they could not have anticipated such a rare cataclysmic event as that genocide. Yet there were plenty of ugly things going on beforehand. Rwanda's Hutu government had long had an official program of discrimination against Tutsis; there was not a single Tutsi head of Rwanda's 143 communes (local governments). Things got worse after a Tutsi-led rebel army invaded Rwanda in 1990. The Hutu government was complicit in massacres of hundreds of Tutsis by Hutu mobs in separate incidents in October 1990, January 1991, and February 1991.[70] Despite these events, the IMF concluded that Rwanda's problem was "structural adjustment," for which it gave the Hutu government a loan on April 24, 1991. (The loan was cut off before being fully disbursed, but it is hard to understand why it was made at all.) Before the genocide, foreign observers noted in the early 1990s the Hutu hate speech and the Tutsis' well-justified fears. The World Bank in 1991 somehow concluded that "Rwanda has made a creditable effort toward social and economic development." The World Bank also made a large loan in 1991, and gave additional credits in 1992–1993. Led by the IFIs, foreign aid to Rwanda increased by 50 percent from 1989–1990 to 1991–1993. Aid worker Peter Uvin, from whom these facts come, described the situation:

> *The development aid system knew of the disintegration of Rwandese society; saw the many Tutsis working for aid agencies or partner NGOs being harassed, threatened, or killed; discussed these matters and surely regretted them; but seemingly felt it was outside its mandate or capacity to intervene, that all it could do was to continue business as usual. Thus aid continued to muddle through, trying to make its usual projects work with a faltering government, until the day the genocide began.[71]*

In what was perhaps the worst timing in the history of foreign aid, the World Bank issued an anodyne report on development in Rwanda in May 1994—while the genocide was in progress. The foreword to the report notes the horrific massacres beginning in April 1994, but goes ahead with its bland recommendations.[72] The report makes no mention of the accelerating persecution of the Tutsis that was taking place while the report was being written in late 1993.[73]

Things have improved over the last decade, as the IFIs are more aware of the problems of corruption, autocracy, and violence. Unfortunately, instead of shunning awful governments altogether, IFIs have made *more* hubristic attempts to transform bad government. So they have continued to be involved recently with some very bad actors under the rubric of "post-conflict reconstruction"—that is, lending in the wake of a civil war. These include Angola and the successor state to Zaire, the Democratic Republic of the Congo.

Maybe there is a case for aiding societies trying to find peace. But note that "post-conflict reconstruction" means you have to do deals with even worse gangsters than under peacetime conditions. And what incentives does it create to give aid money to the men of violence in post-conflict societies, many of whom committed war crimes, while shunning peaceful democratic politicians?

In Angola, a movement away from a Stalinist economic system and toward a market economy in the late 1980s stirred enthusiasm at the IMF and World Bank, but corruption undermined all attempts at economic reform. The abundant oil revenues disappeared somewhere in the Bermuda Triangle of the treasury, the central bank, and the state oil company (Sonangol).[74] President José Eduardo dos Santos is at the end of a long receiving line for plundered oil revenue. The temporary European minority settlers in Angola left behind the "one hundred families" who are the traditional *mestiço/assimilado* elite, who control both the economy and politics.[75] Out of 195 countries, the World Bank ranks Angola as the fifteenth most corrupt country in the world.

The World Bank had already given $180 million to the Angolan government from 1992 to 1999, despite civil war and corruption. Now that peace had finally come to Angola after years of civil war, the country received $421 million in foreign aid in 2002, despite abundant oil revenues for its population of thirteen million.[76]

After the civil war ended, the World Bank did a new report, in 2003. Following the usual language of "catastrophic but improving," it detected that "reformists within the Government have been achieving incremental improvements in the transparency and accountability of public resource management." The World Bank acknowledged that "much more remains to be done."[77]

For its part, the IMF mission "explained" to the Angolan civil servants in 2003 "that a regular reporting and auditing of Sonangol's operations was needed . . . to reduce the risk of corruption and mismanagement."[78] The IMF mission records that "the authorities agreed."

Perhaps the World Bank and IMF efforts could be helpful in making a terrible situation better through the reporting, auditing, and transparency of Sonangol. But the IFI efforts have yet to show up in the World Bank's rating of Angola's corruption, which has stayed unchanged from 1996 to 2004.

Next door, in the Democratic Republic of the Congo (DRC), the latest IMF mission has arrived after the state is starting to put itself back together in the wake of two horrific civil wars. Of course, government is going to be pretty awful right after a war, and movement toward good governance is slow in DRC. The U.S. State Department Human Rights Report for 2003 noted that the new Congolese government's "security forces committed unlawful killings, torture, beatings, acts of rape, extortion, and other abuses, largely with impunity."[79] The IMF mission in 2004 met with two of the four vice-presidents in the coalition government, including Jean-Pierre Bemba (the head of the Uganda-backed Mouvement de la Libération du Congo, accused of massacres in early 2003) and Azarias Ruberwa (the de facto head of the Rwanda-backed Rassemblement Congolais pour la Démocratie, accused of summary executions during a revolt in Kisangani in May 2002).[80] In 2004, the IMF said that "the staff commends the authorities for their steadfast efforts to consolidate peace." The IMF and World Bank note that the autocrats and warlords had completed an interim PRSP "through an extensive consultative process." The rulers promised a shift toward "pro-poor spending."

These are extreme examples that illustrate the IFIs' worst cases: coddling awful gangsters who just call themselves a government. The poor population was going to be liable for IMF loans that were never going to reach them.

What is the IMF's overall record on screening out bad governments? The news is a little better than the situations in Angola, DRC, Haiti, and Rwanda would indicate. We have the World Bank's comprehensive averages of ratings of countries on corruption and democracy from 1996 to 2002, and the time those same countries spent in IMF programs over the same period. The governments rated as among the worst tenth among developing countries in terms of corruption spent an average of 20 percent of the time in IMF agreements, which is significantly less than the average of 41 percent of the time for the rest of the sample. Governments rated as among the worst tenth in terms of dictatorship spent 9 percent of the time in IMF agreements, which is much less than the sample average. So the IMF does show some willingness to lend less to the most awful governments. Unfortunately, once governments get out of the worst tenth, there is no further tendency to penalize bad governments. For example, governments rated among the second-worst tenth on democracy and corruption are no less likely to spend time in IMF programs than the rest of the sample.

The United Nations and Gangsters

The UN has not done any better than the IMF and World Bank in dealing with bad government. An international organization in which it is possible for the Libyan government to chair the Human Rights Commission does not seem to have high standards for good government. Human Rights Watch cites such qualifications of the chairman of the commission as "the abduction, forced disappearance or assassination of [Libyan] political opponents; torture and mistreatment of detainees; and long-term detention without charge or trial or after grossly unfair trials. Today hundreds of people remain arbitrarily detained, some for over a decade."[81]

The United Nations Millennium Project report in January 2005 argues that bad government is not the primary problem facing poor countries, and if there is bad government, it is because of lack of money (a thesis contradicted by the "oil curse" and "aid curse" studies cited earlier): "Many reasonably well governed countries... lack the fiscal resources to invest in infrastructure, social services, and even the public administration necessary to improve governance. Without adequate public sector salaries and information technologies, public management is chronically weak" (p. 34, main report).

Although convinced that bad government was not the problem, the UN report did rule out aid to the four most awful rulers in the world. The report identifies these four governments—Belarus, Myanmar, North Korea, and Zimbabwe—as beyond the pale. This is a pretty small number for bad governments of the world. Even a dictator like Saparmurat Niyazov of Turkmenistan, who so terrorizes his country that he has renamed the months of the year after himself and his late mother, can't get into the UN bad despots club.

The Millennium Project 2005 report then recommends that most others become eligible for the "Big Push" of foreign aid out of the alleged poverty trap, that "well-governed low-income countries be granted 'fast-track MDG status' by the international community and receive the massive increase in development assistance needed for them to implement MDG-based poverty reduction strategies."[82]

The search for the elusive "well-governed low-income countries" casts a broad net. The report lists sixty-three poor countries that are "potentially well governed," and thus potentially eligible for a massive increase in foreign aid. The list includes five out of the seven countries singled out by Transparency International in October 2004 as the most corrupt in the world: Azerbaijan, Bangladesh, Chad, Nigeria, and Paraguay. The list of "potentially well-governed" countries also includes fifteen governments that Freedom House classifies as "not free." Such dictators as Paul Biya of Cameroon, Hun Sen of Cambodia, and Ilham Aliyev of Azerbaijan are on the list. President Aliyev of Azerbaijan has scored a double as most autocratic and most corrupt since he was "elected" to succeed his autocratic father in 2003.[83]

In his book *The End of Poverty,* Jeffrey Sachs emphasizes that many African countries do not have unusually bad governments compared with other countries at their level of income. Unfortunately, what counts for the population's well-being is not how good the government is for its level of income; it is just how good the government is, period. Aid agencies have to face reality: Is money given to a bad government going to reach the poor? Perhaps the reason the country is poor has something to do with bad government?

It could be that donors are just making a pragmatic choice—appeasing the bad government so they can operate in the country on their own and reach the poor. It is true that donors do a lot on their own by bypassing the government. Unfortunately, they also spend massive amounts of their time trying to fix the bad government and work through it—much more than the token amount that the appeasement thesis would predict.

Screening Out Bad Governments

The Millennium Challenge Account of the Bush administration is one interesting experiment in trying to keep money out of the hands of gangsters. The U.S. Millennium Challenge Corporation gives aid only to governments that meet certain standards, such as democracy, investing in their people, freedom from corruption, and freedom from government interference in markets. It is a welcome step compared with giving money to gangsters, and it will be interesting to see how it plays out.

However, there are some potential pitfalls. Can outsiders really tell when government is good and when it is bad? Should outsiders be supporting a government that they decide is good, without a mechanism for feedback from the citizens of that country? There are certainly plenty of extreme cases of bad governments, such as in the examples given in this chapter, and crossing them off the list is a great step that other aid agencies should emulate. Yet there is a middle ground that is treacherous to negotiate. For example, as of June 2005, the Millennium Challenge Corporation had reached agreements on aid programs with two countries—Honduras and Madagascar. In 2004, Honduras's government was ranked by the World Bank as among the worst third in the world for corruption. Madagascar is better; it is smack in the middle on corruption. But the other problem is that these corruption ratings are imprecise. The World Bank reports the margin of error of its estimate, and fifty-seven other countries lie within the margin of error of the Madagascar rating on corruption. The high margin of error reflects the difficulty that different outside rating agencies have reaching consensus on which countries are more or less corrupt. It looks like selecting good governments is not so easy.

Try Again

As the awful examples in this chapter illustrate, the official aid agencies simply don't know how to change bad governments into good governments with the apparatus of foreign aid. Bad government has far deeper roots than anything the West can affect. To make things worse, the aid agencies *need* the poor-country government, even a bad government, to fill the role of aid recipient to keep money flowing.

The aid system continues to pursue the contradictory combination of reforming government, promoting "government ownership" of reforms, and keeping aid money flowing. The current system drives outside observers, like yours truly, so nuts that we are prone to recommending drastic remedies. Right now foreign aid is caught in a nightmarish in-between world in which donors (1) take up much of the time of the government with attempts to impose "good behavior"; (2) insist that the government freely choose to behave; and (3) sometimes bypass the government anyway to do the donors' projects. Observers of aid are sharply divided as to whether aid should bypass government even more, or whether it should bypass it less and try to strengthen low-income governments.

This chapter's reading of the evidence suggests dropping the obsession with always working through the government. However, let's hold fast to opposing shock therapy and universal blueprints, even for the country of foreign aid. Any of these changes should be tried in a gradual, piecemeal, experimental way, and the answers will be different in different countries and different sectors. Large infrastructure projects probably have to be done through governments, although private contracting can be used creatively. Some countries could have sufficiently functional democratic and effective governments so that the aid community could conceivably give the government a blank check. (However, we have seen how difficult it is for outsiders to determine just which governments are in this category.)

For the rest: let political leaders and social activists in the West expose and denounce tyranny in the Rest, but don't expect Western governments or aid agencies to change bad governments into good ones.

Today's system of foreign aid coddles (and probably worsens) bad governments. The long-standing dictator in Cameroon, Paul Biya, gets 41 percent of his government revenue from foreign aid. Under current proposals to sharply increase aid to Africa, that figure would increase to 55 percent.[84]

Let social and economic interactions continue between private citizens of all lands, but Western governments or official aid agencies don't have to deal with corrupt autocrats. When working with the government doesn't get results for the poor, aid agencies should try something else. Can't donors take aid away from bad governments and see if they can get it into the hands of poor people?

And if aid is apolitical on the receiving end, so it should be on the giving end. Can't Western voters demand that their aid agencies direct their dollars to where they will reach the most poor, and not to ugly autocratic friends of the donors?

Even with well-functioning democracies, not everything is done through the government. I could organize a workshop in New York with foreign participants to discuss American economic policies without asking permission from President Bush. I could solicit foreign donations to alleviate poverty in Harlem without checking with the secretary of housing and urban development. Why should donors insist that analogous exercises be run through the government in poor countries?

Some authors argue that aid has to go through even bad governments to promote their political development. This argument is based on the overambitious goals of political transformation, which have repeatedly failed. The argument is not too persuasive if aid aims not at transforming governments but just at helping very poor individuals with their most desperate needs.

The principle is *nonintervention*. Don't reward bad governments by working through them, but don't try to boss them around or overthrow them either. The status quo of both donors and gangsters badly needs some work.

Fela Kuti

Fela Kuti (1938–1997) was not only an internationally famous Nigerian musician, the king of Afrobeat, he was also a courageous political activist. In his songs, he mocked the military rulers who had been such a plague on Nigeria. He said in one song that VIP meant "Vagabonds in Power." Another song was called "Authority Stealing." He also attacked Western racism and meddling in Africa. He was constantly persecuted by the military, beaten with rifle butts, and imprisoned—perhaps because his subversive music was so popular with Nigerians. In his 1977 song "Zombie," he derided Nigerian soldiers as mindless robots obeying orders to harass the population. The enraged army attacked Fela Kuti's compound in Lagos, torturing, raping, and murdering members of his entourage. Soldiers threw his aged mother from a second-story window; she subsequently died from her injuries. Kuti never forgave Olusegun Obasanjo, the military dictator at the time, who never apologized publicly for the attack. In 1979, when Obasanjo transferred power to a civilian regime, Kuti led a march of his followers to Obasanjo's home carrying a mock coffin in protest against his mother's murder. In 1980, Fela Kuti recorded a song called ITT (International Thief Thief), which accused Obasanjo of corruption.

Obasanjo went over to the opposition during the 1990s military dictatorship of Sani Abacha. After the death of Abacha, former military dictator Obasanjo was elected president in 1999. He promised to crack down on Nigeria's notorious corruption, but his Anti-Corruption Commission managed to prosecute only one minor official during Obasanjo's four-year term.[85] He got a second term in 2003, in an election in which European Union observers noted "serious irregularities." He launched yet another anticorruption campaign in 2005, partly motivated by the desire to get relief on Nigeria's high foreign debt. Governments since independence have so mismanaged the country's oil riches that 60 percent of Nigerians remain below the poverty line.[86] Chronic violence between ethnic groups and weak economic performance have marred Obasanjo's presidency. Fela Kuti is no longer with us, but his music remains popular. His courageous struggle for freedom from corruption, and from the heavy hand of the military, lives on.[87]

New York University
Professor Leonard Wantchekon*

I grew up in Zagnanado, a small town in Central Benin of about three thousand people, in the 1960s. It is one of the poorest towns in the country. There was no paved road, and no electricity, but it had one of the oldest elementary schools in the country. Our homes were constructed of straw, earth, brick, cement, or sometimes corrugated aluminum.

My parents, though illiterate, valued education immensely, and in that respect had great ambition for their children. In many ways they went against the grain of custom in the village. Many families had ten or twelve children, often two years apart. My mother decided to have only five children, four boys and one girl, and that she would have them at four-year intervals. All attended school until they were at least fourteen, an extraordinary accomplishment in a region where most frequently only one child from a family of twelve would receive any formal schooling whatsoever.

In Zagnanado, the farther one goes from the village, the easier it is to find a fertile field for one's own use. When my father finally found a good field, it was fifteen kilometers from the village. He fashioned a primitive shelter in a cave in order to store the harvest, and during harvest time he stayed in his field, too far from the village to return. He spent weeks harvesting, far from anyone, and with no means of communication. A man of enormous courage, he slept at night in the cave, alone, surrounded by snakes and monkeys. He only asked that his sons come on weekends to take away as much of the harvest as we could carry, which we then sold to buy books, pencils, and papers for our studies. He also earned extra revenue by taking in laundry from a local government official, but often still had to take on debt to provide his sons with the transportation and school supplies necessary to their studies.

Thirty years later, I realized that Zagnanado has produced ten university professors, thirteen medical doctors, two architects, four diplomats, and at least one hundred more with at least a university degree. At least seven of "our" professors and medical doctors work in the United States, Germany, and France. Zagnanado is also the hometown of Cardinal Gantin, the former dean of the Sacred College of Cardinals in the Vatican, who retired in 2002.

* I have abridged a first-person written narrative that Professor Wantchekon gave me.

Zagnanado and its immediate surrounding towns have a large number of lakes and rivers, with wild animals, and could have been at least a major tourist destination. The story of Zagnanado could also well be the story of the whole of Benin.

Why did such as an impressive collection of personal success and talent not translate into economic prosperity?

I thought the absence of democracy was the root cause of the problem. One year my father was asked to pay taxes amounting to 90 percent of his annual revenue, a level of taxation that was obviously impossible for anyone, but especially so for him, considering his advanced age. He was already quite old at the time, and too sick to work. Officials came to our home in the middle of the night, woke him up, arrested him, and forced him to parade himself throughout Zagnanado denouncing himself: "I am an irresponsible lout, I didn't pay my taxes. Look upon a horrible sight, I didn't pull my weight. I am stupid, and low, I didn't pay taxes." And this was done to the kindest, sweetest, most generous man I ever knew. This was the treatment given to that courageous man who lived alone in a cave for weeks on end to provide for his sons. When it happened I thought, No, it's impossible, it can't happen. And it was then, when I saw my father humiliated in this way, that I resolved to change things in my country. From that point on I was committed to political change.

In 1979 and again in 1985, as a student at the National University of Benin (UNB), I organized pro-democracy movements. I was arrested in July 1985 and fled in December 1986. The pro-democracy movement grew and led to major democratic reforms in the country in 1990. Meanwhile, I immigrated to Canada in 1988 and then later to the United States, in 1992. I enrolled in graduate programs at Laval University and UBC in Canada, and Northwestern University in the United States. I graduated in 1995 and became an assistant professor at Yale University in 1995 and an associate professor at NYU in 2001.

Today, Leonard Wantchekon, now an NYU professor of politics with a global reputation, runs a research institute in Benin devoted to testing what works in development programs for Benin, training the next generation and devising ways to hold the new democratic government of Benin accountable for delivering services to its citizens.

PART II

ACTING OUT THE
BURDEN

CHAPTER FIVE

The Rich Have Markets, the Poor Have Bureaucrats

To err is human,
To really screw up takes a committee.

Anonymous

Foreign aid donors spent two billion dollars in Tanzania during the past twenty years building roads. The road network did not improve. Roads deteriorated faster than donors built new ones, due to lack of maintenance.[1] I have been on my share of bad roads in Africa, roads so bad that you can only creep along them at about five miles per hour. You may think roads are not so critical, but maybe you would change your mind if you were a desperate husband traveling at five miles per hour with a wife in labor, trying to get her to a health clinic to address life-threatening complications. The poor need roads; the aid bureaucracy fails to deliver them. We should be tough on a bureaucracy that fails to turn aid money into critical services for the poor.

The international aid bureaucracy includes the World Bank, the U.S. Agency for International Development and other national government agencies, the regional development banks such as the Inter-American Development Bank, and the United Nations agencies. How well have we foreign aid bureaucrats done through the $2.3 trillion we've spent on the problems of the poor?

The "growth industry" in Tanzania is actually bureaucracy. Tanzania produced more than 2,400 reports a year for its aid donors, who sent the beleaguered recipient one thousand missions of donor officials per year.[2] I myself wasted government officials' time on five continents during my bureaucratic career. Foreign aid did not supply something the poor wanted (roads), while it did supply a lot of something the poor probably had little use for (me and my fellow bureaucrats).

Contrast this with the efficiency of bottom-up Searchers. We have seen that the conditions for markets are often absent, but when they are present, as in rich countries, market Searchers work wonders. It is hard to go ninety miles on a road in Tanzania, but you can book online in about five minutes a nonstop flight from New York to Los Angeles leaving in about an hour and a half from this moment, and be three thousand miles away by this afternoon. No bureaucrats assess your needs for air travel over the next year. You file no reports with strategies or plans for your travel over the next fiscal year. Southwest Airlines is not offering to transform the world; it just searches for a way to get you to Los Angeles right away so you will buy a ticket and contribute to its profits. Despite this lack of bureaucracy, the flight from New York to Los Angeles is available to whoever wants it at a price of $299.

You might think this comparison is unfair. Markets do not supply all goods for the rich. Some goods are public services, such as roads, that have to be supplied by the state. The state does use bureaucracy to meet these needs. Yet the bureaucracy in rich countries works better than the bureaucracy of the aid agencies for the poor. The previous chapter has already shown how better public services go along with democracy, so let me just give an anecdote here. I once had a pothole in front of my house in Takoma Park, Maryland. I got the city bureaucracy to fix the pothole in three easy steps: (1) I called my city councilwoman, Kathy Porter, and asked her to please have the city repair the pothole; (2) the next day, the Takoma Park Public Works bureaucracy was out there filling in the pothole; and (3) actually, there was no third step. This worked because the city bureaucracy is accountable to elected politicians such as Kathy Porter, who is accountable to me and other voters. Kathy Porter is a Searcher. She built her political career in Takoma Park on responding to constituents. Today, she is entering her eighth year as mayor of Takoma Park. Of course, rich-country democracy doesn't always work this well, but it works well enough to get many public services to its rich citizens.

This example shows that bureaucrats are not automatically ineffective. Markets themselves use bureaucracies. Southwest Airlines, like all corporations, has a corporate bureaucracy that organizes its delivery of travel services to the customers. The difference from aid bureaucracy is that the corporate bureaucrats are accountable to those same customers—if they don't deliver the goods, they go out of business. The market forces corporate bureaucracies to use Searchers to find out how to deliver services most cheaply for the highest degree of customer satisfaction.

The tragedy of poverty is that the poorest people in the world have no money or political power to motivate Searchers to address their desperate needs, while the rich can use their money and power through well-developed markets and accountable bureaucracies to address theirs. The foreign aid bureaucracy has never quite gotten it—its central problem is that the poor are orphans: they have no money or political voice to communicate their needs or motivate others to meet those needs.

To make things even worse, aid bureaucrats have incentives to satisfy the rich countries doing the funding as well as (or instead of) the poor. One oversight in the quest to help the poor was the failure to study the incentives of its appointed helpers. The bureaucratic managers have the incentive to satisfy rich-country vanity with promises of transforming the Rest rather than simply helping poor individuals. Internal bureaucratic incentives also favor grand global schemes over getting the little guy what he wants.

This is not to say that self-serving incentives determine everything in either markets or bureaucracies. People take pride in doing good work, achieving results, and helping others in both private and public organizations. Many aid agency staffers are hardworking, caring, honest professionals dedicated to helping the poor. The question is whether the incentives work *for* or *against* the well-intentioned workers. In private markets, incentives and pride in doing good work reinforce each other. In democratic bureaucracies, political incentives are on the same side as the professional norms of good performance. In aid bureaucracies, unfortunately, the political incentives too often work against the professionals trying to get results.

Understanding the bureaucratic obstacles to serving the interests of the poor can point the way toward more effectively helping the poor. This chapter is a modest step toward shining a light into some of the bureaucracies' dark corners, and motivating others to do the same, in order to begin to change incentives for the helpers to deliver results rather than plans. This chapter will suggest some hypotheses as to why aid agency bureaucracy works badly, and then test these hypotheses with as many case study examples as possible. Unfortunately, in this area I have to rely more on case studies and even anecdotes than systematic data, as bureaucratic behavior is harder to quantify than other things this book covers.

Bottom-up Feedback Again

The beauty of the market's focus on the individual is that customer choice gives feedback to suppliers. If flights to Los Angeles on Southwest are fully booked and you attempt to book an additional seat, that's a signal to Southwest to schedule more flights or raise prices. The wonder of markets is that they reconcile the choices of myriad individuals. A price that clears the market is like a heating thermostat. When the house gets too cold, the thermostat automatically turns on the heat. If the house gets too warm, the thermostat turns off the heat. If you still feel too cold at the current setting of the thermostat, you change it. *You* decide if you are too cold, and *you* control the thermostat. The market works in the same way—if there is excess demand, the price goes up; if there is excess supply, the price goes down. Democracy also features feedback. If a citizen or civic lobby observes a problem and calls a public official to get it fixed, it often gets fixed. If the government does something that really pisses off the majority of the population, the voters scream loudly enough that the government changes its behavior.

To see how unique a well-working feedback system is, consider a mix-up that once happened to me. My companion and I were going to sleep on a cold night under a dual-control blanket. Each of us could control the warmth on our own side of the blanket. We got the controls mixed up so that I was unknowingly controlling her side and she was controlling my side. I felt too warm and turned the control down, which made her side colder, so she turned her control up, which made my side even hotter, which made me turn down my control even more, which made her side even colder, which made her turn her control up . . .

The difficulty of foreign aid agencies is that a bureaucrat is controlling the thermostat to the distant blanket of some poor person, who has little ability to communicate whether she is too hot or too cold. The bureaucratic Planners get little or no feedback from the poor. So the poor foreign aid recipients get some things they never wanted, and don't get things they urgently need. Searchers can do better by getting out in the field, talking to the poor, designing feedback mechanisms such as surveys, and experimenting with what works in local conditions.

Me Principal, You Agent

Not that there are easy solutions in foreign aid. The aid problem is inherently difficult. Rich-country politicians control the foreign aid agencies. To make the relationship between rich-country politicians and aid bureaucracies more precise, think of principals and agents (an agent is anyone who acts on behalf of another person, the principal—there is a lot of research in economics about this setup). Think of the rich-country politician as the principal and the aid bureaucrat as the agent. The big problem already noted is that the principal is the rich-country politician and not the real customers, the poor in poor countries. Voters in the rich country and their representatives are the ones who choose the actions of the foreign aid agency. They love the Big Plans, the promises of easy solutions, the utopian dreams, the side benefits for rich-country political or economic interests, all of which hands the aid agency impossible tasks.

But even if voters and their representatives were more focused on feasible actions to help the poor, problems would remain. In the usual principal-agent setup, the principal cannot execute all of a task himself, so he delegates part of it to an agent, who will perform it on his behalf. For example, a store owner cannot man the cash register all the time, so she hires an employee. But the principal and the agent do not have the same interests. The store owner wants the employee to serve as many customers as energetically as possible to maximize store profits. The employee wants to conserve his energies for after-hours barhopping. The owner and the employee can resolve the incompatible goals by writing a contract that gives the agent the incentive to do what the principal wants. The employee gets rewarded if he serves the customers, and gets fired if he blows them off.

However, principal-agent contracts do not work if the principal cannot observe performance by the agent. With no ability by the principal to monitor the agent, the agent has no incentive to work hard for the principal's interests.

These problems become a nightmare under the Planner's mind-set, where there is some utopian objective such as ending world poverty. The rich-country politician could judge the aid agency based on the overall poverty outcome—but that assumes a known relationship between foreign aid efforts and poverty reduction. On the contrary, because the poverty outcomes in the Rest depend on many factors besides the bureaucracy, the aid agency's contribution in the field is invisible.[3]

Pity the aid agency for having an almost impossible problem. The agency must indulge the dreams of the rich-country principals of transforming the Rest. The agency must work with local government institutions and local elites who themselves may not care about poverty reduction. There is uncontrollable variability about poverty outcomes, due to such unanticipated factors as political upheavals, droughts, or export price declines. Although rational principals could control for the difficulty of the environment, conditional evaluation requires inside knowledge that only the aid agencies themselves have.

Again, the invisibility of individual aid agency efforts and outcomes is at the core of the problem. To see how visibility matters, suppose you are the agent and your principal is the dinner guest you have invited over to your home. Compare the cleanliness of your dining room and your attic.

The dining room is observable to your dinner guest. The attic is not. Your dining room is a lot cleaner than your attic. You devote much more effort to cleaning the dining room than to cleaning the attic. In fact, you may even make the attic messier in the process of cleaning the dining room, shoving dining room junk up into the attic. If someone comes up with a utopian plan to transform your attic, nobody will ever know if it succeeded or not. When nobody can tell whether aid agency efforts make a difference, the aid agency managers have only weak incentives to exert effort. This goes back to one of the key predictions of this book: visibility gives more power to Searchers, while invisibility shifts power to Planners.

The problem with aid is that the poor are mostly invisible. Foreign aid and other development efforts take place in the attic of the rich people's world. Does the ineffective utopian vision survive in foreign aid because nobody is paying much attention? Let us see if we can make aid perform better by throwing open the attic to public view.

The Kids Contribute Some Bathroom Humor

Trying to do everything with foreign aid creates a situation with many principals and many agents. Principal-agent theory says that multiple principals (many rich-country governments and issue lobbies) weaken the incentives for the agent (the international agency). The messianic urge of the West to solve all of the Rest's problems creates multitudinous objectives for the aid agency. Each principal (say, each issue lobby) influences the agent to pursue its objectives and neglect the other principals' objectives; together, this weakens incentives for the agent to achieve any one objective.[4] Anyone with more than one boss knows this. Whenever one boss complains about your halfhearted performance, you make the excuse that you were working for the other boss.

The solution to this particular problem is to have fewer objectives. If the aid business were not so beguiled by utopian visions, it could address a more realistic set of problems for which it had evidence of a workable solution. A further step would be to have each aid agency specialize more in some subset of these workable solutions.

Foreign aid is also complicated by having many agents—many different aid agencies who answer to different bosses. Operating in the Bolivian mountains are the International Monetary Fund, the World Bank, the Inter-American Development Bank, USAID, the U.S. Drug Enforcement Administration, the UK Department for International Development (DFID), just about every other rich country's aid agency, multiple NGOs, and Bono. None of the agencies is responsible for a particular outcome, and the effects of their individual efforts are unobservable. They jointly affect what happens to economic development in Bolivia. When something goes wrong in Bolivia, such as the economic and political crisis in 1999–2005, after years of effort by these agencies, which one is to blame? We don't know, so no one agency is accountable. This weakens the incentive of agencies to behave.

Consider the following analogy, inspired by a discussion with my kids that drew upon their deep reserve of bathroom humor. Suppose a child is uncouth. When he is on a school elevator that contains only one other child, should he suppress flatulence? The answer is yes, to avoid extreme disapproval from the other child. But now suppose he is on a crowded elevator. The incentive to suppress, as my kids analyze this sensitive subject, is not as strong, since the other children on the elevator won't know whom to blame.

A dysfunctional bureaucracy is an agency or group of agencies where no one is to blame: "that's not my department." Principals don't know whom to hold accountable when something goes wrong. The problem is more severe the more general the objective, and thus the more agents that could have contributed to the outcome.

This is the flaw in exercises in international cooperation such as the Millennium Development Goals. All the rich-country governments and international aid agencies are supposed to work together to achieve the MDGs. So when the goals are not attained, no one agent can be held accountable. This weakens the incentive of any one agent to break its neck to reach the goals. Collective responsibility for goals doesn't work for the same reason that collective ownership of farmland in China didn't work.

Yet going along with collective responsibility is an optimal strategy for individual aid agencies to protect themselves from the hostile political environment facing foreign aid. With success on the big goals of foreign aid so dependent on many other factors besides aid agency effort, it is understandable that aid agencies want to share the blame with as many other agencies as possible if something goes wrong.

The free market in rich countries solves the problem of many principals and many agents. There are many firms (agents) supplying goods to many consumers (principals). A decentralized search by both firms and consumers through the free market creates a number of matches. Each match creates a temporary principal-agent relationship between the consumer and the firm. If the firm's product is defective, the consumer knows whom to blame and can ask for his money back. The firm thus will have an incentive not to make a bad product. With nothing analogous to the marketplace in foreign aid, the many principals don't know from which of the many agents to demand their money back.

As the previous chapter notes, bureaucracy works better—though, God knows, far from perfectly—in countries with governments democratically accountable to their citizens. The analogue to market feedback in democracy is voter feedback. If the citizens don't get results from government bureaucracy, they complain to politicians who depend on the citizens' votes. The politicians (principals) try to design bureaucracies (agents) with incentives to deliver results to the voters. In rich-country democracies, bureaucracies are more likely to be assigned a simple, doable task (Takoma Park Public Works, U.S. Government Veterans Affairs, the State Highway Department, Social Security) rather than visionary ambitions. Politicians will blame bureaucracies (and voters will blame politicians) if they fail to deliver results (potholes fixed, veterans' benefits delivered, new roads built, retirement checks issued).

To Repair a Pothole

Now consider a poor person in the countryside of Tanzania who wants to get a pothole repaired in front of his house. As we saw in the beginning of this chapter, Tanzanians have not enjoyed good roads. In contrast to the ease with which I got my pothole fixed in Takoma Park, the poor Tanzanian has no way of getting anyone to act in his behalf. The Tanzanian government looks to foreign aid for financing of public services. This poor person somehow communicates his desires to "civil society representatives" and/or nongovernmental organizations (NGOs), who articulate his needs through the government of Tanzania to the international donors. The national government solicits a "poverty reduction support credit" (PRSC) from the World Bank (also known as the International Bank for Reconstruction and Development, or IBRD) and a Poverty Reduction and Growth Facility (PRGF) from the International Monetary Fund (IMF).

To get loans from the IMF and the World Bank, the government must complete a satisfactory Poverty Reduction Strategy Paper (PRSP), in consultation with civil society, NGOs, and other donors and creditors. Although they do advocate free markets, the IMF and World Bank show a curious affinity for the national Planners who will create a Poverty Reduction Strategy Paper.

The World Bank then follows a series of internal steps to approve a PRSC, including preparation of a Country Assistance Strategy (CAS), a pre-appraisal mission, an appraisal mission, negotiations, and board approval, all in accordance with the Comprehensive Development Framework (CDF), Operational Directive (OD) 8.60, Operational Policy (OP) 4.01, and Interim PRSC Guidelines. The government also seeks qualification for the Enhanced Heavily Indebted Poor Country (Enhanced HIPC) Debt Initiative so that the new loan doesn't simply go to service old loans. The creditors and the government conduct a debt-sustainability analysis (DSA). The HIPC, PRSC, and PRGF require numerous reform conditions, such as participation of the poor in designing projects, poverty-reducing government expenditure monitored through annual "public expenditure reviews" (PERs), fiscal deficit targets, revenue-mobilization targets, and structural reforms such as implementation of a Financial Information Management System (FIMS) in the government, financial sector reform in line with the Basel standards and the eleven areas of International Standards and Codes recommended by the IMF and World Bank, control of money laundering, and privatization, lowering trade barriers in ways governed by the World Trade Organization (WTO), perhaps by applying the Integrated Framework for Trade-Related Technical Assistance to Least Developed Countries. The PRSP plan may or may not include money that could finance road repair for this poor person. The amount of money for road maintenance will depend on a prioritization of various needs for expenditure in a multi-year "medium-term expenditure framework" (MTEF).

Meanwhile, if beleaguered Tanzanian government officials have any time left, the PRSP Sourcebook also suggests that they cost out all the various ways the government is making progress toward the Millennium Development Goals for poverty, hunger, infant and maternal mortality, primary education, clean water, contraceptive use, AIDS, gender equality, and the environment. Meanwhile, other international bodies will review the Tanzanian PRSP, such as the United Nations Development Program (UNDP), the African Development Bank (AfDB), the United Nations Conference on Trade and Development (UNCTAD), the Food and Agriculture Organization (FAO), the World Trade Organization (WTO), the World Health Organization (WHO), the International Labour Organization (ILO), the European Union (EU), the United Nations Children's Fund (UNICEF), as well as NGOs and the national aid agencies such as those from Austria, Belgium, Canada, Finland, France, Germany, Ireland, Italy, Japan, Netherlands, Norway, Spain, Sweden, Switzerland, United Kingdom (DFID), and the United States (USAID). If IBRD, IMF, UNDP, FAO, WTO, EU, WHO, AfDB, DFID, and USAID approve the PRSP and release new funds to the national government, then the government will allocate the money in accordance with the MTEF, PER, CDF, PRGF, PRSC, and PRSP, after which the money will pass through the provincial governments and the district governments, and the district government may or may not repair the pothole in front of the poor person's house.

The analysis points to possible improvements: Have aid agencies specialize more in solving particular problems in particular countries, rather than having each agency responsible for everything. Then hold each agency responsible for progress on its particular problem, which might encourage it to cut red tape. And give the poor Tanzanian Kathy Porter's phone number.

> *No matter how hard you try, every once in a while,*
> *something is going right.*
>
> > *Corollary to Murphy's Law*[5]

Success

Don't abandon all hope. Even with all the possible bureaucratic pitfalls to making aid work, it sometimes *does* work. There *are* successful projects in the World Bank's portfolio, for example. The World Bank in the early 1990s helped fund the Food for Education program to keep Bangladeshi girls in school by giving their parents cash payments in return for school attendance (this is the kind of program that could help Amaretch in Ethiopia). Female enrollment doubled in the areas covered by the program. Another World Bank project in Bangladesh helped reduce the percentage of malnourished children from 13 percent to 2 percent in the areas covered. The World Bank's Peru Rural Roads Project helped Andean villagers get their crops to market in one tenth the time it used to take before the project.[6]

In 1991, the World Bank co-financed a ten-year $130 million project in China to control tuberculosis deaths. Local TB clinics tested 8 million people for TB during 1991–2000. Of these, 1.8 million tested positive. Doctors gave TB patients the proven regimen of streptomycin and other drugs. Because it is critical that patients take their medicine regularly (a weak point in many previous anti-TB programs), the project assigned health workers to watch patients do so. (This is the DOTS, "directly observed treatment, short course," approach successfully pioneered by the World Health Organization.) Local units reported on caseload and treatment to provincial and central committees, which made possible continuous evaluation of whether the program was working. The program was a success: the cure rate for TB increased from 52 percent to 95 percent. Chapter 5 discusses other health success stories.

The WHO and UNICEF supported a child nutrition project in the Iringa region of Tanzania beginning in 1983. The project held community health days in which all the children got a weight-for-age calculation to identify which children were malnourished. The project also trained village health workers and traditional healers to recognize the signs of malnutrition. Feeding centers got food to undernourished children. In the five years of its operation, the program reduced severe malnutrition by 70 percent and moderate malnutrition by 32 percent. The World Bank and other donors started similar projects in other parts of Tanzania in the 1990s.[7]

Foreign aid likely contributed to some notable successes on a global scale, such as dramatic improvement in health and education indicators in poor countries. Life expectancy in the typical poor country has risen from forty-eight years to sixty-eight years over the past four decades (see figure 20 below). Forty years ago, 131 out of every 1,000 babies born in poor countries died before reaching their first birthday. Today, 36 out of every 1,000 babies die before their first birthday. Kids enrolled in primary school in the typical

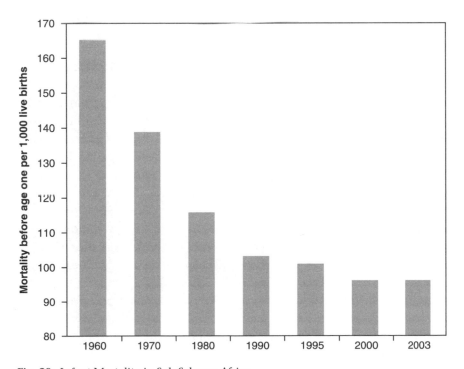

Fig. 20. Infant Mortality in Sub-Saharan Africa

poor country went from 65 percent of their age group in 1960 to 100 percent today. (There are a number of countries below 100 percent enrollment, but more than half of poor countries have 100 percent enrollment—hence the "typical" poor country has 100 percent enrollment.) The corresponding ratios for secondary school were even more dramatic: only 9 percent in 1960, 70 percent today. Despite the zero-growth payoff to aid in Africa, there has been a fall in infant mortality and a rise in secondary enrollment (see figure 21) in that most aid-intensive continent.

Organizations such as the IMF and the World Bank do succeed in attracting professionals who are dedicated to the mission of poverty reduction. Employees with strong norms of professional conduct do perform better than suggested by the more cynical analysis of aid agency incentives to please the rich. Even if aid didn't work well at the top, agents at the bottom sometimes made it work anyway. Professional fieldworkers can discover projects that do convey real benefits to poor people—e.g., better economic policy; better health, education, and sanitation; and better access to water, sanitation, and electric power.

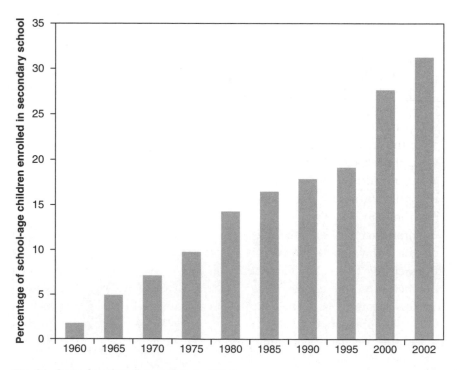

Fig. 21. Secondary Enrollment Rate in Africa

Maybe aid even works on average in some sectors, such as health, education, and water and sanitation. For example, maybe aid agencies had something to do with the improvement in water and sanitation in Africa. From 1970 to 2000, the percentage of the population with access to clean water went from 20 percent to 60 percent, and the access to improved sanitation went from one sixth to two thirds in the typical African country. Attributing these successes to aid is conjectural because there has not been enough of a scientific attempt in aid agencies to evaluate the impact of aid projects, but at least it lends some suggestive hope that aid can sometimes work.

Predictions of Bureaucratic Behavior

The concepts discussed earlier suggest that we bureaucracies will devote effort more to activities that are more observable and less to activities that are less observable. By the same token, we bureaucrats will perform better when we have tangible, measurable goals, and less well when we have vague, ill-defined dreams. We will perform better when there is a clear link from effort to results, and less well when results reflect many factors besides effort. We will perform better when we have fewer objectives, and worse when we have many objectives. We will perform better when we specialize in particular solvable problems, and less well when we try to achieve utopian goals. We will perform better when there is more information about what the customers want, and less well when there is confusion about such wants. We will perform better when agents at the bottom are motivated and accountable, and less well when everything is up to the managers at the top.

All of these positive factors shift power from Planners to Searchers. When aid efforts meet these criteria, Searchers offer the bureaucracy visible results that will burnish its external image, protecting it in a politically hostile environment.

Unfortunately there are large areas of aid efforts that do not meet the criteria for favorable opportunities for success, leaving power in the hands of Planners. We expect bureaucracies to do worse than private firms at matching their supply of services to their customers' demands, since bureaucracies are less accountable to their intended customers—the poor. The lack of a scientific approach to evaluating actions in the bureaucracies may also reflect the same lack of accountability.

Aid agencies will perform better when they can recruit dedicated professionals, and less well when there are political pressures to hire staff based on other criteria. Professionals will be easier to attract when the achievement of well-defined specific tasks can bolster professional morale.

We can use these predictions to speculate how we got some of the success stories just noted. Perhaps health interventions are more successful because the outcomes are specifically defined and easily observable—you can keep track of deaths from disease. Particular diseases can be monitored; you get feedback from how well the agency is doing on a particular disease, and adjust accordingly. The health field may also benefit from having a large organization with the narrow goal of improving health—the World Health Organization (WHO). Where there are visible indicators of success, even top-down efforts can work. The WHO's vaccination campaigns, which get part of the credit for the fall in infant mortality, involved a lot of top-down control, but there was feedback from the bottom through measures of vaccination coverage. Similarly, educational enrollment ratios can be monitored easily, and so effort at increasing enrollment gets rapid feedback. Likewise, nutrition projects can monitor the weight and height of children and thus get better feedback on whether their efforts are working. The prominence of the specific health, education, and nutrition goals for most of the history of foreign aid and the agreement of virtually all principals on these goals helped facilitate achievement here. The successes of expanding access to clean water and sanitation reflect the aid agencies' greater success at visible infrastructure projects than at more intangible (and less visible) goals.

Moving outside of projects, aid that promotes piecemeal reforms, in areas such as cutting red tape or ensuring better banking regulation, has visible results—such as the number of days to start a new business, the number of new businesses started, or the number of bank failures. We can hope for better results from piecemeal policy advice than from aid that promotes comprehensive reforms, where nobody can tell what is causing what.

The link from efforts and inputs—medicines, vaccination, food, construction of classrooms and water infrastructure, power generation, regulation simplification, etc.—to results is simpler and clearer in health, education, nutrition, water, electrification, and piecemeal policy reform than with other more general goals, such as how to achieve overall economic growth. It is easier to tell in these sectors what customers want—starving children obviously want food. Searchers have the inside track when there is the hope of visible results in these areas, in spite of bureaucracy above and around them.

Of course, it would be circular reasoning just to attribute any success in aid to Searchers and any failure to Planners. Instead, we have specific testable predictions based on how piecemeal an outcome is, how visible it is, and how much individual accountability is feasible. A piecemeal, visible, and individually accountable outcome, such as clean water for a village, is more likely to be addressed by Searchers, while a general, invisible, and unaccountable outcome, like a contribution to economic growth, is more likely to be addressed by Planners. The areas with piecemeal, visible, and individually accountable outcomes are more likely to experience success, while areas where objectives are general, efforts are invisible, and individual accountability is infeasible (or evaded) are more likely to experience failure.

This story is plausible but includes some speculation because the aid agencies didn't have enough incentives to evaluate (independently) what was working and why.

Aid Volume

In other areas the emphasis on observable indicators was less productive. Given that the goal was the development and transformation of poor countries, the aid agency somehow had to show progress toward that millennial vision. When the contribution of the agency to development *output* is unobservable, the agency planners try to advertise the volume of their *inputs* to development. One visible indicator of input that foreign aid agencies advertise is the volume of money they disburse. What Judith Tendler wrote about foreign aid back in 1975 is equally true today:

> A donor organization's sense of mission, then, relates not necessarily to economic development but to the commitment of resources, the moving of money.... The estimates of total capital needs for development assistance in relation to supply seem to have been the implicit standard by which donor organizations have guided their behavior and judged their performance...the quantitative measure has gained its supremacy by default. Other definitions of success and failure of development assistance efforts have been hard to come by.

Longtime World Bank president Robert McNamara cut his teeth in a previous life on the combined military intervention and aid program in Vietnam. McNamara had an infamous penchant for using numbers to monitor success in the Vietnam War, such as the body counts. Once he got to the World Bank, his numerical measure of success was less gruesome—it was loan volume: "we proposed to double the Bank's operations in the fiscal period 1969–73 compared to the previous 5-year period 1964–68. That objective has been met" (McNamara, 1973).

Advocates for the world's poor throughout the decades have focused on increasing the *volume* of foreign aid. The recommended increase displays a strange fixation on *double:* "the current flow of ODA [Official Development Assistance]...is only half the modest target prescribed by the internationally accepted United Nations Strategy for the Second Development Decade" (McNamara, 1973). "A cut of just 10 percent in military spending by the countries of the North Atlantic Treaty Organization would pay for a doubling of aid" (World Bank, World Development Report, 1990). "If we are serious about ensuring a beneficial globalization and meeting multilateral development goals we have all signed on to, we must double ODA from its current level of about $50 billion a year" (World Bank president James Wolfensohn, 2001). A World Bank technical study on the cost of meeting the Millennium Development Goals concurred on doubling: "An increase in foreign aid of an amount equal to current foreign aid...is about the right order of magnitude for achieving the development goals" (World Bank, 2002). Aid mounted throughout the period when agencies were emphasizing volume (see figure 22).

British prime minister Tony Blair and the chancellor of the exchequer Gordon Brown placed an increase in foreign aid, especially to Africa, high on the agenda of the G8 meetings in 2005. The recommended increase: double. In his 2005 book, *The End of Poverty,* Jeffrey Sachs called for a doubling of aid in 2006, then nearly a doubling again by 2015.

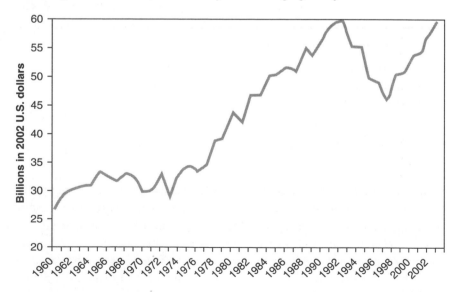

Fig. 22. Foreign Aid 1960–2003

Aid had declined in the first half of the 1990s, perhaps explained by the end of the cold war and a weariness with meager results. However, a new wave of aid expansion commenced in the new millennium and shows no sign of abating under the international war on terrorism.[8] The G8 did indeed agree in July 2005 to double aid to Africa.

The only problem is that foreign aid volume is an input to development, not an output. It seems strange that bureaucrats and politicians would focus on the input—total aid dollars spent. The Hollywood producers of *Catwoman*, which won an award for being the worst movie of 2004, would not dare to argue with moviegoers that the movie wasn't so bad because they had spent $100 million on making it. We can understand the emphasis on aid volume only as reflecting the pathology that in aid, the rich people who pay for the tickets are not the ones who see the movie.

This particular pathology has a solution, at least in theory. The rich-country monitors of aid agencies should disqualify aid disbursements (and the spending they finance) as a measure of success. The aid agencies have tried to deemphasize aid disbursements themselves, but in vain, given the political payoff to advertising disbursements. Aid critics have to persuade the rich-country public and politicians not to reward agencies for how much money is mobilized; what matters is results.

Yosemite Sam in the Tropics

The managers at the top of aid agencies had the incentive to show observable effort to the rich-country public. This caused them to produce many visible frameworks, task forces, reports, and meetings of statesmen. The World Bank evaluation of its activities in 1997 cited "the Interagency Task Force on an Enabling Environment for Social and Economic Development" that "followed up on two key conferences held during 1994–1995: the Copenhagen Social Summit (March 1994) and the Fourth World Conference on Women (September 1995)." During 1994–1996, the World Bank "chaired ninety formal meetings and provided substantial input to thirty-eight formal meetings chaired by other donors." Likewise, the United Nations Development Program (UNDP) discussed in a report its success at arranging meetings:

Trust Fund resources have been used to support the preparation and dissemination of social sector expenditure reviews in seven African countries.... Five of these reports have already been finalized and a workshop has been or will be held to discuss their findings and recommendations. Preliminary findings of these studies were shared in three regional meetings, co-sponsored by UNDP and UNICEF, which served to sensitize policy-makers about the 20/20 initiative and prepare them for the international meeting which took place in Hanoi in October 1998.[9]

In 2005, the UN Millennium Project issued its report, summarizing the meetings of ten different task forces, which in turn built upon a previous task force on poverty and development that had issued a report in 2004, summarizing meetings hosted by the UN Economic Commission for Africa (with the assistance of UNDP Ethiopia) and the UN Economic and Social Commision for Asia and the Pacific (with the assistance of UNDP Thailand).

Likewise, the aid agencies put a lot of effort into writing reports. They write reports for each other and for the rich-country media. The World Bank and the IMF noted in a 256-page joint report on meeting the Millennium Development Goals in April 2005 that the report drew upon: "Evidence from an OECD DAC Working Party on Aid Effectiveness and Donor Practices (WP-EFF) survey, Strategic Partnership for Africa (SPA) surveys, and the United Nations Economic Commission for Africa (UNECA)—DAC Mutual Review of Development Effectiveness in the Context of the New Partnership for Africa's Development (NEPAD)."[10]

In late 2004 and early 2005, besides the UN's 3,751-page Investing in Development: A Practical Plan to Achieve the Millennium Development Goals, we have the British government's 453-page Our Common Future: Report of the Commission for Africa, plus the latest update of the IMF and the World Bank's 1,246-page PRSP Sourcebook.

The World Bank in 2001 discussed the frameworks produced by different aid organizations, with an output by one organization often serving as an input to another. "The UN Common Country Assessment, the Bank's Economic and Sector Work (ESW), and the IMF's analytical and technical assistance work would contribute to governments' analytical base for PRSPs. [The World Bank] also welcomed the European Union's decision to base its Africa, Caribbean and Pacific (ACP) assistance programs on the PRSPs." In 2002 alone, the World Bank's frameworks included those produced by the International Conference on Financing for Development in Monterrey; the G7/8 Summit on Africa and the Millennium Development Goals in Kananaskis; and the Johannesburg Summit on Sustainable Development. After a bit of a breather, 2005 brought more summits and frameworks, with the Blair Commission for Africa; the Gleneagles, Scotland, G8 Summit on Africa and the Millennium Development Goals, in July; and the UN Millennium Summit on the Millennium Development Goals in September.

The proliferation of summits and frameworks confirms the prediction that aid agencies will skew their efforts toward observable output (these summits and frameworks get a lot of press attention). The frameworks and summits also confirm the prediction that aid agencies will embrace *collective* responsibility, as the summits are occasions for *joint* commitment to general worldwide goals, and the frameworks of different agencies are mutually dependent.

Aid agencies are rewarded for setting goals rather than reaching them, since goals are observable to the rich-country public while results are not. An unintended side effect of the increased activity of NGO issue lobbies has been to expand even further the set of goals that foreign assistance has been trying to achieve. Since no issue lobby takes into account the effect on other issue lobbies of its demands on the scarce aid and administrative resources of agencies, each lobby overemphasizes its goals. This is analogous to the "tragedy of the commons" problem in which too many cows overgraze pastures held in common. To make things worse, each separate aid agency has felt the political pressure to add all of these goals in response to its own rich-country constituency. This is because bilateral aid agencies each have their rich-country publics with multiple goals, and a multilateral agency like the World Bank is fair game for lobbies worldwide. Although this book stresses the virtues of feedback and accountability, it is feedback from the intended beneficiaries that is the desideratum; feedback from rich-country lobbies that don't represent the poor could make things worse rather than better.

The end result is that aid agencies are like Yosemite Sam, firing at random in all directions. Managers at the top feel pressure to promise everything.

For example, World Bank president James Wolfensohn set out his Comprehensive Development Framework in 1999, with a checklist of fourteen items, each with multiple subitems. To his credit, President Wolfensohn recognized that development was complicated. However, as a checklist for World Bank action to address this complexity, it is unworkable. The long list included "capacity building," "property, contract, labor, bankruptcy, commercial codes, personal rights laws," "internationally acceptable accounting and auditing standards," "lessons of practice and history from indigenous peoples and communities," "a strategy for sewerage," [reducing] "the use of wood and fossil fuels," "wind-up radios without batteries," [preserving] "historic sites, artifacts and books, but also the spoken word and the arts," "integrated solutions to rural development," and "appropriate laws."[11] The Johannesburg Summit on Sustainable Development in 2002 upped the ante even further by recommending 185 actions by rich and poor countries, including "efficient use of cow dung."

The UN Millennium Project developed yet another framework in 2005 with the help of 250 development experts, commissioning thirteen reports from ten task forces. All this helped the project to come up with its framework, with its eighteen indicative targets for the eight MDGs, its ten key recommendations (which are actually thirty-six recommendations when you count all the bullet points), "a bold, needs-based, goal-oriented investment framework over 10 years," seventeen Quick Wins to be done immediately, seven "main investment and policy clusters," and ten problems to be solved in the international aid system.

Meanwhile, the aid agencies drive the recipient governments and their own frontline workers insane when they declare each objective to be priority number one. Reaching as many poor as possible would dictate that greater effort go to goals with low costs and high benefits, and that little or no effort go to goals where the costs are very high relative to the benefits. It would recognize that doing more on one goal implied doing less on another goal—politicians and bureaucrats are terrified of the word "tradeoff."

Aid bureaucracies are like my children, who, when asked to choose between a chocolate bar and ice cream when they were young, would say "both." The aid agencies do a little bit on each goal, which forgoes the gains from specialization and leaves low-cost/high-benefit activities underfunded. It follows that the aid community's "do everything" approach thus fails to reach as many people in need as it could. Aid agency managers do talk about setting priorities, but their behavior says otherwise—the political incentives to do token amounts of everything are too strong.

In contrast, the free-market Searchers for the rich provide specialized goods and services that meet consumer needs, not all-inclusive "frameworks" that do everything for the consumer. Consumers pay the cost of asking a product to meet additional goals, and so there is no "tragedy of the commons" excess demand for goals on any one product. Consumers face tradeoffs between alternative products, choosing the one that gives the highest satisfaction for the lowest price.

Economists since Adam Smith have also stressed the efficiency gains from specialization, which suggests that organizations and individuals should focus on a few things and not do others. Since firms can meet consumer goals more cheaply by specializing and having limited objectives, the free market also tends to produce specialized suppliers. You would never go to a dentist who was also an auto mechanic and talk show host. Yet the market has no trouble meeting the multiple objectives of providing consumers with dentistry, auto repair, and talk shows. This is because the decentralized market coordinates through the price system the specialized supplies of each of these services.

Rich democracies also feature bureaucracies that are more specialized than those in foreign aid. Each interest group can concentrate on the bureaucracy addressing their issue. Local governments handle local issues, national government national ones.

Part of the solution is changing the rich-country political marketplace that aid agencies face. If Western governments and NGOs really want to make poor people's lives better, it will take some political courage to admit that doing everything is a fantasy. The rich-country public has to live with making poor people's lives better in a few concrete ways that aid agencies can actually achieve.

Good Observables

Some of the glossy reports produced by aid agencies are worthwhile. The World Bank and the IMF have a happier intersection of the visibility imperative and the needs of poor countries in their research-based efforts. Both institutions have large research departments devoted to studying development issues, staffed by researchers whom the outside academic community respects professionally. They publish extensively in competitive academic journals. This is an example of the bottom-up staff observing professional norms, accountable to the outside world for their efforts, with the power and motivation to perform well. This book draws heavily on the work of IMF and World Bank researchers.

Outside of the research departments, there are many other outposts of professionals in the aid agencies devoted to rigorous analysis of development problems. Such professionals produce many valuable reports and studies on development. The judgment of the outside world provides an incentive for them to publish something useful.

The key publication of the IMF is the World Economic Outlook. This is a high-quality analysis of the state of the world economy and its prospects. It is widely covered in the business press when it comes out.

The flagship report of the World Bank each year is the World Development Report. The 2004 World Development Report studied the determinants of government delivery of services such as health and education. Shanta Devarajan, director of the World Development Report 2004, said, "Services can work when poor people stand at the center of service provision—when they can avoid poor providers, while rewarding good providers with their clientele, and when their voices are heard by politicians—that is, when service providers have incentives to serve the poor."[12] The 2002 World Development Report was on institutions for prosperity. Roumeen Islam, director of the World Development Report 2002, has written about the need to adapt institutions to local conditions and traditions, as well as the need for donors and governments to get feedback from the citizens. These examples show that some Searchers in the World Bank *are* aware of the need for feedback from the poor.

Both the IMF and World Bank produce reports on individual poor countries, which are available on their Web sites. Together these reports make up the world's best supply of information on the economic situation of individual countries—most of them are ignored by the American press.

Low-Maintenance Development

Unfortunately, the incentives to produce observable output also create mismatches of the aid agencies' services and the poor's needs. As exemplified by the Tanzanian story that opens the chapter, the downside of the agencies' success at visible road building is their failure on (less visibly) maintaining those roads. For decades, aid reports bewailed the neglect of operating supplies and maintenance after infrastructure projects were completed. Donors consistently refuse to finance maintenance and operating supplies, with the idea that this is the responsibility of recipient governments, even though there is intense client demand for these goods.

Besides the visibility bias toward new construction, the underfunding of maintenance reflects the elusive goal of "sustainability" (best summarized by that tiresome cliché about giving a man a fish versus teaching him to fish). Donors envision the local government taking over the project, which they think is necessary to make it last.[13] This intuition was once appealing, but the decades of evidence show that that dog won't hunt. As Michael Kremer of Harvard and Edward Miguel of Berkeley argue, trying to make the project "sustainable" usually guarantees that it will *not* be "sustained." Since we have already seen the weak commitment of many governments to development, and the inability of donors to transform governments, the takeover of the project usually doesn't happen. But donors keep flailing away at this infeasible but inflexible objective.

This is another example of how having a grandiose instead of a modest goal makes things worse rather than better. By aiming at the unworkable goal of "sustainable projects" (meaning new projects combined with changing the government's behavior so it can take over those projects), the donors failed at the simpler tasks of providing well-maintained roads, children with textbooks, and clinics with medicines.

Here is one way to make aid work better: aid donors should just bite the bullet and permanently fund road maintenance, textbooks, drugs for clinics, and other operating costs of development projects. Politically dysfunctional governments that don't do maintenance can concentrate on other things.

The World Bank's periodic reports on Africa show they know about the low-maintenance problem but are prevented by their grandiose goals from fixing it: "Vehicles and equipment frequently lie idle for lack of spare parts, repairs, gasoline, or other necessities. Schools lack operating funds for salaries and teaching materials, and agricultural research stations lack funds for keeping up field trials. Roads, public buildings, and processing facilities suffer from lack of maintenance" (World Bank, 1981). "Road maintenance crews lack fuel and bitumen . . . teachers lack books, chalk . . . health workers have no medicines to distribute" (World Bank, 1986). "Schools are now short of books, clinics lack medicines, and infrastructure maintenance is avoided" (World Bank, 1989). "Typically, 50 percent of the rural road network requires rehabilitation" (World Bank, 1995). "Many countries suffer chronic shortages of current funding, especially for operations, maintenance, and nonwage inputs" (World Bank, 2000).

World Bank researchers Deon Filmer and Lant Pritchett estimate that the return on spending on instructional materials in education is up to fourteen times higher than the return on spending on physical facilities, but donors continue to favor more observable buildings over less observable textbooks.[14] This has undercut the donors' success on increasing educational enrollments noted earlier. Quantity of education has gone up, but quality remains low.

Coordination

From the earliest days of aid, the emphasis of all participants has been on coordination of all the aid agencies. After reading the literature, one can hardly say "aid" without adding "coordination." One reason that aid bureaucracy is so excessive is that multiple aid agencies are all trying to do everything, which means they are duplicating each other (each aid agency has the incentive to take on multiple goals to satisfy its own constituency). In 1969, an aid commission said, "A serious effort is necessary to coordinate the efforts of multilateral and bilateral aid-givers and those of aid-receivers"

(Pearson Commission, 1969). Thirty-six years later: "The multilateral agencies are not coordinating their support" (UN Millennium Project report, 2005).

These continued calls for coordination and complaints about lack of coordination illustrate that everyone knows it is desirable but is unable to change anything to achieve it. Of course, the Planners' answer is a Plan:

> [The government should negotiate] an external assistance strategy... *that explicitly identifies the priority sectors and programs for donor financing.... More detailed external assistance strategies can then be developed for key areas through sectoral working groups in which representatives of major donors and line agencies participate....* Agreeing on financing priorities for individual donors within the framework of a global external assistance strategy, *rather than through bilateral agreements.*[15]

This suggestion worsens rather than improves one of the main problems with multiple, uncoordinated donors—the huge strain the donors put on the few decision-makers in the recipient government. The donors pour a huge flow of aid money, donor missions, and projects into a funnel. The narrow part of the funnel is the administration in the recipient government. To do another plan to coordinate all the previous plans would demand even more of this administration.

Coordination plans have failed to achieve coordination for four decades. Coordination is impossible under the current aid system, when every agency reports to different bosses who have different agendas. Once again, we see the Planners flailing away at an insoluble problem. Some of the recommendations already made about focusing on solvable problems—such as donor specialization and bypassing government—would alleviate the coordination hornet's nest.

Collateral Benefits, Collateral Damage

The agencies are less effective at helping the poor not just because of little voice or feedback from the intended beneficiaries but also because there are noisy rich clients—the rich countries that actually pay the bills. Since aid agencies need to please the electorate in rich countries, the agencies often strive to produce side effects for rich countries at the same time they are transforming the Rest. Thus, rich-country donors restrict some part of aid to purchases from their own country's exporters ("tied aid"). The United States requires recipients to spend the aid receipts on products from American companies for about three quarters of its aid.[16] Other donor nations have similar restrictions (although the share of tied aid is not as high as that of the United States). Tying of aid lowers its value to the recipient because it restricts choice on what products can be purchased and from whom. Technical assistance to poor countries is even worse, since rich countries typically insist that their own nationals be the technical advisers. Hence, a good part of technical assistance aid is simply flowing back to some rich-country consultant handing out the kind of deep insights that come from two weeks' acquaintance with a poor country. (Tying of aid shows rich-country hypocrisy, but this hypocrisy is not the reason why aid fails to raise growth—see chapter 2.)

Aid agencies are also attentive to the need to reward political allies of the rich countries with aid. The frequency with which a recipient country votes with the donor in the UN, and whether the recipient is an ex-colony of the donor, affects how much aid that country gets.[17] After September 11, 2001, agencies gave new aid to allies in the war on terror, such as Central Asia, Pakistan, and Turkey.

Evaluation

If a bureaucracy has a rich donor mandate vague goals for it *and* is not accountable to its intended beneficiaries, the poor, then the incentive for finding out what works is weak. Although evaluation has taken place for a long time in foreign aid, it is often self-evaluation, using reports from the same people who implemented the project. My students at NYU would not study very hard if I gave them the right to assign themselves their own grades.

The World Bank makes some attempt to achieve independence for its Operations Evaluation Department (OED), which reports directly to the board of the World Bank, not to the president. However, staff move back and forth between OED and the rest of the World Bank; a negative evaluation could hurt staffs' career prospects. The OED evaluation is subjective. Unclear methods lead to evaluation disconnects such as that delicately described in Mali:[18] "it has to be asked how the largely positive findings of the evaluations can be reconciled with the poor development outcomes observed over the same period (1985–1995) and the unfavourable views of local people (p. 26)."

Even when internal evaluation points out failure, do aid agencies hold anyone responsible or change agency practices? It is hard to find out from a review of the World Bank's evaluation Web site. The OED in 2004 indicated how eight "influential evaluations" influenced actions of the borrower in thirty-two different ways, but mentioned only two instances of affecting behavior within the World Bank itself (one of them for the worse).[19]

The anthropologist James Ferguson offers a rare detailed case study of an aid project by an independent outsider. A Canadian International Development Agency/World Bank project was to help farmers in the mountains of Lesotho (the Thaba-Tseka region) to gain access to markets and develop modern methods of livestock management and crop production. The project would lend Western expertise at livestock management and cash-crop production and would build roads to enable beneficiaries to carry their products to market.

The only problem was that the beneficiaries were not that interested in farming, since they mainly were migrants working in South Africa. They already had access to markets, where they had long since learned that cash-crop production was not competitive given the region's poor agricultural conditions. The Canadian/World Bank Thaba-Tseka project sought to improve livestock and food production. The project would improve livestock production by scientific range management, dividing the land into eight controlled grazing areas, with grazing associations to control overgrazing through resting and rotation of livestock. The project designers promised that scientific range management would eventually allow the land to support twice its current animal population, with each animal becoming 20 percent heavier. The only catch was that the project had no legal authority to restrict access to grazing, as land in Lesotho is publicly owned and livestock owners are free to graze the open range. Scientific range management didn't happen.[20]

The project promised to increase food yields by 300 percent. Instead, a pilot potato project had losses due to bad weather, disease, and mismanagement. Other cash-crop experiments fell victim to the area's "killing frosts and hail, and erratic and infrequent rainfall." The project managers complained that the local people were "defeatist" and didn't "think of themselves as farmers." Perhaps the locals didn't consider themselves farmers because they were *not* farmers—they were migrant workers in South African mines.[21]

The main accomplishment of the project was the building of roads that brought South African lorries carrying grain *into* the region (driving the few existing local farmers out of business).

Aid agency watchers should be tough on such disasters, if only with the aim of strengthening the accountability lobby in foreign aid, so we can shift power from Planners to Searchers. The way forward is politically difficult:

truly independent scientific evaluation of specific aid efforts; not overall sweeping evaluations of a whole nationwide development program, but specific and continuous evaluation of particular interventions from which agencies can learn. Only outside political pressure on aid agencies is likely to create the incentives to do these evaluations. A World Bank study of evaluation in 2000 began with the confession, "Despite the billions of dollars spent on development assistance each year, there is still very little known about the actual impact of projects on the poor."[22]

After years of pressure, the IMF created an Independent Evaluation Office in 2001. The World Bank in 2004 laudably created a Development Impact Evaluation Task Force. The task force will use the randomized controlled trial methodology discussed in chapter 2 to assess the impact of selected interventions on the intended beneficiaries. The task force has started two dozen new evaluations in five areas (conditional cash transfers in low-income countries; school-based management; contract teachers; use of information as an accountability tool for schools; and slum upgrading programs). It remains to be seen if the evaluation results change the incentives to do effective programs in the operational side of the World Bank.

Evaluation—with consequences for a bad evaluation—is one of the keys to accountability of aid. You evaluate what we bureaucrats accomplish, and you hold us responsible for it. Accountability for aid would transfer power from Planners to Searchers—maybe then somebody could figure out how to keep potholes fixed in Tanzania.

Participation Through Planning?

If one problem in foreign aid is that the poor have little power to hold anyone accountable for meeting their needs, the World Bank and the IMF to their credit now show some awareness of this problem. They seek some role for the poor's choices. They have recently put increased emphasis on "participation by the poor." It is good that there is some awareness of the feedback problem with the poor.

However, it just shows how stubborn bureaucratic incentives are that the chosen vehicle for bottom-up participation is a detailed central government plan (the PRSP, Poverty Reduction Strategy Paper, already mentioned). The multivolume PRSP Sourcebook of the World Bank suggests some pretty detailed planning—the PRSP needs to include a medium-term expenditure framework (MTEF) in which:

The sector ministries prepare medium-term strategic plans that set out the sector's key objectives, together with their associated outcomes, outputs, and expenditure forecasts (within the limits agreed upon by the Cabinet). These plans should consider the costs of both ongoing and new programs. Ideally, spending should be presented by program and spending category with financing needs for salaries, operations and maintenance, and investment clearly distinguished.[23]

Alas, even when we visualize the poor participating, we can't give up our central planning. Such planning inevitably implies giving *more* power to the Planners at the top, not less. The last thing poor countries need for greater democratic accountability is a plan that strengthens already strong authoritarian officials.

The officials who talk about "participation" and "local ownership" can't seem to let themselves shift power to the locals—the bureaucratic incentives against it are too strong. The African founder of a private school where he lives once told me about the frustration in dealing with Planners who paradoxically seek "participation." The founder had started a high-quality private school in Africa, with many scholarships for poor children. He started it with his own money, but sought to expand activities and scholarships further by getting outside donor funding. He approached one of the world's largest official aid agencies with a proposal for funding. They turned down his proposal. The founder asked them why. They wouldn't tell him, saying that he had to demonstrate "local ownership" of the project by coming up with his own ideas without regard to what they would approve or reject. He lost his temper, saying that he could waste a lot of time submitting proposals to try to figure out what they would approve, or they could just have a frank discussion of what their criteria for project approval were. Finally, the aid agency official told him that his proposed pupil-teacher ratios were too low. Their planning incentives were to show as many students as possible reached with an aid grant, and they suggested a pupil-teacher ratio of fifty to one. This contradicted the founder's objective of fostering high-quality education in Africa, and he told them to get lost.

The appeal of planning to aid visionaries is so strong that they map out top-down plans at the same time that they emphasize "local ownership" and emphatically deny that they favor top-down planning. To supplement the above example, consider the following explanation by the UN Millennium Project of how it goes about implementing the MDGs (which it describes as "open and consultative, involving all key stakeholders").[24] The head of the UN Millennium Project denied to me in person that this is a top-down plan, so I quote from it at length so you can judge for yourself:

In each of these countries, the Project and local research partners built upon international best practices to identify . . . the input targets that would be needed for the country to achieve the MDGs by 2015. These estimates cover hundreds of interventions . . . that need to be provided to meet the Goals. . . . The second stage of the planning process will be for each country to develop a long-term (10–12 year) framework for action for achieving the MDGs, building upon the results of the MDG needs assessment. . . . This MDG framework should include a policy and public sector management framework to scale up public spending and services, as well as a broadly defined financing strategy to underpin the plan. The third stage of the planning process will be for each country to construct its medium term (3–5 year) poverty reduction strategy (PRS) and, where appropriate, its Poverty Reduction Strategy Paper (PRSP) based on the long term MDG plan . . . and should be attached to a Medium Term Expenditure Framework (MTEF). . . . Fourth, both the 10-year framework and three-year PRS should include a public sector management strategy. . . . Bringing together a wide variety of inputs from expert resources, the Millennium Project secretariat has been coordinating a multi-step process to develop a methodology for country-level MDG needs assessments.

Far from promoting "participation," planning patronizes and diminishes the poor, who have little voice to say what they want and need. Unfortunately, decades of participation rhetoric have not changed the balance of power in foreign aid. At some point the donors just have to trust the recipients to be self-reliant enough to follow their own interests, to seize the opportunities created by aid. Certain kinds of aid can create opportunities for the poor and maximize payoff by letting the poor self-select, that is, show willingness to exert effort toward making the best of the opportunity.

I once got a big boost from such an aid program. The National Science Foundation (NSF) gave me a three-year fellowship to get an economics Ph.D., with tuition paid plus a stipend. Without this, I couldn't have gotten a Ph.D. The NSF did not send me missions of NSF staff to look over my shoulder as I was studying. They did not ask me to attend meetings of "stakeholders" to write a Ph.D. Promotion Strategy Paper. They had no conditions at all other than my enrolling in school and not flunking out. They allowed me the dignity of self-reliance. I could have wasted the opportunity by skipping my courses and spending all my time going to Woody Allen film festivals. But the NSF trusted the choices of the Ph.D. candidates, who the NSF thought would act in their own best interests with the opportunity given to them to get a Ph.D. The NSF could have this confidence because the applicants for the fellowships were self-selecting: only those who are willing to do the hard work of getting a Ph.D. apply.

Similarly, scholarships or matching grants for poor individuals or entrepreneurs could promote true "participation" in which the poor make their own choices. If you really want to put the poor in the driver's seat, aren't there any ways to do so directly? Could you give many more scholarships to poor students? Could you give matching grants to poor entrepreneurs who put their own money at stake to start a new business? Could you have village elections that select (or reject) aid projects? Could you give the poor "aid vouchers" that they could spend on aid agency services of their choice? None of these are easy answers, and all have pitfalls, but new thinking is needed. The final chapter explores these ideas further.

As for aid agency staff, a more effective way to listen to the poor than costing out a Big Plan would be to have aid agency specialists spend time learning about a particular sector in a particular region. In other words, have aid agency staff be sufficiently specialized to be effective Searchers. Aid bureaucracies tend to do the opposite: they reassign staff frequently across countries and across sectors, producing generalists who are much better at producing Big Plans than local solutions. They opt for universality rather than specificity, for worldwide "best practices" rather than what works in each locale. As James C. Scott points out, Planners are impatient with local peculiarities: "the lack of context and particularity is not an oversight; it is the necessary first premise of any large scale planning exercise."[25] To change practice, we must persuade the aid agencies to give up their utopian planning in favor of piecemeal intervention. This is not easy when the power and prestige of the existing aid agency managers may depend on keeping the planning approach.

Prior Lives

One characteristic of private markets is that they foster innovation: new products, new business techniques, new financial instruments, in short, new and better ways of doing things. Searchers learn not to repeat prior mistakes; Planners with no feedback keep doing the same failed plans.

In the movie *Groundhog Day,* a television reporter played by Bill Murray is condemned to endlessly repeat the day on which he must report on whether a groundhog sees its shadow. The aid agencies seem to be stuck in a similar lame cycle of repeating themselves, as table 3 shows. Bill Murray escapes his torment only when he is able to resolve his relationship with his beautiful producer, played by Andie MacDowell.

The lack of historical memory in the aid community inhibits people from learning from mistakes. Moreover, the unchanging approach to many of these desirable objectives shows again that aid agencies keep throwing in more and more resources to try to reach a predetermined, although unattainable, goal.

Table 3. Plus ça Change, Plus c'est la Même Chose

Aid idea	Stone Age	Iron Age	Silicon Age
Donor coordination	"a cooperative enterprise in which all nations work together through the United Nations and its specialized agencies" (Truman, 1949)	"Aid coordination . . . has been recognized as increasingly important . . ." (World Bank, 1981)	"[The donors need] to ensure better coordination and stronger partnership in . . . development cooperation." (World Bank, 2001)
Increasing aid volume	"an increase in the per capita national incomes cannot be brought about without . . . a sum of money . . . of about $3 billion a year" (UN Expert Group, 1951)	"the current flow of ODA . . . is only half the modest target prescribed by the internationally accepted United Nations Strategy" (World Bank President Robert McNamara, 1973)	"If we are serious about . . . meeting multilateral development goals we have all signed on to, we must double ODA from its current level of about $50 billion a year." (World Bank President James Wolfensohn, 2001)
Selectivity about whom you give aid	"objective No. 1: To apply stricter standards of selectivity . . . in aiding developing countries" (President John F. Kennedy, 1963)	"the relief of poverty depends both on aid and on the policies of the recipient countries" (Development Committee Task Force, 1985)	"[the World Bank] should increase its selectivity . . . by directing more assistance to borrowers with sound policy environments" (World Bank, 2001)
Increase in poverty emphasis	"far greater emphasis on policies and projects which will begin to attack the problems of absolute poverty" (McNamara, 1973)	"an even stronger emphasis on poverty reduction in [the World Bank]'s programs" (World Bank, 1990)	"increasing the focus . . . on the overarching objective of poverty reduction" (World Bank, 2001)
Country ownership	Development policy is "the responsibility of the recipient alone" (Partners in Development, 1969)	"novel approaches to community involvement in service provision" (World Bank, 1981)	"greater national ownership of development programs" (World Bank, 2001)
Debt relief	"the debt-servicing problem, already severe in the early 1960s, has [become] increasingly difficult" (World Bank, 1970)	"more concessional reschedulings for the poorest debtor countries" (G7 Summit, 1990)	"further national and international measures . . . including, as appropriate, debt cancellation" (Monterrey Consensus, UN, 2002)

Differences Among Aid Bureaucracies

I took most of my examples of aid agency bureaucracy from the World Bank because of my personal familiarity with its operations. However, there are differences between the international organizations, which give some insight into when aid succeeds and fails. The International Monetary Fund is somewhat more successful in achieving its narrow goals, although there have been failures (see next chapter). The World Bank is more prone to meaningless frameworks and goal proliferation, but it is actually among the better aid agencies, as some of the positive examples I have given illustrate.

There are also differences between national aid agencies. USAID brazenly states its objective is to further "the foreign policy goals of the United States."[26] The United Kingdom's aid agency, the Department for International Development (DFID), says its objective is helping the world's poor and it is more committed to independent evaluation of its projects than most other aid agencies.

Going to the other extreme, I have just read some UN documents on what they label "The Open-Ended Ad-Hoc Working Group on Integrated and Coordinated Implementation of and Follow-up to the Outcomes of the Major United Nations Conferences and Summits in the Economic and Social Fields." This open-ended ad hoc working group faces some challenges, as it coordinates the follow-up to nine reports on country-level coordination, four reports on the PRSPs, eleven reports on the Bretton Woods Institutions (aka the World Bank and IMF), eleven reports on the MDGs, the annual reports of the Administrative Council on Coordination, reports from the five regional commissions of the UN, reports from five other specialized UN agencies, and the follow-up to eighteen UN world conferences.[27] The working group labels the background papers for its efforts "non-papers." (I am not making this up; see http://www.un.org/esa/coordination/ecosoc/paper says that the work of the open-ended ad hoc working group

> should be consistent with the provisions of resolution 50/227 and the follow-up mechanisms decided upon by the respective United Nations conferences and summits and should respect the interlinked nature of their outcomes as well as the thematic unity of each conference. . . . [C]ross-sectoral thematic issues for further consideration throughout the existing structure should be decided upon at the intergovernmental level and should focus on implementation, bearing in mind that the process of integrated and coordinated follow-up to the outcomes of the United Nations conferences and summits in the economic, social and related fields should be fair and balanced and should respect the principle of multilateralism and the principles contained in the Charter of the United Nations.

To be fair, there is incomprehensible language also in private-sector documents, such as investment prospectuses or engineering designs. The difference is that in private-sector documents, the jargon actually has some meaning to specialists. In UN documents, the jargon has no substantive content for anyone.

To help "focus the work of the UN," non-paper one sets out twelve "cross-cutting themes" previously set out by the Economic and Social Council (for example, theme twelve is "participation, democracy, human rights, accountability and partnership with major groups and non-governmental organizations"). Non-paper one then goes on to list eleven "areas calling for greater attention" identified by the secretary general (e.g., "greater coherence in United Nations action in support of Africa's development"). Finally, the non-paper wraps up with ten new "cross-cutting themes" that emerged from recent UN conferences, many with multiple sub-themes. Non-paper three lists all the UN non-conferences on which it is based.

Just as other aid agencies like to produce observable output, the UN holds big world summits. UN officials are travel weary from attending all these utopian summits: Environment and Development (three summits), World Food Summit (two), World Summit for Children (two), World Assembly on Ageing (two), World Conference Against Racism, International Conference on Financing for Development, UN General Assembly Special Session on AIDS, UN Conference on Human Settlements (three), UN Conference on the Least Developed Countries (three), Millennium Summit, World Summit for Social Development (two), World Conference on Women (five), Global Conference on Sustainable Development of Small Island Developing States (two), International Conference on Population and Development (two), and the World Conference on Human Rights. Officials who participate in these summits mean well, but the reason these summits are repeated so often is that previous summits haven't accomplished their goals.

Another sign of the ineffectiveness of the UN is its dubious economic analysis, in contrast with the higher-quality analysis cited above at the IMF and the World Bank. To take one of the worst examples, the analysis by the UN Commission on Trade and Development (UNCTAD) of the predicament of the least-developed countries (LDCs) is the Rube Goldberg diagram in figure 23. Poor countries may not be in a poverty trap, but UNCTAD itself seems to be trapped in some kind of intellectual maze, with arrows flying in all directions.

What makes the UN worse than other aid bureaucracies? Conditions for bureaucratic behavior are even more unfavorable for the UN because an unwieldy General Assembly with "one nation, one vote" runs it. Answerable equally to 191 member states (many of whom are undemocratic), the UN has an especially severe problem of multiple principals and collective responsibility. The multiple principals have political goals such as making sure the UN employs a sufficient number of staff from their country. Perhaps because of this constraint, the UN has been less successful than the World Bank and IMF in attracting high-quality professionals. The voting power of the large group of undemocratic states makes the UN susceptible to coalitions of tyrants. Since the UN does not actually represent anyone in particular, nobody is paying much attention to what it does. (I may have been the

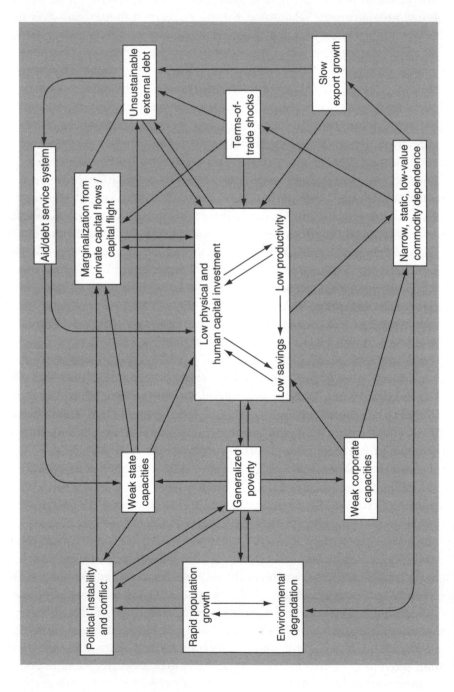

Fig. 23. UNCTAD Explains Poverty

first person to have voluntarily read some of the documents I have just quoted.) Except for a few high-profile things that the rich countries want the UN to do, the UN is operating in the attic.

Making Progress

This chapter discusses why we aid bureaucrats who are often unable to supply what the poor so desperately need. The analysis points the way to some improvements. Again, extreme humility is in order because of all the efforts to reform aid in the past. My suggestions for improvement are no doubt flawed, but they may be less flawed than those of the status quo. I aim these remarks at the Searchers out there on the ground, as well as the reformers who seek to shift power away from Planners and toward Searchers.

A big part of the problem probably originates with the rich-country governments who set the mandates of the aid agencies. Dear rich-country funders, please give up your utopian fantasies of transforming the Rest. Don't reward aid agencies for setting goals that are as impossible as they are politically appealing. Please just ask aid agencies to focus on narrow, solvable problems. For example, let them focus on the health, education, electrification, water problems, and piecemeal policy reforms to promote the private sector—where they have already had some success—and fix some remaining problems such as the refusal of donors to finance operations and maintenance.

Collective responsibility for Millennium Development Goals or any other goals does not work. Hold aid agencies individually responsible for what their own programs achieve, not for global goals. Letting different agencies specialize in different areas would also lessen the coordination problem.

To facilitate both specialization and effectiveness, consider ways that aid agencies (including NGOs) could compete to supply development services, so that those who were best at doing a particular something in a particular country would "win the contract" to do that something. Those who failed to deliver something reliably and effectively would lose the contract, and could concentrate on something that they were better at doing.

How to tell who is doing a good job? Aid agencies need independent evaluation of the effects on the poor of their programs to motivate them to find the things that work. What aid agencies do today is mostly self-evaluation. Even the commendable steps toward independent evaluation taken by the World Bank and IMF still keep the evaluation unit within the organization. Sixty years after the founding of the World Bank and IMF, independent evaluation is long overdue. How about if aid agencies and international organizations put some of their budgets into an escrow account, which would fund independent evaluators (themselves chosen by actors who had no stake in the evaluation outcome) to look at a random sample of their projects and programs?

Academic researchers could play more of a fruitful role even in the absence of official independent evaluation. Academics could do public service by applying their techniques to evaluate the projects, programs, and approaches taken by aid agencies. They do this already in publications in academic journals, in aid agencies' own research departments, and in consulting assignments for aid agencies. However, none of these outlets is adequate to the task at the moment. What gets published in academic journals is selected on very good scientific criteria, but journals tend to undervalue research that is unoriginal but relevant to evaluating aid agencies.

Aid agency research departments and consultants have incentives not to deviate too far from the party line of aid Planners, even though they manage to produce some good research anyway. More independence for aid agency researchers would help. One idea would be for all aid agencies to contribute to a research fund, which would set up an independent research outfit to study aid and development policy.

Businessmen are also a great untapped resource for aid watching. One can imagine schemes for giving private business a stake in aid outcomes, so that they formed part of the army of watchers for good results. Think of what could happen if an army of independent aid watchers, including those from inside the country receiving the aid, were keeping tabs on the aid agencies.

Please understand that the foreign aid problem is inherently difficult because of the complexity of development, the weak power of the poor, and the difficulty of getting feedback from beneficiaries and of learning from failure. Throw into the trash can all the comprehensive frameworks, central plans, and worldwide goals. Just respond to each local situation according to what people in that situation need and want.

The sad part is the poor have had so little power to hold agencies accountable that the aid agencies have not had enough incentive to find out what works and what the poor actually want. The most important suggestion is to *search* for small improvements, then brutally scrutinize and test whether the poor got what they wanted and were better off, and then repeat the process.

It hasn't worked to tell the poor what to do. Just screen aid recipients to select those likely to act in their own interest, give them incentives and opportunities to better their lives, and then trust in their self-reliance, with no further strings attached. Programs like this are already working. The Food for Education program in Bangladesh lets poor families choose whether to keep their daughters in school, making this choice more possible by offering the families food and money to do so. The Progresa program in Mexico (domestically conceived and operated) similarly creates opportunities for the poor by giving cash payments to parents who keep children in school, and gets nutritional supplements to the children.

There should be much further exploration of mechanisms that give control of aid resources directly to the poor and let them choose what they most want and need. Participation should mean more buying and voting power in the hands of the poor in aid, not strategies or frameworks. This is not easy, but I suspect this is the future of foreign aid.

The aid agencies need tough love from the critics—who must not abolish them but must pressure them so that aid reaches the poor. This may in itself seem utopian—haven't we already tried for fifty years to make aid work?

But progress happens in public policy. The good news about the noisy anti-globalization protesters, the hardworking NGOs, the rock bands and the movie stars, and the rich-country governments' increased interest in the Rest coming after 9/11 is that the constituency for the poor is growing. It's time for the rich-country public to insist that aid money actually reach the poor. Isn't it past time that donors got held accountable for actually fixing the impassable roads that keep Tanzanians from saving the lives of sick children and pregnant women?

Private Firms Help the Poor in India

Diarrhea is another deadly disease often overlooked by foreign well-wishers for the poor. A baby suffering from diarrhea and the dehydration it induces suffers from rapid heartbeat, sunken eye sockets, indentations in the skull, and reduced nutrient supply to tissues and vital organs. If the baby survives, the diarrhea contributes to her malnutrition—the child will be stunted and abnormally thin. Commonly, a baby suffering from diarrhea-induced dehydration goes into shock and dies. Preparing food with unwashed hands spreads the bacteria and viruses that cause diarrhea.

In 2005, C. K. Prahalad, a University of Michigan Business School professor, wrote a fascinating book, *The Fortune at the Bottom of the Pyramid: Eradicating Poverty Through Profits*. He shows how private firms can sometimes find it in their own interest to help solve some of the problems of the poor that are traditionally addressed by aid agencies. The Searchers in a free market do much better than aid agencies in solving specific problems of the poor, although having a profit incentive to do so is not the typical case. Still, Prahalad's book is a good reminder of what we know from free markets—self-interested behavior can do good things for others.

Prahalad gives the example of Hindustan Lever Limited (HLL), a subsidiary of the giant multinational Unilever. HLL sold a very simple product, soap, which it realized could find a larger market if it was tied to preventing diarrheal diseases of the poor. Hand washing with soap is critical to preventing the spread of the viruses and bacteria that cause diarrhea. HLL realized that if it could promote increased awareness among the poor of the benefits of antibacterial soap, a product with which HLL dominated the Indian market, it could significantly increase sales.

Getting people to use soap is not as easy as it sounds. Poor people are not well informed about the science of disease transmission. Most poor people wash their hands only if they are visibly dirty, not when their hands are covered with invisible germs after using the latrine or changing a baby's diaper. Invisible germs on hands are the main transmission mechanism for diarrhea. HLL had to change behavior. To realize this market potential, HLL also had to find ways of gaining the poor's trust in its health-promoting product. Working with the government, aid agencies, and NGOs, it started educational programs, including a program called Lifebuoy Swasthya Chetna, (Lifebuoy Glowing Health), which sent out two-person teams to show schoolchildren how they could avoid stomach, eye, and wound infections by washing with Lifebuoy soap. The teams enlisted the village doctors to speak to the children's parents about how hand washing with soap could prevent diarrhea and other health complications. Lifebuoy Swasthya Chetna formed health clubs in the village.

Sales of HLL's antibiotic soap did indeed increase, and on its way to profits it also succeeded in persuading villagers to use a product that protected them against disease.

CHAPTER SIX

Bailing Out the Poor

The secret isn't counting the beans; it's growing more beans.

Roberto Goizueta (1931–1997)

I am walking through one of the many slums in Addis Ababa. I pass residences made of mud walls and thatched roofs, some with holes in the roofs and walls, set off against more prosperous residences made from concrete blocks. Some residences feature neat flower gardens in front, as if defying demeaning poverty stereotypes that would rule out such touches. A smiling grandmother invites me into her modest dwelling of sticks and mud, offering coffee to the surprise guest, to the delight of a crowd of curious children. Poverty is here, as children in rags are playing in the red dirt beside a stream containing raw sewage. These slum dwellers are not among the 12 percent of Ethiopians with access to healthy sanitation facilities.[1] The children seem unusually thin and short for their age, as is to be expected in a country in which about half of all children are malnourished.[2] Food production in Ethiopia suffers from soil erosion and periodic drought. Some of the children could be AIDS orphans, as the AIDS crisis in Ethiopia is severe. Only 14 percent of children are immunized against childhood diseases, which no doubt has something to do with why 17 percent of them don't live to see their fifth birthday.[3]

Across town, the minister of finance and economic development of Ethiopia, Sufian Ahmed, is meeting with six men (and one female secretary) from the IMF to plan the future of Ethiopia's economy. They discuss the government's revenue and spending. The meeting is part of the IMF's "Fifth Review Under the Three Year Arrangement with the Poverty Reduction and Growth Facility." The economy is recovering from a major drought. Tax revenue has been lower than expected, as have external loans. To stay within the limits agreed with the IMF, Ahmed has cut government spending. The IMF staff approve of the spending cuts, although they urge Ahmed to protect "poverty-targeted expenditure." (It is unclear how they decided what was "poverty-targeted," since almost *any* spending that brings *any* results would lower poverty in such a poor society.) In reaction to the drought, the government is developing a "food security program." The IMF staff suggests that the government be careful that food security spending doesn't endanger "macroeconomic stability,"[4] although the report encouragingly indicates that otherwise "the staff welcomes the food security program."

The IMF specifies mandatory targets for Ethiopia for international foreign exchange reserves, for the net domestic credit of the central bank, for domestic financing of the government deficit, for government arrears on paying its bills, and for government external borrowing. Other agreements of Ahmed with the IMF include reforming the tax system (including computerization of the taxpayer identification number and introduction of the value-added tax); limiting defense spending; limiting the government wage bill; consolidating regional and federal budgets and extrabudgetary accounts; reconciling fiscal and monetary account statistics; letting the market determine the exchange rate; provisioning by commercial banks for overdue loan repayments; privatizing the Commercial and Business Bank (CBB); restructuring the Development Bank of Ethiopia (DBE); restructuring the National Bank of Ethiopia (NBE); increasing the autonomy of the NBE; reforming the Commercial Bank of Ethiopia (CBE) based on an audit by the international firm KPMG and a detailed plan agreed upon with the IMF that specifies numerical performance targets, limits any delinquent loan from CBE to two renewals, and transfers co-financed loans from the CBE to the DBE; liberalizing trade as a preliminary step in the Integrated Framework for Trade Development in the least-developed countries; rewriting the investment code to limit the role of government to electricity transmission, the postal service, and the national airline; tracking debt-relief resources so that they are used for poverty reduction; and improving the compilation of statistics on the balance of payments, monetary indicators, international reserves, and agricultural and industrial production. The government should do all this while consulting with the poor, civil society, nongovernmental organizations, private individuals, and the foreign donors on what it should do to reduce poverty, in the context of the Annual Progress Report (APR) on the PRSP. From January 2001 to November 2003, the minister of finance has benefited from twenty-one separate background papers prepared by the IMF to give him technical advice, on topics ranging from income tax legislation to the interbank foreign exchange market.

Has the International Monetary Fund been an effective agency to serve the poor in far-flung corners of the globe? The IMF is an interesting case study for testing the following hypotheses: (1) agencies work better with few goals rather than many goals; (2) unaccountable agencies are worse than accountable agencies; (3) top-down Planners suffer from information shortages about reality on the ground. And, indeed, as we will see, the IMF's effectiveness has benefited from its having fewer goals than other agencies of Western assistance (1), but its effectiveness has suffered a lot from lack of accountability (2) and from the lousy information available to top-down Planners (3).

The West first set up the IMF to prevent large trade imbalances and unstable currencies in the West. In this initial phase of the IMF's work, it was very successful. It then shifted toward bailing out countries in the rest of the world. On balance, the IMF has done useful short-term bailouts of poor countries experiencing financial crises, but it has done worse at promoting long-term development. Moreover, things have gotten worse over the past two decades, as the IMF's mission statement has grown more and more bloated, its conditions more and more numerous, and its interventions more and more intrusive. The IMF has no mechanism that holds it accountable to the poor for acting in their long-term interest or improving their welfare. It places excessive confidence in very shaky statistics on the countries' problems it seeks to correct. Although it has accomplished many good things, its performance today resembles more and more the coercive Planners' dreams of the White Man's Burden.

The World's Most Powerful Creditor

The International Monetary Fund, headquartered in Washington, D.C., is the West's most powerful agency for dealing with many poor countries. The IMF supervises poor-country finances. When the governments of poor countries can't pay their import bills or service their debts to Western creditors, the IMF arrives to straighten things out. The Fund arranges a new schedule of debt repayments that the country can manage. It lends the government short-term money (to be repaid within two to four years) to tide it over its cash squeeze.[5] The Fund also negotiates with the government a series of spending cuts or tax increases to enable the government to make the necessary repayments (including of its own loans).

The IMF has a lot of money. It has $157 billion in resources available to lend, of which $96 billion was actually out on loan in August 2004.[6] It gets its money from subscriptions by all of its members (most countries of the world) and then keeps the money rotating among borrowers.

The IMF's description of its function stresses the benefits of its activities to poor countries: "A main function of the IMF is to provide loans to countries experiencing balance-of-payments problems so that they can restore conditions for sustainable economic growth. The financial assistance provided by the IMF enables countries to rebuild their international reserves, stabilize their currencies, and continue paying for imports."[7]

Part of the IMF's role is to enforce "financial discipline," i.e., get countries to pay their bills and repay their creditors. Credit enforcers are always unpopular, but they do play a valuable role. If borrowers could default on their loans without fear of consequences, lenders would not make loans. Loans can finance productive investment that borrowers can't finance on their own. Loans can tide countries over bad times; countries can repay loans during good times. In the private market, collection agencies' combination of threats and negotiation facilitates borrowers' access to the benefits of future loans. The IMF client maintains its access to future Western loans by following IMF dictates, meanwhile getting an IMF loan to ease the pain (or more accurately, to postpone the pain to when it can repay the loan). Critics unfairly vilify the IMF because of the stereotype of the evil creditor squeezing the last drop of blood from the debtor. The international system including the IMF helped make a large market in lending to poor countries possible. The IMF *is* preferable to the earlier Western method for collecting debts—sending in gunboats to seize the poor country's customs revenues, or even invading the country to take over the government.

As for IMF conditions on its loans, you could understand them as a way to ensure that the loan is repaid. If your ne'er-do-well cousin asks for a loan, you may decide to give it only on condition that he change his behavior in a way that makes it likely that he will pay back the loan—that he stop drinking, that he get a job, etc.

The IMF has had some notable successes. It helped South Korea and Thailand with financial squeezes in the 1980s, after which they had rapid growth. The IMF bailout of Mexico in 1994–1995, although much criticized at the time, worked well. The Mexican government repaid the loans in advance, and economic growth resumed. Most recently, the IMF handled the 1997–1998 East Asian financial crisis with some success, especially, again, in South Korea.

The IMF recruits talented Ph.D.'s in economics, who observe strong norms of professional analysis. It has an outstanding research department, as well as other specialized departments that provide valuable technical advice to poor countries on their fiscal and financial systems. The IMF has been a good source of economic advice to countries on the wisdom of government solvency and the folly of excessive government debt and deficits.

(One backward country is currently not heeding this advice, the one whose capital is the same city in which the IMF is located.)

But the IMF's more ambitious attempts to reform poor economies have had more mixed success. Even the core function of enforcing financial discipline is flawed by an intrusive Planner's mentality that sets arbitrary numerical targets for key indicators of government behavior. Like all Planners, the IMF fits the complex reality of economic systems into a Procrustean bed of numerical targets that have little to do with that complexity. The conditions on its loans often roil internal politics in a way that is much too intrusive. And in the end, it is not even clear that the conditions contribute to repayment of the loans.

The IMF does not force country governments to enter its agreements; they do so willingly. If IMF agreements are sometimes counterproductive, why do governments enter into such agreements? Usually it is because the government is myopic—a financial crisis makes it desperate for a loan right away, no matter what the long-term consequences. The IMF is often the only way to get such a loan.

So Many Pesos, So Few Dollars

The standard IMF loan is a "standby arrangement." The IMF loan is conditional upon the government's getting its finances in order so it can pay the loan back quickly.

The IMF's approach is simple. A poor country runs out of money when its central bank runs out of dollars. The central bank needs an adequate supply of dollars for two reasons. First, so that residents of the poor country who want to buy foreign goods can change their domestic money (let's call it pesos) into dollars. Second, so those poor-country residents, firms, or governments who owe money to foreigners can change their pesos into dollars with which to make debt repayments to their foreign creditors.

What makes the central bank run out of dollars? The central bank not only holds the nation's official supply of dollars (foreign exchange reserves), it also makes loans to the government and supplies the domestic currency for the nation's economy. In accounting lingo, the central bank has two assets, foreign exchange reserves and credit to the government, and one liability, domestic currency.

In many poor nations, the government's main source of finance for any excess of spending over tax revenues is credit from the central bank (the other main source is foreign borrowing; more on that later). The central bank extends credit to the government and prints up a corresponding amount of currency to hand over to the government as the proceeds of the loan. The government spends the currency, and the pesos pass into the hands of people throughout the economy.

But are people willing to hold the currency? The printing of more currency drives down the value of currency if people spend it on the existing amount of goods—too much currency chasing too few goods. People don't hold pesos whose value is falling—this is like a savings account with a negative interest rate. So they take the pesos back to the central bank to exchange them for dollars. Since they are unwilling to hold more pesos, they exchange pesos for dollars until the amount of pesos they hold is the same as it was before. At the end, the central bank holds more credit to the government and fewer dollar reserves, with the same amount of pesos outstanding. The effect of printing more currency that people don't want is to run down the central bank's dollar holdings.

This was the insight of early IMF official Jacques Polak, the father of IMF financial programming. The central bank's holdings of dollars runs low because the central bank prints too many pesos, which people then want to exchange at the central bank for its dollars.[8]

There will often be a panic element to buying dollars from the central bank in this situation. People's willingness to hold pesos is the key variable. When the public begins to suspect that the central bank is printing too much money for its existing holdings of dollars, it will rush to buy up its dollars before the supply runs out. Too few dollars for the outstanding stock of pesos is kind of like the *Titanic* with too few lifeboats. People will rush for the lifeboats (i.e., rush to buy dollars), and the stock of dollar reserves at the central bank will fall. People wanting to buy dollars for imports or to service foreign debts will then be out of luck. The country then calls on the IMF.

Excessive money printing also affects another important goal of IMF programs—controlling inflation. Too much money chasing too few goods will drive up the prices of those goods, causing inflation. Again, the key is how much money people are willing to hold relative to buying goods. If their desire to keep money in their wallet increases, that money won't be out on the town chasing goods.

The last insight of IMF financial programming is that excessive government deficits cause excessive printing of money. The government finances its deficit by borrowing from the central bank, which finances the loan by printing money. So the standard IMF prescription to build up reserves again is to force a contraction of central bank credit to the government, which requires a reduction in the government's budget deficit.

This all sounds very technical and neutral, but the IMF then gets involved in how the government is spending the money (i.e., which items to cut). It often forces the government to do unpopular things, such as cut subsidies for bread or cooking oil. People in the country receiving the IMF loan often blame the IMF when the government does those things, and they take to the streets to protest IMF-enforced austerity. One big trouble sign in IMF stabilization plans is their disturbance of domestic politics.

IMF Riots

Quito is a favorite destination of IMF staff, who gave Ecuador sixteen standby loans over 1960–2000. In the year 2000, the latest IMF loan's austerity measures induced reductions in teacher salaries and increases in fuel and electricity prices.

On January 22, 2000, three thousand protesters from Ecuador's indigenous groups occupied Congress, while more than ten thousand demonstrated outside. The government of democratically elected president Jamil Mahaud confronted them with more than thirty-five thousand soldiers and police. The leaders of the armed forces saw the handwriting on the wall, however, and deposed Mahaud on January 23, 2000, in favor of his vice-president, Gustavo Noboa. Noboa insisted he would continue with the IMF reforms.

In May 2000, teachers in Ecuador went on strike for five weeks to protest salary reductions. The government dispersed a demonstration of teachers in the capital with tear gas and riot police. On June 15, 2000, protest groups organized a general strike, which included teachers (again), government employees, doctors, oil workers, and unions. There was another tear gas confrontation between riot police and protesters in Quito. The army sent a unit under Colonel Lucio Gutiérrez to break up the protests. Colonel Gutiérrez instead sided with the indigenous protesters and attempted an unsuccessful coup. The army put down the coup and fired Gutiérrez.

Noboa temporarily managed to survive the protests, and the country wound up complying with the IMF conditions. The protesters got revenge at the next election, in November 2002, when the voters elected as president former coup leader and populist hero Lucio Gutiérrez.

By February 2004, the indigenous groups began protesting against Lucio Gutiérrez for once again cozying up to the IMF. On April 20, 2005, Gutiérrez, like his many predecessors, fled the presidential palace for good.[9]

Ecuador was not alone in protesting against the IMF. In the first nine months of 2000 alone, there were demonstrations against IMF programs in

Argentina, Bolivia, Brazil, Colombia, Costa Rica, Honduras, Kenya, Malawi, Nigeria, and Zambia.[10] We cannot always conclude that the protesters are representative of the majority, but at the very least, it is a sign of the impact of the IMF on domestic politics.

We still haven't exhausted the roll call of IMF involvement in domestic politics. There is an association between IMF involvement and the most extreme political event: total state collapse. Of course, prior to disappearing into the parallel universe of social collapse these governments were already very sick at the time they were getting IMF loans. It is unclear how much blame the IMF bears for subsequent collapse in these unfortunate countries, but financial indiscipline was the least of their problems. Liberia spent 77 percent of the period 1963–1985 in an IMF program, before finally collapsing into anarchy after 1985. Somalia spent 78 percent of the decade 1980–1989 in an IMF program, after which the warlords tore the country apart.

Table 4 shows that of all eight cases worldwide of state failure or collapse, seven of them had a high share of time under IMF programs in the ten years preceding their collapse. Statistically, spending a lot of time under an IMF program is associated with a higher risk of state collapse.

The IMF should have been more careful imposing its comprehensive reforms on such fragile political systems. At best, the IMF doing a program in these countries was like recommending heart-healthy calisthenics every morning for patients with broken limbs. The IMF feels its mandate requires it to help any and all countries in financial difficulty. However, the Planners' mentality in which the IMF applies the same type of program to all countries is ill matched to such ill societies. In retrospect, it would have been better if the IMF were not involved at all in these cases.

Table 4. All Eight Cases of State Failure Worldwide as of 1990s and Prior IMF Programs

Country	Approximate year of onset of state failure	Time under IMF programs in preceding 10 years (%)
Afghanistan	1977	46
Angola	1981	0
Burundi	1995	62
Liberia	1986	70
Sierra Leone	1990	59
Somalia	1991	74
Sudan	1986	58
Zaire	1991	73
Average		55
Average for all developing countries 1970–90		20

Source for State Failure: Richard Rotberg, 2002

Sierra Leone had a horrific civil war after its state collapse in 1990, following years of heavy IMF involvement. Deranged rebels cut off thousands of civilians' hands to spread random terror. During a pause in the civil war, the IMF entered again to grant loans to Sierra Leone, which spent 83 percent of the period 1994–1998 under an IMF program. Civil war broke out again in 1998, not to be ended until the intervention of UN peacekeeping forces, including British troops, in 2001. The IMF quickly reentered, granting a new loan. Isn't there any society with an illness so advanced that the IMF will decline to prescribe its irrelevant medicine?

Here are some highlights of the IMF program begun in 2001:

- The quantitative performance criterion for end-September 2001 relating to net domestic bank credit to the government was slightly exceeded, reflecting the difficulties we faced in limiting recourse to domestic financing in the context of substantial technical delays in the disbursement of budgetary assistance. ... The structural benchmark relating to the passage of the bill to grant autonomy to the Central Statistical Office by end-September 2001 was, however, missed due to the heavy legislative schedule.

- Progress has also been made in implementing structural reforms and capacity building, although there were significant delays in implementing some key structural reform measures. In the area of economic management, work has continued in developing the medium-term expenditure framework (MTEF).

The Economist Intelligence Unit summed up the Sierra Leone situation as of 2004:

- The rank-and-file [former rebels], particularly in rural areas, remain largely unemployed ... the government still cannot project fully its authority in the diamond mining areas in the east of the country.

- A couple million people internally or externally displaced out of 5 million are coming back to their old homes; meanwhile, traumatized amputees are getting less in benefits than the soldiers who committed the atrocities.

- Indigenous institutions remain weak and, despite the outward appearance of peace and stability following the ending of the war, peace is being maintained by a large, albeit diminishing, contingent of UN peacekeeping troops. With most of the UN peacekeeping force due to be withdrawn by mid-2005 [recently postponed until end of 2005], it is not clear if the president will be able to hold the country together.

IMF management, please phone home for a reality check. There may be some places that you can help, but Sierra Leone is not one of them.

Untidy Numbers

Although we can certainly blame the IMF for messing with fragile countries when it shouldn't, not all criticisms of the IMF are fair. People often blame the Fund for scarce government resources. Governments in poor countries have scarce resources because they are poor, not because of the IMF. Governments cannot live beyond their means on central bank credit, depleting a limited stock of international reserves.

What combination of government spending, budget deficit, and central bank credit makes the books balance? The answer is more imprecise than the IMF acknowledges. The IMF financial programming model is the monetary Planners' equivalent of the Big Push model of the aid Planners. If the numbers are so unreliable, then it is not clear that the IMF conditions are actually increasing the likelihood of its loans being repaid.

Like doctors, the IMF officials cultivate the art of issuing confident pronouncements on the diagnosis and the cure of financial ills. They patiently explain that it's just arithmetic, little more than two plus two. Central bank credit to the government must be no more than the demand to hold currency minus the level of necessary dollar reserves (valued in domestic currency at the current exchange rate). For the banking system as a whole, the expansion of credit (including credit to the government) must not exceed the public's demand to hold currency and bank deposits minus the banking system's foreign exchange reserves. If credit is too high, the system will lose foreign exchange reserves as people turn in unwanted money at the central bank for dollars.

There are two problems here: (1) inadequate knowledge of what is really happening on the ground, and (2) complexities that are not captured by the financial programming model.

Planners everywhere like to manage by the numbers. The planning arithmetic is not as straightforward as it appears. Accurate information on all of the items in the central bank balance sheet are as hard to come by in many poor countries as an honest customs collector.

I can remember visiting the central bank of The Gambia in one of my first trips for the World Bank. The figures for currency outstanding, central bank credit, and international reserves were in a ledger book, which I saw with my own eyes. The figures were in pencil. The figures showed signs of having been erased and recalculated several times. The sum at the bottom was not equal to the sum of the entries in the column. My faith in central bank accounting suffered.

The IMF's standard training manual on financial programming gives the example of Turkey's central bank accounts. A mysterious item pops up, called "other items, net," which balances central bank assets (foreign exchange reserves plus domestic credit to the government) with central bank liabilities (currency and deposits by banks). Nobody knows what an "other items, net" is or where it will wake up tomorrow morning. The change in "other items, net" was one fourth of the change in domestic credit from one year to the next in the Turkey example from the IMF training manual.[11] This figure is about average for all of the data on central bank accounts in all countries over the last four decades.

The IMF's own numbers are not internally consistent. The IMF reports data in two ways: in its statistical publication, International Financial Statistics (IFS), and in the country reports that IMF staff prepare when they are designing a program for a country. The two sets of numbers measure the same concepts, such as the key variable net international reserves (local currency equivalent). Yet the numbers are often at odds.

I randomly assembled a sample of the most recent country reports that reflected active IMF programs, as shown on the IMF Web site in February 2004, and compared their data with that available in IFS at the same time. Table 5 shows very distinct estimates in some countries for net international reserves in the monetary survey.

All these monetary uncertainties mean that the IMF staff set program targets for central bank credit, foreign exchange reserves, and money supply based on shaky numbers. The money supply number is very important because it determines how much credit expansion is safe without losing dollar reserves or increasing inflation.

Table 5. Estimates of Local Currency Equivalent Net International Reserves in December 2002 in Monetary Survey by IMF International Financial Statistics (IFS) and IMF Country Desk

Country	Date of report	IFS	Country desk	Percentage difference
Bulgaria	Feb. 2004	9,881	9,892	−0.1
Burundi	Feb. 2004	18,405	21,100	−12.8
Gabon	Feb. 2004	1.9	36.1	−94.8
Lesotho	Jan. 2004	3,770	3,201	17.8
Mali	Jan. 2004	324	285	13.7
Turkey	Oct. 2003	−6.6	−6.5	1.6
Uruguay	Aug. 2003	20,831	−31,044	−167.1

GDP growth plays a big role in projecting how much money demand or other important variables will grow. In March 2003, IMF staff put Mali's GDP growth in 2001 at 1.5 percent. By August 2003, it had raised the 2001 number to 3.5 percent. Just five months later, in January 2004, IMF staff now put Malian growth in 2001 as 13.3 percent! This is not to say the IMF is incompetent at statistics; it is just that any statistics are very shaky in very poor countries.

Things get worse on the arithmetic that says the government budget deficit must equal its sources of financing. Government spending minus revenue yields one estimate of the budget deficit. Adding up all the sources of financing the deficit (central bank credit, foreign borrowing, etc.) yields another. The numbers do not agree. IMF programs will include an "adjustment" to reconcile the two. In the official statistics from the IMF's Government Finance Statistics, the "adjustment" is equal to 55 percent of domestic credit on average.[12] So we are not sure exactly how much the government deficit or domestic credit is now, and thus are not sure how much the government has to cut it.

Just as the IMF should not be blamed for all budgetary austerity, an IMF program also is not *necessary* for the budget to be balanced. If the IMF were not there, the government would still be constrained by its available revenues and whatever loans people were willing to give it. If it was an irresponsible spender, private lenders would not lend to it. The government could print money, but the revenues from doing so would be limited and come at the price of a high inflation rate, which is usually unpopular. The government on its own doesn't have the same dependence on shaky statistics that the IMF does because it will be constrained by real resources, even if it doesn't know how much it has. You may not know the balance in your checking account due to sloppy bookkeeping, but if you spend too much, your checks will bounce. Is the IMF's shaky accounting an improvement on what the government would do without the IMF?

Unstable Behavior

The second problem is that planning the macroeconomic program depends not just on accounting but also on the behavior of people inside and outside the economy. Remember, for example, that the effect of expanding central bank credit to the government and printing money would cause people to turn the extra money in to the central bank for dollars, depleting international reserves. But what if people decided they wanted to hold more currency, for whatever reason? The IMF estimates the desire to hold currency by assuming that the ratio of currency to gross domestic product will remain stable. Unfortunately, after examining data on all IMF borrowers for all available years, I found the historical path of this ratio to be more like that of a drunken unicyclist.

A supply of money greater than the demand to hold that money could also drive up prices. Again, it is uncertain how the actual supply of money compares with what people willingly hold. This may be why the IMF has had difficulty predicting inflation under its programs of financial discipline and restructuring. Post-program inflation under the IMF was higher than the program targets on average in the 1990s for a worldwide sample of countries.[13]

Conversely, what if people holding domestic currency suddenly panicked and wanted to turn it in for the central bank's dollars? It's not always clear why they panic, but it happens. International reserves would drop precipitously for reasons unrelated to government budget deficits. Many economists think that this is a good description of the East Asian financial crisis of 1997–1998. East Asian countries were not running large government deficits, yet they suffered currency panics and disappearing foreign exchange reserves all the same.

Another loophole in the relationship between budget deficits and foreign exchange reserves is that the government finances its deficit not only with central bank credit but also with foreign debt. The willingness of foreign investors and banks to buy government bonds is another unknown. This is not so relevant for the poorest countries, or with countries that just have a bad rep as politically unstable or as profligate spenders—they don't qualify as "emerging markets," to use Wall Street jargon. But other poor countries do qualify as emerging markets; private investors and banks help finance these countries' government deficits by buying government bonds. One Web site suggests that there were about forty-five emerging markets (countries), together accounting for 2.6 billion people.[14] A sudden surge in demand for government bonds by foreign investors could allow the governments of these countries to cut back their use of central bank credit, building up dollar reserves without any need for fiscal austerity. Conversely, a flight out of government bonds in emerging markets—as happened after the Mexico crisis in 1994, the East Asian crisis in 1997–98, the Russia crisis in 1998, and the Argentina crisis in 2001—could suddenly force governments to use central bank credit again, running down foreign exchange reserves.

How much do you need to cut central bank credit when the desire to hold domestic currency jumps around like my dog, Millie, after swallowing a jalapeño? How much do you need to cut deficits when the willingness of foreigners to hold government bonds is oscillating? The desire to hold currency or government debt may itself depend on the government's policy on cutting central bank credit or budget deficits. It is circular—if the government is willing to cut the deficit and cut central bank borrowing, then people will be willing to hold more currency and hold more government debt, which lessens the need to cut deficits and central bank borrowing. Finding out where this complex process reaches equilibrium is more complicated than jet-lagged IMF staff can capture by adding up numbers on a spreadsheet.

The moral of the story is that IMF prescriptions about how much to cut central bank credit and government deficits are often based on shaky foundations. The IMF should give up its pretensions that it understands the whole complicated system of financial equilibrium—this is another strain of the disease of utopian social engineering.

Is the IMF a Wimp?

The real test of the IMF's approach is whether it gets results on stabilizing macroeconomic disorder. On average, one of the big surprises is that the IMF has been weak in enforcing its conditions on macroeconomic misbehavior.

Let's analyze the IMF and the World Bank adjustment loans together because they play the same role of promoting "structural adjustment" (i.e., the reforms to straighten out finances and promote free markets) and because World Bank adjustment loans often support financing for IMF programs. The key number is what happens to the budget deficit. Remarkably, budget deficits did not improve from one adjustment loan to the next over 1980–99.[15]

Next, let's broaden the definition of bad government policy to include a variety of indicators: (1) whether the inflation rate is above 40 percent; (2) whether the dollar is trading on the black market for foreign exchange at more than a 40 percent premium over the official rate; (3) whether the official exchange rate is more than 40 percent out of line with the competitive rate that facilitates exports; and (4) whether interest rates are controlled at more than 5 percent below the rate of inflation. If any of these conditions is met, economic policy is classified as bad. These are exactly the kind of bad economic policies targeted by the IMF and the World Bank. That is, the IMF and the World Bank give "structural adjustment loans" on the condition that all of these problems be corrected. Yet the fraction of structural adjustment loan recipients violating one or more of these conditions did not decrease from one structural adjustment loan to the next (see figure 24).

What explains this surprise? One possible explanation is the IMF's tendency to wipe the slate clean with each new loan, especially if new officials are in power in the recipient country. Even though an IMF loan is supposed to be a short-term or medium-term bailout, the countries often don't seem to stay bailed out. Other countries fail to fulfill the conditions on old loans and yet get new loans anyway. Countries such as Ecuador and Pakistan went for more than two decades receiving one IMF loan after another, even though they had never completed any previous IMF program (meaning they didn't fulfill the conditions to get a second or later installment of a loan commitment).[16] A slew of examples in Africa had the same problem, which was to contribute to the African debt crisis.

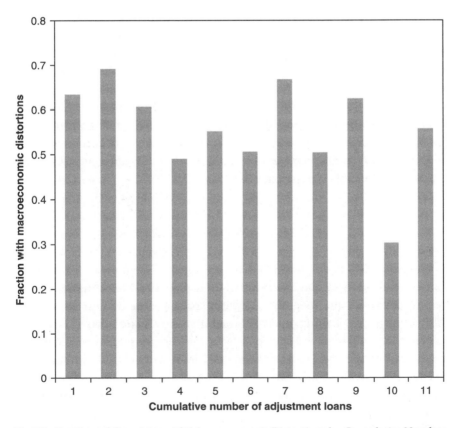

Fig. 24. Fraction of Countries with Macroeconomic Distortions by Cumulative Number of Adjustment Loans

The IMF's relationship with its clients is capricious. First, the IMF is tough on cutting budget deficits and causes riots. Then a new government comes in and again runs a high deficit, which the IMF then tries to bring down again (the deficit, not the government).

Debt and Consequences

The IMF also monitors government debt because it knows that a heavier debt load will increase future government deficits by increasing interest costs on the debt. Too high a debt will also make the creditors unwilling to continue lending.

The IMF has its own self-interest in this—if the country owes too much, it can't pay back the IMF. The IMF protects itself against this with a stipulation in its loan agreements that the government always pays it *first*, before other creditors. Still the IMF fails in its mission if a country becomes insolvent. Part of the IMF's role is to head off this denouement by persuading the government to borrow no more than a reasonable amount. But what is a reasonable amount? The IMF has a difficult time finding the answer to this question.

Then there is the problem of repaying the IMF loans themselves. The capricious relationship just described between the IMF and some of its clients means that first installments of IMF loans are made, but true macroeconomic adjustment does not happen. This does not augur well for countries being able to repay the IMF loans.

Bailing Yourself Out

One way the IMF has adjusted to this situation is to keep making new loans to repay the old loans. Once a country is in deep to the IMF, with the country owing the Fund due to previous bailout packages, it is hard to get out. Although the IMF bailing out Wall Street investors is controversial, the real problem is that it is bailing itself out. If the IMF did not make a new loan, the country might not repay the previous IMF loan. The IMF often drags in its sidekick, the World Bank, just across Nineteenth Street in Washington from the IMF, which makes an "adjustment loan" to the country as part of the bailout package.

One sign of this self-repayment is the high loan repetition rate for the Sisters of Nineteenth Street. The probability of getting a new loan does not go down with the number of IMF and World Bank adjustment loans already received. (See figure 25.)

The IMF's Independent Evaluation Office highlighted this problem of "prolonged use" of IMF money.[17] It defined a "prolonged user" as a country that was under an IMF program for seven years out of any ten-year period. Forty-four countries met this definition of IMF addiction over the period 1971–2000. Prolonged use has become more common in recent years. In 2001, loans to prolonged users accounted for half of all IMF lending.

As usually happens with addiction, the IMF habit of repeat lending includes some self-deception. The IMF made overly optimistic projections

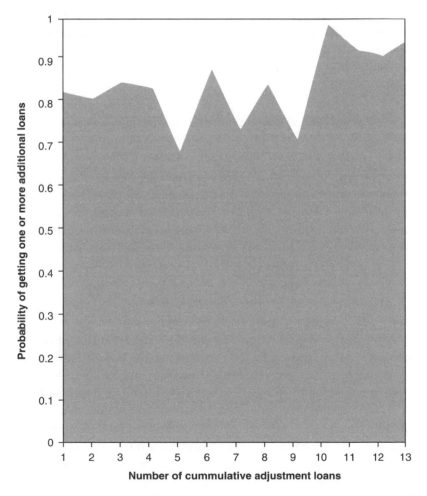

Fig. 25. Repetition Rates of Structural Adjustment Lending After Given Number of Loans, 1980–1999

of the prolonged users' GDP and/or export growth. It granted waivers of its conditions on its loans to repeat offenders. As the Independent Evaluation Office describes this process of fooling yourself into lending: "Internal incentives in the IMF encourage overpromising in programs. This results from both the relatively short time frame of programs, forcing optimistic assumptions about the pace of adjustment.... This led to a tendency to downplay risks. Even when, as was often the case, they were well identified during the internal review process, the assessment of risks was not candidly presented to the Executive Board." The Evaluation Office noted that repeat lending by the IMF tended to weaken the leverage the Fund had over countries to enforce its conditions.

The IMF displays one of the classic symptoms of Planner's disease: in many countries, it keeps doing the same thing over and over again to reach a never-reached objective. The repetition itself shows the failure of previous attempts at "short-term stabilization."

Heavily Indebted Poor Country Crisis

Repeated lending also does nothing to make the debt repayable, as debt keeps mounting without countries becoming more able to service the loans. One embarrassment happened with the poorest countries, which received many IMF loans as well as World Bank "structural adjustment loans," also meant to restore financial discipline. The poorest countries also received loans from Western governments and export credit agencies. Their debt load became so extreme that after 1996, the IMF and the World Bank, for the first time in their history, forgave part of their own loans. The IMF and the World Bank called these impoverished borrowers the Heavily Indebted Poor Countries (HIPCs). Among poor countries receiving above-average amounts of IMF and World Bank structural adjustment loans, seventeen of the eighteen became HIPCs, whose debt the IMF and the World Bank partly forgave. Among poor countries who had less than the average IMF and World Bank borrowing (measured by number of loans), only eight of seventeen became HIPCs. This could reflect the maddening selection problem again—that sick economies were both more likely to pile up debt and to turn to the World Bank and the IMF for help. However, this does not reflect wise lending by the IFIs, since a good part of the HIPC debt that had to be forgiven was directly from the IMF and the World Bank—even in such "successful" cases as Ghana and Uganda. Far from helping the poor countries achieve a reasonable debt load, the IMF and the World Bank were themselves contributing to the excessive debt of the HIPCs.

HIPCs qualified for debt relief by meeting some of the same conditions that they had failed to meet (or first met and then backtracked on) when getting the original loans. As of March 2005, debt-reduction packages have been approved for twenty-seven nations, providing fifty-four billion dollars' worth of debt relief—a reduction by about two thirds of their outstanding debt.[18]

HIPC debt forgiveness was supposed to be a once-and-for-all solution that would solve the debt problem. The IMF and the World Bank often had optimistic forecasts for GDP growth in the HIPCs. This hoped-for growth would have allowed the HIPCs to keep the ratio of debt to GDP from surging again. But the debt relief did not spur growth.

Bolivia is an example. The country had been an IMF ward ever since the first HIPC relief in 1998. The IMF and the World Bank projected rapid growth in Bolivia in per capita income over 1999–2003; instead living standards declined (see figure 26).

The failure of debt relief to spur growth was a problem because the failure of the original loans to spur growth was what had caused the debt problem

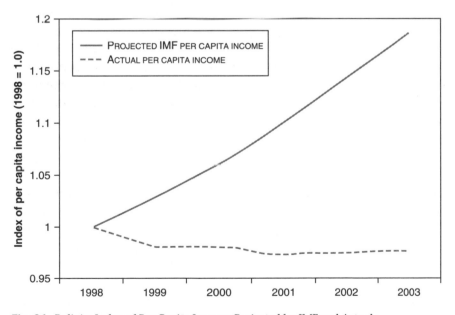

Fig. 26. Bolivia: Index of Per Capita Income Projected by IMF and Actuals

in the first place. We have already seen that Africa, a favorite destination of repeated IMF and World Bank lending, also failed to have the growth that would have enabled it to service its debt. This is a general pattern: the growth in program countries fell short of the IMF's own targets. On average for IMF programs in the 1990s, the target GDP growth was 4 percent, but actual growth was only 2 percent.[19] Since population growth was also about 2 percent, this meant that the actual growth of income per person was close to zero.

The supposed once-and-for-all debt relief in 1996 was superseded by Enhanced HIPC in 1999, which gave deeper debt relief to more nations. However, even Enhanced HIPC was not enough. The G8 Summit in July 2005 decided to give 100 percent debt cancellation (worth forty billion dollars) to eighteen low-income countries that had already qualified for HIPC debt relief, including Bolivia and fourteen African countries.

Low-income countries have had debt problems since the 1960s, yet still the IMF and the World Bank have insisted on making repeated loans to very shaky borrowers.[20] This is yet another of our numerous examples of the aid community pouring in resources at a fixed objective—financing "development" with aid loans. The IMF and the World Bank kept making new loans to repay old loans, even though countries were having ever-increasing difficulties at repayment.

At this point, the ever-escalating degree of debt forgiveness has destroyed low-income debt as a believable instrument to finance anything. The borrowers have little incentive to repay when they see the debts periodically forgiven (what economists call "moral hazard"). Calling a loan to the poorest countries a "loan" has become ever more fictional. The World Bank, which is an aid agency, should just give the poorest countries grants, not loans (this was one of the better ideas of the Bush administration on foreign aid). The IMF, which is not supposed to be an aid agency, should get out of the business of loaning money to the poorest, least creditworthy countries altogether. Is there any reason to keep bailing out countries that chronically fail to stay bailed out?

Cry, Argentina

Another of the IMF's recent embarrassments was Argentina's default on its government debt in December 2001. The IMF was deeply involved in the elusive quest for Argentine financial stability, with fifteen standbys from 1958 to 1999. After unhappy decades of financial chaos, Argentina had a decade of financial stability after 1991. It was the star pupil of the IMF, even as other IMF clients such as Mexico, Russia, Brazil, and the East Asian countries experienced crises. But Argentina began to get into trouble in 1999. President Carlos Menem, who presided over Argentina's near decade of financial stability, increased public spending in his quest to get a third term in office. When this quest failed, electoral politics among other contenders took over. In the understated language of a former top IMF official, Michael Mussa, "election-year concerns further depressed the normally low level of interest Argentine politicians . . . attached to measures of fiscal prudence."[21] Argentina borrowed heavily from emerging-market investors in 1999 and 2000. By this point, the game was up—Argentina would not honor its commitments to private foreign lenders. In the quaint language of emerging markets, private lenders would "take a haircut." At this point, the IMF should have pulled the plug. Instead, it put together a forty-billion-dollar rescue package that included fourteen billion dollars from the IMF itself, five billion dollars from the Inter-American Development Bank and World Bank, one billion dollars from Spain, and a projected twenty billion dollars from private lenders—announced on January 12, 2001.

In 2001, lenders demanded interest rates on Argentine government debt that were ten percentage points higher than comparable loans elsewhere. If our team was behind by late 2000, the game was a rout in the first half of 2001. Deposits in the banks and international reserves collapsed. By August 2001, as Mussa put it, "prospects for a favorable outcome were pure fantasy." The IMF should have curtailed its scheduled payouts under the January 2001 package.

Instead, in August 2001, the IMF increased its payout to Argentina by more than five billion dollars and offered three billion dollars more to support Argentina's rescheduling payments to its private creditors. As Mussa put it, there was "a failure of moral courage, to decline substantial additional support for policies that no longer had any reasonable chance of success."

The only effect of the August 2001 package was to postpone by a few months the Argentine default on eighty-one billion dollars owed to foreign bondholders. Argentina defaulted on its debt in stages in November–December 2001. Riots in late 2001 spread from the provinces to Buenos Aires. Rioters smashed store windows and looted. The president resigned. Political farce ensued, as three interim presidents took office and resigned in the space of ten days.

After much bluster on both sides in the wake of the default, Argentina put out a take-it-or-leave-it offer to pay bondholders thirty-five cents on the dollar in February 2005, a loss for creditors of unprecedented scale in recent experience. The majority of bondholders took the offer. The IMF in past debt crises has often played the role of referee between creditors and borrowing governments. Perhaps scarred by its own Argentine miscalculations, this time it stayed on the sidelines.[22]

International Monetary Paradise

The IMF sometimes plays a useful role in the world's financial system—it helps countries facing a temporary shortage of cash get off their backs. The world needs some kind of an international financial crisis manager like the IMF.

But the IMF fudged its mission beyond short-term crisis bailouts to be a repeat lender to deadbeat governments, with the idea that it was promoting "structural adjustment." Even worse, it became a long-run lender to the poorest countries through its loans with the Orwellian name "Poverty Reduction and Growth Facility" (PRGF)—the new name for structural adjustment loans. The IMF is now getting involved in programs to broaden "country ownership" of its adjustment loans, to strengthen "popular participation," and to put a "more explicit focus on poverty reduction."[23] No amount of rhetoric can paper over the contradiction between the IMF dictating conditions and "popular participation." We will tell you what to do, as well as promise you that you are doing it of your own free will.

The participation fad indicates that the disease of bureaucratic babble is spreading to the IMF. The Fund is even concerning itself with environmental policy, which is about as far from its central mission as you can get.[24]

The extremely long list of conditions the IMF attaches to its PRGF loans, as exemplified by the Ethiopia example at the beginning of this chapter, makes each loan an attempt to engineer paradise rather than do piecemeal reforms. The IMF seems more and more to be trying to do everything, a lot like the aid bureaucracies we looked at in the previous chapter.

Conclusions

Although the IMF has benefited from having a narrower mandate than other development agencies, it, too, suffers from lack of accountability to its intended poor beneficiaries as it seeks to reform the economy from the top down. The simplicity of its mandate is outweighed by the heavy-handed way it is applied. The IMF's confident pronouncements about what governments should do has some patronizing echoes of the White Man's Burden, in which (in the words of William Pfaff) "the native peoples of Asia, Africa, and the Americas were expected to acknowledge Western truth against native error."[25]

The IMF needs to find a way to drastically simplify its dealings with poor countries in ways that reduce its intrusion. First, there are some poor countries that are so politically and institutionally dysfunctional that the IMF should not be involved with them at all. The fiasco of low-income debt has shown how ineffective the IMF conditions were at ensuring repayment of loans in the poorest countries. The IMF's natural niche seems to be the emerging markets, not the poorest countries. The latter includes most countries in Africa, where the IMF should just head for the exit and let traditional aid agencies operate.

Second, the IMF needs to find a way to get rid of its intrusive and complex conditionality. We have seen that its conditions are not effective in making sure the loans are repaid anyway, so it's hard to argue that they are essential for the functioning of the IMF. One possibility is that the IMF could just make bailout loans when it judges—as any lender does—that the loan is likely to be repaid. How the borrower manages to repay the loan is up to it, just as how I spend my money is of no interest to my Visa company. The IMF has an enforcement mechanism in that it can refuse to lend in the future to a country that fails to pay it back. Also, the IMF has the leverage that it is the creditor that is paid first, and so private creditors will not lend if a country is not serious about repaying the IMF. (This didn't work to prevent the HIPC debacle, but that was because the poorest countries—which I have argued the IMF should not lend to anyway—did not have access to private creditors.) Suppliers' credits are the lifeblood of trade, and having these cut off is a very effective threat. This is a lot like the multilateral punishment strategy for networks of merchants that chapter 3 discusses. This is the same as the enforcement mechanism in the private market—if you fail to repay your creditors and declare bankruptcy, you won't be able to get new loans for a long while. If all this is not enough, the IMF may need to supplement the refusal-of-new-lending sanction with some other market-based device, such as requiring that some kind of collateral be put up by the government. The movement away from intrusive conditionality and toward simple credit payment enforcement would prevent the IMF from getting involved in poor-country politics, which has been so disastrous, as shown by the IMF riot phenomenon.

The IMF needs to shed its excessive self-confidence that it knows in detail what is best for the poor, based on an analysis of the whole economy that shares the presumptions of utopian planning. It should go back to its narrow mandate of financial stabilization. The talented professionals at the IMF *could* play the simplified role of bailout creditor effectively, making a useful contribution to the well-being of emerging-market countries.

Water Pipe

In the Great Rift Valley of Ethiopia, I visited a village far from the big dreams and Big Plans the West has for the Rest. A British nongovernmental aid organization called Water Aid, which receives funds from official aid agencies, had inaugurated a new project in this village. This agency seemed to be acting more like an explorer and less like a foreign aid planner. Water Aid had discovered a way to get clean water to some very poor villages in the Great Rift Valley. They built a water pipe to carry clean water from springs on top of the mountains bordering the Great Rift Valley to villages down in the valley. The project was run entirely by Ethiopians, with representatives from the villages sitting on the board of the agency.

At a bustling water tap in one village, the villagers watered their cattle and collected drinking water for a nominal fee paid to Water Aid, to be used for maintenance of the system. Previously the villagers had walked two miles every other day to collect water from a polluted river. Villagers, especially children, had been getting sick from the contaminated water –with some of them dying. Children had been kept out of school, farmers away from farming, all to pursue the all-consuming and backbreaking task of fetching water.

Now life was better. Some of the money of the rich *had* reached the desperate poor.

CHAPTER SEVEN

The Healers: Triumph and Tragedy

Oh tear-filled figure who, like a sky held back
grows heavy above the landscape of her sorrow. ...

Rainer Maria Rilke, "O lacrimosa," Translated by Stephen Mitchell, 1995

In 1989, a team of field researchers in southern Uganda, near the Tanzanian border, stumbled on an older man living by himself in a thatched hut. The man himself was incoherent, but neighbors told his story: his wife and eight children had all died of AIDS. Asked about the man's future, villagers said, "He will not marry again."

Fourteen years later, I am sitting in a health clinic in Soweto, South Africa, talking to a sad young woman named Constance. Constance tells me she is HIV-positive and is too sick to work to support her three children. Even when she is feeling better, she cannot find a job. The father of her children is also unemployed, and she rarely sees him. Constance didn't tell her mother that she is HIV-positive, for fear that her mother and stepfather would eject her and her children from the household. She says her stepfather complains bitterly about her not working and not contributing to the maintenance of her children. Left unspoken between us is Constance's fate, and the fate of her three children when she succumbs to AIDS.

Southern Uganda was one of the places where AIDS first appeared in the early 1980s, but in the years since then, the epidemic has spread to most of southern and eastern Africa. South Africa is the most recent casualty of its spread. Thirty percent of pregnant women in their twenties test HIV-positive in South African antenatal clinics.

A third of the adult population is now HIV-positive in Botswana, Lesotho, Swaziland, and Zimbabwe. In other eastern and southern African countries, between 10 and 25 percent of the adult population is HIV-positive. AIDS is spreading also to African countries outside of the "AIDS corridor," which now runs from Ethiopia to South Africa. In Africa as a whole, there are 29 million HIV-positive people. Tragedies like that of the man in southern Uganda and Constance have happened many times over the past decades, and will happen many more times in the future. More than 2 million people in Africa died from AIDS in 2002. Their places in the epidemic were taken by the 3.5 million Africans newly infected in 2002.

AIDS gets attention. Celebrities and statesmen—ranging from Bill Clinton and Nelson Mandela to Bono and Ashley Judd—call for action. The anti-globalization activists also focus on AIDS. Oxfam calls for access to life-saving drugs for AIDS patients in Africa. American activists at international AIDS conferences (such as American health secretary Tommy Thompson at a conference in Barcelona in 2002) shout down anyone not responding with sufficient alacrity, *pour encourager les autres*.

The foreign aid doyens have also woken up to the problem. The actors include the UN agency UNAIDS, the World Bank's multicountry program to fight AIDS in Africa, the World Health Organization's Commission on Macroeconomics and Health, and the Global Fund to Fight AIDS, TB, and Malaria.

In his 2003 State of the Union Address, President George W. Bush announced the release of fifteen billion dollars in foreign aid to fight AIDS. The initiative was passed by Congress, and Bush signed it into law on May 27, 2003.

It is great that public figures are publicizing the needs of AIDS victims. Many people feel compassion in the face of the death sentence of millions of HIV-positive people in Africa, and in the face of fear that the epidemic will keep spreading.

Yet behind this recent Western attention to AIDS is a tale of two decades of neglect, prevarication, incompetence, and passivity by all those same political actors and aid agencies. By the time researchers found the incoherent victim in southern Uganda in 1989, and even years before that, the West had all the information it needed to predict (and virtually every expert did predict) that AIDS would kill tens of millions of people worldwide, above all in Africa, if nothing was done.

Paradox of Evil and the White Man's Burden

Scholars of religion talk about the paradox of evil, which says you cannot have all three of the following conditions hold: (1) a benevolent God; (2) an all-knowing and all-powerful God; and (3) evil things happening to good people. If you have (1) and (2), then why would God (3) let bad things happen to good people?

Similarly, in the White Man's Burden, you cannot have all the following hold: (1) the White Man's Burden is acting in the interests of the poor in the Rest; (2) the White Man's Burden is effective at resolving poor people's problems; and (3) lots of bad things, whose prevention was affordable, are happening to poor people. If (3) happens, then either (1) or (2) must not hold. Religion is a matter of faith in an invisible Supreme Being, so the contradictions inherent in the Paradox of Evil are more easily tolerated by true believers. Foreign aid is not a faith-based area, however. It is a visible policy with visible dollars meant to help visible people.

The breakdown of the aid system on AIDS is a good test case of the paradox of evil in foreign aid. It reflects how out of touch were the Planners at the top with the tragedy at the bottom, another sign of the weak power of the intended beneficiaries. It shows how ineffective Planners are at making foreign aid work. It is hard to imagine anything more in the interest of the poor than preventing the spread of a fatal disease. Today, the Western aid community has finally woken up to AIDS. Now that community has moved from inaction to ineffective action. Aid for AIDS still appears mismatched to the choices of the poor.

Health Triumphs

The failure on AIDS is all the more striking when we consider that health is the area where foreign aid has enjoyed its most conspicuous successes.[1] Maybe the part of the White Man's Burden that addresses disease offers a more hopeful picture than the malfunctioning bureaucracy in other areas. The healers are working on an issue where the needs and wants of the poor are more obvious—they don't want to die—and so feedback is less critical. The outcomes are more observable, as deaths tend to get noticed by others.

The successes may tell us about the ability of aid agencies to be effective when they have narrow, monitorable objectives that coincide with the poor's needs and with political support in the rich countries for an uncontroversial objective like saving lives. As the previous chapters argue, areas with visible individual outcomes are more likely to put Searchers in charge—in contrast to the power of Planners in areas where nobody can be held individually accountable, such as economic growth. I also hypothesize that Searchers are more likely to succeed at their narrow goals than the Planners are to succeed at their more general goals.

A vaccination campaign in southern Africa virtually eliminated measles as a killer of children. Routine childhood immunization combined with measles vaccination in seven southern African nations starting in 1996 virtually eliminated measles in those countries by 2000. A national campaign in Egypt to make parents aware of the use of oral rehydration therapy from 1982 to 1989 cut childhood deaths from diarrhea by 82 percent over that period. A regional program to eliminate polio in Latin America after 1985 has eliminated it as a public health threat in the Americas. The leading preventable cause of blindness, trachoma, has been cut by 90 percent in children under age ten in Morocco since 1997, thanks to a determined effort to promote surgery, antibiotics, face washing, and environmental cleanliness. Sri Lanka's commitment to preventing maternal deaths during childbirth has cut the rate of maternal mortality from 486 to 24 deaths per 100,000 births over the last four decades. A program to control tuberculosis in China cut the number of cases by 40 percent between 1990 and 2000. Donors collaborated on a program to wipe out river blindness in West Africa starting in 1974, virtually halting the transmission of the disease. Eighteen million children in the twenty-country area of the program have been kept safe from river blindness since the program began. An international effort eradicated smallpox worldwide. Another partnership among aid donors contributed to the near eradication of guinea worm in twenty African and Asian countries where it was endemic. Beginning in 1991, a program of surveillance, house spraying, and environmental vector control halted transmission of Chagas' disease in Uruguay, Chile, and large parts of Paraguay and Brazil. Worldwide, as we see in chapter 3, infant mortality in poor countries has fallen and life expectancy has increased.

Many of these programs benefited from donor funding and technical advice. In Egypt's fight against childhood diarrhea, for example, it was a grant from USAID and technical advice from the World Health Organization (WHO). In China's campaign against tuberculosis, it was a World Bank loan and WHO advice. In Morocco, the drug company Pfizer donated antibiotics to fight trachoma. Although the aid agencies have not calculated the aid impact in a scientifically rigorous way, the broad facts support the belief that aid was effective in many of the above health interventions. Alas, instead of expanding success in the many health areas where it had triumphed, the international health community was going to get bogged down in its equivalent of Vietnam: AIDS.

The Coming Storm

The health successes make the failure on AIDS stand out even more. As with any contagious disease, early action is far more effective than later action.

A bucket of water is enough to put out a campfire; it takes more to put out a forest fire.

On the plus side, it was the West that solved the scientific problem of what caused AIDS, making prevention efforts possible. Unfortunately, this knowledge did not translate into effective prevention in Africa.

The World Bank advertises that it is now the "world's single largest funder of AIDS programs" (the same claim is made by the World Health Organization and by the U.S. Agency for International Development). The World Bank doesn't mention that it did a total of one project dedicated to AIDS before 1993 (an eight-million-dollar loan to Mobutu in Zaire in 1988). The World Bank today endorses the WHO calculation that Africa needs one billion dollars a year in AIDS-prevention spending. Yet over the entire period 1988–99, the World Bank spent fifteen million dollars a year on all AIDS projects in Africa. In 1992, a World Bank study noted that the Bank "has done little to initiate prevention in countries in which the risk of spread is high."

Why did the West not act more vigorously early on in the AIDS crisis? Was it because people didn't know how bad the crisis would become, because action was ineffective, or simply because it took millions of deaths to make it a headline issue worth responding to?

The defense that the West didn't know is not credible. As long ago as 1986, AIDS in Africa was attracting international attention. On October 27, 1986, an article in the *Times* of London said: "A catastrophic epidemic of AIDS is sweeping across Africa ... the disease has already infected several millions of Africans, posing colossal health problems to more than 20 countries. ... 'Aids has become a major health threat to all Africans and prevention and control of infection ... must become an immediate public health priority for all African countries,' says report published in a leading American scientific journal."

Signs of the coming epidemic appeared even earlier. A sample of prostitutes in Butare, Rwanda, in 1983 found that 75 percent were infected. A later study by the group that reported this statistic dated the general awareness that Central Africa was at risk for the spread of AIDS back to 1983 as well.[2]

The World Bank did its first AIDS strategy report in 1988. The report said the crisis was urgent. It presciently detected "an environment highly conducive to the spread of HIV" in many African countries. It noted that the epidemic was far from reaching its full potential and that "the AIDS epidemic in Africa is an emergency situation and appropriate action must be undertaken now."[3] Yet the effort at the time was underwhelming: the World

Bank made a grant of one million dollars to the World Health Organization (WHO) in the 1988/1989 fiscal year to fight AIDS.

A 1992 World Bank retrospective on the 1988 strategy damns it with faint praise: "In view of the 1988 decision to deal with AIDS using existing resource levels and the small PHN [Population, Health, and Nutrition] staff that has had to handle a steadily increasing work program, we conclude that the agenda in the 1988 Strategy Paper has been reasonably well implemented."[4]

The World Bank's 1993 World Development Report, whose theme was health, notes that "At present, most national AIDS programs are inadequate, despite international attention and the significant effort by WHO to help design and implement plans for controlling AIDS." Translation: it's the WHO's fault.

An article in 1991 in the World Bank/IMF quarterly magazine predicted that thirty million people would be infected worldwide by the year 2000 if nothing was done.[5] The actual figure would turn out to be forty million, but the point is: more than a decade ago many knew that a catastrophic epidemic was under way.

The 1992 World Bank study, while noting the lack of progress, did sound the obligatory refrain that progress was under way, not least because "countries have been informed of the Bank's increasing attention to AIDS."

The World Bank itself was directing the tiny flows of AIDS financing to "currently affected countries," while "little has been done by the Bank to prevent AIDS in less affected countries with a high potential for spread."[6] The 1992 report closed with the curious admonition that "AIDS should not be allowed to dominate the Bank's agenda on population, health, and nutrition issues in Africa." Raising this issue early in the epidemic is strange, when an ounce of prevention *is* worth a pound of cure. Now AIDS work has crowded out treatment of other equally lethal threats to Africans because its spread was not averted. The best way to have kept AIDS from "dominating the Bank's agenda" was to have prevented its spread.

Perhaps we can better understand the aid community's difficulties on prevention if we realize that prevention was not very visible to the rich-country public. Although insiders knew that a horrific AIDS crisis was brewing in Africa in the late 1980s and early 1990s, this attracted little attention from Western media or politicians. Part of the problem was probably that aid agencies didn't know what to do to address the crisis, but the above examples show little evidence that they were searching for answers. Only *after* a truly massive number of people were infected with HIV did AIDS gain the sufficient level of visibility for action.

Not Following Your Own Advice

By 1998, the World Bank had done ten stand-alone AIDS projects. Researcher Julia Dayton was hired by the Bank to analyze its programs.[7]

Dayton found that only half of the fifty-one World Bank projects with AIDS components promoted condom use or financed condom purchases. To understand this omission, consider another Dayton finding: almost none of the fifty-one projects did any economic analysis of what an effective AIDS interventions was.

Dayton also found that World Bank country teams were missing in action on AIDS. AIDS was already reaching epidemic levels in Côte d'Ivoire, Haiti, Kenya, and Zambia in the 1990s. The World Bank's Country Assistance Strategy Documents in the 1990s for those countries did not describe HIV prevalence or transmission, recommend STD- or HIV/AIDS-prevention or care, or in fact analyze HIV/AIDS at all. Ironically for aid agencies that often are trying to do everything, "everything" sometimes leaves out some high priorities.

Day of Judgment

Shortly after Dayton's report was issued, the World Bank produced another AIDS report. The World Bank Africa vice-president wrote in the introduction to this 2000 report that "AIDS is completely preventable." He gave a prediction that "those who look back on this era will judge our institution in large measure by whether we recognized this wildfire that is raging across Africa for the development threat that it is, and did our utmost to put it out. They will be right to do so."[8] He could have spared us the use of the future tense.

The World Bank did produce a Monitoring and Evaluation Operations Manual, prepared jointly by UNAIDS and the World Bank.[9] The manual sensibly warns that "the more complex an M&E system, the more likely it is to fail." It then spends fifty-two pages laying out its extremely complex M&E system. This includes the ten-step M&E program (step 3: "NAC [National AIDS Councils] and stakeholders engage in an intensive participatory process to build ownership and buy-in, particularly for the overall M&E system and programme monitoring"). There is also the list of thirty-four indicators (none of which involves monitoring "core transmitters"), the nineteen-point terms of reference for the M&E consultant to the NAC, and the "summary terms of reference for specialized programme activity monitoring entity." The accepted scientific standard for any program evaluation, the randomized controlled trial, did not make it into the manual.

The Kitty Genovese Effect

Winston Moseley killed Kitty Genovese, a twenty-eight-year-old bar manager, in Queens, New York, in 1964. Her murder is the first news story I remember from my childhood. As Moseley first stabbed Kitty, neighbors heard her screams but didn't call the police. Moseley drove away and then came back and stabbed her some more, till she died. Police later identified thirty-eight neighbors who saw or heard part of the attack. The eyewitnesses' failure to call police became a symbol of the callousness of urban America. I think my mother showed me the newspaper to illustrate the wickedness of big-city folks.

The last thing I want to do is defend such bad Samaritans, but economists point out that the callousness of each individual was not as great as their group behavior suggests. All the neighbors agreed that saving Kitty's life would have been worthwhile. Outraged commentators pointed out that only one out of those thirty-eight people had to call the police, but that was exactly the problem. Calling the police would have had some cost to the individual, who may later have had to testify and may have feared retribution from the associates of the killer. Each of the thirty-eight people might have been willing to bear this cost to save Kitty's life, but preferred that someone else make the call. With so many witnesses to the scene, each person calculated a high probability that someone else *would* make the call and save Kitty. Therefore, each person did nothing. If there had been only one witness, and if that person had known he was the only witness, he would have been more likely to call the police.

The Kitty Genovese effect is another plausible example of the problem of collective responsibility I mention in chapter 5, which leads to bureaucratic inaction. Each development agency is one among many responsible for solving crises in the poor countries. Each agency may altruistically care about the poor. Suppose that action by one agency will be enough to solve a problem, and all agencies will share in the glory of the triumph; it is difficult to tell which agency's effort made the difference. If effort is costly and diverts resources away from other organizational goals, each agency will prefer that some other agency make the effort. The more agencies that could act, the less likely that action will occur.

The Genovese effect can also operate within aid bureaucracies. Each department might wish that results happen, but would prefer that some other department achieve them, with glory for all. Departments then get into the game of shifting responsibility for difficult tasks onto other departments, which drives the leaders of even the most results-oriented agency insane.

Action does become more likely as the status quo deteriorates due to inaction. The crisis could eventually become big enough to outweigh the option of waiting for someone else to act. In the Kitty Genovese example, a neighbor did eventually call the police. Kitty was dead by then.

A story like this could help account for the long period of inaction on the AIDS crisis, until the crisis was so severe that finally aid agencies acted.

Orphans in the Storm

Mary Banda, about sixty-five, lives in Lusaka, Zambia.[10] Five of her eight children have died from AIDS. In Zambia, adult children usually care for their aged parents. AIDS reversed the equation for Mary Banda. Instead of her children caring for her, she is caring for eight orphaned grandchildren, ranging in age from six to twenty.

Mbuya (Grandmother) Banda doesn't get much help from her three surviving children. One of her children is in South Africa, and Mbuya hasn't heard from her. Her youngest daughter is unmarried and unemployed. Her remaining daughter is married, but does not work; her husband can only sporadically find work. She comes around with a bag of mealie meal (cornmeal) every now and then.

The biggest problem is finding food for the orphans. Mrs. Banda sells groundnuts by the road, and grows a little maize, sweet potato, and greens. It is never quite enough. Only two of the children are in school, where they are sometimes refused entry because they lack fees, shoes, and uniforms.

When her children became sick from AIDS, she tried traditional healers as well as the hospital. Mary Banda believes her children died from witchcraft—a sign of the need to adjust to local conditions with prevention messages. Her four deceased daughters were businesswomen buying secondhand clothes in Lusaka and exchanging them for groundnuts in the villages, and then reselling the groundnuts in Lusaka. She believes villagers jealous of their success bewitched her daughters through their feet. She blames her son's death on witchcraft from jealous rivals after his work promoted him. She wishes her children had seen a witchdoctor to get preventive medicine to put on their feet.

Discussion of African beliefs in witchcraft is taboo in aid agencies, as nobody wants to reinforce ill-informed stereotypes. Unfortunately, political correctness gets in the way of making policy, as conventional public health approaches may not work if people *do* believe that witchcraft causes illness and turn to traditional healers. Americans and Europeans also believed in witches when they were at similar levels of income as Africa (and many Americans still do today; hence the spiritualism section at the Barnes & Noble bookstore in Greenwich Village—one of the intellectual capitals of the United States—is three times the size of the science section). Moreover, many American evangelicals believe divine intervention can cure illness.

Beliefs in invisible malign forces in Africa are not so surprising when a virus visible only to scientists is killing previously healthy young people. Princeton political scientist and ethnographer Adam Ashforth documented the widespread belief in Soweto, South Africa, that witchcraft causes many symptoms of illness, including symptoms similar to AIDS.[11] AIDS-prevention efforts would do much better to work with traditional healers on fighting HIV transmission than to ignore beliefs in witchcraft because of political sensitivities.

Mrs. Banda speaks for her generation of Mbuyas: "I'm an old woman who's suffering. When I was young, I never thought such cruel things could happen. When I think about it, I pray and cry, but I don't like to cry because it'll upset the children."

At least Mrs. Banda's grandchildren have her to care for them. A group even more unlucky is Lusaka's growing population of street children. AIDS orphans with no one to care for them are on the street. The manager of a shelter for abandoned kids, Rodgers Mwewa, noticed the increase in orphaned children coming into Lusaka. The traditional extended-family system of caring for children is breaking down because too many of its adult members are dead. "HIV is destroying families and family bonds," says Mwewa.[12]

The street children don't live long: cars frequently hit them, they get into fights, and they resort to petty crime, drugs, or sniffing glue. They are beaten up by the police. Worst of all, the children sell themselves for sex, and thus sooner or later acquire the HIV virus that killed their parents.

Less anecdotal evidence confirms that orphans in Africa face a rough road. The less orphans can rely on family, the worse off they are. Princeton University scholars Anne Case, Christine Paxson, and Joseph Ableidinger found in a study of orphans in ten African countries that orphans who live with unrelated adults get less schooling than orphans who live with non-parental relatives, who themselves get less schooling than children living with their parents. These effects show up even as discrimination within the household. For example, an orphan living with her aunt and uncle typically gets less schooling than her cousin, the aunt and uncle's child.[13]

Africa's AIDS crisis is leaving a generation of undereducated, undernourished, underparented orphans who will soon be adults. As if Africa's development crisis weren't bad enough for the current generation, the orphans of AIDS complicate development even more.

Treating the Sick

Now that twenty-nine million people in Africa are HIV-positive, compassion would call for treating the sick, right? Yet pity is not always a reliable guide to action. By a tragic irony, compassion is driving the fight against AIDS in Africa in a direction that may cost more lives than it saves. It is political suicide in rich countries to question AIDS treatment. Too bad—what should matter is what helps the poor the most, not what sells politically in rich countries. This political pressure led Planners to fixate on the goal of treatment even when the costs were so prohibitive that it diverted money from cheaper actions that Searchers had found to save many more lives.

The Western aid community is now installing a gold-plated barn door after the horse has been stolen. Foreign aid programs are now starting to finance the "triple-drug cocktail" known as highly active antiretroviral therapy (HAART), which has dramatically lowered AIDS mortality in the West. All of the actors described earlier signed on to financing AIDS treatment. The UN General Assembly Special Session passed a resolution calling for AIDS treatment. This used to be impossible for low-income African AIDS patients, because of high drug prices (ten thousand dollars a year per patient). However, competition from a growing number of generic HIV/AIDS drugs has cut prices, which are now as low as $304 per year per patient.[14] This caused leaders of international aid agencies, such as former WHO director-general Grö Harlem Brundtland, to ask, "Does anyone deserve to be sentenced to certain death because she or he cannot access care that costs less than two dollars a day?" The WHO started a "3 by 5" campaign to get three million HIV-positive patients on antiretroviral therapy by the end of 2005.

Saving lives is not so simple. First of all, the focus on drug prices understates the expense and difficulty of treatment. Three hundred and four dollars is just the price of the first-line therapy drugs per year. The population first needs to be tested to see who is HIV-positive. Patients need to have their viral load tested to see if they should start taking drugs and, after taking them, if the drugs are working to decrease the viral load. The drugs are toxic, with potentially severe side effects. Health workers need to adjust the combination of drugs when side effects are too extreme. Patients need counseling and monitoring to make sure they are taking the medicine (if there is less than full adherence to treatment, the virus builds up resistance to the drugs). Patients also need treatment for the opportunistic infections that afflict AIDS sufferers. So treatment is more expensive than just the cost of the drugs. The World Health Organization is working with a figure of $1,500 per year per patient for delivering treatment to prolong the life of an AIDS patient by one year. Even if the WHO can drive down the price of the drugs further, the cost per year would still be $1,200. Other experts use similar figures.[15] But is even this number too high to justify giving a person another year of life?

The advocates for treatment stress the universal human right for HIV-positive patients to have access to life-saving health care, no matter what the cost. This is a great ideal, but a utopian one. There are also other ideals—first of all, prevention of the further spread of AIDS. And what about the universal human right for health care for other killer diseases, freedom from starvation, and access to clean water? Who chose the human right of universal treatment of AIDS over the other human rights? A non-utopian approach would make the tough choices to spend foreign aid resources in a way that reached the most people with their most urgent needs.

Poor people have many other needs besides AIDS treatment. The total amount of foreign aid for the world's approximately three billion poor people is only about twenty dollars per person per year. Is the money for AIDS treatment going to be "new money" or will it come from these already scarce funds? President Bush's 2005 budget proposal increased funding for the American AIDS program (especially treatment), but cut money for child health and other global health priorities by nearly a hundred million dollars (later reversed after protests).[16]

Bush's cut in other health spending was particularly unfortunate when two and a half times as many Africans die from other preventable diseases as die from AIDS. These diseases include measles and other childhood illnesses, respiratory infections, malaria, tuberculosis, diarrhea, and others. World-wide, in 2002 there were 15.6 million deaths from these causes, as opposed to 2.8 million deaths from AIDS.[17]

A well-established public health principle is that you should save lives that are cheap to save before you save lives that are more expensive to save. That way you save many more lives using the scarce funds available. Prevention and treatment of these other diseases cost far less than AIDS treatment.

Granting life through prevention of AIDS itself costs far less than AIDS treatment. A years' supply of condoms to prevent HIV infection costs about fourteen dollars. In a 2002 article in *The Lancet,* Andrew Creese from the World Health Organization and co-authors estimated that AIDS-prevention interventions such as condom distribution, blocking mother-to-child transmission, and voluntary counseling and testing could cost as little as one to twenty dollars per year of life saved, and twenty to four hundred dollars per HIV infection averted (even though this study may overstate the confidence that these things always work). Other studies come up with similar estimates.[18]

Then there are other diseases for which Searchers have found cheap interventions (although we have seen that the Planners' domination of aid often interferes with making these things work). The medicines that cure TB cost about ten dollars per case of the illness. A package of interventions designed to prevent maternal and infant deaths costs less than three dollars per person per year. Worldwide, three million children die a year because they are not fully vaccinated, even though vaccines cost only pennies per dose. One in four people worldwide suffers from intestinal worms, though treatments cost less than a dollar per year. A full course of treatment for a child suffering even from drug-resistant malaria costs only about one dollar. In fact, Vietnam, a relatively poor country, reduced deaths from malaria by 97 percent from 1991 to 1997 with a campaign that included bed nets and antimalarial drugs.[19] A bed net program in Tanzania also reduced mortality significantly.[20] (The availability of such cheap remedies makes it all the more tragic that malaria is still so widespread—we are back to the second tragedy of the world's poor.)

Overall, the World Bank estimates the cost per year for a variety of health interventions like these to range from five to forty dollars, compared with the fifteen-hundred-dollar cost of prolonging the life of an AIDS patient by a year with antiretroviral treatment. The $4.5 billion the WHO plans to spend on antiretroviral treatment for one more year of life for three million could grant between seven and sixty years of additional life for five times that many people—fifteen million. For the HIV-positive patients themselves, you could reach many more of them to prolong their lives by treating the opportunistic infections, especially TB, that usually kill AIDS victims.

Other researchers come up with similar numbers. For example, Harvard economics professor Michael Kremer noted in an article in *The Journal of Economic Perspectives* in 2002: "for every person treated for a year with antiretroviral therapy, 25 to 110 Disability Adjusted Life Years could be saved through targeted AIDS prevention efforts or vaccination against easily preventable diseases."

A group of health experts wrote in the prestigious medical journal *The Lancet* in July 2003 about how 5.5 million child deaths could have been prevented in 2003, lamenting that "child survival has lost its focus." They blamed in part the "levels of attention and effort directed at preventing the small proportion of child deaths due to AIDS with a new, complex, and expensive intervention."[21]

The WHO expects the added years of life for AIDS patients from antiretroviral treatment to be only three to five years—not exactly a miracle cure.[22] The United Nations Population Division in 2005 similarly estimated that the added years of life from antiretroviral treatment to be a median of 3.5 years.[23] After that, resistance to the first-line treatment (the one with the cheap drugs, which is all that is on the table in Africa, outside of South Africa) builds up and full-blown AIDS sets in. Other estimates are even more pessimistic. The average length of effectiveness of the first-line treatment in Brazil, which has a large-scale treatment program, has been only fourteen months.[24]

The big question is whether poor Africans themselves would have chosen to spend scarce funds on prolonging some lives with AIDS treatment, as opposed to saving many lives with other health interventions. Would the desperately poor themselves, such as those on an income of one dollar a day, choose to spend fifteen hundred dollars on antiretroviral treatment? Should the West impose its preferences for saving AIDS victims instead of measles victims just because it makes the West feel better?

Path of Least Resistance

Getting a complex AIDS and development crisis under control just by taking a pill is irresistible to politicians, aid agencies, and activists. We see here again the bias toward observable actions by aid agencies. The activists' cause plays well in the Western media because the tragedy of AIDS victims even has a villain—the international drug companies that were reluctant to lower the price on life-saving drugs—which makes mobilization for the cause even easier.

AIDS treatment is another example of the SIBD syndrome—rich-country politicians want to convince rich-country voters that "something is being done" (SIBD) about the tragic problem of AIDS in Africa. It is easier to achieve SIBD catharsis if politicians and aid officials treat people who are already sick, than it is to persuade people with multiple sexual partners to use condoms to prevent many more people from getting the disease. Alas, the poor's interests are sacrificed to political convenience. When the U.S. Congress passed Bush's fifteen-billion-dollar AIDS program (known as the President's Emergency Plan for AIDS Relief, or PEPFAR) in May 2003, it placed a restriction that no more than 20 percent of the funds be spent on prevention, while 55 percent was allocated for treatment.[25]

In a fit of religious zealotry, Congress also required organizations receiving funds to publicly oppose prostitution. This eliminates effective organizations that take a pragmatic and compassionate approach to understanding the factors that drive women into prostitution. Programs that condemn prostitutes are unlikely to find a receptive audience when they try to persuade those prostitutes to avoid risky behavior.

To make things even worse, the religious right in America is crippling the funding of prevention programs to advocate their own imperatives: abstain from sex or have sex only with your legally married spouse. Studies in the United States find no evidence that abstinence programs have any effect on sexual behavior of young people, except to discourage them from using condoms.[26] The evangelists' message has not convinced American youth, so the evangelists want to export it to African youth. Moreover, devout women who follow the sex-within-marriage mantra are still at risk if their husbands have sex with other partners without using condoms before or during their marriage. The religious right threatens NGOs that aggressively market condoms with a cutoff of official aid funds, on the grounds that those NGOs are promoting sexual promiscuity. Pushed by the religious right, Congress mandated that at least one third of the already paltry PEPFAR prevention budget go for abstinence-only programs.

The Vatican is also pushing its followers to oppose condom distribution in Africa because of religious doctrine that forbids the use of birth control.[27] These religious follies are one of the most extreme examples of rich peoples' preferences in the West trumping what is best for the poor in the Rest.

While prevention is tied up in religious knots, everyone seems to agree on treatment. The gay community, a group usually not identified with the religious right, is also emphasizing treatment. Activist groups such as ACT UP helped along the push for treatment—in their Web site for the 2002 Barcelona AIDS conference, they mentioned "treatment" eighteen times, but didn't mention "prevention" once.[28] Why do we have a well-publicized Treatment Access Coalition when there is no Prevention Access Coalition? Why didn't the WHO have a "3 by 5" campaign intended to *prevent* three million new cases of AIDS by the end of 2005? The activists have been only too successful in focusing attention on treatment instead of prevention. A LexisNexis search of articles on AIDS in Africa in *The Economist* over the previous two years found eighty-eight articles that mentioned "treatment" but only twenty-two that mentioned "prevention."

Instead of spending ten billion dollars on treatment over the next three years, money could be spent on preventing AIDS from spreading from the 28 million HIV-positive Africans to the 644 million HIV-negative Africans. Thailand has successfully implemented prevention campaigns targeting condom use among prostitutes, increasing condom usage from 15 percent to 90 percent and reducing new HIV infections dramatically. Senegal and Uganda have apparently also had success with vigorous prevention campaigns promoted by courageous political leaders (although the Ugandan government is now backing off from condom promotion under pressure from religious leaders).

If money spent on treatment went instead to effective prevention, between three and seventy-five new HIV infections could be averted for every extra year of life given to an AIDS patient. Spending AIDS money on treatment rather than on prevention makes the AIDS crisis *worse,* not better. If we consider that averting an HIV infection gives many extra years of life to each individual, then the case for prevention instead of treatment gets even stronger. For the same money spent giving one more year of life to an AIDS patient, you could give 75 to 1,500 years of additional life (say fifteen extra years for each of five to one hundred people) to the rest of the population through AIDS prevention.

We should ask the aid agencies why they want to put this much money now into the treatment of AIDS for twenty-nine million people when the same money spent to prevent the spread of HIV might have spared many of the twenty-nine million from infection. This past negligence is *not* an argument for or against any particular direction of action today—we must move forward from where we are now. But it does show how politicians and aid bureaucrats react passively to dramatic headlines and utopian ideals rather than according to where the small aid budget will benefit the most people. Is this what poor people themselves would choose to spend the money on?

Trade-offs

It is the job of economists to point out trade-offs; it is the job of politicians and Planners to deny that trade-offs exist. AIDS campaigners protest that

AIDS treatment money is "new money" that would have been otherwise unavailable, but that just begs the question of where new money is best spent. Why are there not campaigns to spread even further the successful campaigns against children's diarrhea, where a given amount of money—raised from the same sources—would reach many more people than money for AIDS treatment?

The utopian reaction is that the West will spend "whatever it takes" to cover *all* the health programs described above. This was the approach taken by the WHO Commission on Macroeconomics and Health in 2001. This commission recommended that rich countries spend an additional twenty-seven billion dollars on health in poor countries by 2007, which at the time was more than half of the world's foreign aid budget to poor countries. They ramp this number up to forty-seven billion dollars by 2015, of which twenty-two billion would be for AIDS. The commission's report was influential in gaining adherents for AIDS treatment in poor countries.

In an obscure footnote to the report, the commission notes that people often asked it what its priorities would be if only a lower sum were forthcoming, but it says it was "ethically and politically" unable to choose. The most charitable view is that this statement is the commission's strategy to get the money it wants. Otherwise, this refusal to make choices is inexcusable. Public policy is the science of doing the best you can with limited resources—it is dereliction of duty for professional economists to shrink from confronting trade-offs. Even when you get new resources, you still have to decide where they would be best used.

If you want priorities and trade-offs, you can get them in the WHO itself. The WHO's 2002 World Health Report contains the following common sense: "Not everything can be done in all settings, so some way of setting priorities needs to be found. The next chapter identifies costs and the impact on population health of a variety of interventions, as the basis on which to develop strategies to reduce risk."[29]

The next chapter in the WHO report actually states that money spent on educating prostitutes saves between one thousand and one hundred times more lives than the same amount of money spent on antiretroviral treatment.[30]

Getting back to the WHO Commission on Macroeconomics and Health, the commission's sum, according to its own assumptions, did not eliminate all avoidable deaths in the poor countries. These sums, not to mention total foreign aid, are paltry relative to all the things that the world's three billion desperately poor people need. The commission *did* place some limit on what it thought rich countries were willing to spend to save lives in poor countries. *Everybody* places limits on what they spend on health. Even in rich countries, people could maximize their chances of catching killer diseases early enough for treatment by, say, having a daily MRI. Nobody, except possibly Woody Allen, actually does this, because it's too costly relative to the expected gain in life and relative to other things that rich people would like to spend money on. Virtually nobody was advocating AIDS treatment in Africa when the drug cocktail cost more than ten thousand dollars per year. Everybody, except political campaigners, knows that money, whether "new" or "old," is limited.

A political campaigner giving a graphic description of AIDS patients dying without life-saving drugs is hard to resist, making the trade-offs described earlier seem coldhearted. But money should not be spent according to what the West considers the most dramatic kind of suffering. Others with other diseases have their own chronicles of suffering. The journalist Daniel Bergner describes the relentless wailing of mothers in Sierra Leone who have lost a child to measles, the wailing that never stopped in a village during a measles epidemic. The high fever of measles stirs up intestinal worms, which spill out from the children's noses. Sores erupt inside their mouths. The parents in desperation pour kerosene down the children's throats. The graves of the dead children lie behind their parents' huts, mounds of dirt covered by palm branches.[31]

Take also the small baby dying in his mother's arms, tortured by diarrhea, which can be prevented so easily and cheaply with oral rehydration therapy. *Many* deaths can be prevented more cheaply than treating AIDS, thus reaching many more suffering people on a limited aid budget. Nobody asks the poor in Africa whether they would like to see most "new" money spent on AIDS treatment as opposed to the many other dangers they face. The questions facing Western AIDS campaigners should not be "Do they deserve to die?" but "Do we deserve to decide who dies?"

Constance, the HIV-positive mother from Soweto whom I mention at the beginning of this chapter, had an interesting perspective on priorities. When I asked her to name Soweto's biggest problem, she did not say AIDS or lack of antiretroviral treatment. She said, "No jobs." Finding a way to earn money to feed herself and her children was a more pressing concern for her than her eventual death from AIDS.

The more sophisticated way to deny that trade-offs exist is to insist that each part of the budget is necessary for everything else to work. When asked to choose between guns and butter, the canny politician insists that guns are necessary to protect the butter. In the AIDS field, strategic responses gave us the mantra "prevention is impossible without treatment." The proposition rests on the plausible reasoning that people will not come forward to be tested (most HIV-positive Africans do not know they are HIV-positive) unless there is hope of treatment. Some bits of evidence support this intuition, but the notion has not really been subjected to enough empirical scrutiny. Moreover, it is also plausible, and there is also a little evidence, to support the idea that treatment makes prevention more difficult. There is evidence that people in rich countries engaged in riskier sexual behavior *after* HAART became available.[32] Prevention campaigns did work in Senegal, Thailand, and Uganda without being based on treatment. Finally, there remains the risk that treatment with imperfect adherence will result in emergence of resistant strains of HIV, so that treatment itself will sow the seeds of its own downfall.[33]

Dysfunctional Health Systems

Admittedly, these trade-offs are oversimplified. Cost-effectiveness analysis—which compares different health interventions according to their estimated benefits (years of lives saved) and costs (drugs, medical personnel, clinics, hospitals) gives us these numbers. This is the mainstream approach in the international public health field. Many of the advocates for treatment, such as Grö Harlem Brundtland and WHO staff, buy into this approach. They just fail to follow the logic through to the conclusion that you could save many more lives spending on other health interventions—including AIDS prevention—with what they propose to spend on AIDS treatment.

Lant Pritchett of Harvard's Kennedy School and Jeffrey Hammer and Deon Filmer of the World Bank criticize these cost-effectiveness calculations for the oversimplifications they are. Just because it costs a dollar to treat a person's illness, it doesn't follow that giving a dollar to the national health system will result in treating that person. We have already seen what a difficult time international aid planners have in getting even simple interventions to work.

Despite the health successes noted earlier, Filmer, Hammer, and Pritchett talk about "weak links in the chain" that leads from the donor's dollar to the person's treatment. The second tragedy of the world's poor means that many effective interventions are not reaching the poor because of some of the follies of Planners mentioned in previous chapters.

Because of the insistence on working through governments, funds get lost in patronage-swollen national health bureaucracies (not to mention international health bureaucracies). In countries where corruption is as endemic as AIDS, health officials often sell aid-financed drugs on the black market. Studies in Cameroon, Guinea, Tanzania, and Uganda estimated that 30 to 70 percent of government drugs disappeared before reaching the patients. In one low-income country, a crusading journalist accused the ministry of health of misappropriating fifty million dollars in aid funds. The ministry issued a rebuttal: the journalist had irresponsibly implied that the fifty million dollars had gone AWOL in a single year, whereas they had actually misappropriated the money over a *three-year* period.

I have heard from multiple sources of AIDS money disappearing before it reached any real or potential victims. In Cameroon, the World Bank lent a large amount for AIDS, which the health ministry handed out to local AIDS committees. Critics allege there was virtually no monitoring and no controls and are not quite sure what the local committees did, except for vaguely defined "AIDS sensitization." In one alleged case, a local committee chair threw a large party for his daughter's wedding under the category of "AIDS sensitization."

Many doctors, nurses, and other health workers are poorly trained and poorly paid. The AIDS treatment campaigners are oblivious to these harsh realities of medical care in poor countries. The worst part about the heartfelt plea for money for AIDS treatment is that it will save many fewer lives than campaigners promise.

Of course, similar arguments would also weaken the case for the allegedly more cost effective health interventions on illnesses such as diarrhea, malaria, and measles. They do not work everywhere as well as they should, as the rest of this book makes clear. But this complication does not strengthen the argument for funding AIDS treatment in Africa. The cheap interventions have some successes, as noted earlier. They are cheap because they are simpler for Searchers to find ways to administer—a measles vaccination has to happen only at one given point just for each child. A bed net impregnated with insecticide has to be handed out just once to each potential malaria victim, along with the information on how to use it, then impregnated again periodically.

The treatment of AIDS with drugs is vastly more complicated and depends on many more "links in the chain": refrigeration, lab tests, expert monitoring and adjusting therapy if resistance and toxic side effects emerge, and educating the patient on how to take the drug. In Europe and North America, 20 to 40 percent of AIDS patients do not take their drugs as prescribed. Resistance will emerge if there are lapses from the correct regimen. Even with good intentions, government bureaucrats currently do a poor job making sure that drug supply matches demand in each locale.

Unfortunately for the patients, it is critical that AIDS treatment not be interrupted by drug shortages (critical both for effectiveness and for preventing resistant strains from developing). A 2004 article in the *Journal of the American Medical Association,* while generally positive about treatment in developing countries, sounded some concerns:

> *Finally, how will the tens of thousands of health care professionals required for global implementation of HIV care strategies be trained, motivated, supervised, resourced, and adequately reimbursed to ensure the level of care required for this complex disease? To scale up antiretroviral therapy for HIV without ensuring infrastructure, including trained practitioners, a safe and reliable drug delivery system, and simple but effective models for continuity of care, would be a disaster, leading to ineffective treatment and rapid development of resistance.*[34]

Even doing the huge amount of testing required to find out who is HIV-positive and eligible for treatment would likely overwhelm health budgets and infrastructure in poor countries.

The tardy response to the AIDS crisis has meant that it has built up to an unbearable tragedy—to the point that it's now too late to save many millions of lives. Spending money on a mostly futile attempt to save all the lives of this generation of AIDS victims will take money away from saving the lives of the next generation, perpetuating the tragedy. The political lobby for treatment doesn't mention that no amount of treatment will stop the crisis. The only way to stop the threat to Africans and others is *prevention,* no matter how unappealing the politics or how uncomfortable the discussion about sex. The task is to save the next generation before it is again too late.

Let's commend the campaigners wanting to spend money on AIDS treatment in Africa for their dedication and compassion. But could they redirect some of that compassion to where it will do the most good?

Feedback and Idealism Again

Why did the health system fail on AIDS when foreign aid successes are more common in public health than in other areas? The AIDS crisis was less susceptible to feedback, and the interests of the poor were not coincident with rich-country politics. The necessary actions were in the area of prevention, which doesn't involve just taking a pill or getting a shot, as in many of the other successes. The donors showed shamefully little interest in researching the sexual behavior that causes AIDS to spread or in which prevention strategies work to change that behavior. Donors should have asked, "How many people have we prevented from becoming HIV-positive?"

A patient who is already HIV-positive is a highly visible target for help—a lot more visible than someone who is going to get infected in the future but doesn't yet know it. The rich-country politicians and aid agencies get more PR credit for saving the lives of sick patients, even if the interests of the poor would call for saving them from getting sick in the first place. This again confirms the prediction that aid agencies skew their efforts toward visible outcomes, even when those outcomes have a lower payoff than less visible interventions.

The politicians and aid agencies didn't have the courage to confront the uncomfortable question of how to change human sexual behavior. The AIDS failure shows that the bureaucratic healers too often settle for simply handing out pills.

Heroes

The AIDS disaster in Africa features many ineffective bureaucrats and few energetic rescuers. But there are a few heroes. A group called HIVSA works in Soweto, South Africa, helping people like Constance. Its energetic director, Steven Whiting, was formerly an affluent interior designer. He stumbled on the AIDS issue by chance when he got the contract to renovate the head-quarters of the Perinatal HIV Research Unit at the largest hospital in Soweto. He was so moved by what he saw there that he decided to quit his job and devote his efforts full time to fighting AIDS.

HIVSA does the little things that make a difference. It provides the drug nevirapine to block transmission of the HIV virus from mothers to new-borns. Doctors give just one dose during labor, an intervention that is highly cost effective compared with other AIDS treatments. To follow up, HIVSA provides infant formula to HIV-positive new mothers, since breast-feeding can also transmit the HIV virus to newborns. Less tangibly, HIVSA provides support groups meeting in health clinics throughout Soweto to help HIV-positive mothers confront the stigma of HIV and their many other problems. (One hint of such problems: the signs all over the clinics announcing that no guns are allowed inside the clinics.) When the mothers visit the clinics, they get a free meal and nutritional supplements. Mothers and HIVSA staff work in community gardens attached to each clinic to provide food. HIVSA staff are almost all from the Soweto community and are HIV-positive.

Constance has problems that are overwhelming, but her most recent baby was born HIV-negative, thanks to nevirapine. HIVSA's free meals, nutritional supplements, and emotional support make her life a little more bearable.

If only all the West's efforts at fighting AIDS were so constructive at giving the poor victims what they want and need. The West largely ignored AIDS when it was building up to a huge humanitarian crisis, only to focus now on an expensive attempt at treatment that neglects the prevention so critical to stop the disaster from getting even worse.

Prostitutes for Prevention

Prostitutes in Sonagachi, the red-light district of Calcutta, India, form a world unto themselves. Social norms about female sexual behavior in India are such that prostitution carries an even larger stigma in India than elsewhere. Cut off from the wider world, prostitutes have their own subculture, with an elite of madams and pimps. As in any subculture, its members strive for status. Prostitutes who aspire to greater status attain it most commonly by attracting long-term clients.

Many well-intentioned bureaucrats have tried to help the prostitutes by "rescuing" them and taking them to shelters to be trained in another profession, such as tailoring. However, sex work pays a lot better than tailoring, and former prostitutes face harassment and discrimination in the outside world. Hence, most "rescued" women returned to prostitution. But the advent of the AIDS epidemic in India and the well-known role of prostitutes in spreading AIDS caused increased concern about these failures.

Dr. Smarajit Jana, head of the All India Institute of Hygiene and Public Health, had another idea in 1992. He and his team would learn the subculture of the prostitutes and work with it to fight AIDS. They formed a mutually respectful relationship with the madams, pimps, prostitutes, and clients. They noted the class system within Sonagachi. By trial and error, and with feedback from the prostitutes, Dr. Jana and his team hit upon a strategy for fighting AIDS. The strategy was awfully simple in retrospect: they trained a group of twelve prostitutes to educate their fellow workers about the dangers of AIDS and the need to use condoms. The peer educators wore green medical coats when they were engaged in their public health work, and they attained greater status in Sonagachi. Condom use in Sonagachi increased dramatically. By 1999, HIV incidence in Sonagachi was only 6 percent, compared with 50 percent in other red-light districts in India.

The project had other, unexpected consequences. The increased confidence of the peer educators and the media attention on the success of prevention efforts led the community to aspire to greater things. The prostitutes formed a union to campaign for legalization of prostitution and a reduction in police harassment, and to organize festivals and health fairs. Dr. Jana's approach based on feedback from the intended beneficiaries succeeded when so many other AIDS prevention programs had failed.[35]

PART III

THE WHITE MAN'S ARMY

CHAPTER EIGHT

From Colonialism to Postmodern Imperialism

The curious task of economics is to demonstrate to men
How little they really know
About what they imagine they can design.

F. A. Hayek, The Fatal Conceit:
The Errors of Socialism, *1988*[1]

Imperialism is coming back into fashion in the West. Western journalists report locals harboring nostalgia for colonialism in Sierra Leone or even for white-minority regimes in Zimbabwe. Other prominent Western journalists write about "The Case for American Empire."[2]

Prominent political scientists James Fearon and David Laitin of Stanford wrote in the spring of 2004:

> The United States is now drawn toward a form of international governance that may be described as neotrusteeship, or more provocatively, postmodern imperialism. The terms refer to the complicated mixes of international and domestic governance structures that are evolving in Bosnia, Kosovo, East Timor, Sierra Leone, Afghanistan and, possibly in the long run, Iraq. Similar to classical imperialism, these efforts involve a remarkable degree of control over domestic political authority and basic economic functions by foreign countries.

Fearon and Laitin conclude that "the current, ad hoc and underrationalized arrangements ought to be reformed in the direction of neotrusteeship."[3]

Altogether, five different articles in *Foreign Affairs*, the bible of the policymaking elite, in the past few years have considered some variant of "postmodern imperialism" for ailing states.[4] In a similar vein, political scientist Stephen Krasner (also of Stanford) writes in the fall of 2004:

> *Left to their own devices, collapsed and badly governed states will not fix themselves*
> *because they have limited administrative capacity, not least with regard to maintaining*
> *internal security. Occupying powers cannot escape choices about what new governance*
> *structures will be created and sustained. To reduce international threats and improve the*
> *prospects for individuals in such polities, alternative institutional arrangements*
> *supported by external actors, such as de facto trusteeships and shared sovereignty, should*
> *be added to the list of policy options.*

He concludes: "De facto trusteeships, and especially shared sovereignty, would offer political leaders a better chance of bringing peace and prosperity to the populations of badly governed states." Secretary of State Condoleezza Rice appointed Stephen Krasner to be head of policy planning at the State Department on February 4, 2005.

As Naomi Klein wrote in *The Nation* on May 2, 2005, the U.S. State Department has an interesting new office:

> *On August 5, 2004, the White House created the Office of the Coordinator for*
> *Reconstruction and Stabilization, headed by former U.S. Ambassador to Ukraine Carlos*
> *Pascual. Its mandate is to draw up elaborate "post-conflict" plans for up to twenty-five*
> *countries that are not, as of yet, in conflict. . . . Pascual told an audience . . . in October,*
> *will have "pre-completed" contracts to rebuild countries that are not yet broken. . . . The*
> *plans Pascual's teams have been drawing up . . . are about changing "the very social fabric*
> *of a nation." . . . The office's mandate is not to rebuild any old states . . . but to create*
> *"democratic and market-oriented" ones. . . . Sometimes rebuilding, he explained, means*
> *"tearing apart the old."*

Stephen Krasner and Carlos Pascual wrote an article for *Foreign Affairs* in July/August 2005 explaining further how all this would work. Like their foreign aid counterparts, Krasner and Pascual are Planners:

> *During U.S. or other military or peacekeeping operations, the new office will coordinate*
> *stabilization and reconstruction activities between civilian agencies and the military. As*
> *part of the military's planning effort, interagency civilian teams will deploy to regional*
> *combatant commands to develop strategies for stabilization and reconstruction. This type*
> *of involvement will help make certain that assumptions about civilian reconstruction*
> *capabilities remain realistic. After the planning stage, advance civilian teams will deploy*
> *with the military to help direct stabilization and reconstruction.*

Further, they said, there will be coordination with the other kind of foreign aid, the one that involves USAID, the World Bank, and the IMF. Krasner and Pascual offer the hope that "the United States will have enabled more people to enjoy the benefits of peace, democracy, and market economies."[5]

It used to be that everybody agreed that colonialism was bad. Frustration with disastrous postcolonial outcomes in Africa has led many to imagine a colonial past of peace and prosperity. More sophisticated scholars have also challenged the conventional wisdom of evil colonialism. Harvard historian Niall Ferguson, whose work on every topic but this one I greatly admire, says that there is "such a thing as liberal imperialism and that on balance it was a good thing...in many cases of economic 'backwardness,' a liberal empire can do better than a nation-state."[6]

Such ambitious claims have provoked this economist to venture outside of normal economics territory, to considering economic development as pursued through military occupation, invasions, and nation-building. Certainly this part of the book is looking at a set of actors different from those in the rest of the book—most of the advocates of foreign aid are horrified at the idea of imperialism and colonialism, new or old, and so this chapter is less relevant for them. Yet the neo-imperialists represent an influential approach to ending world poverty that needs to be addressed.

Following the familiar escalation syndrome, failed intrusions of the West provide the motivation for the West to become even more intrusive. Aid failed in the sixties and seventies because government was bad, and the West used that to justify structural adjustment to induce governments to change in the eighties and nineties. Structural adjustment failed to change governments in the eighties and nineties, so now some in the West entertain replacing national government altogether with "trusteeship" or "shared sovereignty" for the most extreme failures.

This chapter argues that the old conventional wisdom was correct—the previous imperial era did not facilitate economic development. Instead, it created some of the conditions that bred occasions for today's unsuccessful interventions: failed states and bad government. The West sowed further mayhem with chaotic decolonization, especially the arbitrary way the West drew borders. Although many will deny the relevance of colonial experience to today's allegedly more humanitarian exercises, I argue that there are many lessons to be gained from the previous wave of Western intervention in the Rest—as many problems were created by colonizers' incompetence as by their exploitation. It is at least ironic that some offer a new White Man's Burden to clean up the mess left behind by the old White Man's Burden.

This is not to say that the West was the only driving force that created bad governments in the Rest—this would exaggerate the West's negative impact just as the White Man's Burden exaggerates the West's positive potential. There was plenty of despotism and vicious politics before the West ever showed up. Nor is the West the only source of imperial conquest— remember, say, the Aztecs, the Muslims, and the Mongols?

The colonialists left behind independent states with arbitrary borders that had little chance to build up popular legitimacy. Sometimes these governments comprised little more than an independence agitator, an army, and a foreign aid budget. Although they had shallow roots, the new states brought benefits to their new leaders. The new rulers could use the inherited colonial army to levy high taxes on natural resources or any other valuable economic activity, and they had a tradition of autocratic colonial rule and economic planning. It was not surprising that most of these new states were unfriendly to both economic and political freedoms.

Sponsoring Native Autocrats

To make things worse, colonial administration had reinforced autocracy. The preferred method of colonial administration had been "indirect rule," relying on native rulers or intermediaries. Columbia University professor Mahmood Mamdani labels this system in Africa "decentralized despotism." Indirect rule was inevitable given that the colonizers were unwilling or unable to put more than a few Europeans in the colonies to administer them. There were enough Europeans with power to mess up the pre-colonial arrangements (which were far from the blank slate Europeans presumed), but not enough to create anything resembling beneficent institutions. Destruction is always easier than construction.

In 1893, the Covenanted Civil Service for India had only 898 positions for Brits to rule a continent of around 300 million. The entire Indian civil service (the rest of which was Indian) was 4,849 officials. After the Indian Mutiny in 1857, the government increased the number of British troops, but it was still only 78,000 by 1885 (to go along with 154,000 Indian troops).[7]

Earlier, regarding the East India Company of the eighteenth century, Edmund Burke described how arrogant Brits messed up India: "a few obscure young men, who having obtained, by ways which they could not comprehend, a power of which they saw neither the purpose nor the limits, tossed about, subverted, and tore to pieces . . . the most ancient and most revered institutions of ages and nations."[8]

In Africa, the ratio of Europeans to population was also scanty:[9]

Table 6. European Officials and Native Population in Africa, 1939

	European officials	Native population in millions
British Nigeria	1,315	20.0
Belgian Congo	2,384	9.4
French Equatorial Africa	887	3.2
French West Africa	3,660	15.0

These few whites were not abundantly qualified to create new nations from scratch. They set low standards of performance, mitigated only by their consistent failure to attain them. A Belgian professor described Belgian colonial administrators in the Congo as: "too young and incompetent; they are sent out, without knowing the native language, without serious training, without a probationary period, to a distant place where they are usually alone. Isolated, powerless, able only with difficulty to leave their headquarters, they do not travel enough in their district, they do not get to know the villages."[10] (Sort of reminds me of myself as a young World Bank official!)

These raw recruits had to be "tax collectors, census takers, policemen, judges, agronomists, road builders, sanitationists, and wise counselors," all while they were often sick. The Igbo in Nigeria derisively referred to British district officers as "student magistrates," and performed masquerades in which "Government" was a faceless figure holding a sheet of paper.[11]

Given these administrative limitations, the colonizers in Africa often relied on the "chiefs" to rule for them. But who were the "chiefs"? The colonizers, displaying a room-temperature IQ about the locals, didn't know how to deal with the many non-chief societies in Africa. Igboland in Nigeria was a non-state society, with decentralized village self-government. Other examples were the slash-and-burn agriculturalists of northern Uganda and the pastoral communities of the East African Rift Valley. The British appointed chiefs anyway, sometimes choosing one of the village heads to rule over the others. In 1930 in Tanganyika, colonizers adapted the rule that "every African belonged to a tribe, just as every European belonged to a nation." Officials said, "Each tribe must be considered a distinct unit . . . each tribe must be under a chief," although "most administrators knew that many peoples had no chiefs." Earlier German practice in Tanganyika had also invented chiefs. Understandably unhappy with outsiders imposing their leaders on them, Africans started two rebellions directly caused by "indirect rule": the Maji-Maji revolt in Tanganyika and the rebellion against "warrant chiefs" (those "warranted" by the colonial officials) in Igboland.[12] Women, who were among the main victims of the new order, led the latter revolt.[13]

Even when chiefs existed, they had limited powers before colonial times. There were only loose confederations of the Akan peoples of Ghana, the Ashanti and the Fanti. The chiefs of these confederations had limited powers, acting with the concurrence of their counselors. A chief who acted on his own could expect to lose his throne. The colonizers took over the decentralized system of rule in Africa, yet removed the checks and balances on that rule. The restored Ashanti Confederacy of 1935 under the British lacked the counselors who had previously shared power with the chief. The confederacy quickly abolished "youngmen's associations," another traditional check on chiefly power.[14]

A European observer in Nigeria noted, "The chief is the law, subject to only one higher authority, the white official stationed in his state as advisor. The chief hires his own police... he is often the prosecutor and the judge combined and he employes the jailer to hold his victims in custody at his pleasure. No oriental despot ever had greater power than these black tyrants, thanks to the support which they receive from the white officials who quietly keep in the background."[15]

Thus Europeans may have actually increased despotism in Africa. According to Professor Mamdani, nowhere in Africa had there been "centralized judicial institutions with exclusive jurisdiction over an area," which colonialism created as "customary." The British governor of Sudan described his policy of restoring "tribal chiefs" as aimed at "making the Sudan safe for autocracy."[16]

The Europeans delegated to the "chiefs" the collection of taxes and the supervision of forced labor. In the Buganda Agreement of 1900, the British gave the chief the right to assess and collect taxes, and to hand out justice. The chief was to draft one laborer for every three households for a month each year to maintain the roads. In French colonies, the chief's duties included "collection of taxes, requisitioning labor, compulsory crop cultivation and provision of military recruits." In the Belgian Congo, chiefs were to enforce "forced labor, compulsory cultivation, conscription, labor recruitment, and other state requirements."[17] The chiefs often took advantage of their unchecked powers to collect extra taxes and labor for themselves. A missionary in German Tanganyika estimated the ratio of taxes the chiefs collected to taxes turned over to the colony as seven to one. In northern Nigeria, Lord Frederick Lugard, the British architect of indirect rule, tried to end abuses by paying the emirs a salary.[18] Like later aid agency recommendations to end corruption by raising civil servant pay, the salaries did not stop the abuses. There was no reason to expect them to—in either case—without effective checks on the ability to extract loot. The Europeans kept their despots accountable, not to their subjects but to Europeans. In Buganda, the struggle with the Europeans over the Kabaka's right to appoint chiefs forced the prime minister of Buganda to resign in 1926.

When the French conquered the kingdom of Segu in what is now Mali in 1890, they deported the Tukolor rulers to Senegal, put in a chief from the friendly Bambara dynasty, subsequently questioned his loyalty and executed him, and then appointed a rival Bambara, before finally abolishing the chiefdom altogether—all within three years. Both the British and French indulged the urge to appoint "the right native" to colonial positions.

University of Cambridge professor John Iliffe notes in his magnificent history of Africa that even the French and Belgian system labeled "direct rule" in Africa was really indirect rule. While the French and Belgians were at the top of the pyramid, they appointed *chefs de canton* drawn from the local population (chosen as usual for their loyalty to the colonizers), who in turn relied upon village chiefs.[19]

Despite the pretensions of the colonizers to control things, opportunistic locals easily bamboozled them. In Igboland, the elderly collaborators with the British rewrote "customary law" to their own advantage, often at the expense of women and the young. It was no accident that women led the revolt against chiefs in Igboland. Even European district chiefs who took direct decisions had to rely on native clerks and interpreters. One of the latter in Dahomey established his own court, in which he took bribes to reach a decision before presenting it to the colonial administrator, claiming "the white man will believe anything he says." In Buganda, the chiefly allies of the British exploited the 1900 agreement to distribute the kingdom's land among themselves.[20] Like today's donors and postmodern imperialists, the colonizers were outside Planners who could never know the reality on the ground. Like their modern-day counterparts, colonizers often unwittingly destabilized the balance of internal power.

Before the scramble for Africa, there had been educated Africans who had some power in colonial regimes. Missionaries founded a university in Sierra Leone, the Fourah Bay College, in 1827. West Africans sent their children there, as well as to London law schools. Many of these graduates held positions in the colonial administrations, including legislative posts in the Gold Coast and Lagos as early as the 1850s. Educated Africans made up nearly half of the senior posts in the 1890s in these two colonies. After the scramble added interior territory to what had previously been coastal enclave colonies, the British and French betrayed their educated African allies. The colonizers decided they needed traditional rulers to hold the interior, and removed from power the educated Africans on the coast. Sir George Goldie of the Royal Niger Company in 1898 said power must be shifted from "the educated strata to traditional chiefs." The educated turned in frustration to Pan-Africanist ideologies and later played an important role in independence movements. As if they had not created enough divisions already, the colonialists left behind a legacy of mistrust between the educated class and the traditional rulers. (A rare exception to this mismanagement of traditional rulers was Botswana, where the British left largely intact the traditional structures of the ethnically homogeneous Tswana tribes. The first president, Seretse Khama, had earned a law degree in Britain and was a traditional ruler.)

Another consequence of favoring elderly traditional rulers under colonialism was the exacerbation of Africa's long-standing generational conflict between young and old males. Professor Iliffe emphasizes that a persistent theme in Africa's history was the scarcity of labor relative to abundant land, which led societies to maximize fertility. One institution to increase fertility was polygamy, which left older men and younger men competing for the same women. Indirect rule shifted power in favor of elderly autocrats by removing some of the checks and balances on them. In independent Africa, some part of the political conflict would turn out to be the revolt of younger males, who sometimes triumphed over their elders by their advantage at using political violence.[21]

Some colonies outside of Africa also used indirect rule. The Dutch compelled native rulers in Indonesia to maintain coffee plantations and pay coffee tribute to them around the beginning of the nineteenth century, using forced labor.[22] In Bengal, the British retained the landed aristocracy, the zamindars, to collect taxes for them, paying a fixed sum for a given area. They even appointed zamindars where there was no landed aristocracy to begin with, creating an elite from scratch. Today the formerly zamindar-controlled regions do worse on many development outcomes than other parts of India.[23]

Elsewhere in India, the British had more direct rule, although they still delegated tax collection to Indian "collectors." A system more akin to indirect rule operated in the more than six hundred princely states in India, where the British claimed "paramountcy" but were content to just leave a resident to advise the prince.[24]

Beneficent but Crazy

It is common to attribute the defects of colonialism purely to Western exploitation. Today's nation builders would claim that they are more altruistic than the colonizers. However, there were humanitarian instincts at work during colonialism similar to those in today's nation-building (just as there are some self-interested objectives today). Moreover, the specific problems created by colonialism seem to reflect more Europeans' incompetence than their avarice.

Certainly there was change over time from the era of annihilation of indigenous people and African slavery in the sixteenth through eighteenth centuries to the more beneficent empires of the nineteenth and twentieth centuries, just as nation-building today is more beneficent than colonial rule. Kipling wrote "The White Man's Burden" at the height of the imperial era in 1898. Before that, the British government ban on the slave trade in 1807 inaugurated a more humanitarian imperial era. The British agreed to take over Sierra Leone in 1808 from a chartered company, which had failed to make the country a haven for freed slaves (most of whom had died). The British acted out of humanitarian concern, including the desire for a base to prevent the slave trade. In Freetown, the British resettled slaves their warships had intercepted in transit. Christians back in Britain gave donations to support the Sierra Leone settlements. Like Save the Children later, the charity stressed the person-to-person link. For a gift of five pounds, the missionaries would baptize the freed slave on the receiving end with the name of the donor.[25]

White imperial benevolence was a strong staple of propaganda back home to justify the colonies. Thomas Macaulay told the House of Commons during the debate on the India Bill of 1833: "[India will be] the imperishable empire of our arts and morals, our literature, and laws.... I see bloody and degrading superstititons gradually losing their power.... I see the public mind of India, that public mind which we found debased and contracted by the worst forms of political and religious tyranny, expanding itself to just and noble views of the ends of government."

The imperialists early on had ideas that would later become "development economics." The governor-general of India from 1828 to 1835 spoke of the "improvement" of India, "founding British greatness on Indian happiness."[26] A British commentator on India concurred in 1854: "when the contrast between the influence of a Christian and a Heathen government is considered; when the knowledge of the wretchedness of the people forces us to reflect on the unspeakable blessings to millions that would follow the extension of British rule, it is not ambition but benevolence that dictates the desire for the whole country."[27]

The nineteenth-century economist John Stuart Mill saw the British empire as furnishing what sounds like a colonial combination of the Big Push and structural adjustment: "a better government: more complete security of property; moderate taxes; a more permanent... tenure of land... the introduction of foreign arts... and the introduction of foreign capital, which renders the increase of production no longer exclusively dependent on the thrift or providence of the inhabitants themselves."[28] Refuting criticism that Manchester capitalists dictated imperial policy, Lord Palmerston said in 1863, "India was governed for India and...not for the Manchester people."[29]

In India, the British doubled the area under irrigation from 1891 to 1938, introduced a postal and telegraph system, and built forty thousand miles of railroad track.[30] Railways had been part of India's "development plan" since the 1820s, the key to "opening up" the country to commerce.[31] The Indian civil servant Charles Trevelyan in 1853 had told a Commons committee that railways would be "the greatest missionary of all."[32] The development efforts were not any more successful than today's foreign aid or nation-building, however: Indian income per capita failed to rise from 1820 to 1870, grew at only 0.5 percent per annum from 1870 to 1913, then failed to grow again from 1913 to independence in 1947.[33]

In the American empire in the Philippines, American teachers and their Filipino successors imparted at least a rough education, raising literacy and making English the lingua franca in the ethnically fragmented islands. Americans also contributed dams and irrigation facilities, mines and timber concessions, roads, railways, and ports, legal reforms, a tax system, and currency reform. They nearly wiped out cholera by teaching Filipinos to boil water, reduced malaria by controlling mosquitoes, and controlled smallpox by compulsory vaccination. They advocated increased production of rubber, hemp, sugar, tobacco, and lumber.

The imperialists also built railways throughout Africa, using public money because of the lack of private interest (except in the Belgian Congo). The French built the first railway in Senegal in 1883. Later railways in French West Africa connected plantations in the interior to ports on the coast. The copper mines of the Belgian Congo shipped ore south after 1910, putting out a spur to meet the railways emanating from South Africa. The British empire planner Cecil Rhodes called railways and the telegraph "the keys to the continent."[34] Railways reduced Africa's ancient curse of high transport costs by as much as 90 percent.[35] The advent of roads in the twentieth century reduced the transport cost from farms to railheads by a similar amount.[36]

Among other benevolent actions, the French colonial minister Albert Sarraut launched a program in 1923 to improve general hygiene and medical care in the African colonies, including clinics, training centers, maternity homes, and ambulances. He aimed to enable the most deprived segment of the population in the remote bush to gain access to medical care. Other programs about the same time included "pilot farms" to disseminate agricultural knowledge.

European medicine made a lot of progress against smallpox and sleeping sickness in the first half of the twentieth century. Colonial maternity clinics also contributed to a fall in infant mortality. The end result was that death rates fell and population rose in the twentieth century in colonial Africa.

Colonizers had much more uneven performance on providing public education, for which there was a lot of demand by Africans eager to get ahead. In 1949–1950, 33 percent of children were in primary school in the Belgian Congo, 26 percent in Kenya, 16 percent in Nigeria, and only 6 percent in French West Africa. Secondary education was far worse, enrolling only 1 to 2 percent of young Africans in 1950.[37]

Cocoa and coffee farms took hold under the British and French colonizers in Africa, bringing benefits to the locals. The colonizers' railways (and later roads) facilitated the access of African cocoa and coffee farmers to the world market.[38] Cocoa in Ghana fueled per capita growth somewhat more rapidly than in British India: 1.3 percent per annum from 1870 to 1913.[39]

However, even with the best of motives, colonial officials suffered from all the same problems that characterize today's White Man's Burden: excessive self-confidence of bureaucrats, coercive top-down planning, desultory knowledge of local conditions, and little feedback from the locals on what worked. Under the theory that "whites know best," colonialists forced development schemes on the locals rather than respecting their economic choices. A British colonial directive on Uganda in 1925 went: "Natives to be informed that three courses are open: cotton, labor for Government, labor for planters. . . . [T]hey cannot be permitted to do nothing." There were also forced cotton-growing schemes in Congo, Nyasaland, Tanganyika, and Upper Volta.

Perhaps force was necessary because the natives were choosing to grow high-yield food crops such as millet while they were "doing nothing." The obsession with cotton often displaced these high-return food crops.[40]

The British pursued a similar policy in Sierra Leone, where they imposed a tax on huts to try to spur production of cash crops such as oil palm. One district commissioner said that the tax was necessary for the natives to "rouse them from their apathy and indolence and to bring them more in touch with civilizing influences." When the natives resisted being taxed for their own good, British soldiers and native auxiliaries killed the resisters.[41]

British colonial officials' next bright idea in Sierra Leone was to introduce long-staple cotton to replace the short-staple cotton already grown by local farmers. The results were disastrous: heavy rain eroded long-staple fields. The peasants had not chosen their methods by accident: intercropping short-staple cotton with food crops controlled erosion, kept down plant pests, and preserved food security. The short-staple cotton was suitable for locally produced cloths.

The local British officials also introduced irrigated rice in Sierra Leone, whose yields rapidly declined due to irrigation's by-products of acidity and salinity. Local farmers were already getting high yields from rice grown in mangrove swamps. Not yet convinced of their own fallibility, the Brits introduced tractors into Sierra Leone in the 1950s. The tractors never paid for themselves, which was not surprising given the missing imperative to economize on abundant labor. Tractor farms produced 4 percent of Sierra Leone's rice output, but took 80 percent of the colonial Department of Agriculture's spending.

In Malawi's Shire Valley from 1940 to 1960, British officials tried to teach the peasants how to farm. They offered the standard solution of ridging to combat soil erosion, and were at a loss to understand why Malawian farmers resisted the tried-and-true technique of British farmers. Unfortunately, ridging in the sandy soils of the Shire Valley led to *more* erosion during the rainy season, while exposing the roots of the plants to attacks by white ants during the dry season.[42]

A famous colonial project was the Tanganyika Groundnuts Scheme of the 1940s. A subsidiary of Unilever, which manufactured soap from vegetable oils, suggested growing groundnuts (peanuts) in Tanzania during British shortages of cooking oil and other foods. However, the Unilever subsidiary didn't think a private project could handle the ambitious scheme. The socialist food minister in postwar Britain, John Strachey, embraced the project. The government created a public corporation and appointed Major General Desmond Harrison to what they saw as a military operation. Major General Harrison set up headquarters at Kongwa, an area of marginal rainfall. Henry Stanley had described the area as "an interminable jungle of thornbushes." Clearing the jungle required teams of two bulldozers linked by naval anchor chains (which were late in arriving because a British official back home thought the order for ship anchors for the middle of Tanzania was a joke). This Fitzcarraldo territory was home to bees so vicious that they put some bulldozer operators in the hospital. The bulldozers' work still left the roots, which ate up the root-cutting equipment. Out of the original proposal of 3.25 million acres, the project cleared ten thousand acres.

Still, the project continued. Plantable when moist, the ground turned into concrete by harvesting time in the dry season. Since groundnuts grow underground, this was a problem. The project had bought four thousand tons of peanuts for seed. After two seasons, the project produced two thousand tons of peanuts. Faced with a state enterprise that had turned four thousand tons of peanuts into two thousand tons, the British government finally cancelled the project.[43]

Despite (or because of) these heroic efforts, African growth under the imperialists was modest: 0.6 percent per annum from 1870 to 1913 and then 0.9 percent per annum from 1913 to 1950.[44] Looking at Africa, India, and other Asian colonies besides India together, we see that the gap between Europe and its colonies grew during the colonial period (figure 27). After independence, Africa continued to fall further behind Europe, while India and other Asian colonies kept up with European growth. It is hard to see any positive overall effect of colonial rule compared to independent states.[45]

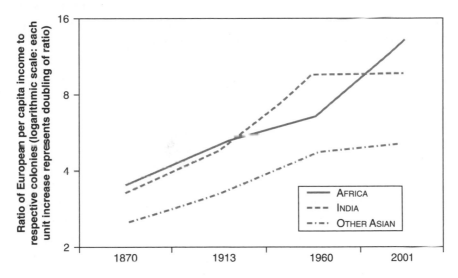

Fig. 27. Ratio of Europe's Income to Colonies

Benefits of Not Being Colonized

It is also interesting that the notable East Asian success stories—China, Japan, Korea, Taiwan, and Thailand—were never completely colonized by Europeans. In contrast, East Asia's main disappointment, the Philippines, was colonized by Spain and the United States.

The few areas of the world that were not formally colonized by Europeans provide an interesting, although imperfect, counterfactual to what would have happened in the absence of the White Man's Burden. They are imperfect as a test of colonialism because these areas were not chosen randomly—they wound up that way because of factors that influenced their social evolution. There was also some degree of European control in some of these territories, like the infamous European enclaves in China. Korea and Taiwan did spend some part of the twentieth century as colonies of Japan.

I compare the non-colonies to European colonies that were not settled by Europeans. The colonies settled by Europeans are a special case, discussed in an earlier chapter. The non-settlement colonies are a more natural experiment of European intervention from afar. The non-colonies had more rapid increases in secondary education from 1960 to 2001. Growth per capita from 1950 to 2001 was 1.7 percentage points higher in the non-colonies than the non-settlement colonies, a huge difference for a fifty-one-year period. By 2001, income was 2.4 times higher in the non-colonies than in the former non-settlement colonies.

Brown University economist Louis Putterman argues that having a long history of statehood (which was one thing that prevented colonization in many cases) was favorable for seizing economic opportunities in the postwar era, and that may be the reason for the different outcomes in the non-colonies compared with the colonies. Naturally formed states outperformed artificial colonial creations.

The difference in per capita income in 2001 conceals very high variance of outcomes among the non-colonies. China, Japan, South Korea, and Taiwan had spectacular growth in income, Thailand and Turkey only slightly less impressive growth, and Iran and Saudi Arabia had a windfall gain in oil income. On the negative side, North Korea's Stalinist development strategy gave a very different outcome than the development path of its former countrymen in South Korea. Afghanistan was a disaster of tribal strife, communism, and foreign intervention. Bhutan, Ethiopia, and Nepal were hardly poster children for the benefits of escaping European control, either. We will never know what would have happened to Tibet if China had not swallowed it in 1951. So absence of the White Man's Burden did not ensure paradise. It just gave a better result on average than colonialism (and the better result is statistically distinguishable from colonies, despite the high variance of non-colonial outcomes; see figure 28).

National self-help doesn't always work—disasters can be homegrown as easily as miracles. Economic miracles are uncommon under any circumstances, but they seem to be more likely among non-colonies than colonies. Hence, the big success stories of the last four decades include a preponderance of places never colonized by Europeans, which tells us a little something about the benefits of escaping the White Man's Burden.

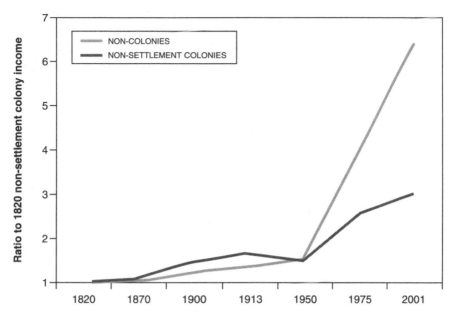

Fig. 28. Per Capita Income in Non-settlement Colonies Versus Non-colonies

To illustrate some of the problems left behind by the colonialists and nation-builders, as well as how they meshed with later Western interventions, consider one case study.

Abused the Most and the Longest

In 1483, Diogo Cão, a Portuguese ship captain sailing off Central Africa, came upon a river. Asking the locals the name, they told him Nzere, the river that swallows all others. He Europeanized the name as Zaire, which Mobutu would later take as the "authentic" name of the unlucky country the Portuguese had found.

Cão was more interested in profits than nomenclature. He established relations with the local king, Nzinga Mbemba, whom he dubbed Alfonso I, of the powerful Kongo kingdom. The Kongo people (also known as Bakongo) practiced ironworking, copperworking, weaving, pottery, and carving of wood and ivory. The Kongo also had slavery, which didn't bother the Portuguese priests, although the Kongo polygamy did. Soon the Portuguese were trading guns and luxury manufactures for Bakongo slaves and ivory. The Portuguese demand for slaves was so insatiable that the Kongo raided neighboring peoples, who retaliated in kind. The warfare of slave raiding weakened the kingdom, but it managed to survive until the late nineteenth century, when the Belgians arrived.[46] The Portuguese (later joined by Dutch, French, and British slavers) established slave-exporting ports at Boma, on the Zaire (aka Congo) River, and at Luanda, sending slaves (including many Bakongo) by the boatload to the sugar plantations in Brazil and the Caribbean.

Belgian King Leopold's abuses of the Congo from 1877 to 1908 are well known (see the great book *King Leopold's Ghost,* by Adam Hochschild). Belgian king Leopold said that his aim for the Congo Free State was "to bring civilization to the only part of this globe where it has not penetrated, to pierce the darkness that envelops entire populations . . . a crusade worthy of this age of progress."[47] Impressed by his ideals, European powers awarded him the Congo at the Berlin Conference. The borders they established showed their usual arbitrariness. For example, they divided Tutsis between the Belgian Congo and German East Africa, an area that included what would become Rwanda and Burundi. This would have deadly consequences a century later.

The Belgians exacerbated ethnic tensions. Every individual was given a tribal label that was written on his pass, hardening tribal identities that were previously fluid.[48] Some ethnic groups resisted those perceived as Belgian favorites. The Kongo in Leopoldville formed an Alliance of the Bakongo People (ABAKO) to protect their interests against the Lingala-speaking migrants to Leopoldville from upriver.[49]

The Belgians were not so good at preparing Congo for independence. They didn't even consider independence until 1956, when Belgian law professor A.A.J. Van Bilsen published a "thirty-year plan" to turn Congo over to the Congolese.[50] Not wanting to have the Belgians in town that long, ABAKO and its leader, Joseph Kasavubu, called for immediate independence in the same year. The Belgians finally allowed elections in 1957, but only at the local level—which meant that most political parties formed along ethnic and regional lines. ABAKO took 133 out of the 170 council seats in Leopoldville, while other ethnic parties won elsewhere.[51]

On January 4, 1959, Belgian troops forcibly dispersed an ABAKO political rally. Riots broke out, with thousands of people breaking into European stores and looting. The Belgians panicked, hastily turning the Thirty-Year Plan into the Six-Month Plan. The Congo became independent on June 30, 1960.

At independendence, qualified leaders were in short supply. Only seventeen Congolese in 1960 had a university degree. Joseph Kasavubu had a strong base in Leopoldville and the lower Congo River. The other main contender, Patrice Lumumba, was a high school dropout, former beer salesman and postal clerk, whose main qualification was his oratory.[52]

Chaos ensued. Within days the Force Publique mutinied against their Belgian officers, who quickly headed for the next flight out. So did many Belgian civilians after mutineers beat and raped whites. The new government was an awkward coalition, with Kasavubu as president and Lumumba as prime minister. Seeking someone to fill the empty slots at the Force Publique, Lumumba reached far down the ranks to an obscure non-commissioned officer named Joseph Désirée Mobutu (who, like Lumumba, had not finished secondary school).[53]

Desperate to keep the country together when the provinces of Kasai and Katanga announced secession, Lumumba cast about for global allies. Soviet and American agents in Leopoldville schemed to get the Congo in their camp. UN troops arrived, but had no brief to intervene in intra-Congolese conflicts. Not satisfied with what the United States and the UN were offering, Lumumba solicited Soviet support to fight the Katanga secession. Kasavubu and Mobutu were not happy, nor was the paranoid CIA. Kasavubu announced on the radio that he was firing Lumumba in September 1960, while Lumumba announced on another station that he was firing Kasavubu. Mobutu staged a brief coup and later flew Lumumba off to Katanga, with state agents beating him up on the plane and eventually assassinating him. CIA machinations allegedly had some role in these events.

Further bizzare twists occupied Congolese politics from 1961 to 1965. A Marxist revolt broke out in eastern Congo, the former home of Lumumba, intriguing the Marxist Internationale enough to earn a visit from Che Guevara. Che was disgusted at the poor military skills, womanizing, and drinking of one of the young Marxist leaders, named Laurent Kabila.[54] By 1965, Congolese politics were deadlocked along ethnic and regional lines. Mobutu staged another coup, this time for keeps. Kabila retreated into a tiny Marxist mini-state west of Lake Tanganyika, financed by gold mining and ivory, and kidnapped for ransom four Western students from naturalist Jane Goodall's primate research center in Tanzania.[55]

Compensating for economic mismanagement, Mobutu came up with a name change for the country, Zaire, the old Portuguese mispronunciation of the Nzere (Congo) River. A lonely democratic opposition emerged, led by the courageous Étienne Tshisekedi, who endured at Mobutu's hands multiple arrests, torture, and banishments over the next few decades.

Little more needs to be said about Mobutu's notorious looting of the Congo's natural resources, and his ability to attract aid from Western donors, which enabled him to buy off potential opponents and finance villas on the Riviera. In the end, it took an armed rebellion instigated by Uganda and Rwanda to oust Mobutu in 1997. Rwanda sought to defeat the Interhamwe—the Hutu militia that carried out the genocide of eight hundred thousand Tutsis in Rwanda in 1994—who had taken refuge in the Congo. The Rwandans had local allies because there was a substantial population of Congolese Tutsis in eastern Congo.[56]

Unfortunately for the Congolese, Ugandan president Yoweri Museveni had gone to the University of Dar es Salaam with Laurent Kabila, the dissolute rebel who had last been active three decades earlier.[57] Museveni and Rwandan president Paul Kagame (another friend of the glad-handing Kabila) decided to install Kabila as the new president, although he had little or no role in the rebellion that ousted Mobutu. Kabila turned out to be something less than the Congolese George Washington. His autocratic ways (he quickly banned the party of Étienne Tshisekedi) and his failure to control the Interhamwe alienated even his foreign backers. Uganda and Rwanda started a second rebellion that was eventually to involve six neighboring states backing and opposing the Kabila government. The foreign forces, as well as a medley of local military bands, further looted the Congo (now called the Democratic Republic of the Congo [DRC]) of minerals. From August 1998 to November 2002, an estimated 3.3 million Congolese died as a result of the war, making it the world's deadliest conflict since World War II.[58]

Unknown parties assassinated Laurent Kabila in 2001. His hastily installed successor was thirty-two-year-old Joseph Kabila, the son of the incompetent autocrat. Joseph didn't prove to be any more democratic than his father (he also banned the party of Étienne Tshisekedi),[59] but he was a lot better at relations with the international donors and foreign invaders. A peace deal brought together assorted rebels and warlords into a coalition government under Joseph Kabila, which the ever-hopeful international community deemed a Government of National Unity. The foreign aid spigot reopened, and UN troops arrived, starting a new quasi-colonial experience for the DRC. The World Bank strategy since 2001 was "to promote 'early wins' to build a track record for the then new Government."[60] It didn't explain why it wished on the Congolese people a government made up of political actors who had demonstrated only an exceptional ability to use violence.

The income of the average Congolese today is the equivalent of twenty-nine cents a day. The World Bank has lent $1.5 billion to the Congolese "government" since 2001. It's not clear what benefits the money brought to the Congolese people when channeled through the warlords and autocrats.

As many as 3.4 million Congolese are still refugees.[61] After five centuries of European intervention, the DRC is still today contesting the record for worst and longest misgovernment.

Many of the problems since independence are admittedly homegrown. I am not sure that the DRC would be a prosperous place if the Europeans had never come. But after five centuries of European violence, slavery, paternalism, colonialism, exploitation, and aid to prop up bad rulers after independence, the DRC is an extreme example of why the West's successive interventions of exploitation, colonization, foreign aid, and nation-building have not worked out well.

White Mischief

If you thought European colonization was bad, decolonization was not much better. Planners did decolonization as a crash utopian program to create whole new nations overnight. The decolonizers decided the boundaries of the decolonized from on high. The Europeans did this with little consideration for of the wishes of the locals, usually just keeping the colonial borders, even when they were of very recent invention, or having European officials make up a partition line. One thing today's nation-builders could learn from their colonial predecessors: once you get in, it's very hard to constructively get out.

The West decided what *a nation was,* determining the boundaries of the new nations. It decided which peoples got their own nation and which did not. The results are as bad as with other Western top-down schemes in the Rest. The West imposed its map of the world on a quilt of thousands of linguistic groups, religious creeds, tribes, and racial mixtures. The West's drunken parallelograms did not give nations to some existing ethnic nationalities (e.g., the Kurds) while creating other nationalities (e.g., the Iraqis) where none existed before.

The resulting "nations" started their ill-starred journey with ethnic and nationalist grievances. Nations whose territory is disputed by different groups are like landowners whose property rights are insecure. The insecure landowner will divert effort away from investing in the fertility of the soil or constructing a lovely house and toward litigation and shotgun defense of his property. Nations with insecure borders will have more civil and international wars. They will devote more effort to defense and less effort to investing in the productive potential of the nation. Gangsters will exploit ethnic hatreds to promote their own self-serving agendas.

As George Bernard Shaw said: "A healthy nation is as unconscious of its nationality as a healthy man of his bones. But if you break a nation's nationality it will think of nothing else but getting it set again. It will listen to no reformer, to no philosopher, to no preacher, until the demand of the Nationalist is granted. It will attend to no business, however vital, except the business of unification and liberation."[62]

This is not to say that all of the nationalist and ethnic conflicts are the West's fault. No matter how the West drew the map, there would have been some conflict. No scheme of Western mapmaking would have led to utopia.

However, the West has plenty to answer for. As David Fromkin's wonderful history of the Middle East after World War I, *A Peace to End All Peace,* puts it, Woodrow Wilson's speeches about what *would not* happen during Western drawing of borders of the Rest was an excellent prediction of what *would* happen. Wilson said "that peoples and provinces are not to be bartered about from sovereignty to sovereignty as if they were chattels or pawns in a game," and definitely "not upon the basis of the material interest or advantage of any other nation or people ... for the sake of its own exterior influence or mastery." Then the West bartered about peoples as if they were pawns in a game, for the sake of its exterior influence or mastery. It partitioned territory for the sake of short-term gain with little thought of the long-run consequences for the people living there. Even after decolonization, the West played with peoples as chess pieces in pursuit of the West's own security aims, frustrating the right of peoples to choose their own destiny.

The political crises that make the headlines today, such as the Israeli-Palestinian conflict, the war in Iraq, the Kashmir dispute, the war on terror, and brutal civil wars in Africa, have some roots in past Western treatment of peoples as "pawns in a game." Look behind a modern-day headline and often you will find the machinations of some long-forgotten colonial planner.

There are three different ways that Western mischief contributed to present-day grief in the Rest. First, the West gave territory to one group that a different group already believed it possessed. Second, the West drew boundary lines splitting an ethnic group into two or more parts across nations, frustrating nationalist ambitions of that group and creating ethnic minority problems in two or more resulting nations. Third, the West combined into a single nation two or more groups that were historical enemies.

Alberto Alesina and Janina Matuszeski of Harvard and I have analyzed statistically whether countries with artificial borders do worse on economic development.[63] We have two measures of colonial mischief in forming countries. The first is the percentage of the population that belongs to ethnic groups that the borders split between adjacent countries. The percentage partitioned is strongly correlated with the ethnic heterogeneity of the population, which previous studies have identified as another determinant of underdevelopment. This is plausible, since the more heterogeneous the population, the more likely it is that arbitrary borders will split more ethnic groups. To make sure that the share of partitioned peoples is not just proxying for ethnic heterogeneity, we control separately for heterogeneity. Former colonies with a high share of partitioned peoples do worse today on democracy (see figure 29 for illustration), government service delivery, rule of law, and corruption. Highly partitioned countries do worse on infant mortality, illiteracy, and specific public services such as immunization against measles, immunization for DPT (diphtheria-pertussis-tetanus), and supply of clean water.

Our second measure of artificial borders is more exotic, if not crazy. We reasoned that "natural" nations would determine their borders by some complex organic process, again depending on factors such as the spread of a unifying culture or the location of ethnic groups. Colonial bureaucrats on the other hand, are more likely to just draw straight lines on a map, without regard to realities on the ground. So we devised a mathematical measure of how wiggly or straight are the borders of every country in the world. We found that artificially straight borders were statistically associated with

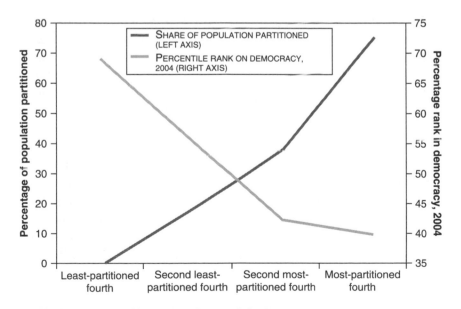

Fig. 29. Democracy and Partiton in Former Colonies

less democracy, higher infant mortality, more illiteracy, less childhood immunization, and less access to clean water—all measured today. The straight hand of the colonial mapmaker is discernible in development outcomes many decades later.

From Sir Mark Sykes to the War on Terror

When today many around the world are blaming the Americans for everything that goes wrong, it's kind of refreshing to go back to an era when everything was the Brits' fault. If only the British had not promised the same piece of land—Palestine, where else?—to three different parties.

The story begins with an Arab sheikh and a British diplomat. The Arab was Emir Hussein ibn Ali al-Hashimi, the sharif of Mecca and Medina. The Hashemite dynasty of Hussein traced its ancestry to the Prophet himself, but hardly attracted allegiance in the Arab world as a whole. During World War I, in which Britain and the Ottoman Empire (which included the Arabs) were on opposite sides, Sharif Hussein was afraid that the Ottomans were about to depose him. He contacted the British in Cairo in 1915 and offered to switch sides. The British war against the Ottomans in the Middle East was not faring well, so they were tempted. Hussein offered a revolt of the Arabs against the Ottomans, mentioning his contacts with rebel secret societies in Damascus. However, there was a catch—the Arab didn't want to exchange one imperial master for another. Hence, Hussein said that the British must promise independence for the Arabs after the war (implicitly assuming he would be their new leader).

Hussein's message caused bewilderment in Cairo. The British commissioner in Egypt, Sir Henry McMahon, contacted London for instructions. The British sent a neophyte diplomat, Sir Mark Sykes, to supervise the negotiations. Sir Mark decided to accept Hussein's terms, with an exception. With Sykes's guidance, McMahon sent a letter to Hussein on October 24, 1915, promising "to recognize and support the independence of the Arabs in all the regions within the limits demanded by the sheriff [namely, the Arab rectangle including Syria, Arabia, and Mesopotamia], with the exception of those portions of Syria lying to the west of the districts of Damascus, Homs, Hama, and Aleppo."[64] The French thought of western Syria—what is today Lebanon—as within their sphere of influence, given their long-standing ties to the Maronite Christians of Lebanon. The British could not afford to offend their French allies. Nobody knew whether McMahon meant also to exclude Palestine. Jews and Arabs later debated what exactly McMahon had meant by "districts," which was not an Ottoman administrative term. Twenty years later, McMahon would say that he did mean to exclude Palestine from Arab control, but that assertion may have been colored by subsequent events. Most historians brave enough to venture an opinion think that at the time, McMahon only meant to exclude Lebanon.[65] McMahon's language was (intentionally?) vague enough to accommodate the Arabs' desire to possess Jerusalem as part of an independent Arab kingdom. Hussein objected even to the exclusion of Lebanon, but agreed to postpone that question until after the war.

But before the end of the war, the British promised parts of Palestine to two other parties. In 1916, Sykes met with French diplomat Charles François Georges-Picot to negotiate the postwar division of the Middle East between the Allies. On February 4, 1916, they secretly reached agreement in Paris. Some of those straight borderlines that Alesina, Matuszeski, and I found to have had bad consequences were drawn by Sykes and Picot in Paris in 1916.

Under the Sykes-Picot Agreement, northern Palestine would go to the French sphere, southern Palestine would go to the British, and central Palestine (including Jerusalem) would be an Allied condominium shared by the British and French (and even Tsarist Russia, but she was kicked out after the Bolsheviks took over).

The British weren't done giving away Palestine. Sir Mark Sykes and others talked to Zionist leaders about their support for the Allied war effort. The British offered a quid pro quo—Palestine. On November 2, 1917, the British foreign secretary issued the famous Balfour Declaration: "His Majesty's government view with favour the establishment in Palestine of a national home for the Jewish people."

Why did Sir Mark Sykes and the Brits promise the same piece of land within two years to three different parties, the Arabs, the French, and the Jews? The British felt desperate about their fortunes in the war, and were eager to have all three peoples on their side. Ironically, in view of all the trouble it would later cause, Mark Sykes got little out of selling Palestine to three different customers. The French had their own life-and-death struggle in the war and hardly needed any inducement to fight with the British. The Arab revolt amounted to deployment of Hussein's son Faisal and a few Bedouin tribesman in the British invading army in Palestine and Syria, far short of the fictional book and movie version of the Arab revolt by T. E. Lawrence ("Lawrence of Arabia"). A small sign of the artificiality of the Arab revolt is that Mark Sykes himself designed the flag of the Arabs as a combination of green, red, black, and white. Variations on this design are today the official flags of Jordan, Iraq, Syria, and the Palestinians. As to the value of the Jews on the Allied side, Mark Sykes had apparently read a few too many of the anti-Semitic conspiracy theories about the Jews' influence on world affairs.

The British Palestinian triple-cross still causes the blood to flow today. Despite Woodrow Wilson's and the League of Nations Charter's idealistic call for national self-determination, the British and the French cared only for their imperial interests.

After the war, the French agreed to give up any claims to Palestine in return for the British recognizing their control over Syria. The British abandoned their protégé Faisal, who had already formed a shaky Arab government in Damascus, but offered Iraq to him as a consolation prize. Faisal and his heirs were to continue in power in an independent Iraq until 1958. However, the imposition of an alien monarch on Iraq, which had been cobbled together from three different Ottoman provinces—containing Kurds, Shiites, and Sunnis—hardly set the stage for stable nationhood. The stage was set for Saddam Hussein, who emerged from a series of military coups after the fall of the monarchy.

To complicate matters further, the British had already promised Faisal's brother Abdullah the Iraqi throne. Abdullah was the only member of the Hashemite family left without a kingdom after the war (the paterfamilias Hussein continued to rule back home in Mecca and Medina, with his son Ali as heir apparent, although *they* were conquered by the rival Saudi family shortly thereafter). After Abdullah threatened to make trouble, Winston Churchill decided to split off the lightly populated part of Palestine east of the Jordan River (called Transjordan and then, simply Jordan) and give it to Abdullah. After Abdullah's assassination in 1951, his grandson King Hussein was to later play a large role in the Arab–Israeli conflict. The Hashemite family is still in power today, under King Hussein's son Abdullah II, with the country known formally as the Hashemite Kingdom of Jordan.

In Syria and Lebanon, the French were supposed to carry out League of Nations mandates that would result in eventual independence. In Lebanon, the French added Tripoli, Beirut, and Sidon to the traditional Maronite area around Mount Lebanon, giving their Maronite Christian allies control of what were majority Muslim areas. This later caused a Christian-Muslim civil war that destroyed the independent state of Lebanon.

The French treated Syria with a heavy hand, more like a colony assimilated to the metropole than a mandate moving toward independence. Arab bitterness at the French betrayal contributed to the emergence of nationalist radicals in Syria after independence.

Table 7. The Children of Sir Mark Sykes

Entity	Some major violent events	Notable political features
Iraq	Kurdish genocide, two border wars with Kuwait and Iran, lots of military coups, then Butcher Saddam for three decades	Model for new version of White Man's Burden in 2005
Israel	Five Arab–Israeli wars	Democracy for citizens, but not so nice for the Palestinians
Palestinians in West Bank and Gaza	Occupation by Israel after 1967, two intifadas, terrorist murders of Israeli civilians	Palestinian Authority receives a lot of American finance to rebuild areas destroyed by American-financed Israeli army
Lebanon	1975–1976 civil war, Syrian occupation, 1982 Israeli invasion	Home of terrorist movements
Jordan	Civil war with Palestinians 1970–1971, wars with Israel	Hashemite dictators still in power
Syria	Invaded Lebanon after its civil war, occupied it, wars with Israel	Good refuge for Nazi war criminals after World War II
Kurdistan	There isn't one, yet	

Back in Palestine, the British took it over as a mandate, inheriting their own problem of how to reconcile the irreconcilable promises they had already made to the Arab and Jewish inhabitants. They were not very successful. At the time, the British were content that they indirectly controlled Palestine, Jordan, and Iraq through the League of Nations mandate system. Combined with some influence in Persia, this gave them a land bridge (and later air routes) from their possession of Egypt all the way to India. Egypt was also the apex of their Cairo-to-Capetown area of control in Africa. It worked out nicely in the head of some British imperial Planner, but at a price we are still paying today.

Of course, the mélange of peoples in the Middle East didn't need British help to hate one another. Much more was to happen to bring the Middle East to its present unhappy state. But the British duplicity about Palestine and Arab independence did not help set the region on a path toward peaceful development. Table 7 summarizes some of the salient events in the region divided up by Sir Mark Sykes.

Partition of India

The British also applied their genius for remaking other people's maps to the Indian subcontinent in 1947. Lord Mountbatten, the viceroy of India who supervised partition and independence, hired a public relations expert to burnish his image for folks back home. After the massacres at partition, four international wars, two genocides, six secessionist movements, and umpteen communal massacres later, it looks like his lordship needed all the PR help he could get.

The burning issue in the partition, of course, was whether and how to award separate rights of national self-determination to Hindus and Muslims (the British ignored the national aspirations of smaller groups such as the Sikhs, which would bring its own bitter consequences). The Congress Party of Gandhi and Nehru campaigned for independence for one unitary Indian state, including Hindus, Muslims, and Sikhs from Peshawar to Dhaka. Mohammed Ali Jinnah was initially a member of the Congress Party, but he left—fearing domination of the Muslim minority by Hindus in the Congress Party. He founded the Muslim League, which called for a separate state for Muslims: Pakistan, or "the land of the pure." But since Hindus and Muslims were mixed together all over the subcontinent, how could you come up with a plan to carve a Muslim nation out of India?

This intermixing was the result of a complex history that included the Muslim Mughal dynasty that the British raj replaced. Until the last days of the raj, there were Muslim princes ruling over majority Hindu princedoms and Hindu princes ruling over majority Muslim princedoms. The only areas with a Muslim majority were in the extreme northwest and the extreme northeast, separated by a thousand miles, and still containing large minority Sikh and Hindu communities. The most populous states of India with a Muslim majority were Punjab and Bengal, both of which Jinnah wanted to include in his Muslim state. But Muslims made up barely more than 50 percent in each state.

To add to the complexity, Muslim areas in the subcontinent had little in common. Bengali Muslims were virtually indistinguishable from Bengali Hindus in every aspect of culture (language, food, clothing, music, etc.) except religion. Muslims within what is now northern India spoke Urdu. Bengali speakers in what became East Pakistan were affronted when Urdu later became the national language of all of Pakistan.

In the Muslim North-West Frontier Province (NWFP), ethnic Pathans (also known as Pakhtuns, Pashtuns, Pushtuns, or Pukhtoons) were separated from their fellow Pathans in Afghanistan by the Durand Line, an arbitrary boundary between Afghanistan and British India laid down by a previous British bureaucrat. Peshawar, the capital of NWFP, was the traditional winter home of the Afghan kings. The Pathans preferred either an independent Pukhtoonwa, uniting all Pathans, or a Pathan-led Greater Afghanistan. At the time of partition, NWFP had a Congress-allied government led by a charismatic advocate of nonviolence, Khan Abdul Ghaffar Khan (the "Frontier Gandhi").

Back in British India, two other provinces of the future Pakistan were Sindh and Balochistan. Sindhi feudal landowners initially opposed the Pakistan idea and only later gave their grudging support under the naïve hope that Sindh would be largely autonomous. Balochi tribesmen (also divided from ethnic compatriots by a colonial boundary with Iran) preferred an independent Balochistan, which would lead to a secessionist attempt in the 1970s, met with murderous repression by the Pakistani state.

As far as Punjab and Bengal were concerned, Congress leaders would not consent to hand them over to the Muslims. This meant the Brits would partition the mosaic of Hindus and Muslims in each state (and Sikhs in the Punjab, which had been a Sikh state at one point). The Unionist government in Punjab prior to partition backed neither the Muslim League nor the Congress Party.

Into this snake pit of conflicting nationalist aspirations came Viscount "Dickie" Mountbatten, a grandson of Queen Victoria (a credential he would cite frequently). Under the theory that his royal brio could smooth over all differences among gentlemen, he put forward an accelerated deadline for independence—on August 15, 1947, just five months after his arrival in India. Nehru recognized a fellow charmer and hit it off with Dickie right away. But the charm offensive did not work on Jinnah, who preferred to argue points with his formidable legal skills. The offended Mountbatten referred to Jinnah as the "evil genius," a "psychopathic case," a "lunatic," and a "bastard," characterizations spread by eavesdroppers to both sides. Mountbatten also referred to Pakistan as a flimsy structure that would fall apart. Mountbatten's wife, Edwina, didn't help the cause of impartiality either, indulging a schoolgirl crush (possibly more) on Nehru.[66]

Pakistan: The Unhappy Family

The unhappiest heir of the Brit Quit of 1947 is Pakistan. Jinnah complained that he got a "moth-eaten" Pakistan, with missing halves of Bengal and Punjab, little of Kashmir, some frontier territory, and two disjointed areas of West and East Pakistan.

The Muslim migrants from India to Pakistan, known as the *mohajir,* later became disillusioned. One of their political leaders, Altaf Hussain, said bitterly in 2000, "My description of the partition as the greatest blunder in the history of mankind is an objective assessment based on the bitter experience of the masses. . . . Had the subcontinent not been divided, the 180 million Muslims of Bangladesh, 150 million of Pakistan and about 200 million in India would together have made 530 million people and, as such, they would have been a very powerful force in undivided India."[67]

As late as 1981, only 7 percent of the Pakistani population were primary speakers of the supposed national language, Urdu (Jinnah himself spoke poor Urdu). So, to sum up, Pakistan wound up as a collection of Balochistan, North-West Frontier Province, Sindh (all of whom entertained secession at various times), East Bengal (which successfully seceded in 1971 to become Bangladesh, although only after a genocidal repression by West Pakistani troops), *mohajir* migrants from India (many of whom regretted the whole thing), and West Punjab (which had its own micro-secessionist movement by the Seraiki linguistic minority).

Democracy never took hold in this rocky soil—the military mounted coups, and no elected civilian ever completed his term of office. Military leaders exploited the unfriendly relations with India to justify military rule and to demand a huge defense budget.

Islam proved imperfect national cement, as many different varieties of Islam competed for the allegiance of Pakistanis. As the Pakistani central bank governor Ishrat Husain put it, "Every conceivable cleavage or difference: Sindhi vs. Punjabi, Mohajirs vs. Pathans, Islam vs. Secularism, Shias vs. Sunnis, Deobandis vs. Barelvis, literates vs. illiterates, Woman vs. Man, Urban vs. Rural—has been exploited to magnify dissensions, giving rise to heinous blood baths, accentuated hatred, and intolerance."[68]

The American support of the anti-Soviet jihad in Afghanistan in the eighties left behind a huge supply of weapons, including Stinger antiaircraft missiles, and extremist groups and terrorists disposed to use them. The Americans didn't bother to clean up after themselves when they lost interest in Pakistan and Afghanistan after the Soviet withdrawal. Today, on the border with Afghanistan, former Pathan scouts for the CIA use the CIA trails from twenty years ago to help Al Qaeda fugitives escape from the Americans.[69] Terrorists move freely from battlefields in Kashmir and Afghanistan to promote Islamic radicalism within Pakistan.

Nevertheless, the American government enthusiastically backs the Pakistani government again today as a reward for the alliance in the war on terror, showering it with World Bank and IMF loans and U.S. foreign aid. Pakistan was the world's largest recipient of foreign aid in 2002: some $2.1 billion. The Americans tactfully overlook unpleasant things such as suppression of democracy, intelligence agencies linked to terrorists, and nuclear proliferation.

Recently it was said in Pakistan: "Fifty-two years ago we started with a beacon of hope and today that beacon is no more and we stand in darkness. There is despondency and hopelessness surrounding us with no light visible anywhere around. The slide down has been gradual but has rapidly accelerated in the last many years.... Violence and terrorism have been going on for years and we are weary and sick of this Kalashnikov culture."[70] These are not statements by an anti-government radical, but those of Pervez Musharraf, the current military leader of Pakistan.

One should not go too far and demonize Pakistan, or dismiss it as a completely artificial state. People of every nation are more complex than what makes national statistics or international headlines. Most Pakistanis are proud of their nationality, with much of which to be proud. The economy has grown despite all obstacles, and a world-class professional elite and talented diaspora achieve a lot. Still, one wishes that their transition from British rule to independence had been a little more constructive, and the American back-and-forth support of military action from Pakistani soil not quite so shortsighted. Pakistan survives in spite of Western bungling.

Capital of the Apocalypse

Sudan was engulfed virtually from the moment of its birth in a civil war between the Arab/Muslim North and the African/Christian/animist South. The British who went to all that grief to partition Muslims and Hindus in India—who were intermixed throughout the subcontinent in one colony—for some reason combined Arab Muslims and African Christians from more defined separate colonies into a single state in Sudan. The British gave in to pressure from educated northerners, who traditionally subjugated southerners. Another version is that the fateful unification of Sudan was determined by a British bureaucratic spat—the British Arabists who managed the North overcame the British Africanists who managed the South. The Brits barely consulted the southerners, who later made their feelings known through civil war.

The British were not ignorant about the North-South difference. A British special commission reported in 1956 that "for historical reasons the Southerners regard the Northern Sudanese as their traditional enemies."[71] For centuries, the Arabs in the North raided the South for slaves. Northern slave raiding peaked in the 1870s, when domestic slavery of southerners in the North became widespread. British colonial rule abolished slavery on paper, but northern slavery continued under other guises: the "slaves" were renamed "servants."[72] The inspector-general of the Sudan for the British in 1898 gave his view on the Africans in the South: "These god-forsaken swine do not deserve to be treated like free and independent men."[73]

Sharing these enlightened views, Arab northerners used to call African southerners "slave" (*abid*) to their faces. The northerners are more discreet now but still use the word in private or jokingly in public. As Sudanese scholar Francis Deng explains, "The term abid...is the exact equivalent of 'nigger' in American popular usage."[74]

The British treated the South as separate for decades before independence, even banning migration between the North and the South. Without consulting southerners, they reversed this policy less than a decade before independence. A British bureaucrat, civil secretary Sir James Robertson, decreed the unity of Sudan in a memo of December 16, 1946.[75] Out of that memo came a half century of civil war.

The British gave the South promises of constitutional protection in the new Sudan, through autonomy in a federal system, but didn't keep the promises. The Sudanese replaced eight hundred British colonial officers in the run-up to independence. Only eight of the eight hundred new officials were southerners. Northern military officers moved into the South.[76] On January 1, 1956, Sudan became independent. The National Assembly appointed a constitutional commission to design the structure of the new state; only three of its forty-six members were southerners.[77] A historian later summed up the "the shambles of independence, when international intervention circumvented the self-determination process, the general populace was denied a final vote on their own future, and a decision on the form of government under which the Sudanese were to live as one people was deferred to a never-realized future."[78] A civil war lasted until a settlement in 1972, killing five hundred thousand Sudanese.[79]

After a decade of peace, civil war began again in 1983. Sudanese president Jafar Numeiry imposed the Islamic penal code, the Shari'a, on the whole country in a bid to get Islamist support for his faltering regime. Just as the British let down the South at independence, now it was the turn of the Americans to coddle the North and shun the South. In 1983, Numeiry was Washington's man. The Americans saw him as a strategic ally against Qaddafi in Libya and the Soviet-backed Marxists in Ethiopia. The friendship with Numeiry started under Jimmy Carter, whom Numeiry made grateful with his support of the Camp David Peace Accords. Reagan continued the policy of friendship with northern Sudan, which he lucidly explained at a press conference: "We do know that Colonel Qaddafi has been and will continue to be a destabilizing force in the region, so nothing would surprise us, and we do know that Sudan is...Sudan is...Sudan is...one of those countries in that region of Africa."[80]

Numeiry got nearly $1.5 billion in U.S. aid before his fellow officers kicked him out in 1985.[81] U.S. friendship continued with the northern Islamists who succeeded Numeiry. The World Bank did its part, lending eight hundred million dollars to the northern regimes in the period 1983–1993. Only after the first Gulf War did the Islamist regime finally outlive its usefulness and become a pariah on the list of terrorist states.

The southern rebels in Civil War II were led by John Garang. Garang further strengthened Washington's resolve to cozy up to the North when he accepted arms and refuge wherever he could get them, which included Libya and Soviet-backed Ethiopia. Moreover, Garang was far from a saint, with his own human rights abuses and massacres. The people of the South were the pawns in a game played by others, caught between the ruthless rebels and Western-supported northern governments perpetrating atrocities against the South.

Sudan Today

Yet history keeps repeating itself. In the new millennium, with the war on terror and to some extent before, the northern Sudanese government and the U.S. government decided to make amends. President George W. Bush certified Sudan as making progress toward peace and humanitarian assistance, although he noted the government's poor cooperation with humanitarian relief. Bush's certification enabled Sudan to restart a relationship with the IMF and the World Bank. The International Monetary Fund praised five years of economic reforms by the government in its 2002 report, and commends the government because "the authorities have given a high priority to poverty reduction."[82] The World Bank's chief economist for Africa praised Sudan as one of Africa's economic success stories.

Meanwhile, back in the real Sudan, there was still an Islamist dictatorship, the civil war went on despite perpetual peace negotiations, and the old horrors kept recurring. A 2002 Médecins sans Frontières report notes in the Western Upper Nile region "that repeated displacement and continued fighting, coupled with lack of access to health care and humanitarian aid, are slowly killing off the region's people."[83] A peace deal between North and South was finally announced in 2004, and signed in 2005. John Garang joined a national unity government, but died soon after in a helicopter crash.

However, just as Sudan settled one civil war, another burst of violence made headlines in 2004–2005, in the province of Darfur. The Janjaweed (Arab militias) attacked Africans, some of whom had rebelled against discrimination and maltreatment. African villagers fled into Chad. Counting those displaced within Darfur, 2.5 million people have lost their homes and 400,000 have died, either at the hands of the Janjaweed or indirectly from starvation and ill health in the horrendous refugee camps.[84] The Janjaweed terrorized civilians with arsons, rapes, and massacres.[85]

Meanwhile, there wasn't energy left over from civil war for any economic development. Per capita income stayed stagnant for decades. In 1994 it was below what it was at independence in 1956. Ten percent of Sudanese children will not live to see their fifth birthday. Only one out of every seventy-one Sudanese has a phone. Twenty-eight percent of Sudanese children attend secondary school. While much of the world achieved universal primary enrollment, only a little over half of Sudanese kids go to elementary school.[86] Sudan has four million internal refugees.[87] The expansion of oil exports from Sudan has led to an upturn in per capita income since 1994, but oil is often a curse in the long run, as we have seen. Through all the horrors, aid kept flowing to Sudan, with a total of twenty-three billion dollars in today's dollars over 1960–2002.

Conclusions

Western intervention in the government of the Rest, whether during colonization or decolonization, has been on the far side of unhelpful. The West should learn from its colonial history when it indulges neo-imperialist fantasies. They didn't work before and they won't work now.

Ghana Finds its Swarthmore*

Patrick Awuah was born in Ghana in 1965. He came of age just as Ghana was going through its worst times. When he was seventeen, the long economic decline was reaching its nadir. The military government was destroying the economy with draconian price controls on consumer goods. Patrick's mother was a wholesaler offering essential consumer goods such as soap. The price controls put the consumer price of soap below what Patrick's mother paid her suppliers for the soap.

Patrick was lucky to find an escape route. Although his family could afford to put up only a hundred dollars for his college education, he got a scholarship to study at Swarthmore, and left Ghana. He pursued a double major of engineering and economics. A fledgling software company hired Patrick fresh out of Swarthmore. The name of the company was Microsoft.

Seven years later, Patrick was a Microsoft millionaire and looking for ways to help his native country. He decided first to get an MBA at Berkeley. Then he moved back to Ghana to start a private university in Accra, called Ashesi University. "Ashesi" means "beginning" in the local Fanti dialect. Patrick put up his own funds, raised money from old colleagues at Microsoft, and gave free tuition to half of the entering class, smart kids from poor families. Twenty percent of the students are from the most extreme poverty. The other half, from richer families, paid four thousand dollars a year in tuition. Patrick built an impressive facility with good computers, Internet connections, and classrooms.

I have visited Ashesi three times, and I was overwhelmed by the enthusiasm and talent of the students. The curriculum marries liberal arts to computer science and business. Patrick Awuah's goal is to teach the students to solve problems, not just engage in rote memorization. He wanted to build the "Swarthmore of Ghana." "We want to train people as critical thinkers," he says. One of his

---

* This section is based on an interview with Patrick Awuah by journalist Dyan Machan.

most satisfying moments came when a student sent him an e-mail, "Mr. Awuah, I am thinking now."

Patrick's main surprise has been the lack of interest of the official aid agencies in his university. It is a mystery why a Ghanaian Swarthmore, started and run by a Ghanaian, that offers scholarships to young West Africans eager to improve their talents, would not attract support from Western donors. Despite donors' ideals of "local ownership" and "participation," I have come across several other incidents of the aid community rejecting worthy projects initiated and led by Africans, including a homegrown university in Burundi (meanwhile financing 88 percent of government spending for the gangsters who ran Burundi), and a master's scholarship program for Africans run by two leading African professors in American higher education.

Still, Patrick doesn't let lack of aid funds stand in his way. Morale is high among his staff. "Ashesi people are proud because it's going to have a place in Ghana's history," Patrick Awuah says.

Professor Kingsfield goes to India

Jayanth Krishnan, a professor at William Mitchell College of Law in Minnesota, tells the story of Indian legal education in his paper "Professor Kingsfield Goes to India."[88] In the 1950s, the Ford Foundation began spending millions of dollars to promote legal education in India. India's democratic constitution impressed Ford, and the Foundation decided to train Indians in Western legal doctrine to spread respect for democratic institutions and rule of law. Ford sent a number of distinguished American law professors to India to try to set up American-style law schools in the 1950s and 1960s.

Perhaps because the American professors were not professional development consultants, they told Ford that its idea was crazy. The American law school model did not translate well to India, and it was unlikely to have much effect if it did. Caste divisions, patronage politics at both the national and university level, and low respect for law professors and students plagued Indian legal education at the time. Law professors and students did little to earn respect, with frequent absenteeism and low academic standards, as noted by both American and Indian commentators. Practicing lawyers took and paid bribes and tied up cases in court for long periods to maximize fees. Harvard Law professor Arthur von Mehren suggested that the majority of the population failed to embrace the legal system because the laws on the books were of Western rather than indigenous origin. But Ford forged ahead, with a large grant to the Banaras Hindu University law faculty in 1964.

Another American law professor evaluated the program at Banaras in 1971. He concluded that it had failed; most of its graduates did not even go into law practice. The Ford Foundation, to its credit, drastically cut back its legal education efforts in India after the 1971 report. One of those who observed the failure of the Ford experiment was N. R. Madhava Menon, a little-known Indian law professor at Delhi University who had met some of the American consultants in the 1960s. After a year's sabbatical spent at Columbia, Professor Menon started a legal aid clinic at Delhi in 1971 as a way both to provide law students with real-world experience and to raise the prestige of law schools among the population. After several years of educational experiments of mixed success, Menon proposed a new type of law-school in 1982. He suggested a grueling five-year program that would yield students both a B.A. and a law degree, emulating the demanding and highly regarded engineering and medical schools in India. He proposed mixing in experience at legal aid clinics. He tried to sell his idea to universities all over India, but they universally turned him down. The Ford Foundation considered his proposal, but having been burnt once already, it declined to get involved again. Fortunately for Menon, others within the Indian legal profession were disenchanted with the state of legal education in India, and began to advocate a new independent law school. Menon's dream finally came to pass when, on September 1, 1986, the Bar Council of India and the state government of Karnataka appointed him to a new National Law School of India, in Bangalore, Karnataka. The new school drew on some American ideas, such as the use of the case study method, but Menon made sure the school was mostly Indian. The first class to enroll was a big success, and Menon now sought funding to build new facilities to replace the school's ramshackle buildings in Bangalore. He later got a large grant—from the Ford Foundation.

Today the National Law School is the leading law school in India, with huge numbers of applications for every slot in its entering class. As India has embraced globalization, National Law School graduates are in high demand in the private sector. The school has steadily expanded to keep up with demand. Menon reached the mandatory retirement age in 1998, but the school has continued to thrive since. The leaders of other Indian states soon came calling to have Menon set up law schools in their states. Menon started a similar school in Calcutta, West Bengal. Besides West Bengal, four other Indian states imitated the Menon model with new law schools. Today Professor Menon is heading up a National Judicial Academy in Bhopal to train judges beginning their careers.

CHAPTER NINE

Invading the Poor

As our commerce spreads, the flag of liberty will circle the globe and the highway of the ocean—carrying trade to all mankind—will be guarded by the guns of the republic. And as their thunders salute the flag, benighted peoples will know that the voice of liberty is speaking, at last, for them ... that civilization is dawning at last, for them.

United States Senator Alfred Beveridge, *1898*[1]

The neo-imperialism of the previous chapter has been possible only because of another important aspect of the Western quest to save the poor, military force. The U.S. Army occupies Iraq and Afghanistan to spread democracy and capitalism and create benevolent states. The U.S. government justifies its military interventions to promote development as part of the "war on terror," "nation-building," or "regime change."

In post-invasion Iraq, the U.S.-led Coalition Provisional Authority (CPA) in 2003 drew up one of the most radical free-market reforms ever attempted anywhere. Stanford economist John McMillan likened it to the "big-bang" free-market programs that had failed in the ex-Communist countries. *The Economist* wrote in 2003 that the intention of the CPA for Iraq was to "abruptly transform its economy into a virtual free trade zone."[2] Naomi Klein wrote in September 2004 in *Harper's* magazine about the attempt to transform Iraq from the blank slate of post-invasion "Year Zero" into a "neocon utopia." CPA chief Paul Bremer announced the layoffs of five hundred thousand soldiers and state workers, the privatization of two hundred state enterprises, no restrictions on foreign investment in the non-oil sector, minimal taxes, and no import tariffs. USAID gave a contract in 2003 to the KPMG consulting firm Bearing Point to create a free market from scratch in Iraq. A twenty-four-year-old American named Jay Hallen was put in charge of launching Iraq's new stock exchange. A twenty-one-year-old college senior named Scott Erwin, a former intern to Dick Cheney, wrote home that he was "assisting Iraqis in the management of finances and budgeting for the domestic security forces."[3] This is what structural adjustment looks like when it has an army and a navy.

Harvard historian Niall Ferguson suggested in a 2001 book (and quoted this suggestion again in his 2004 book) that:

> *the United States should be devoting a larger percentage of its vast resources to making the world safe for capitalism and democracy...the proper role of an imperial America is to establish these institutions where they are lacking, if necessary...by military force....Imposing democracy on all the world's "rogue states" would not push the U.S. defense budget much above 5 percent of GDP. There is also an economic argument for doing so, as establishing the rule of law in such countries would pay a long-run dividend as their trade revived and expanded.*[4]

If it were not for the U.S. Army trying to promote economic development, it would seem presumptuous for me as an economist to comment on military interventions. Yet even without recent rhetoric, military intervention is too perfect an example of what this book argues you should *not* do—have the West operate on other societies with virtually *no* feedback or accountability. The military is even more insulated from the interests of the poor than aid agencies are. People don't give reliable feedback at gunpoint. Invading soldiers and covert destabilization are not great ways to ascertain local peoples' interests. The poor on the receiving end have few votes on whether they want the Americans to save them. Military interventionists are inherently Planners; armies do not have Searchers.

Economists must protest against military policies when they make it even more unlikely that Western economic assistance will achieve benefits for the poor. During the Guatemalan civil war, USAID gave aid to train rural leaders in order to give more political voice to peasants. At the same time, the CIA supported the military's counterinsurgency campaign, which suppressed peasant activism in the name of fighting the Marxist guerillas. A later study found that the U.S.-trained Guatemalan military murdered more than 750 of the U.S.-trained rural leaders.

This chapter will ask questions such as: Did this military intervention done by Planners promote peace, democracy, and development? Were our guys the good guys? I use a mixture of episode analysis and case studies to shed light on these questions.

Cold War

The laboratory this chapter will use to study such interventions is the cold war. Various American presidents felt they had to fight the cold war in poor countries. Anyone fighting a Soviet-backed regime was a "freedom fighter" to be supported by American military aid. Some regimes considered too sympathetic to the Soviets were overthrown through CIA engineering.

I focus on the cold war because the interventions are old enough for an evaluation of long-run consequences. People who discuss military intervention today often dismiss the cold war as an aberration. Today advocates of Western military intervention see it as trying to introduce democratic capitalism. In the cold war, by contrast, the Americans tried to convince third world nations that a better system than communism was … democratic capitalism. In the bad old days of the cold war, Americans embraced some dictators as allies. In today's war on terror, the Americans embrace some dictators as allies. The various military interventions of the United States even involve some of the same people: for example, Vice-President Dick Cheney was chief of staff to Gerald Ford during the Angola intervention of 1975, and was influential as a congressional leader in support of the Contras in Nicaragua and Jonas Savimbi in Angola in the 1980s. John Negroponte was on the front line of the war against Nicaragua Contras as U.S. ambassador to Honduras in 1981–85 and was U.S. ambassador to Iraq in 2004–5. Perhaps the cold war experience offers some lessons for today. I will briefly review today's humanitarian military interventions at the end of the chapter to see if they are a dramatic improvement on cold war interventions.

The advocates of American military intervention during the cold war had good intentions. Communism *was* an evil economic and political system. The Soviets did their own meddling in poor countries, which *could* have required meddling by the Americans in response. Perhaps military action *may* have been necessary to get rid of some evil governments imposed by the Soviets.

However, even political opponents of evil governments show little gratitude for American invasion to modernize them. I won't comment on how necessary military intervention was for American security or for winning the cold war, just as I have nothing to say about whether today's military interventions are necessary for American national security. I *will* comment on the consequences of cold war interventions for the poor countries themselves, which may have some lessons on the likely consequences of today's military interventions. Given the reality that the White Man's Burden weights the interests of the rich more than the poor, slight benefits for the West were enough to justify high costs to the Rest. The list in table 8 will help get us started.

Let me be a little more systematic and document how much peaceful democratic capitalism these countries have today. As of 2004, the typical nation described in table 8 was in the bottom 15 percent on democracy, the

Table 8. Some Cold War Interventions

Intervention	Negative consequences	Silver lining for United States
Vietnam War, 1961–1975	Fifty-eight thousand American dead; Communists still rule Vietnam; one of poorest countries in world; millions of Vietnamese dead	Explosion of Vietnamese restaurants in the United States
Cambodia, 1970–1973; support of pro-American military ruler; American invading and bombing	Khmer Rouge genocide; Vietnamese invasion; today one of poorest, most corrupt, most tyrannized nations	Cambodian food is good, too
Arming mujahadeen against Soviets in Afghanistan from 1979 on	Civil war and chaos in Afghanistan continued after Soviets withdrew; destabilization of Pakistan; former mujahadeen supported perpetrators of September 11 attacks	CIA got practice for when it had to fight mujahadeen after September 11
CIA-backed coup in Guatemala in 1954	Decades of civil war and death squads; genocide against Indian population	Market for Guatemalan handicrafts boomed in United States
Korean War, 1950–1953	2.5 million Koreans killed in North and South; left behind rogue state of North Korea, the only nation that can achieve famine and a nuclear arsenal at the same time	Thank God for American ally South Korea!
CIA-backed coup in Iran in 1953	Shah's tyranny; Khomeini's revolution; hostage crisis; Iran still ruled by clerics seeking nuclear weapons	Talented Iranian exiles became available to work in international organizations run by United States
Backing Liberian dictators 1945–1985 with massive foreign aid in return for American military base and Voice of America broadcasting station	Liberia collapses after 1985 into horrific and violent anarchy under born-again warlord Charles Taylor, who also fueled civil wars in Sierra Leone and Côte d'Ivoire	American television evangelist Pat Robertson could pursue lucrative business deals with Mr. Taylor
Backing Haile Selassie in Ethiopia against Soviet-backed Somalia	Military overthrows Selassie and aligns itself with Soviets; two decades of civil war; Ethiopia still one of poorest countries in world	Live Aid concert to help Ethiopia in 1985 gave valuable experience to Live 8 musicians to help Africa twenty years later
Switching to backing Somalia against Soviet-backed Ethiopia	Devastation of Ethiopia-Somalia with war and famine; collapse of Somali state and descent into chaos; fiasco of American intervention of 1994	Black Hawk Down was great book and movie
Backing army of El Salvador against Marxist rebels in 1980s	Twelve-year civil war kills seventy thousand; right-wing death squads rape and murder such dangerous guerillas as American Catholic nuns	Salvadoran refugees became cheap housekeepers for desperate housewives
Backing Contras in Nicaragua against Soviet-backed Sandinistas in 1980s	Civil war in Nicaragua with atrocities on both sides; Nicaraguan economy destroyed by corrupt leftists	Corrupt leftists thrown out in 1990, so now have corrupt rightists

Intervention	Negative consequences	Silver lining for United States
Assassination of Lumumba; support for pro-Western Mobutu in Zaire	Mobutu loots billions; collapse of state; civil war with intervention by virtually all of Zaire's neighbors; abysmal poverty	Needed stimulus to American and Swiss banking industry
Backing Jonas Savimbi against Soviet-backed Angolan government in 1975 and again in 1980s	Government wins anyway; civil war continues after Soviets and Cubans leave and American aid ends; Savimbi is power-hungry warlord; land mines outnumber people; spectacular misery today despite great mineral wealth	Can't think of any

bottom 18 percent on rule of law, the bottom 22 percent on economic freedom. Statistically, the cold war countries in table 8 have far worse institutional outcomes than other developing countries on all six dimensions that World Bank researchers measured in 2004: democracy, political stability, government effectiveness, regulatory quality, rule of law, and corruption.

There is a selection problem with cold war interventions, just as there is in other aspects of the White Man's Burden. The countries the Americans selected for intervention during the cold war were already messed up—they were already at war, already under the threat or reality of Communist revolution, or might have been at war anyway without American intervention. Moreover, since both sides of the cold war intervened in many of these cases, it's hard to tell if it's the Americans' or the Communists' fault that the countries wound up how they did. But, remember, Americans say we *won* the cold war. Whose victory is it when most of the poor countries where (and allegedly, on whose behalf) the Americans fought the cold war are still in such bad shape? A cursory reading of table 8 makes it hard to believe that things would have been even *worse* without American intervention.

Still, to try to get beyond the limitations of a superficial survey of interventions and outcomes, I turn to two more detailed case studies to see how American intervention worked out.

NICARAGUA

You...will know how to read the bitterness in my verses....
my grief for remote memories and black misfortunes...

Nicaraguan poet Rubén Darío, "Nocturne,"
Translated by Lysander Kemp, 1983

Both the Right and the Left adopted the Contra war in Nicaragua in the 1980s as one of their defining achievements. To the Right, Reagan's support for the "freedom fighters" eventually forced the Communist Sandinistas from power, achieving a victory in the last days of the cold war. The Left saw itself as successful in cutting off Reagan's military aid for the thugs murdering the Nicaraguan peasants. Soon after the cutoff, the Contra war in Nicaragua ended. In the left's view, the heroic nationalists, the Sandinistas, stayed in power until they surrendered it voluntarily after losing an election. Both the Left and the Right were correct about part of the situation—the Left that the United States should not have intervened, and the Right that the Soviet-backed Sandinistas were bad. Conversely, neither the American Left nor the Right was well qualified to decide for Nicaraguans what was best for them— the Left wished the Sandinistas on them, while the Right wished on them the equally appalling Contras. Nicaragua was left only with the kind of woes described decades earlier by its national poet Darío.

Cold War in Quilalí

None of the conservatives or liberals in Washington had ever heard of Quilalí, a small municipality in the mountains of northeastern Nicaragua, near the Honduran border. During the war, a CIA-supplied land mine laid by the Contras, whom Reagan called "the moral equal of our Founding Fathers," blew up a passenger bus in Quilalí. Seventeen people died: ten men, two women, and five children. The youngest victim was four-month-old Juan Carlos Peralta. At the wake in Quilalí, relatives surrounded the table on which Juan's corpse was laid out, wrapped in a white cloth. Flowers surrounded his body and a candle burned at his feet. His father could not attend the wake—he had died when the Contra land mine blew up the bus. Juan Carlos Peralta's mother could not attend either—the same explosion had left her in critical condition.[5]

The killing of innocents was not an accident. The human rights organization Americas Watch in the 1980s talked about abuses by both Sandinistas and Contras, but singled out the Contras for the "deliberate use of terror" in the countryside. This terror campaign included sowing CIA-supplied land mines without regard for civilian lives. The Contras wanted to bring home to the peasants that the Sandinistas had brought a war upon them and could not protect them. Not all Contra violence was at a distance; the Contras executed on the spot any civilian associated with the Sandinistas, including schoolteachers and coffee bean pickers.

A lot of the Contras' military victories consisted of overrunning peasant cooperatives, when their spies indicated the enemy soldiers were away, and opening up on the dwellings with AK-47s. Inés Delgado remembers the attack on El Coco cooperative in Quilalí on December 18, 1983: "People were killed when they ran out of ammunition and the Contras slit their throats. They sprayed gunfire inside one house and killed the children hiding under the bed. They cut out the eyes of a visiting doctor."[6]

The American government knew about Contra atrocities. Somehow they needed the homicidal Contras to defend against the "mounting danger" to the "security of the United States."[7] The president did not specify how this nation of 3.4 million people with an average annual income of $420 could threaten the world's most powerful nation, although he did mention they might "interdict our vital Caribbean sea lanes" (impoverished Communists hassling cruise ships?)[8]

The bereaved family of the infant Juan Carlos Peralta could have sympathized with their neighbors in Quilalí, the Galeano family. During the war, State Security agents of the Sandinista government took away the Galeanos' adult son, Catalino Galeano, from the family home in Quilalí. He was never seen again. This disappearance was not the only one that happened during the Sandinista years. The Sandinistas, idealized as nationalists by the American and European Left, invested a lot in their State Security apparatus, with Cuban, Soviet, and North Korean advice. The former dictator Somoza had about three hundred secret police; the Sandinistas had more than three thousand.[9]

The Galeano family in Quilalí was unpopular with State Security (the national head of which was the aptly named Lenin Cerna) because it included many Contra sympathizers. The clan had even more Contra sympathizers after Francisco Galeano, who had fought with the Sandinistas against Somoza, was arrested by State Security, tortured at a prison known as La Perrera, and castrated after watching his wife being gang-raped by their captors. Juan Carlos Peralta and Catalino Galeano of Quilalí were two of the 30,865 Nicaraguans who died during the Contra war.[10]

Contrary to the legend of the American Left that the Contras were CIA mercenaries from the ranks of the former National Guard, the Contras had significant popular support in the northeastern mountains (despite their violence against civilians). Besides the land question, the population's grievances included forced sales to the state of their grains and livestock at cheap prices (nice to maintain cheap food for those more politically influential people in the cities) and long lines for rationed goods that were often unavailable (the hallmark of Soviet economic systems everywhere).

However, the Left was right that the CIA made a bad situation worse. Injecting lethal weapons into this fracas was not a great boon to the people of Nicaragua. According to one of the founding Contras, the CIA made them "capable of inflicting great harm on Nicaragua." The CIA trained the Contras "in guerrilla warfare, sabotage, demolitions, and in the use of... assault rifles, machine guns, mortars, grenade launchers, and ... Claymore mines." The CIA accomplished this even though CIA director William Casey mangled the name of the country, saying something like "Nicawawa," prompting an outburst from an aide: "You can't overthrow the government of a country whose name you can't pronounce!"[11]

President Ronald Reagan's vision of Central America didn't reflect reality in the mountains: "If the rest of this century is to witness the gradual growth of freedom and democratic ideals, we must take actions to assist the campaign for democracy. ... Since the exodus from Egypt, historians have written of those who sacrificed and struggled for freedom—the stand at Thermopylae, the revolt of Spartacus, the storming of the Bastille, the Warsaw uprising in World War II."[12]

Reagan got Congress to approve making war on the Sandinistas only to interfere with Sandinista arms supplies to the Marxist guerrillas in El Salvador. Congress even passed an amendment (the Boland Amendment) to the covert aid bill that forbade American assistance "for the purpose of overthrowing the government of Nicaragua." So Congress gave aid to Contras, whose purpose was overthrowing the government of Nicaragua.[13]

Double-talk continued to characterize the Contra question in the U.S. Congress. After further political debate on Contra aid, the Senate reached a compromise on "humanitarian aid" for the Contras. The solons' creative definition of "humanitarian" included trucks, helicopters, and communications gear," as long as this equipment was not "used to inflict serious bodily harm or death."

According to author Lynn Horton, whose brilliant work is the source of much of the material on Quilalí here, cooperatives were not the place to be in Quilalí. The Sandinistas resettled peasants from the mountains to join self-defense militias for the Sandinista cooperatives in the valleys.[14] On July 28, 1986, forty Contras attacked one river valley co-op after they got word that the army was away on mission. They killed six residents, including three children, and wounded twenty-five. Repelled by this kind of humanitarian initiative, Congress finally cut off aid to the Contras in 1987. The cutoff had more to do with the Reagan administration's misbehavior in the Iran-Contra Affair than the Contras' misbehavior.

President Oscar Arias of Costa Rica negotiated a peace plan for Nicaragua (with support from other Central American presidents), for which he received the Nobel Peace Prize. As part of the deal, the Sandinistas agreed to democratic elections, which both they and impartial international observers thought they would win.

But the Nicaraguan people and the people of Quilalí were not fans of schoolboy socialism and never-ending war. In the February 25, 1990, elections, the candidate of the united opposition, Violeta Barrios de Chamorro, the widow of a martyr in the struggle against Somoza, carried 55 percent of the popular vote against Daniel Ortega's 41 percent.

Postwar Quilalí

Between May and September 1990, about five hundred ex-Contras and one thousand civilian families returned to Quilalí from their refuge in Honduras. The Organization of American States provided some aid to ex-Contras, such as kitchen utensils, tools, zinc roofs, and cash payments of fifty dollars. The ex-Contras found a Quilalí where, partly through their own actions, the infrastructure was ruined and about one third of the land lay fallow. The war had killed 300 Quilalí residents, leaving behind 900 widows and orphans. Another 185 were permanently handicapped. In a 1991 survey, only 23 percent of Quilalí's people drank milk regularly and 30 percent ate any kind of meat, while 70 percent lived in overcrowded housing (defined as 4 to 10 people sleeping in the same room). Nearly half of the people over age ten were illiterate; only half of the children attended elementary school.[15]

Chamorro didn't keep a promise of land grants to the ex-Contras. Nor did the United States show interest in the plight of their former allies. The ex-combatants, with their usual directness, took matters into their own hands. In Quilalí, twenty-five families of ex-Contras invaded lands of the Panali cooperative on February 18, 1991, saying they were claiming the plots of land the government had promised them during demobilization. Cooperative members confronted them, and there was a standoff between two groups of peasants armed with machetes. Years later, the conflict was still not resolved, and the ex-Contras continued their occupation of the land. They couldn't get bank loans since they didn't possess land titles. The co-op members who lost their lands to the ex-Contras didn't get any compensation.[16]

This episode was symptomatic of the confused land question on a national scale. Pre-revolutionary owners of expropriated land, cooperative members, ex-Contras, ex-Sandinistas, and speculators who had bought land from any of the above, competed for the same plots of land. The Chamorro government confused things even more with its own land reform program. Ex-Contras, ex-Sandinistas, and even mixtures of the two again took up arms in some parts of the countryside to agitate for land. The IMF in 2003 summarized this situation as "inadequate protection of property rights."[17] With such uncertainty about who owned the land, agricultural production did not rebound strongly after the new government took power.

Economic growth in Nicaragua in the post-revolutionary era, while at least not as calamitous as it was under the Sandinistas, was anemic (see figure 30).

Nicaragua failed to recover despite the boatloads of aid money that arrived in the nineties: aid inflows averaged 40 percent of Nicaragua's income from 1990 to 1999. The World Bank, Inter-American Development Bank, and the International Monetary Fund once again offered their assistance (they had withdrawn in the early 1980s under heavy American pressure—the World Bank refers to Sandinista misrule and American intervention as "economic and political disarray in the 1980s").[18]

Nicaraguan politics remain chaotic. Of the first two post-Sandinista presidents, Violeta Chamorro and Arnoldo Alemán, the much-abused Nicaraguans say, "It took the Sandinistas twelve years to make a saint of Somoza; it took Violeta only five years to make saints of the Sandinistas; Alemán has needed only two years to make a saint of Violeta."[19]

Daniel Ortega lost two more presidential elections after he lost to Chamorro. The current president, Enrique Bolaños, put his predecessor, Alemán, in jail for gross corruption. The IMF in 2003 said Nicaragua's problem was one of "weak governance and rule of law" and "an inefficient public sector."[20]

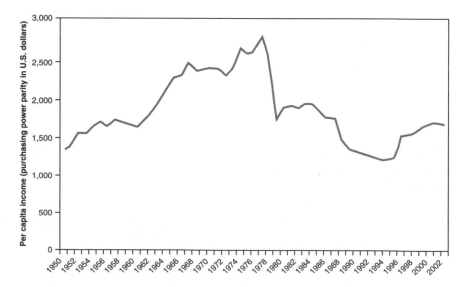

Fig. 30. Nicaragua Per Capita Income, 1950–2002

As we pursue new interventions for the war on terror, Americans have largely forgotten the land in which one of the most famous standoffs of the cold war took place.

ANGOLA

How many dead in this war? How many homes abandoned, how many refugees in neighboring countries, how many separated families? For what? When I think of all the suffering, the individual hopes destroyed, futures torn apart, I feel anger, impotent anger.

Angolan Novelist Pepetela[21]

Henry Kissinger expressed concern about the proxy standoff in December 1975 in Angola, featuring Soviet-backed and American-backed independence movements: "I do care about the African reaction when they see the Soviets pull it off and we don't do anything. If the Europeans then say to themselves, 'If they can't hold Luanda, how can they defend Europe[?]'"[22] Such imaginative thoughts about America's reputation for saving Africa and Europe from communism motivated the decades of mayhem to follow in Angola.

White Man in Angolan History

Angola's tragic relationship with her European would-be saviors dates back a ways. Luanda was a slave port for the Portuguese beginning in the sixteenth century, well before its twentieth-century incarnation as the front line in the cold war. The Portuguese sent slave raiders from Luanda into the interior to buy slaves from African intermediaries, then shipped off the slaves to Brazil and Cuba. (Some of the descendants of those Cuban slaves would go back to Angola four centuries later, as part of Castro's expeditionary force to fight in the civil war.)

The first victims of the Portuguese in the sixteenth century were the Mbundu people, who in the late twentieth century would be backers of the Marxist guerillas fighting for independence, the Popular Movement for the Liberation of Angola (MPLA, in Portuguese). By the eighteenth century, the Portuguese had reached into the interior plateau of Angola, the *planalto,* and begun enslaving the Ovimbundu people. The Ovimbundu were the base for the National Union for Total Independence of Angola (UNITA, in Portuguese).[23] The small Portuguese population on the coast was mostly men, with the usual result that a population of mixed race, known as *mestiços*, had sprung up. By the late nineteenth century, a small group of Africans were attending mission schools and learning to speak Portuguese fluently. They were known as *assimilados*. The *assimilados* and *mestiços* played a leadership role in the colony as government officials and traders.

However, by the 1920s, the Portuguese had changed their minds and decided to sharply limit the role of Africans in government, in favor of Portuguese settlers. Under the dictatorship of António Salazar, from 1932 to 1968, Portugal sought to incorporate Angola as an overseas extension, giving aid to white Portuguese settlers to move there. The dregs of society, such as ex-convicts, were the most likely to take up the offer; they became known as the self-explanatory *degredados*. The restrictions on upward mobility of the *assimilados* and *mestiços* in favor of the white *degredados* explains why the former groups became leaders in the anti-colonial insurrection against the Portuguese. Together with the Mbundu ethnic group, the *assimilados* and *mestiços* founded the MPLA.

The Ovimbundu had a different history with the Portuguese. The increasing encroachment of the whites on the Ovimbundu homeland on the *planalto,* including the continuation of the slave trade inside Angola, created tensions between the two groups. White settlers were attracted into the *planalto* by the mild climate at three thousand to six thousand feet, which one settler called "perpetual springtime." A random incident sparked a full-scale Ovimbundu rebellion against the Portuguese in 1902. The Ovimbundu saw the *assimilados* and *mestiços* as part of the colonial establishment, and thus part of the enemy. Using African troops from other parts of Angola, the Portuguese suppressed the rebellion within a few months, punishing the Ovimbundu leaders with banishment. One of those punished was royal counselor Sakaita Savimbi. His grandson, Jonas Savimbi, would be the leader of the Ovimbundu during the 1975–2002 Angolan Civil War.

After that, in the course of the twentieth century, the *mestiços* and the Ovimbundu switched positions, with the former becoming hostile to the Portuguese and the latter becoming compliant subjects. The Ovimbundu would agree to work in the homeland of the Mbundu on white-owned coffee plantations when the local people refused. The Mbundu, *mestiços,* and *assimilados* scorned the Ovimbundu as scabs.[24]

The first leader of the MPLA, founded in 1959, was Mário de Andrade, an educated *mestiço* and a poet. The second leader was an *assimilado* and poet named Agostinho Neto, who became the first president of independent Angola in 1975. At a time when European powers granted other African colonies independence, Portugal insisted that Angola remain a colony.

The MPLA and UNITA thus began a guerilla war for independence in the 1960s, starting with an uprising in 1961.

Ironically, the biggest surge in white settlement of Angola came in the last twenty-five years of the colony's existence, from the end of World War II until independence in 1975. High coffee prices after World War II brought large profits to new white settlers, who started even more coffee plantations in the interior. By 1975, there were 335,000 whites in Angola, 5 percent of the population. The whites made up most of the economy's managers, commercial farmers, business owners, and technicians.[25]

Even more than in other African colonies, the colonizer made a mess out of decolonization. In 1975, after a socialist government came to power in Portugal, the colonizer hastily handed over power in Angola to whoever would take it, leaving the guerilla movements to fight it out among themselves. The white community fled en masse back to Portugal, amputating most of Angola's economy. Angola has never recovered from the double blow of civil war and settler exodus.

Civil War in 1975

The inability of three egotistical Angolan leaders to agree on power sharing or elections was the proximate cause of the Angolan civil war in 1975. MPLA leader Agostinho Neto, UNITA leader Jonas Savimbi, and Holden Roberto (who led a movement called the National Front for the Liberation of Angola [FNLA in Portuguese]—based mainly on the Bakongo ethnic group in the north)—decided to fight it out.

Three Angolan leaders, three white sponsors. The subsequent civil war became more destructive because of the intervention of the Soviets, the Americans, and the South Africans in Angola. The Soviets uncorked a massive arms flow to the MPLA. The Americans' typical reaction to Soviet arms flows was offering arms to whoever was fighting the Soviet-backed people. It didn't bother the Americans that one of these fighters they supported, Jonas Savimbi, himself solicited Communist support when he visited Eastern Europe, North Korea, North Vietnam, and China in 1965.[26] He stayed in China from July to November 1965, getting guerilla training along with eleven other members of UNITA (later known as the "Chinese eleven").[27] He subsequently incorporated some features of Maoism into his movement, above all a personality cult and a dictatorship of the proletariat. (Savimbi was the proletariat.) In Kissinger's worldview, American support of the Maoist Savimbi in 1975 was critical to preventing "a massive shift in the foreign policies of many countries" away from alliances with America, which would be "a fundamental threat over time to the security of the United States."[28]

Communist countries such as China, Romania, and North Korea also supported the third Angolan leader, Holden Roberto. Kissinger nevertheless decided that Roberto's FNLA was the most "pro-Western faction," and decided to give most of the covert support to him.[29] The FNLA would disappear from the stage of history after losing the civil war, with most of its former supporters joining the MPLA. The American support to UNITA and the FNLA in 1975 was sixty-four million dollars.[30] The head of the CIA's Angola task force, John Stockwell, later admitted the classic Planner's shortcoming: "The glaring weakness of the program was a lack of information about our allies and about the interior of Angola. We were mounting a major covert action to support two Angolan liberation movements about which we had little reliable information."[31] Two consecutive assistant secretaries of state for Africa predicted the failure of covert action in Angola; Kissinger forced them both out of their jobs.[32]

The MPLA happened to control the capital, Luanda, at the moment that Portugal formally withdrew on November 10, 1975, so they portrayed themselves as the "legitimate" government of Angola, fighting UNITA and FNLA "rebels." A great many credulous countries around the world bought into this charade and recognized the MPLA as the "government of Angola."

China withdrew its support of the FNLA once South Africa intervened on the anti-MPLA side. South Africa invaded Angola from Namibia in October 1975, in support of UNITA; Cuba followed up on earlier support for the MPLA by sending troops in November 1975. The FNLA desperately tried to reach the capital before independence, but the MPLA and Cuban forces turned them back using Soviet-supplied rocket launchers known as "Stalin's Organs."

News of American covert support for UNITA and the FNLA leaked in late 1975, provoking Congress to pass a law forbidding American military aid to Angolan political factions (the Clark Amendment). The South Africans were unwilling to bear the burden of supporting UNITA alone, and they withdrew.[33] UNITA lost the civil war in 1975 and retreated into its rural Ovimbundu bases, to fight another day.

Jonas Savimbi and the Reagan Doctrine

Angola again came into cold war prominence after Reagan became the U.S. president and decided to provide aid to insurgents fighting Soviet-allied regimes (the "Reagan Doctrine"). Reagan's man on Africa, Chester Crocker, said that aid to Savimbi "would be the African version of the 'America is back' message of the Reagan presidency."[34] According to this cold war Planner, supplying Savimbi and UNITA with land mines was "standing tall," giving the Americans a "place where we can achieve victory, a psychological victory."[35]

In one of the most bizarre episodes of the cold war, the Reagan administration sponsored an organization called Democratic International, which brought together the Contras in Nicaragua, UNITA in Angola, the Islamic mujahedin in Afghanistan, and anti-government rebels in Cambodia.[36] Representatives of these disparate groups met in Jamba, Angola, Savimibi's base, in the summer of 1985. The lack of democratic credentials of these groups was perhaps most extreme for the Cambodian contingent, which had allied itself with the genocidal Khmer Rouge to fight the Vietnamese-backed Cambodian regime.[37] None of the other groups could be called excessively democratic, either. Reagan said of the Democratic International in 1988: "there is something in our spirit and history that makes us say these are our own battles and that those who resist are our brothers and sisters."[38]

Savimbi was to democracy what Paris Hilton is to chastity. He was tarnished by such documented incidents as: (1) murdering dissidents, including burning alive a couple and their three children; (2) kidnapping foreign aid workers as hostages; (3) using famine as a weapon of war, such as attacking UNICEF and Catholic Relief Services food convoys to drought victims; and (4) establishing the personality cult that demanded total obedience to *O Mais Velho* (The Eldest One).[39]

On February 1, 1986, Jeane Kirkpatrick, Reagan's representative to the UN, called Savimbi, "One of the few authentic heroes of our time." Ronald Reagan welcomed Savimbi to the White House in 1986, saying that American support would enable UNITA to win "a victory that electrifies the world and brings great sympathy and assistance from other nations to those struggling for freedom."[40]

The Reagan administration got Congress to repeal the Clark Amendment, allowing military aid to let loose the dogs of war in Angola. Chester Crocker explained the motivation: "Repeal changed the equation we faced. It would send a signal—a useful one—to Moscow, Havana, and Luanda that we had options if they continued to use our diplomacy as a cover for the pursuit of unilateral, military objectives. Now we could threaten to raise the price. Now we had the basis to acquire a stake of our own."[41] The price of a stake of our own, Crocker later acknowledged, was a "wrecked Angola," and the deaths of "an estimated 350,000 Angolans." But Angolans don't vote in U.S. elections.

Crocker declared victory when the MPLA and UNITA signed a peace agreement on May 31, 1991: "I knew that we were celebrating the end of an era. Angolans could now begin to shape their own destiny after centuries of foreign domination, living with foreign legacies and foreign conflicts."[42]

War to the Death

The foreign legacies in Angola were to have a longer shelf life than Crocker's premature obituary. The Americans again showed their habit of not cleaning up after themselves. Their protégé Savimbi quickly violated the peace agreement after he lost an election to the MPLA.

The civil war that the cold war fueled would outlive the cold war by a decade. UNITA got new sources of funding by capturing diamond mines, whose revenues it used to buy arms on the black market. Ironically, the main source of weapons for UNITA was the late Soviet bloc, which sold its surplus weapons after the end of the cold war.

The civil war kept on, by the end killing 750,000 Angolans (7 percent of the population) and displacing 4.1 million people.[43] Peace came to Angola, long after the West stopped paying attention, only when MPLA forces killed in battle that authentic hero of our time, Jonas Savimbi, on February 22, 2002.

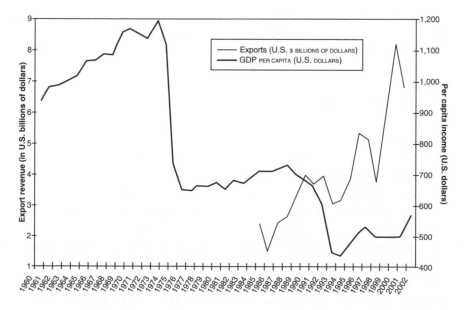

Fig. 31. Angola: Per Capita Income and Export Revenues

The combination of outside meddling, inside mismanagement, and civil war left the Angolan economy six feet under along with Jonas Savimbi. Even the surge in export revenues due to new oil discoveries did not help its recovery (see figure 31). The MPLA's blend of Soviet central planning and kleptocracy contributed to the disaster.

Today Angola is dependent on food aid, and it exports hardly anything besides oil (which Western companies extract on behalf of the government; during the civil war, Cuban troops defended American companies' oil wells against American-backed UNITA rebels). Provincial capitals have been without electricity for ten or more years.[44] Twenty-six percent of children die before reaching their fifth birthday, the third highest rate in the world.[45] AIDS already infects 5.5 percent of the adult population. It is spreading rapidly.[46]

Nation-Building in the Americas

A previous incarnation of the utopian internationalism of the cold war was the American effort to stabilize unruly republics in the Americas. The United States did direct military interventions in Mexico, the Caribbean, and Central America to spread democracy and free markets in the late nineteenth and early twentieth centuries. After bombarding Veracruz during the Mexican Revolution in 1916, Woodrow Wilson said, "The United States had gone to Mexico to serve mankind."[47]

Haiti is again illustrative. Chapter 4 discusses how the legacy of slavery left a toxic division between mulattoes and blacks in Haiti, forever destabilizing Haitian politics. Throughout the nineteenth century, the two factions called on foreign intervention to help them defeat their rivals. Americans, British, and Germans were often eager to intervene anyway to protect the business interests of their citizens. Historian Hans Schmidt noted, "US Navy ships visited Haitian ports to 'protect American lives and property' in 1857, 1859, 1868, 1869, 1876, 1888, 1889, 1892, 1902, 1903, 1904, 1905, 1906, 1907, 1908, 1909, 1911, 1912, and 1913."[48]

Finally, tired of all those round trips, the U.S. occupied Haiti from 1915 to 1934. Haiti's second colonial masters, according to Gendarmerie Commandant Smedley Butler, were "trustees of a huge estate . . . the Haitians were our wards and that we were endeavoring to develop and make for them a rich and productive property."[49] This patronizing attitude was only rarely contradicted, for example by the American journalist who pointed out that the Haitian mulatto elite was "so many layers in culture above the army or navy man and his wife that the visiting American must feel ashamed of his country's representatives."[50] But Haitians united again in resistance against the foreign invaders, and the Americans left in 1934.

The Americans left behind a newly trained Haitian army, the Garde, with black soldiers and mostly mulatto officers. Mulattoes dominated political office until 1946, when the black majority of the Garde revolted with a new vision of black pride and power, the *noirist* movement. After further political instability, a leading *noirist*, François Duvalier, defeated his mulatto opponent in the elections of 1957.[51] Papa Doc Duvalier would rule until his death, in 1971, after which his son Baby Doc ruled until 1986.

After the fall of the Duvalier family, a mixture of military regimes tried to stave off the coming to power of the populist Jean-Bertrand Aristide, who was finally elected president in 1990. Another U.S. military intervention in 1994 restored Aristide to power after a coup.

The second U.S. occupation of Haiti was less ambitious than the first, obsessed above all else with avoiding American casualties. The writer Bob Shacochis pointed out the novelty of an invasion to protect the invading soldiers from those they were invading.[52]

After the United States spent two billion dollars to restore Aristide to power,[53] U.S. support weakened in Aristide's democratically challenged second term. Aristide government ministers diverted aid money into corrupt takings, as had their many predecessors. The World Bank in 2002 ranked Haiti as the world's second most corrupt country out of 195 countries rated.[54] After an armed rebellion in February 2004, Aristide took the traditional Haitian path into exile.

Aristide's jet had barely disappeared over the horizon when the World Bank convened a meeting of donors. The Bank announced "a joint government/ multi-donor Interim Cooperation Framework (Cadre de Coopération Intérimaire, or CCI)."[55] In July 2004, the CCI believed that Haiti was now "primed to tackle many urgent and medium term development needs."[56] *The Economist* in June 2005 quoted people a little closer to reality, such as diplomats stationed in Port-au-Prince, as saying that Haiti was on the verge of being a "failed state." *Foreign Policy* magazine in August 2005 classified Haiti as a failed state, ranking it as more dysfunctional than the likes of Afghanistan, North Korea, and Zimbabwe.[57] The long years of military intervention have failed to produce anything constructive in Haiti.

As far as promoting democracy, one study on the historical record of American nation-building says that it doesn't usually work. Carnegie Endowment for International Peace scholars Minxin Pei and Sara Kasper analyzed sixteen American nation-building efforts over the past century.[58] Only four were democracies ten years after the U.S. military left—Japan and

Germany after resounding defeat and occupation in World War II, and tiny Grenada (1983) and Panama (1989). Besides those already mentioned, the long list of twentieth-century intervention disasters includes Cuba (1898–1902, 1906–1909, 1917–1922), the Dominican Republic (1916–1924, 1965–1966), Nicaragua (1909–1933), and Panama (1903–1936).

Peace Enforcement

What about today's "humanitarian" military interventions to bring peace, democracy, and prosperity to the Rest? I don't review them in detail because they are too recent to judge properly their long-run effects on the Rest. Anyway, other writers have already covered humanitarian intervention well (in particular, I recommend David Rieff's 2002 book, *A Bed for the Night: Humanitarianism in Crisis*). I will just review briefly here how the new interventionism (or, as the U.S. government now calls it, "peace enforcement")[59] has many of the same faults as cold war interventions, not to mention many of the same problems as more traditional foreign aid. Just as the argument for more aid money presumes that there is some all-knowing Planner who can get the right technical fix to the right place, the argument for humanitarian intervention presumes an omniscient and disinterested military force coming from outside. The triple tragedies of UN peacekeeping in Bosnia, Somalia, and Rwanda in the 1990s showed that such a force does not exist. The peacekeeping system then (which still exists today) could not get right the decisions about whether and how to intervene.

Like the cold war interventions, the new humanitarian interventions were distorted by serving the interests of the West rather than the supposed beneficiaries in the Rest. The French (motivated by their strategic interest in maintaining a French zone in central Africa, which was allegedly threatened by English-speaking Tutsi rebels)[60] played a shameful role in Rwanda, shipping arms to the Hutu extremists even after the genocide began in April 1994. In April 1994, the French evacuated from Kigali their embassy staff and citizens, some allies in the Huti elite, and even the embassy dog, but left Tutsi employees of the embassy to their fate.[61] Clinton eschewed American or UN military intervention in Rwanda in 1994 to kowtow to right-wing critics of "nation-building," but a few years later, when it became a useful rationale for occupying Afghanistan and Iraq, the right decided it liked "nation-building" after all. Strategic interests also dictated that international peacekeepers avoid casualties to their own forces even if this effort magnified many times the local loss of life, a situation that writer Alex de Waal labels "humanitarian impunity."[62] The widespread Somalian rage at UN/U.S. forces in 1993, shown in the book and the movie *Black Hawk Down,* had a lot to do with the humanitarian impunity that had killed many civilians.

Like the cold war interventions and like Planners' efforts everywhere, the interventionists suffer from ignorance of local conditions. The UN team sent to scout out peacekeeping in the former Yugoslavia in 1991 consisted of "two men in a jeep," neither of whom was a Yugoslavia expert.[63] The UN Planners in New York could only fit reports from the field in Rwanda into such preconceptions as "civil war" or "violent chaos," arguing against intervention by not processing the evidence that Hutu extremists were organizing a campaign of extermination against the Tutsis. In Somalia, by contrast, lurid images of gunmen and famine victims argued *for* intervention, exaggerating the crisis (one TV journalist instructed an aid worker to "pick the children who are most severely malnourished" for filming) and fatally ignoring the complexity of clan politics.[64]

Peacekeeping has an even worse problem than foreign aid in dealing with gangsters. The interventionists alternate from one extreme to the other. Either they (1) maintain neutrality between the government and its opponents (operating only with the consent of both parties) or (2) force change on (or terminate) some evil governments. These oscillations seem unrelated to the realities on the ground. Thus, the peacekeepers first followed the principle of consent in Bosnia when Serbs were murdering and raping civilians, then took sides against the Aidid faction in Somalia when the factions were close to equally reprehensible, then maintained neutrality for far too long in Rwanda between the genocidal Hutu government and the Tutsi victims (a policy described by the Czech member of the UN Security Council at the time as "like wanting Hitler to reach a cease-fire with the Jews").[65]

International intervention also suffers from the same collective responsibility system that plagues foreign aid. Peacekeeping could be good, but just who is willing to be accountable for its success or failure? When something goes horribly wrong, like the Rwandan genocide, the UN blames the Western powers, while the Western powers blame the UN and each other. Iqbal Riza, assistant secretary general for peacekeeping at the UN at the time of the Rwandan genocide, more diplomatically uses the passive voice, indicating that "mistakes were made" but nobody made them. Riza also used the bureaucrat's classic "that's not my department" excuse: "Our mandate was not to anticipate and prevent genocide."[66] Nobody pays for mistakes. After presiding over debacles like Rwanda, virtually the entire peacekeeping department of the UN ascended to run the whole organization when Kofi Annan (the former head of peacekeeping) became secretary-general.[67]

Interventionism suffers from the patronizing assumption that only the West can keep the locals from killing each other. Stanford political scientist Jeremy Weinstein notes that peace usually succeeds war because of a decisive victory by one side, not because of negotiated settlements by outsiders. The intuition is simple: military victors are likely to form a more stable government, whereas a coalition of recent antagonists imposed by outside planners is likely to be unstable. Weinstein calculated the likelihood of a stable peace: at least ten years without the resumption of war. UN interventions produced a stable peace only a quarter of the time. With no UN intervention, a stable peace resulted nearly half the time.[68]

In Somalia, the "international community" has sponsored fourteen rounds of fruitless peace talks since the collapse of government in 1991, not to mention the failed UN/U.S. military intervention. Meanwhile, without outside intervention, foreign aid, or even international recognition, the breakaway Republic of Somaliland in the north of Somalia has enjoyed peace, economic growth, and democratic elections over the same period. There can be awful military victors as well as good ones, but local actors are statistically more likely to find peace on their own.

Such common sense has little impact on the overconfidence of the interventionists. The World Bank issued a 2003 report proclaiming that "our new understanding of the causes and consequences of civil wars provides a compelling basis for international action .... International action ... could avert untold suffering, spur poverty reduction, and help to protect people around the world from ... drug-trafficking, disease, and terrorism." With the predilection of the Planner for precise quantification, the report suggests that Western-led military peacekeeping forces, reforms based on Western advice, and Western aid can halve the risk of civil war in poor economies, from 44 percent to 22 percent.[69]

There is a strange confluence of the neoconservatives on the right supporting "regime change" and the humanitarians on the left calling for military intervention in whatever human rights emergency makes the headlines at the moment. As David Rieff notes, this logic would require "endless wars of altruism," given the ubiquity of human rights violations.[70] This is yet another area where the Planners' utopian goals—universal peace, democracy, human rights, and prosperity—substitute for modest tasks that may be more doable by Searchers, such as rescuing innocent civilians from murderous attacks.

The pre–cold war, cold war, and post–cold war record on intervening militarily to promote the more ambitious goals of political and economic development yields a cautionary lesson—don't. Maybe one should never say never, but one should learn from history that the typical Western error is to do too many military interventions in the Rest, not too few.

Silvia

Silvia Neyala Zinga of Huambo, Angola, is not a fortunate person. Her mother, Deofina Chinima, can no longer walk since a mortar shell destroyed her left foot during the Angolan civil war. Her father died fighting in late 1992, after Savimbi again took up arms after losing the election. Her eldest brother, Alberto, has been missing ever since the siege of Huambo by UNITA rebels beginning on January 8, 1993. The only food the family had for long periods was cornmeal donated by the Red Cross. Silvia is two years old.[71]

The best rule of all for Western helpers is, first, do no harm.

Chemist to the Poor

Thirty-nine percent of Ugandans are malnourished. Malnutrition in children and teens causes fatigue, listlessness, reduced immunity to disease, swollen gums, decaying teeth, painful joints, slow growth, and trouble paying attention in school. A pregnant woman who is malnourished is more likely to have a low-birth-weight baby, who has a smaller chance of survival. Some studies estimate that 60 percent of all deaths of children under five are directly or indirectly related to malnutrition. The poor in Uganda eat a diet heavy in carbohydrates (such as cassava and bananas) with little protein.[72]

George Mpango is a chemistry professor on the faculty of Makerere University in Uganda, founded in 1922 by the British. George studied at Makerere himself during the horrific rule of Idi Amin. He saved enough money from tutorials to finance half the cost of a plane ticket to the United States; a wealthy friend of his father paid for the rest. He got a Ph.D. in chemistry at the University of Waterloo, in Ontario, in 1980.

As his father's eldest son, Dr. Mpango returned to Uganda in the late 1980s to fulfill his duties as the head of the extended Mpango family after his father died. He took up a job as assistant professor at Makerere, earning a hundred dollars a month. Coffee trees and cassava on his family farm in the countryside brought in another hundred dollars a month. Dr. Mpango had ideas that could help hungry Ugandans: developing a high-protein biscuit, teaching the next generation of Ugandan chemists, and developing improved varieties of cassava on his family farm. The obstacles were tremendous: Dr. Mpango's lab at Makerere was chronically short of funds, with thirty-year-old chemicals, no new beakers for the past fifteen years, no pH meter, no academic journals since the 1970s, periodic water cutoffs for failing to meet the bills, and not even enough lightbulbs. Aid donors gave unneeded items such as a German chemical reactor, with no instructions on how to use it, and fire extinguishers. "The donors give us what they have, not what we need," said the head of the Makerere chemistry department.

Eventually things looked up for Dr. Mpango. The government changed the policy of free tuition at Makerere to charge tuition for an expanded number of students (shrewdly offering scholarships to the same number who had gotten free tuition before). Students from all over Uganda and neighboring countries came to Makerere to take Dr. Mpango's chemistry classes, which would enable them to get high-paying jobs as chemists for private food companies. Faculty salaries tripled. The high-protein biscuit was now ready for the market; Dr. Mpango also developed an orange juice powder for the local market. He started a private high school back in the family's home village. Despite troubles in the extended family he heads and years of hardship, Dr. Mpango has found a path to his own success and benefits for those around him.*

* Story from chapter 6 of John Stackhouse, *Out of Poverty and into Something More Comfortable*, Toronto: Random House of Canada, 2000.

PART IV

THE FUTURE

CHAPTER TEN

Homegrown Development

I listen with attention to the judgement of all men;
but so far as I can remember,
I have followed none but my own.

Michel de Montaigne (1533–1592)

Twelve-year-old Caleb and I are in Tokyo, in a district called Akihabara. We have visited three temples: a Buddhist one, a Confucian one, and now an Electronics one. We are in an eight-floor electronics department store in a district that is thick with them—blocks and blocks of electronics stores. All the latest electronic gadgets are on display. Huge plasma-screen televisions (Caleb's favorite). MP3 players the size of packs of bubble gum. Laptops the size of a hardback book. Digital cameras the thickness of a credit card. Reclining chairs that give an electronic back massage (my favorite). Customer service is exemplary—a sign in English announces WE CAN HELP YOU WITH OUR PLEASURE.

Japan is famous for its dominance of consumer electronics, not to mention the miracle of its glittering economy. There have been successive phases of rapid and slow growth in Japan, and most recently Japanese growth has slowed. We see in figure 32 (which has a logarithmic scale in which every unit increase means a doubling of income) that these variations are minor in the long run. Starting in 1870, the Japanese economy registered miraculous growth. It recovered quickly from the destruction of World War II to post even more miraculous growth. It became a full democracy after the evil militarist detour of the 1930s and 1940s. Today, income per capita is thirty-two times higher than what it was in 1870. And it did all this without the White Man's Burden—the West never colonized Japan. Instead, Japan had homegrown Searchers.

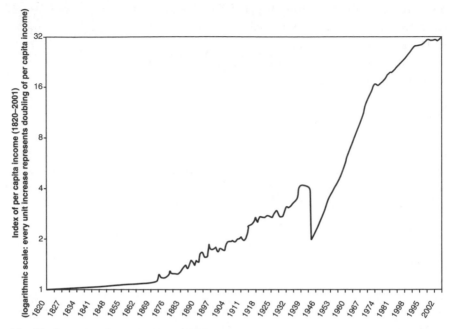

Fig. 32. Japan Per Capita Income, 1820–2001

The first reaction to Matthew Perry's visits to Japan in 1853–1854 was "revere the Emperor; expel the barbarians." But when a group of samurai rebels overthrew the shogun and restored power to the Meiji emperor in 1868, the new catchphrase became "Japanese spirit, Western learning."[1] The young revolutionaries combined patriotism with pragmatism—they realized the West was ahead, and they wanted to borrow Western methods to catch up, while preserving Japanese institutions, culture, and independence. Once in effective power (the Meiji emperor was only fifteen in 1868), they studied Western institutions and technologies. They invited Westerners to Tokyo, and themselves went on long tours of the West. But this was to create no dependence on the West; the watchword was "self-help." (Even the ex-samurai who lost out in the new order established a Self-Help Society.) They had no particular ideology or attachment to any one Western method—their only criterion was to search for things that worked in Japan. One of the leaders of the new government, Yamagata Aritomo, said they wanted "to establish the independence of our country" and "to preserve the nation's rights and advantages among the powers."[2]

The new government faced many economic problems. Searchers found solutions that laid the basis for a miracle. Devoid of revenue bases, it declared a 3 percent tax on the value of land on July 8, 1873. What was more revolutionary was that the emperor declared all land, which had been allocated by village custom, to be the private property of those who farmed it. The government issued certificates of ownership.[3] Land could be bought and sold, and used as collateral for loans—the famous Hernando de Soto formula for unlocking the "mystery of capital." Although externally imposed land reforms have often been disasters, a homegrown reform that respected local custom was more successful.

However, when the land tax was insufficient to cover state spending, the inexperienced rulers printed money. Inflation resulted. Matsukata Masayoshi, the architect of the land reform, became finance minister in October 1881. He cut spending and privatized the many state-owned enterprises, using the revenues of the privatizations to buy back currency issues. In 1882, he created the central bank, the Bank of Japan, with a monopoly over the issuance of paper currency. He eschewed foreign borrowing as a trap that had prompted Western intervention or colonization in other non-European countries (Britain in Egypt, for example). Inflation came to a halt, and private enterprise took off with the privatizations. Matsukata wrote, "The government should never attempt to compete with the people in pursuing industry or commerce."[4] Although such reforms often work badly when imposed from the outside by the IMF today, these homegrown reforms worked.

Other Searchers emerged from the private sector. One of the enterprises that bought up privatized state companies was Mitsui. Mitsui Takatoshi founded a trading firm in the seventeenth century as a combination liquor store and porn shop (a good business formula across the ages). Two hundred years later, what had become a venerable chain of dry goods stores founded the Mitsui Bank in 1876. A key leader of Mitsui was Nakamigawa Hikojiro, who had spent the mid-1870s in London and translated works on economics and American politics into Japanese. Nakamigawa persuaded Mitsui to diversify into industry. They purchased the state-owned Tomioka silk-spinning factory, converting it from a loss maker into a profitable enterprise. The former porn shop also added the Oji Paper Company, the Miike Coal Mine, and the Shibaura Engineering Works (later to crowd the Akihabara district with electronics such as Toshiba) and partially integrated Toyota on its way to becoming one of the world's biggest companies.[5]

Another buyer of privatized state enterprises was Mitsubishi, founded as a steamship line in 1870. Like Mitsui, it bought up mines—copper as well as coal. It leased from the government the Nagasaki Shipbuilding Yard in 1884, where it designed Japan's first steel steamship. In 1890, it purchased eighty acres of marshland next to the Imperial Palace in Tokyo for one million dollars. Ridiculed at the time for buying a swamp, Mitsubishi later realized some profits on what became the downtown Tokyo business district, today worth billions of dollars. To keep its workers happy, it founded the Kirin Brewery. In the twentieth century, Mitsubishi would diversify into just about everything, most famously automobiles and cameras (Nikon). Today, it also makes some of the computer monitors, cell phones, high-definition projection televisions, plasma-screen televisions, DVD players and VCRs that Caleb and I saw in Akihabara.

Heads of Mitsubishi during its formative period included graduates of the University of Pennsylvania and Cambridge University. However, foreign schools could not provide all of the skills that Japan needed to become an industrial power. To make up for the shortage of skilled management talent, Mitsui founded Hitotsubashi University in Tokyo to train future executives. The government founded Tokyo University in 1877, and provided a system of elementary education in the 1880s, which was so successful that enrollment for both boys and girls was close to 100 percent by the close of the Meiji era.[6] Teachers' schools were established to train teachers. The Meiji rulers expressed their passion for education and their break with the past in a declaration in 1872:

> Centuries have elapsed since schools were first established.... Because learning was viewed as the exclusive province of the samurai and his superiors, farmers, artisans, merchants, and women have neglected it altogether.... There shall, in the future, be no community with an illiterate family, nor a family with an illiterate person.... Hereafter... every man shall, of his own accord, subordinate all other matters to the education of his children.[7]

After the militarist epoch of 1931–1945, Japan did have six years of American military occupation, during which it had the usual ambitions to transform Japan from the top down. The American conquerors brought along the patronizing attitudes of the West toward the Rest. Douglas MacArthur compared the Japanese people to "a boy of twelve." John Foster Dulles told Japanese executives that they "should not expect to find a big U.S. market because the Japanese don't make the things we want," although he suggested that maybe they could export cocktail napkins.

The Japanese knew better. The wartime development of heavy and chemical industries left behind advanced technology, engineers, middle managers, and skilled workers that could produce products considerably more advanced than cocktail napkins.[8] The Americans broke up large combines like Mitsui and Mitsubishi to promote competition, but these soon reemerged as economic power centers because the Americans had left untouched the large banks that had become their nerve centers.[9] The

American occupation preserved and perhaps even reinforced the Japanese bureaucracy that was to implement Japan's peculiar state-managed capitalism. Public and private Japanese Searchers soon found the consumer electronics, automobile, steel, and other industries that would fuel Japan's extraordinary postwar export boom.

It is possible that the American post–World War II occupation is one of history's rare examples of top-down transformation of a society by outsiders. If this is true, the example doesn't lend itself to much replication since it took complete annihilation to get the chance to remake Japan. However, most of the evidence points to homegrown factors—the Americans were at most reconstructing an economy that was already advanced. (The same was true of the much-abused example of the Marshall Plan.)

Success and Self-reliance

It is easier to search for solutions to your own problems than to those of others. Most of the recent success stories are countries that did *not* get a lot of foreign aid and did *not* spend a lot of time in IMF programs, two of the indicators of the recent Incarnation of the White Man's Burden (table 9). Most of the recent disasters are just the opposite—tons of foreign aid and much time spent in IMF constraints. This of course involves some reverse causality, as I discuss throughout this book—the disasters were getting IMF assistance and foreign aid *because* they were disasters, while the IMF and the donors bypassed success stories because those countries didn't need the help. This does not prove that foreign assistance causes disaster, but it does

Table 9. Ten Best and Worst Per Capita Growth Rates, 1980–2002

Country	Per capita growth, 1980–2002 (%)	Aid/GDP 1980–2002 (%)	Time under IMF programs, 1980–2002 (%)
	Ten Best Per Capita Growth Rates, 1980–2002		
South Korea	5.9	0.03	36
China	5.6	0.38	8
Taiwan	4.5	0.00	0
Singapore	4.5	0.07	0
Thailand	3.9	0.81	30
India	3.7	0.66	19
Japan	3.6	0.00	0
Hong Kong	3.5	0.02	0
Mauritius	3.2	2.17	23
Malaysia	3.1	0.40	0
Median	**3.8**	**0.23**	**4**

Table 9. (cont.)

Country	Per capita growth, 1980–2002 (%)	Aid/GDP 1980–2002 (%)	Time under IMF programs, 1980–2002 (%)
	Ten Worst Per Capita Growth Rates, 1980–2002		
Nigeria	−1.6	0.59	20
Niger	−1.7	13.15	63
Togo	−1.8	11.18	72
Zambia	−1.8	19.98	53
Madagascar	−1.9	10.78	71
Côte d'Ivoire	−1.9	5.60	74
Haiti	−2.6	9.41	55
Liberia	−3.9	11.94	22
Congo, Dem. Rep.	−5.0	4.69	39
Sierra Leone	−5.8	15.37	50
Median	**−1.9**	**10.98**	**54**

show that outlandish success is very much possible without Western tutelage, while repeated treatments don't seem to stem the tide of disaster in the failures. Most of the recent success in the world economy is happening in Eastern and Southern Asia, not as a result of some global plan to end poverty but for homegrown reasons.

Moreover, the success stories follow a variety of formulas, perhaps an indication of an exploration that reflected each country's unique history and characteristics. South Korea's government intervened in guiding its corporations, while Hong Kong was the poster child for laissez-faire capitalism. China is a unique blend of Communist Party dictatorship, state enterprises, and partial free-market liberalization. India is a long-standing democracy, South Korea and Taiwan more recent democratic converts, while Singapore is not a democracy. All of these cases did realize most of their success from markets, but some were quite far from a laissez-faire model. While I think that free markets and democracy are a big part of the success story of the West, countries sometimes take a circuitous route to get there, or they may conceivably have their own unique recipe.

What we do know from the success stories is that the West played small part in them. As noted earlier, it is also interesting that five of the success stories were never completely colonized by the West, while all of the disasters are former colonies.

Two Special Colonies

Singapore and Hong Kong were British colonies where things turned out better than in other colonies. What was different?

What is unique about these two colonies is that they were unoccupied territories that the British colonized with the permission (or coercion) of the nearby local rulers. Even if the British were disposed to boss around or mistreat the indigenous population, they couldn't, because there was none. The peopling of the two trading stations depended on voluntary migration, mainly from China. Since these colonies depended on trade, the British induced Chinese merchants to settle there. The Brits would hardly have scared the merchants away with exploitation, or any restrictions on trade, so Hong Kong and Singapore were born free traders. The British also left the Chinese communities free to pursue their incomprehensible customs and more or less govern themselves, only intervening if social upheaval threatened. Chinese traders prospered, the richest of them wealthier than the local Brits. Chinese representatives sat on colonial councils as early as 1889 in Singapore and 1880 in Hong Kong.[10]

Starting with a clean slate, culturally homogeneous (the immigrants even largely came from the same region of China, the southern coastal belt that is the same one booming in China today), and committed to free trade, these Chinese microstates started with a much happier colonial legacy than others. This could be ex post facto rationalization, but the colonization of empty territory was fairly unique in colonial experience.

During a visit to Singapore, I shared some guava juice with the Singaporean organizer of the conference I was attending there. We sat on a verandah overlooking a golf course. She told me that she was the first generation in her family to receive a formal education. She has a Ph.D. in economics from an American university, the University of Rochester. Her parents were illiterate when they migrated from southern China to Singapore several decades ago.

As recently as 1974, there were three times as many Singaporeans with no education as there were Singaporeans with a university education. Today, the proportions are reversed. The Organization for Economic Cooperation and Development (OECD) in 1996 certified Singapore's graduation as a developed country. Singapore is the first tropical country to officially become a rich country, according to the OECD. Travelers familiar with the gleaming airport, the efficient subway system, and the immaculate downtown area of skyscrapers can attest to the country's prosperity.

Hong Kong has had equal success at attaining OECD income levels. By 2001, Hong Kong and Singapore had overtaken their erstwhile colonial master (see figure 33).

Hong Kong and Singapore never got significant amounts of foreign aid, nor were they recipients of other Western attention, such as IMF programs or military intervention.

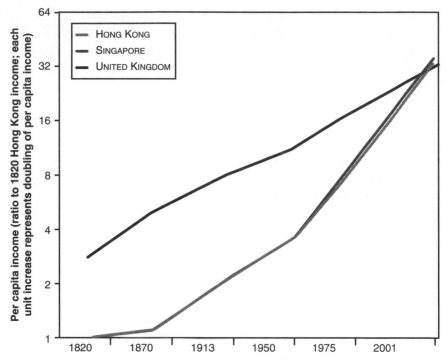

Fig. 33. Per Capita Income in United Kingdom Versus Hong Kong and Singapore

East Asia Dynamo

The success of Hong Kong and Singapore was the leading edge of the well-known success of the East Asian Tigers. I won't belabor the story of their success, since it is so well known—just note a few indicators.

The latest sign of success is in science education. In 2003, about the same number of citizens of East Asian countries received engineering Ph.D.s from American schools as U.S. citizens did.[11] The number of scientific journal articles published in East Asian countries quintupled over 1986–1999. Perhaps reflecting increased scientific expertise, high-technology exports from East Asia took off, growing by a factor of five in a decade (see figure 34).

Taiwan, whose numbers figure 34 above does not include because the cowardly international agencies do not recognize it, has become a remarkable technological success story. The Taiwan Semiconductor Machinery Corporation (TSMC) is the world's largest producer of foundry chips. The Electronics Research and Service Organization (itself started by the Taiwanese government in the early 1970s to get a jump on the IT industry) started

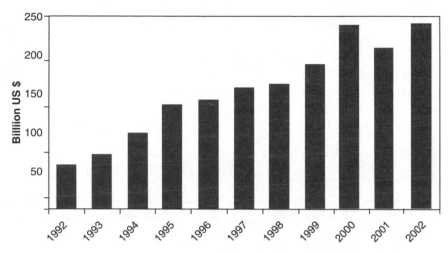

Fig. 34. High-technology Exports of East Asia Six: China, Hong Kong, Korea, Malaysia, Singapore, and Thailand

the TSMC as a joint venture with Phillips of Holland in 1987.[12] Today TSMC has sales of $2.3 billion.[13] Taiwan also produces such complex items as notebook and desktop PCs, video cards, and sound cards. Acer Computers of Taiwan is the world's third-largest manufacturer of PCs, with sales of eight billion dollars.[14] Taiwan's amazing economy has produced ten billionaires.[15]

The Dark Continent Born Again

But what hope could there be for a region impoverished by warlords, civil conflict, unending war, corruption, and brutal tyrants, after futile attempts by the West to influence events?

I am talking about China in the twenty-first century.

There can actually be a lot of hope, as shown by figure 35, which illustrates the launch of China's per capita income late in the twentieth century.

If the West has never had much effect on China, it hasn't been for lack of trying. Long-standing Western enthusiasm for bringing the Middle Kingdom into the modern world has included the usual White Man's Burden brew of Christianity, civilization, and commerce. The Jesuits tried to bring the gospel to the imperial court as long ago as the seventeenth century, packaging it with Western science. The Jesuit Johann Adam Schall got an

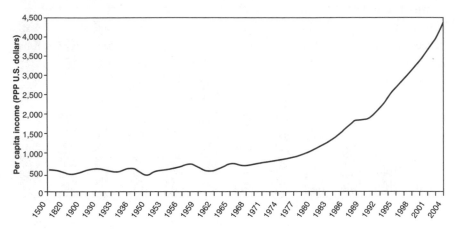

Fig. 35. China Per Capita Income in U.S. Dollars

entrée by predicting the exact time of a solar eclipse on September 1, 1644. (The Chinese astronomers could also predict eclipses, but not so exactly.) The Chinese took the Jesuit astronomy and left the gospel.[16] The Chinese were happy to use Western knowledge and technology, but showed less interest in Western efforts to Christianize and civilize them.

Americans got even more excited about China's development after a recent convert to Christianity, Chiang Kai-shek, consolidated his hold over most of the country during 1927–1931. In a triumph of wishful thinking, the American media (led particularly by *Time* editor Henry Luce, the son of a missionary to China) saw Chiang as a democratic paragon who was leading China into the modern world. Chiang's Wellesley-educated wife, who did publicity tours to the United States, helped Americans visualize a progressive China. Luce said Chiang had "embarked on a vast reformation, partly inspired by the Christian gospel."[17] Chiang-led China was the "protagonist of democracy in the Far East." Americans lent their support through military aid and private contributions funneled through the United China Relief Fund, which fed starving children and promoted industrial development.

A few naysayers, backed up by later historians, noted that Chiang Kai-shek was also a ruthless warlord who came to power by butchering his opponents. Chiang benefited from his long-standing connections to the Shanghai underworld, the Green Gang, whom he employed to massacre his Communist and other rivals in taking over Shanghai in 1927.[18] His underworld friends later helpfully assassinated other enemies, such as the head of the Chinese League for the Protection of Civil Rights (in 1933) and the editor of Shanghai's leading newspaper (in 1934).[19] Chiang installed concentration camps for political prisoners, maintained three secret police forces, and censored the press, publishers, and the universities—all in the name of "Free China." Meanwhile, nationalist officials enriched themselves under his rule.[20] This would not be the last time that the West would idealize its local "partners" in spreading development throughout the world.

China even got an early version of foreign aid. Between 1929 and 1941, the League of Nations provided China with thirty development experts on fields such as health, education, transport, and organization of rural co-operatives. On July 18, 1933, the League appointed a representative to "liase with China's National Economic Council for the purposes of technical collaboration" with the League.[21]

The long involvement of Europeans in China failed to leave much of a mark. The European involvement ended with Mao's victorious revolution in 1949. Then, after Communist tyranny, the "Great Leap Backward," and the Cultural Revolution seemed to have condemned China's people to eternal misery, something unexpected happened in China.

Second Chinese Revolution

I take my teenage daughter, Rachel, shopping for shoes. (Rachel and her teenage girlfriends constitute half of the American shoe market.) I like to turn over the shoes in the store and see where they were made. Almost always they are made in China. Less anecdotally, China now accounts for 63 percent of American imports of women's shoes.[22]

Not that China just exports shoes. I do a quick survey of my apartment. My New York Yankees baseball cap—made in China. My clock radio—made in China. My USB FlashDrive for my computer—made in China. The laptop computer itself—made in China.

The exploration of free markets that started with the end of agriculture communes in Xiaogang in 1978, as told in a previous chapter, spread to industrial as well as agricultural enterprises. On December 24, 2004, the *New York Times* did a story on China's textile enclaves. Datang is China's Socks City, producing nine billion pairs of socks a year, a third of the world's output. As recently as the late 1970s, Datang was a sleepy rice-growing village of less than a thousand people. People sewed socks in their spare time and sold them by the road in baskets. Ms. Dong Ying Hong worked in the 1970s as an elementary-school teacher at nine dollars a month. She gave up her teaching to make socks at home. Today, she is a millionaire as the owner of Zhejiang Socks.

Near Datang, in coastal China, there are other enclaves: Underwear City, Necktie City, Sweater City, and Kid's Clothing City. Hong Kong investors brought modern technology and designs to Necktie City in 1985; the workers at the initial enterprises soon left to start their own necktie companies. China's Communist government discovered ways to promote these enclaves such as handing out public land, giving tax breaks, and building transport infrastructure. What's scary is that China achieved this success even while bound by restrictions on international trade in textiles. Those restrictions expired on January 1, 2005.

China is the most remarkable success story of the last two decades: a very poor nation propelled into an economic powerhouse that scares the Chinese-made underpants off Western companies and other poor countries alike. It is an unconventional homegrown success, failing to follow any Western blueprint for how to be modern. It combines lack of property rights with free markets, Communist Party dictatorship with feedback on local public services, and municipal state enterprises with private ones.

After the market-based reforms started in 1978, what was $59 billion in industrial production in 1978 became $844 billion in 2003. Exports of $44 billion in 1982 became $428 billion in 2003. Enterprises such as Bao Steel adopted cutting-edge technology by sending engineers and managers for overseas training.[23]

Success attracts paternity claims. The World Bank suggests that "support from outside helped make reform happen and contributed to the structure of the reforms." The World Bank is allegedly saving China's poor on a shoestring budget: as of the year 2002, $563 million a year, or about a tenth of a penny per day for each Chinese person.[24]

I visited China in December 2003, amazed at the dynamism of everyone I met and everything I saw. Everyone is working hard, constructing edifices everywhere; everything and everyone is moving at high speed. Where Washington has its one perpetual traffic jam on its Beltway, Beijing has five beltways (with a sixth one under construction). Technology is exploding, with cell phones and computers everywhere.

The Chinese economics Ph.D. students I taught in Beijing and Wuhan Universities were ferocious in their desire to learn. I taught in five days the equivalent of a semester-long course, which exhausted me far more than my Chinese students. I later got a Christmas card from Wuhan University that had the bracing message "Improve oneself, promote perseverance, seek truth, and make innovations."

To be sure, the ultimate economic test of a society is not rapid growth but attaining a high level of income. China's per capita income is still only one sixth of that in the United States. The lack of democracy and the remaining inefficiencies caused by state-owned enterprises, banking-system problems, and other state-induced distortions in the economy are still major worries. The bubble may burst, or China may continue its amazing boom, but change is coming from exploration within.

India

I am hurtling down a street in old Delhi on a bicycle rickshaw. The "street" is barely wide enough to accommodate the rickshaw and the two middle-age tourist-wallahs on the back. The street is also crowded with fruit, vegetable, and flower vendors, motorbikes, wandering children, emotionally disturbed dogs, and two-wheel carts full of bricks pushed by strong men. Hindu temples line the street. We visit one of them. It dazzles with color paintings of gods, inscriptions in an unfamiliar alphabet, burning candles surrounded by flowers, the smell of incense, and carved stone and wood. It should be humbling to arrogant Westerners to realize that Indian civilization goes back more than three thousand years, which is a tad longer than the life of the White Man's Burden.

In any case, India failed to develop during the long period of British tutelage. After independence, foreign aid never amounted to more than about a hundredth of GDP. India initially took a heavily planned, interventionist approach to development, and knew only mediocre growth. The anemic growth was so notorious it even got its own name: "the Hindu rate of growth." India finally discovered its capitalist inner child late in the twentieth century. (See figure 36.)

As it does with China, the West tries to take credit for recent Indian success. In India as in China, the World Bank also congratulates itself on a protégé's rapid economic growth. By its own account, the Bank not only promoted free trade and worked with India's national government, but it also supported the Indian government's decentralization, working with India's myriad state, local, and municipal governments. As in China, the budget for these ambitious achievements was modest: about $1.75 billion in new World Bank lending per year, or about half a penny per Indian per day. How much difference did these modest sums make? The World Bank chief economist suggested their "powerful demonstration effects" enlightened the Indians.

Back on this planet, India had Searchers. Two young entrepreneurs from Delhi, Rajendra Pawar and Vijay Thadani, started a private computer school in the early 1980s. Their National Institute of Information Technology

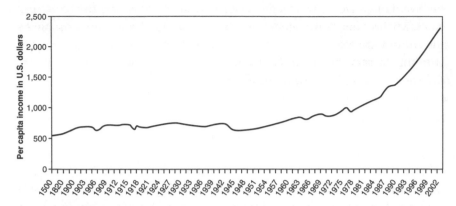

Fig. 36. India Per Capita Income in U.S. Dollars

(NIIT) was an instant hit, so much so that they couldn't accommodate the demand. Their breakthrough idea was to become the McDonald's of computer education, franchising new schools wherever there was the demand. The franchisees were local professionals who carried the NIIT from the largest cities to the smallest towns. NIIT protected its brand name by standardizing class-rooms, teacher training, and advertising, as well as by performing frequent audits and rigorous exams. Today, the tall, bearded forty-eight-year-old Rajendra Pawar leads a company with a stock market capitalization of two billion dollars; eight of his executives are millionaires. Lonely singles seeking matrimony often mention the NIIT degree as a credential in personals ads.[25]

India's famous success at outsourcing IT services for the U.S. market is exemplified by Wipro Ltd., India's most valuable company, at over ten billion dollars in market capitalization.[26] The company provides IT services to 138 of the Fortune 1000 and Global 500 companies, including such famous names as Sony, Nokia, Home Depot, and Compaq. It also runs call centers for the likes of Delta Airlines.[27] This is pretty impressive for an obscure company founded in 1945 as a maker of edible oils. The owner of Wipro, Azim Premji, with a B.A. from Stanford, is the fifty-eighth richest billionaire in the world.[28]

Turkey

I met Fatma two days after September 11, 2001. She lives in a rural village forty miles outside of Ankara, Turkey. I arrived in Ankara just as the planes hit the World Trade Center and the Pentagon back home. After a panic-filled day and night trying to reach my kids, I finally got through and found out they were okay. No planes were flying, so I could not return to the United States. My hosts in Turkey generously arranged some travel in the country-side around Ankara.

On these travels, I encountered Fatma,[29] a dignified middle-aged woman. She was sitting outside her home, a four-room mud-and-stone hut covered with wooden sticks and thatch. She told me of the precarious existence of her family. The only income earner is her illiterate teenage son, who does odd jobs of manual labor. Her husband died two years ago, leaving a large debt to the state welfare agency, which demanded repayment of the debt before it would pay pension benefits. To pay the debt, Fatma had to sell all the family's sheep. Still, some of the debt remained, preventing her from getting a pension. To earn money to feed her aged mother and two deaf and retarded children, she gathers food from the family garden. I can see that what she has described as a two-year-long drought has shriveled its produce. Fatma has some land outside the village, but it is worthless without rain and she cannot afford to dig a well and install an irrigation system. The family makes do on what food Fatma can gather from nature. The charity of neighbors helps the family survive. When I asked her about her hopes or fears about the future, she said she trusted in God to bring better times.

After my visit with Fatma, I went to the village square. The friendly men of the village were very hospitable to the uninvited visitor, offering me a drink of water and then of some unidentified but tasty alcoholic beverage. The men laughed and joked with one another as I asked them about their village. Some of them were of Kurdish descent but had lived in this village in central Turkey for decades. A few women were present, but held back from the conversation. The men pointed with pride to the beautiful local mosque. Some of the people in the square had probably been benefactors to Fatma, under the Muslim tradition of *zakat,* in which observant Muslims give away 2.5 percent of their wealth every year to the poor.[30]

Fatma is needy and poor, but she is better off in a middle-income economy than she would be in a very poor one. Her poverty is not of the same order as that I have seen in Africa. She has a reasonably comfortable home, with a television set and a refrigerator. I hope Fatma's life improved as Turkey's economy recovered strongly from the crisis of 2001. Turkey has had a strong economy for a while.

In 1917, Vehbi Koç, the son of a literary scholar of modest means, opened a grocery store in Ankara, Turkey, with an investment of eight dollars. He was sixteen years old. When he died, in 1996, he was on the *Forbes* list of global billionaires. His company, the Koç Group, went from a small trading firm to a global conglomerate that is one of Turkey's largest private employers. Koç Group produces everything from automobiles, televisions, VCRs, refrigerators, and ovens to matches and tomato paste; it operates banks, insurance companies, tourist properties, and retail chains; it thrives despite the lowering of tariffs and European competition. Koç's son Rahmi took over the business after his father retired in 1984. Rahmi Koç has a B.A. from Johns Hopkins University. In 2004, when he was number 406 on *Forbes*'s list of the world's richest people, Rahmi Koç passed the generational reins of the company along to his son, Mustafa Koç.[31] With consumer choice the guide for Koç that it never was for the White Man's Burden, Koç has prospered.[32] In 2002, its exports rose 45 percent, to $2.6 billion.

From 1970 to 1995, the share of manufactures in Turkey's exports rose from 9 percent to 74 percent.[33] Turkey's manufacturing sector as a whole has grown at a robust 5.6 percent per year from 1966 to 2003.

Turkey is one of the success stories of the twentieth century (see figure 37). Never colonized or occupied by the West, it recovered from the collapse of the Ottoman Empire and a war with Greece after World War I. It has known steady growth ever since. Notwithstanding periodic macroeconomic crises,

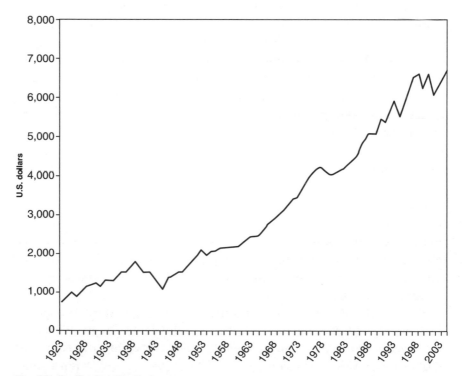

Fig. 37. Turkey Per Capita Income

conflicts with the Kurds, and military coups, Turkey is today a stable democracy. Students from the country are flooding the graduate schools of the United States, getting top faculty positions at prestigious American universities, or going back to Turkey to teach at very well regarded universities there.

Turkey's government is negotiating with the European Union the conditions of its accession to the Union, promising the epic moment of economic and political unity of Western Christendom and what Europeans used to view as the Eastern infidels. Turkey is not just catching up to the West, it is rubbing out the line between the West and the Rest.

Botswana

In 1968, the South African company De Beers discovered significant diamond deposits in Botswana. Botswana's government negotiated a partnership agreement with De Beers. Whereas other governments with valuable minerals usually nationalized them, Botswana's government acted shrewdly in enlisting De Beers's expertise at diamond mining and marketing. In 1976, the De Beers Botswana Mining Company (Debswana) discovered another huge diamond pipe at Jwaneng, in southern Botswana, the largest diamond discovery in the world since the original South African discoveries at Kimberley. Botswana renegotiated the original agreement with De Beers, giving it close to 80 percent of the profits from diamonds. In 1986, Botswana sold to De Beers its stockpile of diamonds (previously withheld from the world market to keep prices high) in exchange for cash and an unprecedented 5.2 percent of the shares of De Beers itself, including the right to name two directors of the De Beers board. Botswana's economy grew at the world's fastest rate over the last four decades, despite its dependence on diamonds, an outcome very different from that of other diamond producers, such as Sierra Leone and Angola.[34] Botswana's tiny manufacturing sector expanded rapidly at the same time, registering 8.7 percent growth from 1966 to 2003. Cattle was another important prop for exports and domestic income. In the new millennium, Botswana is diversifying its economy to include other products besides diamonds and is coping with a terrible AIDS crisis.

Botswana may have benefited from strong pre-colonial institutions of consultations of chiefs with citizens (in *kgotlas* that were sort of like town hall meetings). Other favorable factors were benign neglect by Britain during the colonial period, the absence of ethnic conflict because of the relative homogeneity of the Tswana people, and clear indigenous property rights based on cattle holdings.[35]

Botswana shows a possible path for homegrown development for many African countries. The abundance of natural resources in Africa has been a curse due to their capture by corrupt dictators. We saw in chapter 4 that natural resources are historically associated with bad government. But historical tendencies are not ironclad laws; some countries can break free. Botswana shows that if Africans can get good government from their rulers, the abundance of natural resources can be turned into a blessing.

Not all African countries are resource rich, but many are. Angola's natural resources to produce food crops, coffee, sisal, oil palm, sugarcane, tobacco, citrus fruits, fish, hydroelectricity, diamonds, and oil should make it rich. People produced all of these things in the colonial period, but the abrupt departure of the Portuguese at independence and the outbreak of civil war destroyed this potential. Railways built by the Portuguese formerly reached into the mining regions of DRC and Zambia for lucrative cross-border transit to the Angolan port of Benguela. The railway has not functioned since independence. Peace in the DRC and Angola could open the door to tapping this potential again, if citizens' demands for better government were realized.

Chile

I saw just how well integrated Santiago, Chile, was into the world economy when I visited some of the local espresso bars during a visit to Chile's central bank. Barely clad young waitresses took orders, handed out the cups, and collected generous tips. Combining sex, caffeine, and commerce seemed like the epitome of the best and worst of today's global economy.

A purer vision of the benefits of Chile's development came during a visit to a shantytown in Santiago. Accompanied by some idealistic upper-class students who ran a charity renovating shantytown dwellings, I visited some clean, orderly homes amid well-kept streets. I talked to a grandmother whose cement dwelling was adorned by hanging pots of flowers, a television, and comfortable furniture. Poverty was here, but it was quite muted by comparison with other shantytowns I had visited around the world. Chile's economic growth has benefited poor as well as rich.

Chile is an exception to the current Latin American travails (see figure 38). After Salvador Allende's socialist detour in 1970–1973, the brutal military government of Augusto Pinochet instituted free-market reforms. Macroeconomic crises plagued the military regime, but the free-market reforms eventually paid off in the 1980s. Democracy returned, but both leftist and rightist

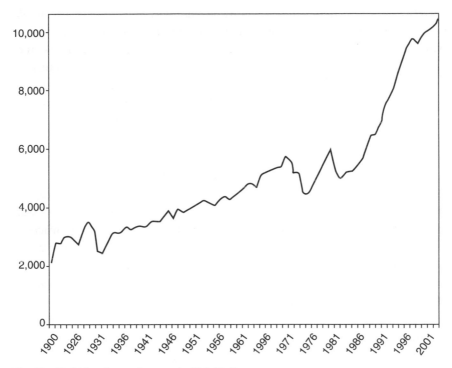

Fig. 38. Chile Per Capita Income in U.S. Dollars

political parties agreed to keep the free-market model. Today, Chile is a stable free-market democracy.

On July 23, 2003, Congress approved a free-trade agreement between Chile and the United States, which took effect on January 1, 2004. Chile exported a diverse range of products to the United States in 2004, such as fish, fresh fruit, wood, wood products, copper, and clothing.[36] The success of the fresh fruit industry is typical of Chile's exploration for its niche in the world economy. Exploiting its Mediterranean climate and its opposite Southern Hemisphere growing season, it seized on the chance to export gourmet fresh fruit to the North Americans.

When I recently flew to Chile during the U.S. summer, my flight was crowded with American college students bringing their skis and tourist dollars to Chilean winter resorts. The road from the airport to Santiago was a new four-lane highway that put to shame the traffic-choked trip from Manhattan to LaGuardia on the other end. In a nice example of South–South globalization, Senegalese singer Youssou N'Dour was playing on the radio in the taxi.

When it suited them, Chileans borrowed freely from American economic models, as implemented by the famous Chicago Boys—disciples of Milton Friedman trained at the University of Chicago. A disproportionate number of my colleagues ever since graduate school have been Chileans—most of whom are now back in Chile, running the economy and government. Foreign aid, the World Bank, and the IMF were never more than trivial players in Chile during its discovery of a free-market democratic model.

Homegrown Development

The success of Japan, China, the East Asian Tigers, India, Turkey, Botswana, and Chile is turning into a comic relic the arrogance of the West. Americans and Western Europeans will one day realize that they are not, after all, the saviors of the Rest.

Even when the West fails to "develop" the Rest, the Rest develops itself. The great bulk of development success in the Rest comes from self-reliant, exploratory efforts, and the borrowing of ideas, institutions, and technology from the West when it suits the Rest to do so.

Again, the success stories do not give any simple blueprint for imitation. Their main unifying theme is that all of them subjected their development searching to a market test, using a combination of domestic and export markets. Using the market for feedback and accountability seems to be necessary for success. But we have seen in chapter 3 that creating free markets is itself difficult, and the success stories certainly don't all fit some pristine laissez-faire ideal.

We know that gross violations of free markets and brutal self-aggrandizing autocrats usually preclude success. Beyond that breathtakingly obvious point, there is no automatic formula for success, only many political and economic Searchers looking for piecemeal improvements that overcome the many obstacles described in chapters 3 and 4.

Nor is self-reliance a magical panacea for poor people—many unlucky poor people, no matter how hardworking, live in states run by gangsters or simply in complex societies that have not yet discovered the elusive path to development. Western assistance, suitably humbled and chastened by the experience of the past, can still play some role in alleviating the sufferings of the poor. In the next chapter, I examine how Western assistance could do much more than in the past, once it is freed of utopian goals.

Three Classmates from Kumawu

Roland Akosah, Robert Danso-Boakye, and Yaw Nyarko together attended the Tweneboa Kodua Secondary School in Kumawu, a town of about ten thousand people in the Ashanti region of Ghana. It was not easy being a student at this school. Water was out most of the school year. Electricity, when it was working, was on from only 6:00 to 10:00 p.m. There were few books; all the students shared the one or two copies available in the school library. But Yaw Nyarko remembers that the teachers were very dedicated and they taught him and his two classmates a lot.

Together, the three men went on to study at the University of Ghana at Legon, near the capital of Accra. And together, all three left Ghana during the military dictatorship of Jerry Rawlings to get graduate degrees abroad

Roland Akosah, who got an MBA from Wharton, then worked for many years at IBM and United Technologies in the United States, had grown up in poverty; his mother had had no formal education. He decided to return to Ghana and start his own investment bank, Eno International, in 2000. Eno International has raised capital in Ghana and the United States to put money into pharmaceuticals and consumer electronics. It is buying up citrus groves with the aim of eventually starting an orange juice factory.*

With help from family and friends, Robert Danso-Boakye got an M.S. in International Banking and Financing in Edinburgh and a M.Phil. in Economics from the University of Surrey. His mentors persuaded him to return to Ghana in the late 1980s to participate in the new opportunities created by the deregulation of banking. Today he is in senior management at Trust Bank in Accra.

Yaw Nyarko got a Ph.D. in Economics on a scholarship from Cornell University. He became a well-known expert in game theory, writing articles such as "On the Convexity of the Value Function in Bayesian Optimal Control Problems." After a stint at Brown University, he joined the Department of Economics at NYU, where today he

---

* The details on Roland Akosah are taken from Dyan Machan, *Forbes Magazine*, "Ghana's Moment," and from background notes Machan generously provided.

is my colleague. He is also the vice provost for global affairs at NYU, where he has helped develop an NYU study-abroad site and research site in Accra. It is based at Ashesi University, the dynamic private-university started by Patrick Awuah, and the University of Ghana at Legon. Yaw has donated his own time to teach economics to the eager undergraduates at Ashesi. He has even more ambitious plans: starting an interdisciplinary research center at NYU called Africa House. Roland Akosah is skeptical about what foreign aid has done for Ghana. "We have a horrible reputation. Not only do people *think* we are panhandlers, we *are* panhandlers. It's up to us to improve our own economy." Yaw Nyarko adds that foreign aid "distorts incentives." He thinks "it makes people look to others to solve their problems."

CHAPTER ELEVEN

The Future of Western Assistance

We shall not cease from exploration
And the end of all our exploring
Will be to arrive where we started
And know the place for the first time.

T. S. Eliot, "Little Gidding,"
Four Quartets, 1943

As development workers Dennis Whittle and Mari Kuraishi once asked, what would the World Bank and IMF shock therapists advise if foreign aid were a country? They would probably abolish state ownership, do rapid privatization and downsizing, let the market work, and put an end to bureaucratic central planning. I would favor a more gradual approach, of piecemeal reforms for the troubled country of foreign aid.

Yes, there is still hope that Western assistance can help poor people in the Rest with some of their most desperate problems.

Official Aid

A big problem with foreign aid has been its aspiration to a utopian blueprint to fix the world's complex problems. If you think I will now offer a utopian blueprint to fix aid's complex problems, then I have done a really bad job in the previous chapters at explaining the problems with utopian blueprints.

Still, I hope there are some useful lessons that could enable Western assistance to make incremental progress. If the utopian goal distracted attention away from holding aid agencies accountable for tangible outcomes, then step one is to give up the utopian goal. The utopian agenda has led to collective responsibility for multiple goals for each agency, one of the worst incentive systems invented since mankind started walking up-right. There has also been the incentive bias toward observability, which has led to unproductive efforts at producing things that made a big splash.

The utopian agenda has also led to an unproductive focus on trying to change whole political systems. The status quo—large international bureau-cracies giving aid to large national government bureaucracies—is not get-ting money to the poor. Conditions on aid don't work to change government behavior.

When you are in a hole, the top priority is to stop digging. Discard your patronizing confidence that you know how to solve other people's problems better than they do. Don't try to fix governments or societies. Don't invade other countries, or send arms to one of the brutal armies in a civil war. End conditionality. Stop wasting our time with summits and frameworks. Give up on sweeping and naive institutional reform schemes. The aim should be to make individuals better off, not to transform governments or societies.

Once the West is willing to aid individuals rather than governments, some conundrums that tie foreign aid up in knots are resolved. Those so unlucky as to have warlords or kleptocrats as leaders will still be eligible for aid. The West can end the pathetic spectacle of the IMF, World Bank, and other aid agencies coddling the warlords and kleptocrats. It can end the paternalism and hypocrisy of conditionality. It can end the inherent contradiction be-tween "country ownership" and dictating conditions from Washington.

Remember, aid cannot achieve the end of poverty. Only homegrown development based on the dynamism of individuals and firms in free mar-kets can do that. Shorn of the impossible task of general economic develop-ment, aid can achieve much more than it is achieving now to relieve the sufferings of the poor.

Put the focus back where it belongs: get the poorest people in the world such obvious goods as the vaccines, the antibiotics, the food supplements, the improved seeds, the fertilizer, the roads, the boreholes, the water pipes, the textbooks, and the nurses. This is not making the poor dependent on handouts; it is giving the poorest people the health, nutrition, education, and other inputs that raise the payoff to their own efforts to better their lives. (Just like a National Science Foundation fellowship to get a Ph.D. once increased the payoff to my own efforts to pursue a career.)

I don't mean to imply that all aid should be for projects. Other areas of aid agencies' possible comparative advantage could include distilling practical knowledge on operating banking systems or stock markets, giving advice on good macroeconomic management, simplifying business regulations, or making piecemeal reforms that promote a merit-based civil service.

Unlike many other aid commentators, I am not saying that it is easy to implement these solutions, that my solutions will work, or even that these solutions are obviously right. No, no, and no. There are good reasons why these solutions are not happening already. It is partly because of the social complexity of making even simple interventions work—which will remain troublesome.

But it is also due to some factors that could be changed. It is partly because the rich countries don't care enough about making aid work for the poor, and are willing to settle for grand utopian Plans that don't work. It is partly because nobody is actually held accountable for making *this* intervention work in *this* place at *this* time. My suggestions here could be ludicrously misguided; they should be subject to skeptical examination and ex post facto evaluation just like everything else.

Above all, this book is not a Plan. It points instead to the Searchers with knowledge of local conditions, experimental results from interventions, and some way to get feedback from the poor, who will find out (and are already finding out) all the variable and complicated answers of how to make aid work.

I will plunge recklessly ahead with some suggestions, just because the current system is unacceptable. This book has presented some historical lessons that could guide the Searchers.

Fix the incentive system of collective responsibility for multiple goals. Have individual accountability for individual tasks. Let aid agencies specialize in the sectors and countries they are best at helping. Then hold the aid agencies accountable for *their* results by having truly independent evaluation of their efforts.

Perhaps the aid agencies should each set aside a portion of their budgets (such as the part now wasted on self-evaluation) to contribute to an international independent evaluation group made up of staff trained in the scientific method from the rich and poor countries, who will evaluate random samples of each aid agency's efforts. Evaluation will involve randomized controlled trials where feasible, less pure statistical analysis if not, and will at least be truly independent, even when randomized trials and statistical analysis are not feasible. Experiment with different methods of simply asking the poor if they are better off. Mobilize the altruistic people in rich countries to put heat on the agencies to make their money actually reach the poor, and to get angry when the aid does *not* reach the poor.

With specialization on a small number of tasks and the fear and reward induced by independent evaluation, maybe agents of aid will be willing to keep exploring different means of fixing a problem, such as malnutrition, until they get it working. Agents of aid can experiment with different delivery mechanisms: an NGO, private firms, social entrepreneurs who scout out ways to help the poor, maybe even a decently functioning local government agency. Specialization on modest tasks and evaluation for whether you have accomplished them will transfer power from Planners to Searchers.

Although I think the existing bilateral or multilateral aid agencies and poor-country governments have done a bad job, they might be able to perform better once they are held accountable. Official aid agencies and national government bureaucracies should remain on the list of possible vehicles for delivering development services. Again, all that matters is what works to get help to the poor.

How to fix the bias toward observability? If you evaluate tangible results, won't that just increase the bias toward doing things that are observable? Here I think we need a healthy dose of pragmatism. It is hard to think of any incentive system that is going to successfully reward invisible effort toward producing invisible outcomes. Give it up. A cow will always be a cow. Instead try to find where useful interventions intersect with observability. Let international aid agencies go ahead and do the observable things, but make sure that the evaluators hold these agencies accountable for getting results for the poor with those things. The evaluators will give zero marks for empty public gestures such as summits and frameworks.

In making these reforms, there are many pitfalls. Reformers have to gird themselves for all the ways the wily aid bureaucracies will appear to be making the necessary changes while preserving the politically powerful status quo. The aid bureaucracy is marvelously skilled at adopting the rhetoric, if not the substance, of any criticism directed its way. Indeed, the aid agencies claim they are already adopting the approach of "managing for results."

Yet another report has shown up on my Web browser, "Managing for Development Results, Principles in Action: Sourcebook on Emerging Good Practice," prepared in April 2005. The unnamed authors call themselves the "Joint Venture on Managing for Development Results for the DAC Working Party on Aid Effectiveness and Donor Practices." Their work is "background information" that is "Forwarded to High-Level Forum on Aid Effectiveness."

Just how much the aid industry still does not *get* the flaws of top-down planning and collective responsibility is shown in how the sourcebook team describes development agencies as already "managing for results": "Development agencies are creating results-based country assistance strategies in close dialogue with each other and with national governments. During this process, multiple agencies negotiate a process for working together to support country outcomes."[1]

There is also the risk that aid agencies will do "cream skimming"—that is, selecting the most promising projects in order to show results, possibly even ones the government would have done on its own without aid. When agencies do this, their aid frees up government resources to be spent on something bad, like the army. This "fungibility" of aid money is something that aid analysts worry about, but perhaps is less of a worry when there are so many things failing. At least make sure that the cows deliver the cream.

The obstacles to reform are formidable. Still, we can try to think of creative aid mechanisms toward addressing the problems, over and above the specialization and evaluation that I discuss here. Many good-hearted people are searching for solutions to the problems of the world's poor, much closer to the bottom than the experts at the top. From some of these efforts, new and promising ideas will emerge, and some are already emerging.

Making PROGRESA

Fifty-year-old Emma García cooks about 250 tortillas a day for her extended family in her smoky dirt-floor kitchen in Buenavista, Mexico. About sixty-two poor and malnourished families live in Buenavista, in the state of Michoacán, with no paved roads, no running water, and no sanitation. The only economic activity in the village is subsistence farming. Children are kept out of school to work in the fields; those who do go to school have trouble concentrating on anything other than their empty stomachs.

In 1997, the Mexican deputy minister of finance, a well-known economist named Santiago Levy, came up with an innovative program to help people like Emma García. Called PROGRESA (Programa Nacional de Educación, Salud y Alimentación), the program provides cash grants to mothers *if* they keep their children in school, participate in health education programs, and bring the kids to health clinics for nutritional supplements and regular checkups. Since the Mexican federal budget didn't have enough money to reach everyone, Levy doled out the scarce funds in a way that the program could be scientifically evaluated. The program randomly selected 253 villages to receive the benefits, with another 253 villages (not yet getting benefits) chosen as comparators. Data were collected on all 506 villages before and after the beginning of the program. The Mexican government gave the task of evaluating the program to the International Food Policy Research Institute (IFPRI), which commissioned academic studies of the program's effects.

The academic findings confirmed that the program worked. Children receiving PROGRESA benefits had a 23 percent reduction in the incidence of illness, a 1 to 4 percent increase in height, and an 18 percent reduction in anemia. Adults had 19 percent fewer days lost to illness. There was a 3.4 percent increase in enrollment for all students in grades one through eight; the increase was largest among girls who had completed grade six, at 14.8 percent.[2]

More anecdotally, people in Buenavista have noticed the difference. Emma García says that she can feed her children meat twice a week now to supplement the tortillas, thanks to the money she receives from PROGRESA. Schoolteacher Santiago Días notices that attendance is up in Buenavista's two-room schoolhouse. Moreover, Días says, "because they are better fed, the children can concentrate for longer periods. And knowing that their mothers' benefits depend on their being at school, the children seem more eager to learn."[3]

Because the program was such a clearly documented success, it was continued despite the voters' rejection of the longtime ruling party in Mexico's democratic revolution in 2000. By that time, PROGRESA was reaching 10 percent of the families in Mexico and had a budget of eight hundred million dollars. The new government expanded it to cover the urban poor. Similar programs began in neighboring countries with support from the World Bank.[4]

The lesson for aid reformers is that a combination of free choice and scientific evaluation can build support for an aid program where things that work can be expanded rapidly. The cash-for-education-and-nutrition segment in itself could be expanded, with suitable local adjustments, to more countries and on a much larger scale than it is now.

Helping Children Learn in Kenya and India

Education promoters have offered a bewildering variety of interventions to educate children: abolishing school fees, providing uniforms, building classrooms, hiring more teachers, training teachers, providing free meals at school, making children healthier with free medicine, providing textbooks and flipcharts, offering remedial education, awarding prizes to teachers whose students perform well, and handing out vouchers for private schools. In the typical utopian program, everything is done at once and it is impossible to learn what works and what doesn't.

Fortunately, some Searchers for solutions have taken a different approach. They study each intervention in isolation, identifying its effects relative to a control group that did not get the intervention. Esther Duflo of MIT and

Michael Kremer of Harvard are pioneers in this approach to development. One researcher studying a project in Western Kenya found that attendance at preschool programs was 25 percent higher when a free breakfast was provided, and test scores were higher even though the meals cut into instruction time.

Did textbooks raise students' performance? More research in the same district in Kenya found that those students who were in the upper 40 percent of the class did have an improvement in test scores after getting textbooks. How to reach the other 60 percent of students? One bright idea was to use flip charts, which were thought to be easier to follow for less literate students. Unfortunately, the same careful research found that flip charts had no effect on test scores. The research giveth, and the research taketh away.

In India, another program to help poorly performing students hired remedial education assistants from the communities to tutor the students. The students in Mumbai and Vadodara got two hours a day of tutoring from the assistants. What were the results? This program did increase test scores, with the most dramatic results among those students who had been doing worst prior to the program. The researchers estimated that the program of hiring remedial education workers from the community achieved ten times the results of hiring more conventional teachers for the same cost.

Another promising idea was to improve teacher incentives. An experiment in Western Kenya had parent groups give prizes to teachers whose students performed the best on standardized tests. Test scores of students covered by the program initially rose, but subsequent monitoring of these students found that they quickly regressed back to the same level as those students not covered by the program. Teachers were apparently "teaching to the test," with no lasting impact on student performance.[5]

The lesson of all this research is that some equally plausible interventions work and others don't. Aid agencies must be constantly experimenting and searching for interventions that work, verifying what works with scientific evaluation. For learning to take place, there must be information. The aid agencies must carefully track the impact of their projects on poor people using the best scientific tools available, and using outside evaluators to avoid the self-interest of project managers.

What Works?

MIT professor Abhijit Banerjee gives other helpful examples besides those already mentioned that have been verified as cost-effective uses of foreign aid: deworming drugs; dietary supplements such as those for iron, vitamin A, and iodine; education in using condoms and treating other sexually transmitted diseases to slow the spread of AIDS; indoor spraying to control malaria; fertilizer subsidies; vaccination; and urban water provision.[6] None of these are keys to development according to some utopian scheme; they are just modest interventions that make people's lives better.

Other evidence on what works has come from cross-country comparisons of country practices and certain outcomes. And not all piecemeal interventions are for social services and projects. James Barth of Auburn, Gerard Caprio of Williams College, and Ross Levine of Brown University found a strong association between banking regulations that force banks to disclose accurate, timely, comparable information on their finances and the level of banking development in a country. They controlled for possible reverse causality and found that the result still held. Contrary to the widespread view that tough official bank supervision is needed to protect savers from rogue banks, they found a *negative* relationship between powers of bank supervisors and development of a healthy banking industry (also controlling for possible reverse causality). If you want to promote healthy banking, which is an ingredient in enabling the poor to help themselves through credit, then these statistical associations point you in the direction of regulating information disclosure rather than having powerful official bank supervisors.[7]

Experiments and statistical analysis are a long way short of a panacea for effective aid. There is also development problem solving that is more like learning to sail than testing a theory of fluid dynamics. Aid agencies must let their staff gain experience in a particular local setting on a particular problem, and then let the experienced staff decide on the ground what is working and what is not. Instead, we see aid bureaucracies shifting staff around before they can gain enough experience, with the result that those agencies are full of generalists without local or specialized knowledge.

How can aid agencies acquire the incentive to do scientific evaluation, statistical analysis, and on-the-ground learning? For many efforts, you can survey the intended beneficiaries—the poor—before and after every project, along with a control group that did not benefit from the project. Disclose publicly all efforts and outcomes. Let a community of observers who care—from both donor and recipient countries—hold the agencies responsible for outcomes. Increase the pressure of free speech and democracy on aid agencies by having vociferous advocates for the poor who practice science rather than public relations. Have rich-country politicians realize that a negative evaluation of a particular aid effort is a learning opportunity, not an excuse to cut foreign aid.

Your ideas are Crazy, but are they Crazy enough?*

On New Year's Eve, December 31, 2004, in Washington, D.C., Dennis Whittle and Mari Kuraishi got married at the stroke of midnight. The wedding was a charming blend: Shaker hymns, a Unitarian minister, Mari's very proper Japanese mother, Dennis's good-old-boy Kentucky father, and the joint giving away of the bride by an international assortment of their friends and relatives.

Dennis and Mari are intellectual as well as romantic partners. They come into this story because of the innovative ideas to which they are devoting their non-wedding hours. They decry the central planning approach of the international aid system and have come up with some practical steps to make it act a little bit more like a free market, making the system match the free-market rhetoric of some of its participants.[8]

They suggest a marketplace instead of central planning, a kind of eBay meets foreign aid. They see three types of actors: (1) social entrepreneurs close to the poor who propose projects to meet their needs; (2) individuals and institutions with technical and practical knowledge, and (3) donors who have funds they want to give away. The current system has huge bureaucracies under (3) doing central planning of (1) and (2). Dennis and Mari envision instead a decentralized market in which each category has many players who seek out players in the other categories and spontaneously form matches (another possible metaphor: aid's version of an online dating service). Projects would compete for funds, technical specialists would compete to be hired, and donors would compete to get results, and thus attract even more funds. All of the players would build reputations based on their past performance delivering results. Players would interact through personal meetings, telecommunications, and the Internet (much like the business networks described in chapter 3). The trust necessary for successful relationships would be built through repeated interactions. Dennis and Mari have put together an Internet platform and a company that would facilitate these matches, called GlobalGiving.com. They summarize their vision:

> The number of potential participants on the project design, funding, and implementation sides have all dramatically risen over the past decades. Official agencies, foundations, and even private companies that want to combat poverty abroad, assist with HIV/AIDS projects, or invest in schools in developing countries all have no place to "shop," so to speak, for projects. On the other side of the equation, people with projects cannot find donors. ... GlobalGiving.com ... treats foreign aid and philanthropy like a

* Borrowed from a quote by Niels Bohr: "Your theory is crazy...but it's not crazy enough to be true."

> *marketplace, where donors and recipients come together to exchange information and resources. ... [R]ecipients post projects that need funding, and individual and institutional donors can provide anywhere from a few dollars to thousands of dollars to the projects they find most worthy.*

This decentralized approach would avoid the coordination problems. It would bypass the narrow administrative funnel in the recipient government through which official aid must pass. It would avoid the strategic manipulation of aid by donor governments and the corruption of recipient governments.

How does this work in practice? Take the schoolteachers in Coimbatore, India, who noticed that their girl students often left school after puberty and thought of a possible solution. As *BusinessWeek* tells the story:

> *The teachers posted a small, bedraggled project on GlobalGiving—so tiny, in fact, that it initially embarrassed Whittle. ... The project ad read: "New Toilet Block for School. $5,000." Within a few weeks, four donors from around the U.S., including a writer from New York City and a banker from JP Morgan, put up the money. In less than three months, the school had its own separate toilet block for girls; the donors had thank-you letters and photos from the kids. Turns out the teachers had guessed right: The girls were dropping out in droves because of the embarrassment they felt once they started menstruating and had no private facilities. Now, two years later, 100 of them have stayed in school because of this tiny addition.*[9]

Remember the networks that substituted for missing institutions to make markets possible, in chapter 3? Think of the power of networks in foreign aid. If local social entrepreneurs, development workers, and rich-country donors were tied together in a network based on repeated interactions, the networks of relationships could find the local social entrepreneurs—like Patrick Awuah, the founder of Ashesi University in Ghana—who had good projects and good reputations. The local social entrepreneurs would be completely in charge, motivated only by the rewards of good reputation if they did deliver results to the poor and the threat of a lost reputation in the network if they didn't.

Think of the potential for creativity if thousands of potential donors, project proposers, technical advisers, and advocates for the poor were freed from the shackles of the large centralized bureaucracy and could find solutions that worked on the ground. This is not a panacea for redesigning all of foreign aid; it is just one promising experiment in how aid could reach the poor.

Development Vouchers

Let's keep getting crazy about market mechanisms. Suppose we issue development vouchers to target groups of the extreme poor, which the poor could redeem at any NGO or aid agency for any development good they wanted—

for example, vaccinations, life-saving drugs, a health worker's visit, an improved cookstove, textbooks, seeds, fertilizer, or food supplements. The official aid agencies would set aside some of their money for an independent "voucher fund" separate from the agencies. The poor would choose both the goods they wanted and the agency they wanted to deliver the goods and would give their vouchers to that agency. The agency could then turn in the vouchers to the voucher fund for real money to cover the costs of providing the development services.

Since the poor would be choosing which agency would deliver the goods, the agencies would feel competitive pressure to deliver results. They would feel cost pressures the way private firms do, trying to deliver more for less. (One study estimates that the least-efficient donor delivers one square meter of primary school space in Guinea for $878, while the most efficient can do the job for $130.)[10] The aid agencies would be forced to act as social entrepreneurs, trying to offer innovative services that would prove attractive to the poor. Any agency that was not delivering what the poor wanted would see its budget go down, as it turned over money to the voucher fund but none of the vouchers came back. The poor would be firmly in charge, giving feedback on what they did and did not want from the aid agencies.

Individual vouchers would not work with development services that had to be chosen collectively to benefit a group, such as roads, health clinics, boreholes, or schools. We could think of vouchers being given to a village rather than to an individual to cover such goods. The villagers could then vote on how to spend the vouchers, so the feedback would be at the village level rather than the individual level. Again, the aid agencies would find out how well they were doing at satisfying the poor based on how many village vouchers they attracted. The vouchers would at long last provide a "market test" and a "voter test" to the aid agencies.

Giving vouchers to the poor may be the stupidest idea ever, except for all the ideas that have already failed in foreign aid. Both the GlobalGiving and the voucher schemes should be treated as experiments that have to be tested to see whether they work. They should be tried on a small scale. Again, let me say that I do *not* have the next utopian scheme to fix aid, because there isn't any. We would have to scrutinize these schemes for results just like we do conventional aid schemes. Do the players in GlobalGiving have the right incentives to give the poor what they need? Could it work on a larger scale than its present modest incarnation? Are voucher markets going to be efficient for small transactions?

We have seen that markets and democracy (such as a village voting on vouchers) require many conditions to work well. One worry is that local elites could cheat the poor by buying up all their vouchers or votes and pursuing projects for the benefit of the elites. We really don't know, but the instinct that something like a market could make aid work better sounds promising.

One idea that is too quickly dismissed is for foreign aid to just give cash grants targeted to the poorest people. This would be the purest solution to letting the poor choose for themselves what they needed. Although there are many potential pitfalls, it's surprising that aid agencies have not experimented with this approach in any serious way. This would be a promising area in which to do a randomized controlled trial.

Rachel Glennerster of the MIT Poverty Action Lab and Michael Kremer of Harvard have another promising idea to give foreign aid in a way that promotes results. They suggest creating a fund that would make an advance-purchase commitment to whoever succeeded in developing a vaccine against malaria. This would remedy the incentives that led to the present pitifully inadequate R&D on malaria. We could think of expanding this idea to other areas of foreign aid. Have worldwide or regional competitions for effective aid projects and programs, with large rewards to be given to the agencies, NGOs, or individuals that an independent panel judged as having designed the most effective aid programs, as measured by results.

Feedback from the Poor

If the main problem with foreign aid is the lack of *feedback* from the poor themselves, and *accountability* to these same poor, then why not attack the problem directly? The World Bank produced a fascinating three-volume publication called *The Voices of the Poor,* from which I have drawn some of the country examples in this book. Why not give the poor voices on whether aid is reaching them?

Americans fought a revolution on the principle of "no taxation without representation." Could Americans and other parts of the West extend that principle to the Rest: "no intervention without representation"? (And I hope I have made clear that nonrepresentative tyrants from the Rest cannot provide such "representation.") Westerners: don't do things to or for other people without giving them a way to let you know—and hold you accountable for—what you have actually done to or for them.

Is aid reaching the poor? Well, let the agents of foreign assistance ask them. Evaluation efforts could include surveys of the poor. Just ask them if they got what they most needed and if they are better off because of an aid intervention, and hold the aid agencies accountable for the results. Hold surveys of the population's well-being both before and after the aid program, to compare the results on specific outcomes.

The main mechanism for feedback and accountability for public services in the West is democracy. Could aid agencies find democratic mechanisms for local communities to vote on what services and projects they wanted? Could independent local watchers make sure the goods actually arrived and delivered what the agencies promised? Myriad volunteers such as local college students could simply monitor a sample of potholes, missing textbooks for schoolchildren, or out-of-stock drugs in health clinics. They could make the call to the responsible party to repair the pothole, supply the textbooks, or restock the drugs. Publicize the results and thus put pressure on the aid donors and their local partners. It is strange that aid agencies talk so much these days about "good governance" in the recipient countries without worrying about "good governance" of their own aid projects.

Aid could better utilize one group of agents who do have an incentive to find things that please the customers: private firms. For example, private firms could provide services that reach the poor, function as watchers, provide funding for poor entrepreneurs, and train aid workers to think like Searchers for customer satisfaction.

A little bit of this is happening already, but not in any systematic way that aid agencies take seriously. Surveys, votes, and watchers are not always reliable, but on average they would be a big step forward from the accountability-free zone that aid agencies now enjoy.

Getting Back to Basics

I don't think these crazy schemes should eliminate official aid agencies. These agencies could work much better if they had more modest agendas and were accountable for those agendas. Again, I emphasize that none of these suggestions is the Big Answer to world poverty, or even on how to fix foreign aid. The only Big Answer is that there is no Big Answer.

The basic principles are much easier to state than to make happen. Agents of assistance have to have incentives to search for what works to help the poor. If you want to aid the poor, then

(1) Have aid agents individually accountable for individual, feasible areas for action that help poor people lift themselves up.

(2) Let those agents search for what works, based on past experience in their area.

(3) Experiment, based on the results of the search.

(4) Evaluate, based on feedback from the intended beneficiaries and scientific testing.

(5) Reward success and penalize failure. Get more money to interventions that are working, and take money away from interventions that are not working. Each aid agent should explore and specialize further in the direction of what they prove good at doing.

(6) Make sure incentives in (5) are strong enough to do more of what works, then repeat step (4). If action fails, make sure incentives in (5) are strong enough to send the agent back to step (1). If the agent keeps failing, get a new one.[11]

It's so obvious, I'm embarrassed even to lay it out. But it's worth laying out only because it is the opposite of the present Western effort to transform the Rest.

Aid won't make poverty history, which Western aid efforts cannot possibly do. Only the self-reliant efforts of poor people and poor societies themselves can end poverty, borrowing ideas and institutions from the West when it suits them to do so. But aid that concentrates on feasible tasks will alleviate the sufferings of many desperate people in the meantime. Isn't that enough?

Think of the great potential for good if aid agencies probed and experimented their way toward effective interventions—such as saving the life of a child with malaria, building a road for a poor farmer to get his crops to market and support his family, or getting food and dietary supplements to people who would otherwise be stunted from malnutrition. Think of the positive feedback loop that could get started as success was rewarded with more resources and expanded further. Think of the increased support for foreign aid if rich people knew that an additional dollar of aid was an additional dollar to meet the desperate needs of the poorest people in the world.

What Can You Do?

The Planners have dominated the past generation of efforts of the West to help the Rest. The utopian Planners cannot transform the Rest—at least, not for the better. While the Rest is transforming itself, the Planners' global social engineering has failed to help the poor, and it will always so fail.

The Planners gave us the second tragedy of the world's poor, that twelve-cent medicines do not reach children dying of malaria, that four-dollar bed nets do not get to the poor to prevent malaria, that three dollars does not get to each new mother to prevent millions of child deaths. Planners made little progress on the first tragedy of the world's poor, that the poor suffer from many calamities that could be averted.

With this historical record, perhaps sixty years of Planners is enough. Maybe it is now time to give the Searchers a chance. Even though the biggest payoff comes from local Searchers who solve their own problems, Searchers from the rich West can do good, specific things for poor people. Searchers can make progress on the second tragedy, which would then make progress possible on the first tragedy. Let the Searchers try their hands at ways for the medicines, bed nets, and aid money to finally reach the poor.

What can you do? There is a role for everyone (both in the West and in the Rest) who cares about the poor. If you are an activist, you can change your issue from raising more aid money to making sure that the aid money reaches the poor. If you are a researcher or student of development, you can search for ways to improve the aid system, or for piecemeal innovations that make poor people better off, or for ways for homegrown development to happen sooner rather than later. If you are an aid worker, you can forget about the utopian goals and draw upon what you do best to help the poor. Even if you don't work in the field of helping the poor, you can still, as a citizen, let your voice be heard for the cause of aid delivering the goods to the poor. You citizens don't have to settle for the grandiose but empty plans to make poverty history. All of you can make known your dissatisfaction with Planners and call for more Searchers.

And could one of you Searchers discover a way to put a firewood-laden Ethiopian preteen girl named Amaretch in school?

Acknowledgments

I have been lucky to get supremely constructive comments on drafts of the book from some knowledgeable and insightful colleagues. Thanks to Scott Moyers, my tough but fair editor, and to production editor Bruce Giffords, to copy editor Jenna Dolan, and to literary agent extraordinaire Andrew Wylie. At Oxford University Press, thanks to Sarah Caro and Jennifer Wilkinson for shepherding this edition to completion. Thanks to my closest longtime intellectual collaborators, Ross Levine and Lant Pritchett, who don't necessarily share all the views expressed here but have greatly influenced my research and writing, including reading drafts and giving pointed comments at many different stages of this project.

I am also very grateful to Angus Deaton for a thorough reading of the draft and exceptionally thoughtful comments on it, although again not necessarily sharing its views. And a big thanks to those who generously gave of their time to read some or all of previous drafts and give enormously helpful feedback: Maryam Abolfazli, Emma Aisbett, Alberto Alesina, Nava Ashraf, Donald Boudreaux, Gerald Caprio, Ron Clark, Michael Clemens, Ravina Daphtary, Jess Diamond, Paul Dower, William Duggan, Kareen El Beyrouty, Stanley Engerman, Helen Epstein, Daphne Eviatar, Kurt Hoffman, Patricia Hoon, Roumeen Islam, Charles Kenny, Peter Lindert, Janina Matuszeski, Taye Mengistae, Edward Miguel, Josepa Miguel-Florensa, Frederic Mishkin, Jonathan Morduch, Stewart Parkinson, Elizabeth Potamites, S. Ramachandran, James Rauch, Kenneth Rogoff, Xavier Sala-i-Martin, Julia Schwenkenberg, Richard Sylla, Leonard Wantchekon, Dennis Whittle, Geoffrey Williams, Michael Woolcock, and Treena Wu.

I benefited greatly from discussions with some really smart people on topics covered by this book: Daron Acemoglu, Carol Adelman, Martha Ainsworth, Abhijit Banerjee, Reza Baqir, Robert Barro, William Baumol, Jess Benhabib, Arne Bigsten, Nancy Birdsall, Peter Boettke, Robert Borens, Eduardo Borensztein, Bruce Bueno de Mesquita, Craig Burnside, Charles Calomiris, Stephen Cohen, Susan Collins, Kevin Davis, Allan Drazen, Esther Duflo, Steven Durlauf, Marcel Fafchamps, Niall Ferguson, Raquel Fernandez, Ricardo Ffrench-Davis, Stanley Fischer, Paul Glewwe, April Harding, Ann Harrison, Ricardo Hausmann, Peter Heller, Arye Hillman, Judith Justice,

Boyan Jovanovic, Ravi Kanbur, Devesh Kapur, Hiro Kohama, Lawrence Kotlikoff, Michael Kremer, Mari Kuraishi, Ruben Lamdany, Adam Lerrick, Ruth Levine, David Levy, Dyan Machan, Bertin Martens, John McMillan, Allan Meltzer, Janvier Nkurunziza, Yaw Nyarko, José Antonio Ocampo, Mead Over, Sandra Peart, Guillermo Perry, Adam Przeworski, Dilip Ratha, Shamika Ravi, Sergio Rebelo, Ritva Reinikka, Ariell Reshef, Mario Rizzo, David Roodman, Dani Rodrik, Claudia Rosett, Frederic Sautet, Anya Schiffrin, Paul Smoke, T. N. Srinivasan, Joseph Stiglitz, Alan Stockman, Judith Tendler, Frank Upham, Nicolas Van de Walle, Ian Vasquez, Michael Walton, and David Weil.

Another big round of thanks to my students at NYU (and some from Columbia), on whom I have tried out some of these ideas in class. I thank also my other colleagues at New York University and the Center for Global Development. Also, I am grateful to audiences in universities, governments, aid agencies, and think tanks around the world who invited me to give lectures to them on some of these ideas over the last few years, and gave me wonderfully useful feedback in person. Any errors that survived the interaction with all these brilliant people are my responsibility.

Notes

Chapter 1. Planners Versus Searchers

1. http://news.bbc.co.uk/1/shared/spl/hi/picture_gallery/04/africa_ethiopian_wood_collector/html/7.stm.
2. On the trail of the celebrity activist, by CNN's Richard Quest, Thursday, August 11, 2005, posted: 10:57 A.M. EDT (14:57 GMT).
3. Gordon Brown speech at National Gallery of Scotland, January 6, 2005, "International Development in 2005: The Challenge and the Opportunity."
4. http://www.msnbc.msn.com/id/8608578/. This reflection occurred to me based on a similar statement by Paul Seabright in his great book *The Company of Strangers: A Natural History of Economic Life*, Princeton, N.J.: Princeton University Press, 2004.
5. Shaohua Chen and Martin Ravallion, "How Have the World's Poorest Fared Since the Early 1980s?" Development Research Group, World Bank Policy Working Paper no. 3341, June 2004, http://www.worldbank.org/research/povmonitor/MartinPapers/How have_the_poorest_fared_since_the_early_1980.pdf, p. 17.
6. www.wfp.org.
7. www.unicef.org.
8. http://www.unaids.org/en/resources/epidemiology.asp.
9. http://www.worldbank.org/watsan/.
10. http://www.sil.org/literacy/LitFacts.htm.
11. http://www1.worldbank.org/education/pdf/achieving_efa/chapter2.pdf, p. 42.
12. World Bank, *Our Dream: A World Free of Poverty* (2000), Washington, D.C.: Oxford University Press and World Bank.
13. UNDP, "Human Development Report on Millenium Development Goals," 2003, overview.
14. Alan Cowell, "In Davos, Spotlight Turns to Africa," *International Herald Tribune*, January 28, 2005, p. 1.
15. United Nations Habitat, "Water and Sanitation in the World's Cities," 2003, http://www.earthscan.co.uk/samplechapters/1844070042Intro.htm and http://portal.unesco.org/education/en/ev.php-URL_ID=37612&URL_DO=DO_TOPIC&URL_SECTION =201.html.
16. Speech at Coast Guard Academy commencement, May 21, 2003.
17. Quoted in William Duggan, *The Art of What Works: How Success Really Happens*, New York: McGraw-Hill, 2003, p. ix.
18. "PSI Malaria Control, the Malawi ITN Delivery Model," February 2005.
19. Karl Popper, *The Poverty of Historicism*, London and New York: Routledge, 1957, p. 61. I am indebted to John McMillan of Stanford for calling my attention to this concept

of Popper's. He and Nassim Taleb (who discussed Popper in his nice book *Fooled by Randomness*) turned me on to reading Popper in general.

20. Quoted in James C. Scott, *Seeing Like a State: How Certain Schemes to Improve the Human Condition Have Failed,* New Haven: Yale University Press, 1998, p. 327.

21. Quoted in *Herald* (Everett, WA), in column by James McCusker, July 5, 2005.

22. Robert Owen, *The Life of Robert Owen: A Supplementary Appendix to the First Volume,* Volume IA, [1858], *Reprints of Economic Classics,* New York: Augustus M. Kelley Publishers, 1967, pp. ii, 5.

23. WHO and World Bank, "Dying for Change," Washington, D.C., 2003, p. 10.

24. Ibid., p. 11.

25. http://www.cdc.gov/ncidod/dpd/parasites/schistosomiasis/ factsht_schistosomiasis.htm

26. WHO and World Bank, "Dying for Change," Washington, D.C.: World Bank, January 2002, p. 21.

27. Deepa Narayan and Patti Petesch, *Voices of the Poor: From Many Lands* (vol. 3), Washington, D.C.: World Bank and Oxford University Press, 2002, p. 383.

28. Ibid., p. 86.

29. Ibid., p. 63.

30. Quoted in Gilbert Rist, *The History of Development: From Western Origins to Global Faith,* London: Zed Books, 1997, pp. 38–39.

31. Quoted in Lawrence James, *The Rise and Fall of the British Empire,* New York: St. Martin's Griffin, 1994, p. 186.

32. Quoted in Klaus Knorr, *British Colonial Theories, 1570–1850,* London: Frank Cass, 1968, p. 380.

33. Quoted in William J. Barber, *British Economic Thought and India, 1600–1858: A Study in the History of Development Economics,* Oxford: Clarendon Press, 1975, p. 138.

34. Niall Ferguson, *Empire: The Rise and Demise of the British World Order and the Lessons from Global Power,* New York: Basic Books, 2003, p. 236.

35. "To the peoples sitting in darkness," in Charles Neider, ed., *The Complete Essays of Mark Twain,* Garden City, N.Y.: Doubleday, 1963.

36. Rist, p. 60.

37. M. J. Bonn, *Crumbling of Empire: The Disintegration of World Economy,* London: Allen & Unwin, 1938, quoted in Knorr, *British Colonial Theories.*

38. Gunnar Myrdal, "Development and Underdevelopment," Cairo, 1956, pp. 63 and 65, quoted in P. T. Bauer, *Dissent on Development,* Cambridge: Harvard University Press, 1971; rev. ed., 1976, p. 70.

39. See Peter Bauer, *Economic Analysis and Policy in Underdeveloped Countries,* Durham, N.C.: Duke University Press, 1957; and Bauer, *Dissent on Development,* Cambridge: Harvard University Press, 1971.

40. Speech by Gordon Brown at a DFID/UNDP seminar, "Words into Action in 2005," January 26, 2005, Lancaster House, London.

41. Multiplying their respective 2003 growth rates by their 2002 Purchasing Power Parity (PPP) GDP in current U.S. dollars. Source: Global Development Network Growth database.

42. http://news.bbc.co.uk/1/shared/spl/hi/picture_gallery/04 /africa_ethiopian_wood_collector/html/7.stm.

43. This quotation makes up the last line of Peter Bauer's classic *Dissent on Development,* 1971.

44. http://www.astdhpphe.org/infect/guinea.html.

45. Demographic and Health Surveys data for 2003, http://www.measuredhs.com/ countries/country.cfm?ctry_id=14.

Chapter 2. The Legend of the Big Push

1. Aart Kraay and Claudio Raddatz, "Poverty Traps, Aid, and Growth," World Bank mimeograph, January 2005; and Bryan Graham and Jonathan Temple, "Rich Nations, Poor Nations: How Much Can Multiple Equilibria Explain?" mimeograph, Harvard University, 2004.

2. Jeffrey D. Sachs, *The End of Poverty: Economic Possibilities for Our Time,* New York: Penguin Press, 2005, p. 191.

3. UN Millennium Project Report, "Investing in Development: A Practical Plan to Achieve the Millennium Development Goals," main report, p. 34.

4. Sachs, *End of Poverty,* p. 226.

5. UN Millennium Project Report, "Millennium Development Goals Needs Assessment," January 2005, p. 119.

6. This implicitly assumes that any periods of missing data showed the same democracy on average as those periods for which data were available. This assumption is problematic, so I try two variants on this approach. First, I recognize that most countries in the sample with missing data were under colonial administration, which is not usually considered a very democratic institution. I make the assumption that colonial control equates to the lowest democracy rating in Polity IV, and try the corrected variable as a measure of democracy. Second, I simply omit any country that does not have at least seventy-five Polity IV observations over 1820–2001 (or 1870–2001). All three variants of the data give similar results. This result echoes a previous result by Daron Acemoglu, Simon Johnson, and James Robinson on what they called the "reversal of fortune" between previously rich places like the Caribbean and previously poor places like North America.

7. This discussion draws upon a joint paper I wrote with Ross Levine of Brown University and David Roodman of the Center for Global Development, called "New Data, New Doubts: Comment on 'Aid, Policies, and Growth' (2000) by Burnside and Dollar," *American Economic Review* 94, no. 3 (June 2004): 774–780. I have used a similar exposition in a paper I wrote called "Can Aid Buy Growth?" in the *Journal of Economic Perspectives* 17, no. 3 (Summer 2003): 23–48.

8. Craig Burnside and David Dollar, "Aid, Policies, and Growth," *American Economic Review* 90, no. 4 (September 2000): 847–68.

9. Another factor in the administration's decision was the personal lobbying by the rock star Bono, who seems to be the most influential figure in the aid policy community.

10. For the full text of Bush's speech of March 14, 2002, see http://www.whitehouse.gov/
    news/releases/2002/03/20020314-7.html. For the announcement of the Millennium
    Challenge Corporation on November 26, 2002, see http://www.whitehouse.gov/
    news/releases/2002/11/20021126-8.html#3. For the quoted passage on the
    motivation behind this new aid, see http://www.whitehouse.gov/infocus/develo-
    pingnations/>.
11. http://www.mca.gov/countries_overview.html.
12. Esther Duflo and Michael Kremer, "Use of Randomization in the Evaluation of
    Development Effectiveness," mimeograph, Harvard and MIT (2003), discuss publi-
    cation bias. A classic paper on this problem is J. Bradford DeLong and Kevin Lang,
    "Are All Economic Hypotheses False?" *Journal of Political Economy* 100, no. 6
    (December 1992): 1257–72.
13. UN Millennium Project Report, "Investing in Development: A Practical Plan to
    Achieve the Millennium Development Goals," overview, box 8, p. 41.
14. Commission for Africa, "Our Common Interest: Report of the Commission for
    Africa," p. 348; www.commissionforafrica.org/english/report/introduction.html.
15. Raghuram G. Rajan and Arvind Subramanian, "Aid and Growth: What Does the
    Cross-Country Evidence Really Show?" IMF mimeograph, April 2005.
16. Todd Moss and Arvind Subramanian, "After the Big Push? Fiscal and Institutional
    Implications of Large Aid Increases," mimeograph, Center for Global Development,
    2005.
17. Jeffrey D. Sachs, John W. McArthur, Guido Schmidt-Traub, Margaret Kruk, Chan-
    drika Bahadur, Michael Faye, and Gordon McCord, "Ending Africa's Poverty Trap,"
    Brookings Papers on Economic Activity, issue 1, 2004, Washington, D.C.
18. See descriptions on the following Nigerian government Web sites: http://nigeria-
    nembassy-argentina.org/nigeria/xsteel.shtml, http://www.nigeria-consulate-ny.org/
    News/Aug03/ajaokuta_prod.htm, and http://www.nopa.net/Power_and_Steel/
    messages/8.shtml.
19. I am indebted to Abijhit Banerjee and Esther Duflo of MIT for the FDA analogy as
    well as for exposition of the randomized control methodology in general.
20. Stephen C. Smith, *Ending Global Poverty: A Guide to What Works,* New York: Palgrave
    MacMillan, 2005, p. 59.
21. Thorsten Beck, Asli Demirgüç-Kunt, and Ross Levine, "Small and Medium Enter-
    prises, Growth, and Poverty: Cross-Country Evidence," World Bank Working Paper
    no. 3178, December 2003.
22. USAID, "Performance and Accountability Report," 2003.

Chapter 3. You Can't Plan a Market

1. Edmund Burke, "Reflections on the Revolution in France," in Isaac Kramnick, ed.,
   The Portable Edmund Burke, Viking Portable Library, New York: Penguin Putnam,
   1999, p. 443.
2. Quoted in Peter Murrell, "What Is Shock Therapy? What Did It Do in Poland and
   Russia?" *Post-Soviet Affairs* 9, no. 2 (April–June 1993): 111–40.
3. Ibid.

4. Ibid.
5. Quoted in Peter Murrell, "Conservative Political Philosophy and the Strategy of Economic Transition," *East European Politics and Societies* 6, no. 1 (Winter 1992): 3–16.
6. Clifford Gaddy and Barry Ickes, *Russia's Virtual Economy,* Washington D.C.: Brookings Institution, 2002.
7. Ibid., p. 176.
8. David E. Hoffman, *The Oligarchs: Wealth and Power in the New Russia,* New York: Public Affairs, 2002, p. 318.
9. http://www.templetonthorp.com/en/news345.
10. UNDP, Russia Human Development Report, 2005.
11. http://www.cdi.org/russia/336-7.cfm.
12. William Easterly, "What Did Structural Adjustment Adjust? The Association of Policies and Growth with Repeated IMF and World Bank Adjustment Loans," *Journal of Development Economics* 76, no. 1 (2005): 1–22.
13. Mark Twain, *The Adventures of Tom Sawyer,* chap. 6.
14. Joseph Stiglitz shared this Nobel Prize for his own extensive work on imperfect markets due to lack of information.
15. http://www.dl.ket.org/latin3/mores/techno/fire/.
16. Paul Seabright, *Company of Strangers,* and Avinash Dixit, *Lawlessness and Economics: Alternative Models of Governance,* Princeton, N.J.: Princeton University Press, 2004, discuss the evidence on biology and trade.
17. Summarized in Stephen Knack, "Trust, Associational Life and Economic Performance," April 2000, World Bank.
18. Quoted in Gary Hawes, "Marcos, His Cronies, and the Philippines' Failure to Develop," in Ruth McVey, ed., *Southeast Asian Capitalists,* Ithaca, N.Y., Cornell University Southeast Asia Program, 1992.
19. Marcel Fafchamps, "Networks, Communities, and Markets in Sub-Saharan Africa: Implications for Firm Growth and Investment," *Journal of African Economies* 10, AERC supplement 2 (2001): 109–42.
20. Ibid., p. 116.
21. Narayan and Petesch, *Voices of the Poor,* vol. 1, chap. 4.
22. Fafchamps, "Networks," p. 119.
23. Nathan Rosenberg and L. E. Birdzell, *How the West Grew Rich,* New York: Basic Books, 1986.
24. Anthony Reid, "Flows and Seepages in the Long-term Chinese Interaction with Southeast Asia," in Anthony Reid, ed., *Sojourners and Settlers: Histories of Southeast Asia and the Chinese,* Honolulu: University of Hawaii Press, 1996, p. 50.
25. Avner Greif, "Contract Enforceability and Economic Institutions in Early Trade: The Maghribi Traders' Coalition," *American Economic Review* 83, no. 3 (1993): 525–48.
26. The preceding three paragraphs except for the Greif paragraph were based on James Rauch, "Business and Social Networks in International Trade," *Journal of Economic Literature* 39 (December 2001): 1177–203.
27. Fafchamps, "Networks," p. 122.
28. This is a central point of Douglas North, *Institutions, Institutional Change, and Economic Performance,* Cambridge, UK: Cambridge University Press, 1990.

29. Narayan and Petesch, *Voices of the Poor,* vol. -2, chap. 8.
30. Ibid., Vol. 1, p. 187.
31. Ibid., Vol. 3, p. 72.
32. Ibid., p. 71.
33. Martin Booth, *The Dragon Syndicates: The Global Phenomenon of the Triads,* New York: Carroll and Graf Publishers, 1999, p. 268.
34. Narayan and Petesch, *Voices of the Poor,* vol. 1, p. 186.
35. Dixit, *Lawlessness and Economics,* pp. 99–110.
36. Narayan and Petesch, *Voices of the Poor,* vol. 3, p. 75.
37. Ibid., pp. 401–2.
38. Ibid., vol. 1, p. 202.
39. North, 1990, p. 88.
40. Ibid., p. 129.
41. World Bank, *Land Policies for Growth and Poverty Reduction,* Policy Research Report, World Bank, Washington, D.C., June 2003, chap. 1.
42. Dixit, *Lawlessness and Economics,* p. 112.
43. Janine R. Wedel, *Collision and Collusion: The Strange Case of Western Aid to Eastern Europe,* New York: Palgrave, 2001.
44. Wade Channell, "Lessons Not Learned: Problems with Western Aid for Law Reform in Postcommunist Countries," Carnegie Endowment for International Peace, Democracy and Rule of Law Project, no. 57, May 2005.
45. Ibid., p. 6.
46. Parker Shipton, "The Kenyan Land Tenure Reform: Misunderstanding in the Public Creation of Private Property," in R. E. Downs and S. P. Reyna, eds., *Land and Society in Contemporary Africa,* Hanover, N.H.: University Press of New England, 1988, pp. 91–135.
47. Discussed in Dixit, *Lawlessness and Economics,* pp. 128–29.
48. Quoted in Duggan, *The Art of What Works,* p. 37.
49. Thorsten Beck and Ross Levine, "Legal Institutions and Financial Development" in Claude Ménard and Mary M. Shirley, eds., *Handbook of New Institutional Economics,* Norwell, Mass.: Kluwer Academic Publishers, 2005.
50. Figures from Ross Levine, private communication.
51. Stephen Haber, "Mexico's Experiments with Bank Privatization and Liberalization, 1991–2003," mimeograph, Stanford University, draft of October 18, 2004.
52. See F. A. Hayek, *Law, Legislation, and Liberty,* vol. 1 (*Rules and Order*), Chicago: University of Chicago Press, 1973, and Robert D. Cooter, "The Rule of State Law and the Rule-of-Law State," in *Annual World Bank Conference on Development Economics,* Washington, D.C.: World Bank, 1996.
53. http://www.festivalcinemaafricano.org/eng/index.php?pag=vis_film&id_film=178, 178, *http : //www.newint.org/issue372/view.htm.*
54. "Mobile Phones and Development: Calling an End to Poverty," *The Economist,* July 9, 2005.
55. Sharon LaFraniere, "Cellphones Catapult Rural Africa to 21st Century," *New York Times,* August 25, 2005, p. A1.

56. John McMillan, *Reinventing the Bazaar: A Natural History of Markets,* New York: Norton, 2002, pp. 94–95.

57. Manish A. Desai, Sumi Mehta, and Kirk R. Smith, "Indoor Smoke from Solid Fuels: Estimating the Environmental Burden of Disease," WHO Environmental Burden of Disease Series, no. 4, 2004.

58. This research was sponsored by the World Bank's 2002 World Development Report, mentioned later as a valuable output of the World Bank.

59. World Bank, *Doing Business in 2005: Removing Obstacles to Growth,* Washington, D.C.: World Bank, International Finance Corporation, and Oxford University Press, 2005, overview, p. 3.

Chapter 4. Planners and Gangsters

1. Federal Research Division, Library of Congress, *Bolivia: A Country Study,* Washington, D.C.: Library of Congress, December 1989.

2. Herbert S. Klein, *Bolivia: The Evolution of a Multi-Ethnic Society,* Oxford: Oxford University Press, 1992, p. 35.

3. Federal Research Division, *Bolivia.*

4. Klein, *Bolivia,* p. 52.

5. Ibid., p. 124.

6. Ibid., p. 152.

7. Ibid., p. 122.

8. Ibid.

9. Ibid., p. 153.

10. Daniel Kaufmann, Massimo Mastruzzi, and Diego Zavatela, "Sustained Macroeconomic Reforms, Tepid Growth: A Governance Puzzle in Bolivia?" in Dani Rodrik, ed., *In Search of Prosperity: Analytical Narratives on Economic Growth,* Princeton, N.J.: Princeton University Press, 2003, pp. 345–48.

11. Ibid., p. 358.

12. Ibid., p. 364.

13. Report No. 26838-BO, "Report and Recommendation of the President of the International Bank for Reconstruction and Development, International Development Association, International Finance Corporation, and the Multilateral Investment Guarantee Agency to the Executive Directors on a Country Assistance Strategy for the Republic of Bolivia," January 8, 2004.

14. "Corraling the Gas—and Democracy," *The Economist,* June 9, 2005.

15. There is a vast body of literature, with such classics as James Buchanan and Gordon Tullock, *The Calculus of Consent: Logical Foundations of Constitutional Democracy,* Ann Arbor: University of Michigan Press, 1962; Mancur Olson, *The Logic of Collective Action,* Cambridge: Harvard University Press, 1965; Anthony Downs, *An Economic Theory of Democracy,* Boston: Addison-Wesley, 1957.

16. Dani Rodrik, "Institutions for High-Quality Growth: What They Are and How to Acquire Them," *Studies in Comparative International Development* (Fall 2000).

17. Philippe Aghion, Alberto Alesina, and Francesco Trebbi, "Endogenous Political Institutions," Harvard University mimeograph, January 2004.

18. W. Easterly, R. Gatti, S. Kurlat, "Democracy, Development, and Mass Killings," New York University Development Research Institute Working Paper, 2004.
19. Daron Acemoglu, "The Form of Property Rights: Oligarchic vs. Democratic Societies," MIT mimeograph, April 2005.
20. Daron Acemoglu and James A. Robinson, *Economic Origins of Dictatorship and Democracy,* Cambridge, UK: Cambridge University Press, 2006.
21. Ibid., p. 27.
22. William Easterly, "The Middle-Class Consensus and Economic Development," *Journal of Economic Growth* 6, no. 4 (December 2001): 317–36.
23. Nathan Jensen and Leonard Wantchekon, "Resource Wealth and Political Regimes in Africa," *Comparative Political Studies,* 2005. See also Michael Ross, "Does Oil Hinder Democracy?" *World Politics* 53 (April 2001): 325–61. Another study confirming this result is Paul Collier and Anke Hoeffler, "Democracy and Resource Rents," Department of Economics, University of Oxford, April 26, 2005.
24. Daniel Kaufmann, Aart Kraay, and Massimo Mastruzzi, "Governance Matters IV: Governance Indicators for 1996–2004." World Bank mimeograph, May 2005.
25. This section is based on W. Easterly and R. Levine, "European Settlers, Inequality, and Economic Development," New York University and Brown University, mimeograph, 2005.
26. Edward L. Glaeser, "The Political Economy of Hatred," Harvard mimeograph, October 26, 2004, http://post.economics.harvard.edu/faculty/glaeser/papers/Hatred.pdf.
27. W. Easterly and R. Levine, "Africa's Growth Tragedy: Policies and Ethnic Divisions," November 1997, *Quarterly Journal of Economics* 112, no. 4 (November 1997): 1203–250; R. La Porta, F. Lopez-de-Silanes, A. Shleifer, and R. Vishny, "The Quality of Government," *Journal of Law, Economics, and Organization* 15, no. 1 (Spring 1999); A. Alesina, R. Baqir, and W. Easterly, "Public Goods and Ethnic Divisions," *Quarterly Journal of Economics* 114, no. 4 (November 1999): 1243–84; and William Easterly, Jozef Ritzen, and Michael Woolcock, "Social Cohesion, Institutions, and Growth," mimeograph, New York University and World Bank, 2005.
28. Daron Acemoglu, Simon Johnson, and James A. Robinson, "Institutions as the Fundamental Cause of Long-Run Growth," in P. Aghion and S. Durlauf, *Handbook of Economic Growth,* New York: Elsevier, 2005; W. Easterly and R. Levine, "Tropics, Germs, and Crops: The Role of Endowments in Economic Development," *Journal of Monetary Economics* 50, no. 1 (January 2003). D. Rodrik, A. Subramanian, and F. Trebbi, "Institutions Rule: The Primacy of Institutions over Geography and Integration in Economic Development," *Journal of Economic Growth* 9, no. 2, (June 2004). Note that some of the results by Acemoglu et al. were challenged on the grounds of faulty data in some excellent work by David Albouy at Berkeley. However, studies that do not use this data still find a causal link between good government and income.
29. Narayan and Petesch, *Voices of the Poor,* vol. 1, p. 181.
30. Ibid., vol. 3, p. 71.
31. Ibid., vol. 2, chap. 8.
32. Ibid., vol. 1, p. 185.

33. Ibid., vol. 2, chap. 8.

34. Ibid., vol. 2, chap. 9.

35. Alberto Alesina and Beatrice Weder, "Do Corrupt Governments Receive Less Foreign Aid?" *American Economic Review* 92 (September 2002): 1126–37.

36. The regression ran the log of aid per capita on the log of population, log of per capita income, and the Kaufmann-Kraay indicator of corruption, all for the year cited. The sample (including all countries that received positive aid inflows) was kept the same between 1996 and 2002. The source for all data is the World Bank's World Development indicators.

37. Deon Filmer, Jeffrey Hammer, and Lant Pritchett, "Weak Links in the Chain: A Diagnosis of Health Policy in Poor Countries," *The World Bank Research Observer,* vol. 15, no. 2 (August 2000), 199–244. Bureaucracies in rich countries where clients don't have much voice could be equally oppressive, like Customs or Immigration in the United States. The U.S. government during the Clinton administration tried to make various agencies more client friendly. According to an anecdote by John Nellis, the response of Customs officials to this initiative was "We don't have clients; we have suspects."

38. http://www.thp.org/prize/89/masire.htm.

39. Judith Tendler, *Good Government in the Tropics,* Baltimore, Md.: Johns Hopkins University Press, 1997.

40. Stephen Knack, "Aid Dependence and the Quality of Governance: Cross-Country Empirical Tests," *Southern Economic Journal* 68, no. 2 (2004): 310–29.

41. Simeon Djankov, Jose G. Montalvo, and Marta Reynal-Querol, "The Curse of Aid," World Bank mimeograph, April 2005.

42. Nancy Birdsall, Adeel Malik, and Milan Vaishnav, "Poverty and the Social Sectors: The World Bank in Pakistan 1990–2003," prepared for the World Bank's Operations Evaluation Department, September 2004.

43. World Bank Ethiopia report, 2001.

44. OECD, *Poor Performers: Basic Approaches for Supporting Development in Difficult Partnerships,* Paris: OECD, 2001.

45. World Bank PRSP Sourcebook 2001.

46. Interim Poverty Reduction Strategy Paper, Joint Staff Assessment, Ethiopia, 2001.

47. http://www.state.gov/g/drl/rls/hrrpt/2003/27716.htm.

48. http://web.worldbank.org/WBSITE/EXTERNAL/COUNTRIES/AFRICAEXT/ 0,,menuPK:258652~pagePK:146732~piPK:146828~theSitePK:258644,00.html.

49. http://lnweb18.worldbank.org/news/pressrelease.nsf/673fa6c5a2-d50a67852565e200692a79/6b834179b3fd616b85256b990077a8a7?Open Document.

50. Daniel Patrick Moynihan. *Maximum Feasible Misunderstanding: Community Action in the War on Poverty,* New York: Free Press, 1969.

51. Ronald Herring, "Making Ethnic Conflict: The Civil War in Sri Lanka," in Milton Esman and Ronald Herring, eds., *Carrots, Sticks and Ethnic Conflict: Rethinking Development Assistance,* Ann Arbor: University of Michigan Press, 2001.

52. Sara Grusky, ed., "The IMF and World Bank Backed Poverty Reduction Strategy Papers." Comments from Southern Civil Society. Globalization Challenge Initiative, May 2000.

53. Scott, *Seeing Like a State,* p. 94.

54. Robert Fatton, Jr., *Haiti's Predatory Government: The Unending Transition to Democracy,* Boulder, Colo.: Lynne Rienner Publishers, 2002, p. 126.

55. World Bank, Country Assistance Strategy for the Republic of Bolivia, January 8, 2004, Report no. 26838-BO, table 10.

56. International Development Association additions to IDA Resources: Thirteenth Replenishment, IDA/SecM2002-0488, September 17, 2002, p. 21.

57. www.imf.org/external/np/exr/facts/prgf.html.

58. Nicolas van de Walle, *Overcoming Stagnation in Aid-Dependent Countries,* Center for Global Development: Washington, D.C., 2005, p. 67.

59. Polity IV database, University of Maryland Political Science Department, www.cidcm. und.edu/inscr/polity.

60. Robert Heinl, Nancy Heinl, and Michael Heinl, *Written in Blood: The History of the Haitian People, 1492–1995,* Lanham, Md.: University Press of America, 1996, p. 7.

61. David Nicholls, *From Dessalines to Duvalier: Race, Colour and National Independence in Haiti,* New Brunswick: Rutgers University Press, 1996, p. 19; Heinl, Heinl, and Heinl, *Written in Blood,* p. 3, gives a higher estimate of the slave population in 1789.

62. Federal Research Division, Library of Congress, *Haiti: A Country Study,* Washington, D.C.: Library of Congress, December 1989, chap. 6.

63. Stanley Engerman and Kenneth Sokoloff, "Factor Endowments, Institutions, and Differential Paths of Growth Among New World Economics: A View from Economic Historians of the United States," in Stephen Haber, ed., *How Latin America Fell Behind,* Stanford, Calif.: Stanford University Press, 1997, p. 55.

64. Heinl, Heinl, and Heinl, *Written in Blood,* pp. 172, 204.

65. Federal Research Division, *Haiti.*

66. Nicholls, *From Dessalines to Duvalier,* pp. 69–72, 77.

67. Heinl, Heinl, and Heinl, *Written in Blood,* p. 158.

68. Michela Wrong, *In the Footsteps of Mr. Kurtz: Living on the Brink of Disaster in Mobutu's Congo,* New York: HarperCollins, 2001, p. 207.

69. World Bank, World Development indicators for 1965–1997, in 2002 dollars.

70. Peter Uvin, *Aiding Violence: The Development Enterprise in Rwanda,* West Hartford, Conn.: Kumarian Press, 1998, p. 65.

71. Ibid., p. 94.

72. Report No. 12465-RW, "Rwanda Poverty Reduction and Sustainable Growth," Population and Human Resources Division, South-Central and Indian Ocean Department, Africa Region, May 16, 1994.

73. Ibid., paragraph xvi of executive summary.

74. Tony Hodges, *Angola from Afro-Stalinism to Petro-Diamond Capitalism,* Bloomington: Indiana University Press, 2001, p. 124.

75. Ibid., p. 37.

76. World Bank, World Development Indicators.

77. World Bank, "Transitional Support Strategy for the Republic of Angola," March 4, 2003, http://www.worldbank.org/ao/reports/2003_Angola_tss.pdf.
78. IMF, "Consultation on Angola," 2003, Article IV, p. 9.
79. http://www.state.gov/g/drl/rls/hrrpt/2003/27721.htm.
80. Economist Intelligence Unit, "Country Profile 2003: Democratic Republic of the Congo."
81. http://www.hrw.org/press/2003/01/libya0117.htm.
82. UN Millennium Project, "Investing in Development: A Practical Plan to Achieve the Millennium Development Goals," January 2005.
83. http://www.underreported.com/mod-ules.php?op=modload&name=News&file=article&sid=1241.
84. Todd Moss and Arvind Subramanian, "After the Big Push? Fiscal and Institutional Implications of Large Aid Increases," Center for Global Development, August 2005.
85. http://news.bbc.co.uk/1/hi/world/africa/3724520.stm.
86. http://news.bbc.co.uk/1/hi/world/africa/4497915.stm.
87. Liner notes from *The Best Best of Fela Kuti*, MCA Records.

Chapter 5. The Rich Have Markets, the Poor Have Bureaucrats

1. World Bank, "Assessing Aid," 1998.
2. World Bank, Africa Development Indicators, 2002.
3. A brilliant review of the feedback problem and principal-agent theory in foreign aid is Bertin Martens, Uwe Mummert, Peter Murrell, and Paul Seabright, *The Institutional Economics of Foreign Aid*, Cambridge, UK: Cambridge University Press, 2002.
4. For a review, see Avinash Dixit, *The Making of Eccentric Policy: A Transaction Cost Politics Perspective*, Cambridge, MIT Press, 1996.
5. http://www.murphys-laws.com/murphy/murphy-laws.html.
6. World Bank, "The World Bank in Action: Stories of Development," Washington, D.C., 2002.
7. Anirudh Krishna with Urban Jonsson and Wilbald Lorri, "The Iringa Nutrition Project: Child Survival and Development in Tanzania," in Anirudh Krishna, Norman Uphoff, and Milton J. Esman, *Reasons for Hope: Instructive Experiences in Rural Development*, West Hartford, Conn.: Kumarian Press, 1997. See also Teresa A. Calderon, "Nutrition Education Training of Health Workers and Other Field Staff to Support Chronically Deprived Communities," Public Health Nutrition no. 6a (2001): 1421–24.
8. Aid statistics from OECD online database (all donors, net disbursements).
9. UNDP, Poverty Strategies Initiative, 1998, http://www.undp.org/poverty/pover-tyarchive/initiatives/psi/.
10. World Bank and IMF, "Global Monitoring Report 2005, Millennium Development Goals: From Consensus to Action," World Bank, Washington, D.C., April 2005, p. 173.
11. http://worldbank.org/cdf/cdf-text.htm.
12. http://econ.worldbank.org/wdr/wdr2004/.

13. See Michael Kremer and Edward Miguel, "The Illusion of Sustainability," mimeograph, Harvard University and University of California at Berkeley, 2003.

14. Deon Filmer and Lant Pritchett, "What Educational Production Functions Really Show: A Positive Theory of Education Spending," World Bank Policy Research Paper 1795, Washington, D.C., 1997.

15. World Bank, *A Sourcebook for Poverty Reduction Strategies*, 2002.

16. OECD policy brief, "Untying Aid to the Least-Developed Countries," July 2001, Paris.

17. Alberto Alesina and David Dollar, "Who Gives Foreign Aid to Whom and Why," *Journal of Economic Growth 5* (March 2002): 33–64.

18. OECD and UNDP, 1999.

19. World Bank, Operations Evaluation Department, "Influential Evaluations: Evaluations That Improved Performance and Impacts of Development Programs," Washington D.C., 2004.

20. James Ferguson, *The Anti-Politics Machine: "Development," Depolarization, and Bureaucratic Power in Lesotho*, Minneapolis: University of Minnesota Press, 1994, pp. 170–71.

21. Ibid., pp. 231, 233.

22. Judy L. Baker, "Evaluating the Impact of Development Projects on Poverty: A Handbook for Practitioners, Directions in Development," World Bank, Washington, D.C., 2000.

23. World Bank, *A Sourcebook for Poverty Reduction Strategies*, 2002.

24. UN Millennium Project, "Investing in Development: A Practical Plan to Reach the Millennium Development Goals," main report, 2005, p. 61.

25. Scott, *Seeing Like a State*, 1998, p. 346.

26. http://www.usaid.gov/faqs.html.

27. http://www.un.org/esa/coordination/ecosoc/wgga/Home1.htm.

Chapter 6. Bailing Out the Poor

1. World Development Indicators, observation for 2000.

2. World Bank, World Development Indicators, observation for 2000 on height for age and weight for height.

3. Demographic and Health Surveys, http://www.measuredhs.com/countries/country.cfm.

4. International Monetary Fund, Federal Democratic Republic of Ethiopia, "Fifth Review Under the Three-Year Arrangement Under the Poverty Reduction and Growth Facility," February 4, 2004, pp. 15, 17.

5. http://www.imf.org/external/np/tre/lend/terms.htm.

6. http://www.imf.org/external/np/exr/facts/finfac.htm.

7. http://www.imf.org/external/np/exr/facts/howlend.htm.

8. Jacques Polak, "The IMF Monetary Model at 40, *Economic Modelling* 15 (1998): 395–410.

9. Juan Forrero, "Ecuador's Leader Flees and Vice President Replaces Him," *New York Times*, April 21, 2005, p. A3.

10. IMF, World Development Movement, "States of Unrest: Resistance to IMF Policies in Poor Countries," September 2000, http://www.wdm.org.uk/presrel/current/anti_IMF.htm.

11. Richard Barth and William Hemphill, with contributions from Irina Aganina, Susan George, Joshua Greene, Caryl McNeilly, and Jukka Paljarvi, *Financial Programming and Policy: The Case of Turkey*, Washington, D.C.: IMF Institute, International Monetary Fund, 2000.

12. This is the median ratio of the absolute value of the adjustment to total domestic financing for all available data 1970–1999.

13. R. Baqir, R. Ramcharan, and R. Sahay, "The Consistency of IMF Programs," mimeograph, IMF, October 2003.

14. http://www.emgmkts.com/research/intro.htm#TheEM.

15. Easterly, "What Did Structural Adjustment Adjust?"

16. Both countries recently completed IMF programs successfully for the first time.

17. IMF, Independent Evaluation Office, "Evaluation of the Prolonged Use of Fund Resources," Washington, D.C., September 2002.

18. http://web.worldbank.org/WBSITE/EXTERNAL/TOPICS/EXTDEBTDEPT/0,,contentMDK:20260411~menuPK:528655~pagePK:64166689~piPK:64166646~theSit-*piPK* : 64166646\sim*theSitePK* : 469043,00.*html*.

19. R. Baqir, R. Ramcharan, and R. Sahay, "The Consistency of IMF Programs."

20. See the chapter "Forgive Us Our Debts," in W. Easterly, *The Elusive Quest for Growth: Economists' Adventures and Misadventures in the Tropics*, Cambridge, Mass.: MIT Press, 2001.

21. Michael Mussa, *Argentina and the Fund: From Triumph to Tragedy* (*Policy Analyses in International Economics 67*) Washington, D.C.: Institute for International Economics, 2002. This section is based on Mussa but differs in emphasis and conclusions in several places; in any case, Mussa should not be held responsible for anything said here.

22. "Argentina's Debt Restructuring: Victory by Default?" *The Economist,* March 3, 2005.

23. http://www.imf.org/external/np/exr/facts/prgf.htm.

24. IMF, "Factsheet: The IMF and the Environment," April 2004.

25. William Pfaff, *Barbarian Sentiments: America in the New Century,* New York: Hill & Wang, 2000, p. 206.

Chapter 7. The Healers: Triumph and Tragedy

1. Center for Global Development, "Millions Saved: Proven Successes in Global Health," Washington, D.C., 2004.

2. Bekki J. Johnson and Robert S. Pond, "AIDS in Africa: A Review of Medical, Public Health, Social Science, and Popular Literature," MISEORE, Campaign Against Hunger and Disease in the World (Episcopal Organization for Development Cooperations), Aachen, West Germany, 1988.

3. World Bank, Africa Technical Department, "Acquired Immune Deficiency Syndrome (AIDS): The Bank's Agenda for Action in Africa," October 24, 1988.

4. Jean-Louis Lamboray and A. Edward Elmendorf, "Combatting AIDS and Other Sexually Transmitted Diseases in Africa: A Review of the World Bank's Agenda for Action," World Bank Discussion Paper no. 181, Africa Technical Department, 1992, p. 29.

5. Jill Armstrong, "Socioeconomic Implications of AIDS in Developing Countries," *Finance and Development* 28, no. 4 (December 1991): 14–17.

6. The World Bank at this time thought the best approach was to target the "core transmitters" of the disease, such as prostitutes. AIDS researcher Helen Epstein has since argued that this was a mistake: that the spread of AIDS in Africa was due mainly to the prevalence of multiple long-term sexual relationships among the general population, which created a sexual network through which AIDS quickly spread. See Helen Epstein, "Why Is AIDS Worse in Africa?," *Discover* 25, no. 2 (February 2004), and Daniel T. Halperin and Helen Epstein, "Sexual Networks Help to Explain Africa's High HIV Prevalence: Implications for Prevention," www.thelancet.com, vol. 364, July 3, 2004.

7. Julia Dayton, "World Bank HIV/AIDS Interventions: Ex-ante and Ex-post Evaluation," World Bank discussion paper no. 389, Washington, D.C., 1998, p. 9.

8. World Bank, Africa Region, "Intensifying Action Against HIV/AIDS in Africa: Responding to a Development Crisis," 2000.

9. http://www.worldbank.org/afr/aids/map/me_manual.pdf.

10. This story comes from Emma Guest, *Children of AIDS: Africa's Orphan Crisis,* London: Pluto Press, 2001.

11. Adam Ashforth, *Witchcraft, Violence, and Democracy in South Africa,* Chicago: University of Chicago Press, 2005, pp. 8–10.

12. Guest, *Children of AIDS,* pp. 144–47.

13. Anne Case, Christina Paxson, and Joseph Ableidinger, "The Education of African Orphans," Princeton University mimeograph, 2003, http://www.wws.princeton.edu/%7Erpds/Downloads/case_paxson_education_orphans.pdf.

14. WHO/UNAIDS, "Report on the Methods Used to Estimate Costs of Reaching the WHO Target of '3 by 5,'" February 10, 2004 , p. 6.

15. Andrew Creese, Katherine Floyd, Anita Alban, Lorna Guiness, "Cost-effectiveness of HIV/AIDS Inverventions in Africa: A Systematic Review of the Evidence," *The Lancet* 359 (2002): 1635–42; Lilani Kumaranayarake, "Cost-Effectiveness and Economic Evaluation of HIV/AIDS-Related Interventions: The State of the Art," in *International AIDS Economics Network, State of the Art: AIDS and Economics,* HIV/AIDS Policy Project, www.iaen.org/conferences/stateofepidemic.php., 2002.

16. http://www.interaction.org/advocacy/budget_request_05.html, FY2005 Foreign Operations Budget Request Summary and Analysis.

17. WHO, World Health Report 2003, Annex 2.

18. See, for example, Emiko Masaki, Russell Green, Fiona Greig, Julia Walsh, and Malcolm Potts, "Cost-Effectiveness of HIV Prevention Versus Treatment for Resource-Scarce Countries: Setting Priorities for HIV/AIDS Management," Bay Area International Group, School of Public Health, University of California at Berkeley, 2002.

19. http://www.massiveeffort.org/html/success_stories__vietnam.html, http://rbm.who. int/cmc_upload/0/000/017/025/vietnam-ettling.pdf.

20. Salim Abdulla, Joanna Armstrong Schellenberg, Rose Nathan, Oscar Mukasa, Tanya Marchant, Tom Smith, Marcel Tanner, Christian Lengeler, "Impact on Malaria Morbidity of a Programme Supplying Insecticide-Treated Nets in Children Aged Under Two Years in Tanzania: Community Cross-Sectional Study," *British Medical Journal*, 322 (February 3, 2001): 270–73.

21. Gareth Jones, Richard W. Steketee, Robert E. Black, Zulfiqar A. Bhutta, Saul S. Morris, and the Bellagio Child Survival Study Group, "How Many Child Deaths Can We Prevent This Year?" *The Lancet* 362 (2003): 65–71.

22. WHO/UNAIDS, "Report on the Methods Used to Estimate Costs of Reaching the WHO Target of '3 by 5,'" February 10, 2004.

23. United Nations Population Division (UNDP), "World Population Prospects," 2004 revision, 2005, p. 22.

24. David Canning, "The Economics of HIV/AIDS Treatment and Prevention in Developing Countries," Harvard School of Public Health, mimeograph, 2005, forthcoming in *Journal of Economic Perspectives*.

25. Center for Health and Gender Equity and Sexuality, Information and Education Council of the United States, "The U.S. Global AIDS Strategy: Politics, Ideology, and the Global AIDS Epidemic," May 2003.

26. Human Rights Watch, "The Less They Know, the Better: Abstinence-Only HIV/AIDS Programs in Uganda," *Human Rights Watch* 17, no. 4a (March 2005).

27. Helen Epstein, "God and the Fight Against AIDS," *New York Review of Books*, April 28, 2005.

28. Barcelona AIDS Conference Reports, "President Bush Is Killing People with AIDS by Lack of Leadership," http://www.actupny.org/reports/bcn/BcnbushAUpr.html.

29. WHO, World Health Report 2002, "Reducing Risks, Promoting Healthy Life," Geneva, 2002, p. 92.

30. Ibid., pp. 123, 132.

31. Daniel Bergner, *In the Land of Magic Soldiers: A Story of White and Black in West Africa*, New York: Farrar, Straus, & Giroux, 2003, pp. 66–68.

32. Dr. Stan Lehman and colleagues, CDC, presentation at XIII International AIDS Conference, Durban, South Africa, 2000.

33. Warren Stevens, Steve Kaye, and Tumani Corrah, "Antiretroviral Therapy in Africa," *British Medical Journal* 328 (January 31, 2004): 280–82.

34. Merle A. Sande and Allan Ronald, "Treatment of HIV/AIDS: Do the Dilemmas Only Increase?" *Journal of the American Medical Association* 292, no. 2 (July 14, 2004): 267. I saw the reference first in an excellent article by Roger Bate, "Slippery AIDS Statistics: Why Loose HIV Numbers Create False Hope and Bad Policy," *Health Policy Outlook*, AEI Online (Washington), May 6, 2005.

35. This account is based on pp. 6–9 Vijayendra Rao and Michael Walton, editors, *Culture and Public Action*, Stanford University Press: Stanford, CA 2004.

Chapter 8. From Colonialism to Postmodern Imperialism

1. F. A. Hayek, *The Fatal Conceit: The Errors of Socialism*, edited by W. W. Bartley III, Chicago: University of Chicago Press, 1988, p. 76.

2. References can be found in Jeremy M. Weinstein, "Autonomous Recovery and International Intervention in Comparative Perspective," Center for Global Development Working Paper no. 57, April 2005.
3. James Fearon and David Laitin, "Neotrusteeship and the Problem of Weak States," *International Security* 28, no. 4 (Spring 2004): 5–43.
4. Sebastian Mallaby, "The Reluctant Imperialist: Terrorism, Failed States, the Case for American Empire," *Foreign Affairs* 81, no. 2 (March/April 2002); Chester Crocker, "Engaging Failing States," *Foreign Affairs* 84, no. 5 (September/October 2003); Stuart Eizenstat, John Edward Porter, and Jeremy Weinstein, "Rebuilding Weak States," *Foreign Affairs* 84, no. 1 (January/February 2005); Stephen D. Krasner and Carlos Pascual, "Addressing State Failure," *Foreign Affairs* 84, no. 4 (July/August 2005); Stephen Ellis, "How to Rebuild Africa," *Foreign Affairs* 84, no. 5 (September/October 2005).
5. Krasner and Pascual, "Addressing State Failure."
6. Niall Ferguson, *Colossus: The Price of America's Empire,* New York: The Penguin Press, 2004, p. 198.
7. D. K. Fieldhouse, *The Colonial Empires: A Comparative Survey from the Eighteenth Century,* New York: Macmillan, 1982, pp. 276–77 .
8. Edmund Burke, speech on Mr. Fox's East India Bill, December 1783, in Isaac Kramnick, *The Portable Edmund Burke,* Viking Portable Library, New York: Penguin Putnam, 1999, p. 374.
9. Mahmood Mamdani, *Citizen and Subject: Contemporary Africa and the Legacy of Late Colonialism,* Princeton, N.J.: Princeton University Press, 1996, p. 73.
10. Robert B. Edgerton, *The Troubled Heart of Africa: A History of the Congo,* New York: St. Martin's Press, 2002, pp. 162–63.
11. John Iliffe, *Africans: The History of a Continent,* Cambridge, UK: Cambridge University Press, 1995, p. 198.
12. Mamdani, *Citizen and Subject,* pp. 79, 41.
13. Iliffe, *Africans,* p. 201.
14. Ibid., p. 201.
15. Mamdani, *Citizen and Subject,* p. 53.
16. Iliffe, *Africans,* p. 201.
17. Mamdani, *Citizen and Subjects,* p. 52.
18. Ibid., pp. 54–56.
19. Iliffe, *Africans,* p. 200.
20. Ibid., p. 199.
21. Ibid., pp. 251–52.
22. Fieldhouse, *Colonial Empires,* p. 161.
23. Abhijit Banerjee and Lakshmi Iyer, "History, Institutions, and Economic Systems: The Legacy of Colonial Land Tenure Systems in India," MIT mimeograph, October 2004; Fieldhouse, *Colonial Empires,* pp. 278–79; and Ravina Daphtary, "Systems of Land Tenure in Bengal: The Unyielding Legacy of the Zamindar," NYU undergraduate thesis, April 2005.
24. Fieldhouse, *Colonial Empires,* pp. 280–83.
25. Bergner, *Land of Magic Soldiers,* p. 29.

26. P. J. Cain and A. G. Hopkins, *British Imperialism, 1688–2000,* 2d ed., Harlow, UK: Longman, Pearson Education, 2002, p. 283.
27. Niall Ferguson, *Empire: The Rise and Demise of the British World Order and the Lessons for Global Power,* New York: Basic Books, 2004, p. 116.
28. Ibid., p. 141.
29. Cain and Hopkins, *British Imperialism,* p. 291.
30. Ferguson, *Empire,* p. 22.
31. Cain and Hopkins, *British Imperialism,* p. 291.
32. James, *Rise and Fall,* p. 175.
33. Angus Maddison, "The World Economy: Historical Statistics," Development Centre of the Organisation for Economic Cooperation and Development, 2003.
34. Cain and Hopkins, *British Imperialism,* p. 308.
35. Iliffe, *Africans,* p. 204.
36. Ibid., p. 212.
37. Ibid., p. 222.
38. Ibid., pp. 203–4.
39. Maddison, "World Economy."
40. Mamdani, *Citizen and Subject,* p. 158.
41. Bergner, *Land of Magic Soldiers,* p. 97.
42. Scott, *Seeing Like a State,* pp. 226–28.
43. Thayer Watkins, "The Tanganyikan Groundnuts Scheme," San José State University Economics Department, at http://www2.sjsu.edu/faculty/watkins/groundnt.htm.
44. Maddison, "World Economy."
45. Ibid. Other Asian colonies are Bangladesh, Burma, Hong Kong, Indonesia, Jordan, Lebanon, Malaysia, Pakistan, Singapore, Sri Lanka, Syria, and Vietnam.
46. "Kongo," in Kwame Anthony Appiah and Henry Louis Gates, Jr., eds., *Africana: The Encyclopedia of the African and African American Experience,* New York: Basic Books, 1999, pp. 1104–5; and Edgerton, *Troubled Heart,* pp. 7–14.
47. Edgerton, *Troubled Heart,* p. 60.
48. Patrick Manning, *Francophone Sub-Saharan Africa, 1880–1985,* Cambridge, UK: Cambridge University Press, 1988, p. 129.
49. *Library of Congress Area Handbook on Zaire,* Washington, D.C.: Library of Congress, 1993
50. "Congo, Democratic Republic of the," in *Africana,* pp. 503–7.
51. *Library of Congress Area Handbook on Zaire.*
52. Ibid.
53. Edgerton, *Troubled Heart,* p. 181.
54. Wrong, *In the Footsteps of Mr. Kurtz,* p. 83.
55. http://www.facts.com/wnd/kabila.htm.
56. Minorities at Risk website, http://www.cidcm.umd.edu/inscr/mar/assessment.asp?groupId=49003.
57. http://www.facts.com/wnd/kabila.htm.
58. http://www.theirc.org/index.cfm?section=news&wwwID=1704.
59. Edgerton, *Troubled Heart,* p. 237.

60. World Bank, "Democratic Republic of the Congo: Transitional Support Strategy," February 4, 2004.
61. UNICEF, "State of the World's Children 2005," pp. 64–65.
62. Quoted in Christopher Hitchens, "The Perils of Partition," *Atlantic Monthly*, March 2003.
63. Alberto Alesina, William Easterly, and Janina Matuszeski, "Artificial Countries and Economic Development," Harvard and NYU mimeograph, 2005.
64. Howard M. Sachar, *The Emergence of the Middle East: 1914–24*, New York: Knopf, 1969, pp. 123–27.
65. Besides Sachar, see also the discussion in Arthur Goldschmidt, Jr., *A Concise History of the Middle East,* 7th ed., Boulder, Colo.: Westview Press, 2002; David Fromkin, *A Peace to End All Peace: The Fall of the Ottoman Empire and the Creation of the Modern Middle East,* New York: Avon Books, 1989; Albert Hourani, *A History of the Arab Peoples,* New York: Warner Books, 1991; and Tom Segev, *One Palestine Complete: Jews and Arabs under the British Mandate,* New York: Metropolitan Books, 1999. I have drawn on all these sources for the text here.
66. Lawrence James, *Raj: The Making and Unmaking of British India,* New York: St. Martin's Griffin, 1997, p. 611f.
67. Quoted in Owen Bennet Jones, *Pakistan: Eye of the Storm,* New Haven, Conn.: Yale University Press, 2002, p. 109.
68. Quoted in William Easterly, "The Political Economy of Growth Without Development: A Case Study of Pakistan," in Dani Rodrik, ed., *Searching for Prosperity,* Princeton N.J.: Princeton University Press, 2003, p. 396.
69. Mary Anne Weaver, *Pakistan: In the Shadow of Jihad and Afghanistan,* New York: Farrar, Straus, & Giroux, 2002, p. 219.
70. Quoted in Bennet Jones, *Pakistan,* p. 281.
71. Francis M. Deng, *War of Visions: Conflict of Identities in the Sudan,* Washington, D.C.: Brookings Institution, 1995, p. 26.
72. Jok Madut Jok, *War and Slavery in Sudan,* Philadelphia: University of Pennsylvania Press, 2001, p. 92.
73. Ibid., p. 96.
74. Deng, *War of Visions,* p. 5.
75. Ibid., p. 87.
76. Ibid., p. 95.
77. Ibid., p. 137.
78. Douglas H. Johnson, *The Root Causes of Sudan's Civil Wars,* Oxford: James Currey, 2003, p. 180.
79. Scott Peterson, *Me Against My Brother: At War in Somalia, Sudan, and Rwanda,* New York: Routledge, 2000, p. 179.
80. Bill Berkeley, *The Graves Are Not Yet Full: Race, Tribe, and Power in the Heart of Africa,* New York: Basic Books, 2001, p. 210.
81. Ibid., p. 213.
82. International Monetary Fund, *Sudan: Final Review Under the Medium-Term Staff-Monitored Program and the 2002 Program—Staff Report,* November 2002, IMF Country Report, No. 02/245, p. 37.

83. http://www.msf.org/content/page.cfm?articleid=84CE9E44-BE8C-4882-83BE7C9305E2B7E4.

84. http://www.savedarfur.org/go.php?q=currentSituation.html.

85. http://www.alertnet.org/thenews/fromthefield/108963973484.htm.

86. Global Development Network Growth Database, August 2003, Social Indicators and Fixed Factors file; www.nyu.edu/fas/institute/dri/index.html.

87. UNICEF, "State of the World's Children 2005," pp. 64–65.

88. Jayanth K. Krishnan, "Professor Kingsfield Goes to Delhi: American Academics, the Ford Foundation, and the Development of Legal Education in India," William Mitchell College of Law Working Paper no. 3, March 2005.

Chapter 9.   Invading the Poor

1. Quoted in http://www.socialstudieshelp.com/USRA_Imperialism_Justify.htm.

2. John McMillan, "Avoid Hubris: And Other Lessons for Reformers," Stanford University mimeograph, July 2004.

3. Naomi Klein, "Baghdad Year Zero: Pillaging Iraq in Pursuit of a Neocon Utopia," *Harper's*, September 2004.

4. Ferguson, *Colossus*, p. 300.

5. Stephen Kinzer, *Blood of Brothers: Life and War in Nicaragua*, New York: Penguin, 1991, p. 364.

6. Lynn Horton, *Peasants In Arms: War and Peace in the Mountains of Nicaragua*, Athens: Ohio University Center for International Studies, 1988, p. 166.

7. The quote is from a Reagan speech made in 1986.

8. World Bank, *Country Assistance Strategy*, 2002.

9. Kinzer, *Blood of Brothers*, p. 179.

10. Horton, *Peasants in Arms*, p. 201.

11. Kinzer, *Blood of Brothers*, pp. 144–45.

12. Robert Kagan, *A Twilight Struggle: American Power and Nicaragua, 1977–1990*, New York: Free Press, 1996, pp. 210, 212.

13. Ibid., p. 218; Kinzer, *Blood of Brothers*, pp. 97–98

14. Horton, *Peasants in Arms*, pp. 233–35.

15. Ibid., pp. 267–69.

16. Ibid., pp. 281 82.

17. IMF, Article IV Report, February 2003, executive summary.

18. World Bank, *Country Assistance Strategy*, December 18, 2002.

19. Worth H. Weller, *If This Soil Could Stop Bleeding: Nicaragua Before and After the Contra War*, North Manchester, Ind.: De Witt Books, 2003, p. 98.

20. IMF, Article IV, 2003.

21. Quoted in Karl Maier, *Angola: Promises and Lies*, Rivonia, South Africa: William Waterman Publications, 1996, overleaf.

22. Quoted in Fernando Andresen Guimaraes, *The Origins of the Angolan Civil War: Foreign Intervention and Domestic Political Conflict*, New York: St. Martins Press, 2001, p. 194.

23. *Library of Congress Area Handbook on Angola;* and Maier, *Angola*.

24. Maier, *Angola*, p. 42.
25. Tony Hodges, *Angola from Afro-Stalinism to Petro-Diamond Capitalism*, Bloomington: Indiana University Press, 2001, p. 37.
26. Library of Congress; and Guimaraes, *Origins*, p. 78 .
27. Library of Congress, and Guimaraes, *Origins*, p. 157.
28. Berkeley, *The Graves*, p. 80.
29. Mark Huband, *The Skull Beneath the Skin: Africa After the Cold War*, Boulder, Colo.: Westview Press, 2001, p. 34.
30. Guimaraes, *Origins*, p. 107.
31. Huband, *Skull Beneath the Skin*, p. 41.
32. Guimaraes, *Origins*, p. 190.
33. Ibid., p. 112.
34. Chester A. Crocker, *High Noon in Southern Africa: Making Peace in a Rough Neighborhood*, New York: Norton, 1992, p. 68.
35. Huband, *The Skull Beneath the Skin*, p. 42; Elaine Windrich, *The Cold War Guerilla: Jonas Sarimbi, the U.S. Media, and the Angolan War;* New York: Greenwood Press, 1992, p. 35.
36. Windrich, *Cold War Guerilla*, p. 35.
37. Ted Galen Carpenter, "U.S. Aid to Anti-Communist Rebels: The 'Reagan Doctrine' and Its Pitfalls," *Cato Policy Analysis* 74 (June 24, 1986), http://www.cato.org/pubs/pas/pa074.html.
38. Windrich, *Cold War Guerilla*, p. 84.
39. Maier, *Angola*, p. 47.
40. BBC News obituary on Savimbi, February 25, 2002.
41. Crocker, *High Noon*, p. 297.
42. Ibid., p. 488.
43. World Bank, *Transitional Support Strategy for the Republic of Angola*, 2003, paragraph 9.
44. Hodges, *Angola*,
45. Data for 2001 from World Bank World Development Indicators.
46. UNAIDS, http://www.unaids.org/en/geographical+area/by+country/angola.asp. Figure as of early 2002.
47. Pfaff, *Barbarian Sentiments*, p. 9.
48. Hans Schmidt, *The United States Occupation of Haiti, 1915–1934*, New Brunswick, N.J.: Rutgers University Press, 1971, p. 31.
49. Ibid., p. 89.
50. Ibid., p. 148.
51. *Library of Congress Area Handbook;* Nicholls, *From Dessalines to Duvalier*.
52. Bob Shacochis, *The Immaculate Invasion*, New York: Viking, 1999, pp. 15, 144.
53. Robert Fatton, Jr., *Haiti's Predatory Government: The Unending Transition to Democracy*, Boulder, Colo.: Lynne Rienner Publishers, 2002, p. 124.
54. World Bank Institute, "Governance Indicators Dataset, 1996–2004," www.worldbank.org/wbi/governance/govdata/.
55. http://lnweb18.worldbank.org/External/lac/lac.nsf/3af04372e7-f23ef6852567d6006b38a3/be0614ec8b422d70852567de0058a2a0?OpenDocument.

56. http://web.worldbank.org/WBSITE/EXTERNAL/NEWS/0,,contentMDK:20226165~menuPK:34457~pagePK:64003015~piPK:64003012~theSitepiPK:64003012~theSitePK:4607,00.html.

57. http://www.foreignpolicy.com/story/cms.php?story_id=3100.

58. Minxin Pei and Sara Kasper, "Lessons from the Past: The American Record on Nation-Building," Carnegie Endowment for International Peace Policy, brief no. 24, May 2003.

59. David Rieff, *A Bed for the Night: Humanitarianism in Crisis*, New York: Simon and Schuster, 2002, pp. 206–7.

60. David Rieff, *At the Point of a Gun: Democratic Dreams and Armed Intervention*, New York: Simon and Schuster, 2005, pp. 65, 69.

61. Michael Barnett, *Eyewitness to a Genocide: The United Nations and Rwanda*, Ithaca, N.Y.: Cornell University Press, 2002, p. 100.

62. Alex de Waal, *Famine Crimes: Politics and the Disaster Relief Industry in Africa*, Bloomington: Indiana University Press, 1997, pp. 185–88.

63. Barnett, *Eyewitness*, p. 31.

64. De Waal, *Famine Crimes*, p. 184.

65. Barnett, *Eyewitness*, p. 134.

66. Ibid., p. 114.

67. Ibid., p. 179.

68. Jeremy M. Weinstein, *Autonomous Recovery and International Intervention in Comparative Perspective*, Center for Global Development Working Paper no. 57, April 2005. Earlier work by political scientist Roy Licklider ("The Consequences of Negotiated Settlements in Civil Wars, 1945–1993," *American Political Science Review* 89, no. 3 [September 1995]: 681–90) found that wars ending in a military victory resulted in recurring war (again measured as another war in the next ten years) 15 percent of the time, while war resumed after a negotiated settlement 50 percent of the time. Other authors making similar arguments include Robert Harrison Wagner, "The Causes of Peace," in Roy Licklider, ed., *Stopping the Killing*, New York: New York University Press, 1993; and Monica Toft, "Peace Through Victory: The Durable Settlement of Civil Wars," unpublished manuscript, Harvard University, 2003 (quoted in Weinstein, *Autonomous Recovery*).

69. World Bank, *Breaking the Conflict Trap: Civil War and Development Policy*, Washington, D.C.: World Bank, 2003, p. 168.

70. Rieff, *At the Point of a Gun*, p. 166.

71. Maier, *Angola*, pp. 11–12.

72. http://pediatrics.aappublications.org/cgi/content/full/102/4/e45; Pediatrics 102, no. 4 (October 1998): e45; Joyce K. Kikafunda, Ann F. Walker, David Collett, James K. Tumwine, "Risk Factors for Early Childhood Malnutrition in Uganda," from, respectively, the Department of Food Science and Technology, Makerere University, Kampala, Uganda; the Hugh Sinclair Unit of Human Nutrition, Department of Food Science and Technology, the University of Reading, Whiteknights, Reading, United Kingdom; the Department of Applied Statistics, the University of Reading, Reading, United Kingdom; and the Department of Paediatrics and Child Health, Makerere University Medical School, Kampala, Uganda.

Chapter 10. Homegrown Development

1. Kenneth G. Henshall, *A History of Japan: From Stone Age to Superpower,* London: Macmillan Press, 1999, pp. 70–71.
2. James L. McClain, *Japan: A Modern History,* New York: Norton, 2002, p. 156.
3. McClain, *Japan,* p. 162; and Andrew Gordon, *A Modern History of Japan: From Tokugawa Times to the Present,* New York: Oxford University Press, 2003, pp. 70–71.
4. McClain, *Japan,* pp. 216–17.
5. Ibid., pp. 232–33; and Randall Morck and Masao Nakamura, "Been There, Done That—The History of Corporate Ownership in Japan," Center for Economic Institutions Working Paper Series no. 2004-4, Institute of Economic Research, Hitotsubashi University.
6. McClain, *Japan,* p. 264.
7. Marius B. Jansen, *The Making of Modern Japan,* Cambridge, Mass.: Belknap Press/ Harvard University Press, 2000, pp. 402–3.
8. John W. Dower, *Embracing Defeat: Japan in the Wake of World War II,* New York: Norton, 1999, p. 537.
9. Ibid., p. 545.
10. Frank Welsh, *A Borrowed Place: The History of Hong Kong,* New York: Kodansha International, 1993, p. 247; and C. M. Turnbull, *A History of Singapore 1819–1975,* Kuala Lumpur: Oxford University Press, 1977, p. 89.
11. http://www.nsf.gov/sbe/srs/nsf05300/pdf/tables.pdf.
12. Alice Amsden, *The Rise of the "Rest": Challenges to the West from Late-Industrializing Economies,* New York: Oxford University Press, 2001, p. 221.
13. http://www.tsmc.com/english/a_about/a_about_index.htm.
14. Amsden, *Rise of the "Rest,"* p. 193, 199; http://www.brandingasia.com/cases/case1.htm.
15. http://www.forbes.com/lists/results.jhtml?passListId=10&passYear=2004&passListType=Person&resultsStart=1&resultsHowMany-1&resultsIIowMany=25&resultsSortProperties=%2Bnumberfield1%2C%2Bstringfield1&resultsSortresultsSortCategoryName=rank&category1=Country+of+Residence&searchParameter1=7Str%7C%7CPatCS%7C%7CTaiwan&categorcategory2=category&searchParameter2=unset.
16. Jonathan Spence, *To Change China: Western Advisers in China,* New York: Penguin Books, 1969.
17. Christopher Jespersen, *American Images of China,* 1931–1949, Stanford, Calif.: Stanford University Press, 1996, p. 37.
18. John King Fairbank and Merle Goldman, *China: A New History,* Cambridge, Mass.: Belknap/Harvard, 1998, p. 284.
19. Jonathan Spence, *The Search for Modern China,* 2d ed., New York: Norton, 1999.
20. Jespersen, *American Images,* p. 120; Fairbank and Goldman, *China,* p. 291.
21. Rist, *The History of Development,* p. 65.
22. For year ending in September 2004, http://www.census.gov/foreign-trade/statistics/product/naics/naicsctry/imports/i316214.html.

23. Amsden, *Rise of the "Rest,"* p. 217.
24. http://lnweb18.worldbank.org/eap/eap.nsf/Countries/China/
    42F2084B942D74C68p. 5256C7600687DBF?OpenDocument.
25. Gurcharan Das, *India Unbound: From Independence to the Global Information Age,* London: Profile Books, 2002, pp. 248–50.
26. http://www.wipro.com/aboutus/whoweare.htm.
27. http://www.businessweek.com/magazine/content/02_47/b3809168.htm.
28. http://www.forbes.com/finance/lists/10/2004/LIR.jhtml?passLis-tId=10&passYear=2004&passListType=Person&uniqueId=1UFS&datatype=Perso-&datatype=Person.
29. Not her real name, but the rest is true.
30. http://www.islamicity.com/mosque/Zakat/.
31. http://www.forbes.com/finance/lists/10/2004/LIR.jhtml?passLis-tId=10&passYear=2004&passListType=Person&uniqueId=HDKF&datatype=Perso-&datatype=Person.
32. Sources on the Koç Group:.
    https://secure.bookinturkey.com/main_en/info/aboutkoc_0.asp?id=1;
    http://www.kocbank.com.tr/kocbank/english/aboutus/default.asp;
    http://www.internationalreports.net/europe/turkey/stay%20close.html;
    Metin Demirsar, "Koç-Sabanci rivalries divide Turkish economy," *Turkish Daily News,* 1996; http://www.vekam.org.tr/en/ogutler.html;
    http://www.bekoelektronik.com.tr/bekoen/kurucu.htm;
    http://www.bekoelektronik.com.tr/bekoen/tarihce.htm;
    Harvard Business School, Koç Holding: Arcelik White Goods, September 1997; available from Harvard Business Online.
33. Amsden, *Rise of the "Rest,"* p. 160.
34. Laura Alfaro, Debora Spar, and Faheen Allibhoy, "Botswana: A Diamond in the Rough," mimeograph, Harvard Business School, March 31, 2003.
35. Michael Houlihan, "Growth and Politics in Botswana, Burundi and Ghana: A Narrative Comparative Account," New York University mimeograph, 2004.
36. U.S. Census Bureau, U.S. International Trade Statistics, by year through October 2004, http://censtats.census.gov/sitc/sitc.shtml.

Chapter 11. The Future of Western Assistance

1. Development Assistance Committee Working Party on Aid Effectiveness and Donor Practices, *Managing for Development Results Principles in Action: Sourcebook on Emerging Good Practice,* 2005, p. 1–11.
2. I am paraphrasing the summary of Esther Duflo and Michael Kremer, "Use of Randomization in the Evaluation of Development Effectiveness," MIT and Harvard University mimeograph, 2004.
3. http://news.bbc.co.uk/1/hi/programmes/crossing_continents/412802.stm.
4. Duflo and Kremer, "Use of Randomization."
5. All of these examples are from Duflo and Kremer, "Use of Randomization."

6. Abhijit Banerjee and Rumin He, "Making Aid Work, MIT mimeograph, October 2003.

7. James R. Barth, Gerard Caprio, and Ross Levine, *Rethinking Bank Regulation: Till Angels Govern,* Cambridge, UK: Cambridge University Press, 2005.

8. Dennis Whittle and Mari Kuraishi, "Competing with Central Planning: Marketplaces for International Aid," Global Giving.com mimeo, 2004.

9. http://www.businessweek.com/magazine/content/04_48/b3910407.htm.

10. Nancy Birdsall and Brian Deese, "Hard Currency," *The Washington Monthly,* 36, no. 3, March 2004, p. 39, quoted in Whittle and Kuraishi "Competing."

11. This is akin to Duggan, *Art of What Works,* p. 167.

Index